Hollywood and the Nazis on the Eve of War

Hollywood and the Nazis on the Eve of War

The Case of *The Mortal Storm*

Alexis Pogorelskin

BLOOMSBURY ACADEMIC
NEW YORK • LONDON • OXFORD • NEW DELHI • SYDNEY

BLOOMSBURY ACADEMIC
Bloomsbury Publishing Inc, 1359 Broadway, New York, NY 10018, USA
Bloomsbury Publishing Plc, 50 Bedford Square, London, WC1B 3DP, UK
Bloomsbury Publishing Ireland, 29 Earlsfort Terrace, Dublin 2, D02 AY28, Ireland

BLOOMSBURY, BLOOMSBURY ACADEMIC and the Diana logo
are trademarks of Bloomsbury Publishing Plc

First published in the United States of America 2024
Paperback edition published 2025

Copyright © Alexis Pogorelskin, 2024

For legal purposes the Acknowledgments on pp. ix–xi constitute
an extension of this copyright page.

Cover design: Eleanor Rose
Cover image: *The Mortal Storm,* 1940, USA, dir. Frank
Borzage © Archives du 7e Art collection/Alamy

All rights reserved. No part of this publication may be: i) reproduced or transmitted in any form, electronic or mechanical, including photocopying, recording or by means of any information storage or retrieval system without prior permission in writing from the publishers; or ii) used or reproduced in any way for the training, development or operation of artificial intelligence (AI) technologies, including generative AI technologies. The rights holders expressly reserve this publication from the text and data mining exception as per Article 4(3) of the Digital Single Market Directive (EU) 2019/790.

Bloomsbury Publishing Inc does not have any control over, or responsibility for, any third-party websites referred to or in this book. All internet addresses given in this book were correct at the time of going to press. The author and publisher regret any inconvenience caused if addresses have changed or sites have ceased to exist but can accept no responsibility for any such changes.

A catalog record for this book is available from the Library of Congress.

ISBN:	HB:	979-8-7651-0810-9
	PB:	979-8-7651-0809-3
	ePDF:	979-8-7651-0812-3
	eBook:	979-8-7651-0813-0

Typeset by Integra Software Services Pvt. Ltd.

For product safety related questions contact productsafety@bloomsbury.com.

To find out more about our authors and books visit www.bloomsbury.com
and sign up for our newsletters.

In loving memory to M.G.P. and M.A.P.

CONTENTS

List of Figures viii
Acknowledgments ix
Prologue xii

Introduction 1

1   A Matter of Timing 7

2   Novelist of War 27

3   Selling *The Mortal Storm* to Hollywood 75

4   In Production, 1939 115

5   In Production, 1940 151

6   June 20, 1940: Did Anyone Have Time to Go to the Movies? 185

7   The Response to *The Mortal Storm*, 1940 229

8   The Response to *The Mortal Storm*, 1941 249

Epilogue 289

Essay on Sources 304
Index 312

FIGURES

1. Example of West's affection for Franklin and the basis for their close working relationship 120
2. Franklin to West as she prepares to leave for several weeks in Europe, June 3, 1938. Her affection for him was clearly reciprocated 121
3. Summary of Bottome's meeting with Franklin's production team held within days of the novel's purchase by MGM 123
4. West advocated making *Good-bye Mr. Chips*, which Franklin at first opposed. Her farewell alludes to their script for the film they had just completed, June 4, 1938 124
5. Summary of Bottome's meeting with Franklin's production team (final page) 131
6. Franklin seeks permission to shoot snow scenes on Mt. Rainier 133
7. West is hospitalized. Franklin insists she rest and forget *The Mortal Storm,* October 4, 1939 137

ACKNOWLEDGMENTS

I owe my fascination with the period of this book, the eve of the Second World War, to my mother, Margaret Griffin Pogorelskin. She lived it and made it come alive for me. She told me, "No one reveals so much about themselves as they do in a parent-teacher conference." She taught the offspring of Harold Ickes, FDR's Secretary of Interior, and his wife, Rose. "Alexis, she was very beautiful, and he loved her very much." She taught the offspring of Ernest K. Lindley, Washington Bureau Chief for the *New York Herald Tribune*, and his wife. Sitting before my mother one evening, Mrs. Lindley broke down. The president, she explained, is going to make Ernest reveal he is running for a third term. Ernest will look like a fool, while FDR denies it and sizes up the reaction.

My mother had come to Washington from Idaho by way of the University of Minnesota. She was a champion debater at the College of Idaho. Senator Borah heard her debate one evening. He offered to pay her way through law school if she agreed to work for him. She declined on the grounds that she did not share his politics. Because of her, this book was in me before I was barely aware of it.

Professor Phyllis Lassner read early drafts and urged me on. She believed in me and the project. She was instrumental in negotiating purchase of Phyllis Bottome's papers by the British Library on which much of it is based. She and her husband Jake, an esteemed Middle Eastern scholar, put me up in Oxford and London where I did much of my research. Her recommendation was instrumental in my becoming the first Vera Brittain Scholar on Women and War, funded by the Society of Women Writers and Journalists (SWWJ). As a result, I spent a month in Chawton House, the manor house of Jane Austen's brother. In its magnificent library, I encountered an unrivaled collection of primary and secondary literature devoted to early British feminists and the abolitionist movement. Standing before the floor to ceiling shelves one morning, I realized that Bottome was the direct heir to those movements and that, imbued with the same moral fervor, she had conceived *The Mortal Storm* to echo *Uncle Tom's Cabin*.

The renowned historian of Hollywood and Sidney Franklin's biographer, Kevin Brownlow, shared with me his correspondence with Franklin, regarding Claudine West and much more. He introduced me to Franklin's great niece, Tory Franklin-Dillon, who in turn opened the producer's archive to me. She provided warm hospitality as I pored over file after file of Franklin's papers. She generously shared her encyclopedic knowledge of Hollywood and its golden age.

I want to thank Steven Carr and David Welky, who provided valuable source material uncovered in the course of their own research into Hollywood. Edward Comstock, Senior Librarian of the USC Cinematic Arts Library, provided me with copies of Bottome's correspondence with Sidney Franklin in 1940. Donald Ritchie, formerly the historian of the US Senate, opened his archives and his photocopier to me. He suggested that I walk down the Hill and see if the National Archives still held material on the Hollywood hearings of 1941. It did. Howard Roger and Michael Cole, past presidents of Temple Holy Blossom's Brotherhood, shared their extensive knowledge of the history of the Temple with me as well as their research on the work of its founder, Rabbi Maurice Eisendrath, who was instrumental in MGM's purchase of *The Mortal Storm*. Sonya Newberg shared with me an account of her family and of her aunt Dr. Blanche Slagerman in particular. Slagerman had been an intimate friend of Claudine West. Joanne Sher tracked down for me all the obscure bits and pieces of information about Claudine West that I have included as well as, no small achievement, her last will and testament. Sister Edith Gottsacker shared her dissertation on Hans Thomsen, Chargé d'Affaires of the German embassy, and much more about that critical player in German espionage on the eve of the Second World War. Kristin Bluemel, an astute and meticulous editor who oversaw publication of my first essay on *The Mortal Storm,* shared with me her extensive knowledge of Bottome and her novel. My dear friend Helen Klier provided sanctuary whenever I came to London to do research. My brother-in-law Michael Iacangelo did the same, generously offering me his pied-á-terre whenever I had an opportunity to do research in Washington, the hometown for both of us. I also want to thank the late Beverly Goldfine, who brought the renowned scriptwriter Sidney Buchman to my attention. Buchman made good in Hollywood after a boyhood spent in the Jewish community of Duluth.

The University of Minnesota provided grants that subsidized some of my research. In the early stages of my work the Society for Study of The Space Between. Literature and Culture, 1914–1945, encouraged me and offered a stimulating intellectual atmosphere in which to try out new ideas. It awarded me a prize for my first (trial) essay on *The Mortal Storm*.

A special thank you to Reeve Lindbergh, who gave me permission to consult her parents' diaries in the Manuscript and Archives Division of Sterling Memorial Library, Yale University.

Finally, I would like to thank an anonymous archivist in the National Archives and Records Administration, College Park, who devoted her lunch hour to help me locate the grave site in France of a Presbyterian minister named Roberts, who died of pneumonia in 1918 on the Western Front.

He was my grandmother's younger brother. Despite her best efforts, we did not succeed.

I list in alphabetical order others whose support and generous assistance contributed to the completion of this book: Susanne Bakken, Pam Enrici, Steve Feinstein, Eleanor Hoffman, Jill Jensen, Chris King, Elizabeth Nelson, Cheryl Reitan, Ravenel Richardson, Leane Rutherford, Rosemary Stanfield-Johnson, Bryan Robert Shechmeister, and Neil Storch (who tracked down Sister Gottsacker).

My gratitude to the archives and archivists where I worked is unbounded. I will discuss them at greater length in the bibliographic essay at the end of this volume.

PROLOGUE

I was 16 and had an important announcement to make. I walked into the kitchen where my parents prepared dinner and shared their workday with each other. "I want to change my name to Freya," I informed them. My mother did not miss a beat. She turned to my father as though I were not even in the room: "Milt, she stayed up last night and watched *The Mortal Storm*."

Her statement was loaded with meaning. I had been found out. For months I had evaded the stricture on my bedtime and snuck downstairs to watch mesmerizing movies of the Second World War that had by now become the source of a secret life that constituted my own private world of adolescent romanticism and anti-Japanese/anti-Nazi heroism. My parents, on the other hand, had just risen in my esteem for their immediate recognition of my treasured, heart-felt reference. It was a draw. I would go unpunished but drop a complicating request in the midst of college applications.

There was still more to the situation. Even at 16, I had perceived a common thread that ran through the movies that mattered most to me: *Good-bye, Mr. Chips* (1939), *Random Harvest* (1942), *Mrs. Miniver* (1942), *The White Cliffs of Dover* (1944), and of course *The Mortal Storm* (1940). They all bore a common stamp. They were produced by Sidney Franklin and employed the same team of writers. But *The Mortal Storm* mattered most of all. As I would learn decades later, it was the first feature film by a major American studio (MGM) to depict the plight of Europe's Jews before the Holocaust. Little did I know that in comprehending among those MGM films the common qualities of literate dialogue, emotional integrity on the part of strong female characters, and the inherent heroism of those who fought the Nazis that I had already found the seeds of the book I would write devoted to that one film.

Years later, when a colleague invited me to participate on a panel devoted to Holocaust film. I tracked down a 1942 reprint of the transcript of the Senate hearings on "Propaganda [for war] in Motion Pictures," September 1941. About 500 pages in length, it reminded me of the typescripts or *stenograficheskie otchëty* of the party congresses of the 1920s which I used in my research on the opposition to Stalin. Such sources carry the voices of my subjects. They are golden.

I sat and read at my dining room table. I had reached the third and final week of the hearings, having gone through more than 300 pages of text. Chairman D. Worth Clark (D-ID) grilled Nicholas Schenck, president of Loew's, Inc., the parent company of MGM, the studio that had produced *The Mortal Storm*. "There is one picture *particularly* [italics mine] that people say propagandizes for war …." I stopped reading and looked at the crowded bird feeder just outside the window. I told myself that if the film Clark referred to was *The Mortal Storm*, then I have a book. I looked back at the page certain of the film Clark was about to accuse Schenck of using to propagandize for war. "*The Mortal Storm*." I knew at that moment a book lay hidden in those words.

Introduction

As war approached in 1939, motion pictures for the first time mattered in American politics. The political debate then centered on two intertwined issues: isolation vs. intervention. By 1940 that meant avoiding involvement in war altogether vs. aiding the British who were to stop the Nazis for us. In the following year the position of the isolationists had not changed. But intervention meant recognizing that we too would probably have to fight.

The newfound role of the movies should have come as no surprise; their significance had been steadily growing for at least a decade. In the 1930s motion pictures acquired a voice in American life. The medium began to narrate the world and navigate values for the 80 million Americans who went to the movies each week. By the end of the decade, newsreels too acquired new significance. They offered images and interpretation of the cataclysmic events abroad. Hollywood had joined the war effort before the rest of the country caught up.

The most critical period for the industry's influence proved to be that between the fall of France and Pearl Harbor, approximately eighteen months. And the films that mattered most in that interval, a number of them released in the summer of 1940, made the Nazis into villains and encouraged support for Roosevelt's foreign policy. Hollywood performed a role that it had never played before, namely, consistent purveyor of a political point of view. The consequences of such engagement could not then be predicted, either for Hollywood or for the country.

Among those films of 1940, one "particularly," to quote D. Worth Clark, Democratic Senator from Idaho, was a "'war propaganda picture'" that "incited hate for the people of another nation."[1] The film Clark denounced as propagandizing for war and demeaning the German nation was the MGM feature released on June 20, 1940, *The Mortal Storm*. Clark had singled it out, without admitting it, because unlike any of the other so-called war pictures made in the last year, it focused on the plight of Europe's Jews under Nazi rule. Other films, such as Paramount's *Escape* and

Twentieth-Century Fox's *The Man I Married* (originally, *I Married a Nazi*), touched on Nazi persecution of the Jews with references to Kristallnacht or the Nuremberg Laws. The entire plot of *The Mortal Storm*, on the other hand, was devoted to Nazi persecution of the Jews. Neither the film nor its subject matter could be overlooked. The premier studio of the day, MGM, had made it. Two of the film's protagonists, Frank Morgan and Jimmy Stewart, had had breakthrough roles the year before, Morgan in *The Wizard of Oz* and Stewart in *Mr. Smith Goes to Washington*.

The Mortal Storm was unique in another way. In those eighteen months before Pearl Harbor, interpretation of it shifted as the political debate shifted; and the question of war became more urgent for the United States. At first seen as a film that argued for intervention, by the fall of 1941, the isolationists, particularly those who were antisemitic such as members of the America First Committee (AFC), aviator Charles Lindbergh, and his isolationist cohort in the US Senate, regarded the film as one of the most dangerous Hollywood had ever made, precisely because of its portrayal of the victimization of Jews. The film's enemies came to see it as a harbinger of Hollywood's intensified defense of the Jews and therefore not only propaganda for war, but a salvo directed at the antisemitism they, especially Lindbergh, began to espouse more openly in the course of 1941. *The Mortal Storm* accomplished all that while obfuscating its intentions behind the word "non-Aryan" substituted for "Jew." Perhaps confusing to some in 1940, by the following year, the term had become interchangeable with "Jew." The use of "non-Aryan," it could be argued, had been a teaser. Hollywood moguls, most of whom were Jewish, intended to use the movies to campaign on behalf of their own. Next time, they threatened, audiences would hear the word "Jew."

The film figured in yet another way in the national debate. It contributed to the discourse on Lincoln and the Civil War, so prominent as the country prepared to fight again. The fascination with the nineteenth-century conflict and its martyred president can be traced back decades. For example, D. W. Griffith made *Birth of a Nation* in 1915 to coincide with the fiftieth anniversary of the end of the Civil War, denouncing the policies of reconstruction implemented with Lincoln absent from the helm. But by the Great Depression and the eve of war, Lincoln and the Civil War found new relevance. Sociologist Barry Schwartz, for example, says of "Lincoln's reputation" that it "peak[ed] during the Great Depression and World War II."[2] Lincoln mattered in the Depression because he reminded that the nation had once before navigated treacherous waters and could therefore do so again.

Lincoln mattered even more under threat of war as the Depression waned. The Spanish Civil War, for example, gave the sixteenth president immediate political relevance. The Americans and other foreigners who formed the Lincoln Brigade invoked the American conflict, making a connection between the fight to preserve a United Front Spain and the one seventy years earlier to preserve the Union. They too battled an insurgency of landowning magnates who exploited the Spanish peasantry reminiscent of the way that Southern plantation owners had revolted to protect their right to exploit African American slaves.

Phyllis Bottome, the British writer who wrote the novel *The Mortal Storm*, on which the film was based, embraced Civil War analogies and astutely sensed the renewed fascination with the war that she encountered on many stays in the United States in the 1930s. She took *Uncle Tom's Cabin* for a model in writing *The Mortal Storm*. Stowe had protested slavery. Bottome decried the potentially lethal antisemitism of the Nazis. Chapter 2 examines the numerous similarities between both novels, arguing that *Uncle Tom's Cabin* is embedded in *The Mortal Storm*.

But there was something more for Bottome in the Civil War analogy than a model for her fiction. The American Civil War even more so than the Spanish Civil War was a fratricidal conflict, pitting brother against brother. By their very nature both conflicts confirmed Alfred Adler's concept of sibling rivalry, which, the psychologist argued, dominated families. Such rivalry could, he implied, expand in a geopolitical context as war. Bottome's best fiction, also examined in Chapter 2, is often driven by the Adlerian concept of sibling rivalry played out as war. Her novel *Private Worlds* (1934) addresses sibling conflict in the First World War, implying that the Great War itself represented such rivalry writ large. *The Mortal Storm* contains sibling conflict that acquires political resonance in the form of Nazis vs. those opposed to them. Siblings in conflict with each other become political rivals as well.

Bottome had fervently embraced Adler and his ideas as far back as 1927. She remained a staunch Adlerian, telling a friend that *The Mortal Storm* in its success as a bestseller helped prepare the way for the reception of Adler's ideas.[3] On the eve of war, the novel suggested the origin of war itself. Evoking the American Civil War even subliminally gave the novel contemporary political significance for its readership in North America, just as analogies with the nineteenth-century conflict filled public discourse when a second war in Europe seemed likely.

The Civil War, in fact, by 1939, the year after the publication of *The Mortal Storm* in the United States, had begun to permeate American popular culture. In that year Hollywood too embraced Lincoln. Jimmy Stewart as Senator Jefferson Smith in *Mr. Smith Goes to Washington* found the strength to fight his corrupt enemies in the Senate heartened by nocturnal visits paid to the Lincoln Memorial. Twentieth-Century Fox released John Ford's *Young Mr. Lincoln* that year, and RKO was finishing John Cromwell's *Abe Lincoln in Illinois*, the latter an adaptation of Robert Sherwood's play by that title which won a Pulitzer Prize in 1939.

The Civil War itself became part of the national discourse at that time. The blockbuster version of Margaret Mitchell's bestseller, *Gone with the Wind*, crowned the country's fascination with the nineteenth century conflict that had "increased exponentially" through the 1930s.[4] That fascination contributed to the popularity of Carl Sandburg's *Abraham Lincoln: The War Years*, published in 1939, and part of his six-volume masterwork on Lincoln, its very breadth a tribute to Lincoln's unique status in the American pantheon. That final volume, suggesting a parallel between Lincoln on the eve of war and FDR in similar circumstances by 1939, encouraged the Pulitzer Prize Committee to give its award for history to Sandburg in 1940. Sandburg therefore won as much for his timeliness as for his scholarship.

Bottome admired Sandburg's work and regarded its popularity, along with that of Steinbeck's *Grapes of Wrath* (1939), whose title recalled *The Battle Hymn of the Republic*, as crucial for Britain.[5] The large readership of such works, she believed, revealed the maturity of the American public. As a result, it would be wise enough to recognize the Nazi menace, leading it to support Britain. But Sandburg's biography held pride of place. She interpreted it as veiled praise of Roosevelt and his commitment to an interventionist foreign policy. In effect, she saw a parallel between the American Civil War and the emerging European conflict of 1939–40. FDR, like Lincoln, was willing to fight to uphold the fundamental values of the nation, its geopolitical unity, and a more inclusive conception of "all men are created equal," the values that her own American abolitionist grandmother Margaret Bottome had defended.

The author of *The Mortal Storm* explained her perception of the American Civil War craze to British diplomat Robert Vansittart, with whom she became acquainted in the battle against appeasement, their political alliance developing into a lifelong friendship. Bottome wrote Vansittart when the filming of *The Mortal Storm* was nearing completion in the spring of 1940: "The six volumes [of Sandburg's Lincoln] are excellent, and so modern in their influences that it is difficult […] to escape the conclusion that one is [now] actually reliving those days."[6] Bottome's phrase, "so modern in their influences," captures the impact of Sandburg's multivolume study of Lincoln on the eve of the Second World War. Sandburg's biography, suggesting a parallel between Lincoln and the current president, helped to elevate FDR's status when he sought an unprecedented third term and increasingly, yet gingerly, guided the nation toward war.

By the late 1930s, for the historically minded reading public, interest in Lincoln's presidency had begun to eclipse the once all-consuming interest in the revisionist approach to the First World War that had also intrigued Americans in the 1920s and 1930s. It became increasingly clear, certainly by the fall of 1941, that the question of America being drawn into another European conflict against her own best interests no longer obtained. How and when would America join the fight encompassed the new uncertainty.

Lincoln again proved eminently relevant to FDR in that uncertainty. The president was aware of the analogy between himself and Lincoln.[7] When Hitler and his allies attacked the Soviet Union, Frank Knox, Secretary of the Navy, urged the president to seize the opportunity and declare war on Germany, soon to be bogged down in Russia. FDR said no. Like Lincoln, he answered Knox, we had to wait to be attacked if he were to carry public opinion with him into war. And so, in the middle of 1941, FDR waited for his own Ft. Sumter.

The Mortal Storm, like *Uncle Tom's Cabin*, can therefore be situated within the broad terrain not only of American protest literature. But Bottome's novel also belonged to the overarching analogy with the Civil War by which Americans framed political debate as the Second World War approached. The Civil War analogy provided substitute discourse for an impending reality, if not too terrible to contemplate, too frightening to name directly. What could not be named could be alluded to through historical analogy or buried in the characters and narration of fiction. Substitute discourse came to operate in the very adaptation of Bottome's novel. The Jews became "non-Aryans," a divisive issue within MGM that is examined in Chapter 5. What the antisemites saw as a threat from the strength and power of the Hollywood moguls in reality revealed the studio heads' fear of controversy and their own identity.

The Civil War analogy took on new meaning after the United States entered the war. The Pulitzer Prize for History in 1942 went to Margaret Leech's *Reveille in Washington*, the story of how the Civil War transformed a provincial backwater into the capital of a nation at war. Reveille, the military call to awake, provided an association with the very decade in which Leech wrote her work. The sleep of the 1930s gave way to the rude awakening of war, the subject of Chapter 1, which follows.

This book is the story of Bottome's work in the American context. A bestseller in Britain, the novel proved as popular on the other side of the Atlantic. Once on screen in 1940, however, it entered the volatile and contentious world of American politics embroiled in controversy over the country's relationship to war abroad. For eighteen months *The Mortal Storm* remained at the center of those debates.

A word on methodology. The author takes inspiration from Glenn Frankel's *The Searchers* and *High Noon* (Bloomsbury, 2013 and 2017), in focusing on a single film whose complex significance has been overlooked. In the case of *The Mortal Storm*, in addition to reflecting the issues that roiled American society and politics, it participated in them.

Helmuth Walser Smith's *The Butcher's Tale. Murder and Anti-Semitism in a German Town* has also inspired this work.[8] Smith "pursues a single, exemplary episode," in his case an antisemitic uprising in the north German town of Konitz in 1900, to reveal "'the environment' […] in which anti-Semitism flourished." He argues, a "small-scale, high-resolution investigation" permits "greater precision than is often possible in a general study."[9] In focusing on *The Mortal Storm*, I have aimed at a "precision" similar to Smith's in recounting the story of Hollywood and the Nazis on the eve of war.

Notes

1. "Propaganda in Motion Pictures," Hearings before a Subcommittee of the Committee on Interstate Commerce, U.S. Senate, Seventy Seventh Congress on S. Res. 152 (September 9–26, 1941) (Washington: U.S. Government Printing Office, 1942), 323. Henceforth Hearings.
2. Barry Schwartz, *Abraham Lincoln and the Forge of National Memory* (Chicago: University of Chicago Press, 2000), xii.
3. Phyllis Bottome (PB) to Lady Violet Bonham-Carter, January 15, 1940. British Library. Additional Manuscripts, henceforth BL Add. Mss. 88921/3/3.
4. Merrill Schlier, "Mr. Lincoln Goes to Washington: The Two Lincolns, Monuments, and the Preservation of Patriarchy," *Quarterly Review of Film and Video*, vol. 31 (2014), 453.
5. PB to Robt. Vansittart, April 12, 1940, BL Add. Mss. 88921/3/3.
6. Ibid.
7. See Kenneth S. Davis, *FDR. Into the Storm, 1937–1940* (New York: Random House, 1993), 565–8 for discussion on this point.
8. Helmuth Walser Smith, *The Butcher's Tale. Murder and Anti-Semitism in a German Town* (New York: W. W. Norton & Co., 2003).
9. Ibid., 21–2.

1

A Matter of Timing

A Work Ahead of Its Time

The Mortal Storm presented a paradox. Its reception as a novel differed so greatly from its reception as a film. As a novel it was considered ahead of its time. On screen, not long after publication, critics charged that the film lagged behind events. The novel's mixed reception proved problematic for its author. Phyllis Bottome had more difficulty selling *The Mortal Storm*, whether to a publisher or to Hollywood, than any other work of fiction she produced in a long and prolific career. Recalling how its controversial subject matter impeded publication, she recounted that Sir Geoffrey Faber courageously stepped forward, publishing the first British edition in 1937 "when it was dangerous to do so, and when [...] very few newspapers would dare to give it good [reviews] if any at all."[1] Faber's firm was a newcomer to British Publishing, barely a decade old; yet the owner took a chance on what might fail commercially. Quite the opposite occurred. The novel proved a bestseller for Faber; and as one of the first paperbacks published by Allen Lane's Penguin Books, it sold over 100,000 copies.

Little, Brown & Co. readily brought out the American edition in the spring of 1938. The novel had an equally successful reception in the United States. *The Saturday Review*, the bellwether of American literary taste, urged readers to add Bottome's novel to their spring reading lists. Donald Gordon, in his "Reader's Almanac," a popular feature of the magazine, enticed subscribers by emphasizing its theme of Nazi-Jewish conflict. He described it as "a novel in which the sons of a German mother's racially 'pure' first marriage find difficulty reconciling love for the gentle and revered Jewish stepfather with newly imbibed Nazi ideals."[2] Gordon had accurately summarized the heart of the novel.

Unlike British readers, the American audience found the story intriguing rather than threatening. But again, the novel appeared to be ahead of its time. Through the summer and fall of 1938, *The Mortal Storm* stood alone on *Publishers' Weekly* bestseller list as the only work of fiction to depict atrocities in Nazi Germany. Little, Brown & Co. in fact advertised it "as the first significant novel torn out of the bleeding heart of modern Europe."[3] If not "dangerous," as Faber considered it in Britain, *The Mortal Storm* was at least provocative for Americans and unique in its fictionalized account of life under the Hitler regime.

Within three years of initial publication, MGM, like Sir Geoffrey, agreed to gamble on the novel's arresting story of a German-Jewish family hounded by Nazis, and brought it to the screen. Such accelerating success, however, failed to impress movie critics. None agreed on when the film should have been made; but all were certain that it belonged on the screen, months, even years earlier.

Most of the New York critics, except for Bosley Crowther, the new film critic for the *New York Times*, concurred on this point. Crowther had recently taken over from Frank Nugent, who since 1936 had produced astute, yet acerbic reviews for the *Times*.[4] His successor took a different approach. Crowther reviewed the film with unqualified praise: "the picture turns out to be one of the most harrowing and inflammatory fictions ever placed upon the screen [...] It strikes out powerfully with both fists [...] it gives no quarter [...] it is magnificently directed and acted."[5] Crowther in fact seemed to think the picture, made seven years after Hitler came to power, was appropriately timed:

> At last Hollywood has turned its camera eye upon the most human drama of our age [...] Although this tragic account has been pieced together out of a seven-year-old record of human suffering, the excellence of the production which Metro has given it-and the innocent forcefulness of a visual presentation imbue "The Mortal Storm" with a sharp and seeming contemporary reality.[6]

Nugent's successor emphasized the very timeliness of the film, that is, its "contemporary reality."

But in short order Crowther rethought that assessment. He had covered New York theater for the *Times* since 1935. New to film criticism, he apparently mistrusted his judgment in another medium. When his colleagues wrote more critically, even agreeing on the film's untimely release, Crowther quickly produced a second review with the provocative title, "Lost Opportunity: Where Was Hollywood When the Lights in Germany Went Out?"[7] The *Times* movie critic now complained that *The Mortal Storm* "reaches the screen so late, so unforgivably late [...] Hollywood has missed the bus. [It] is the sort of picture we should have seen about five years ago [...] If it was to be told at all, why wasn't it told then?"[8] Crowther had clearly reversed himself within days of his original review.

Bill Boehnel in the *New York World-Telegram* allowed for a more recent production date: "Had it been made two years ago it would have been a powerful, timely thunderbolt," he wrote.[9] Howard Barnes in the *Chicago Tribune* suggested an even shorter time frame for the Midwest audience. It could have been made as recently as "six months ago [and] would have been enormously stirring," he argued.[10] *The New Yorker*'s John Mosher made a similar complaint. He suggested, like Crowther in his second review, that Hollywood had "missed the bus."

> So far there have been only a few films, and those minor, rather fumbling, and rather unsuccessful, that have to do with life in Germany since Hitler came into power. "The Mortal Storm" [...] is the first that can be considered of any major consequence as a picture [...] but it does present a story [...] familiar to us by this time [...][11]

Mosher gave no date for when the film's release might have been timely. However good the production, it was by now old hat, he seemed to say. But was it?

Crowther's suggested production date for the film was the least likely. *The Mortal Storm* as film or novel would hardly have been possible five years earlier, that is, in 1935. Bottome only began to write it that year, composing it in defiance of the pacifist mood and atmosphere of political compromise she had confronted in Britain: "I had come from a Europe that was distraught and obsessed between Hitler and Mussolini," she later recounted.[12] Back home in Britain, after residing in Central Europe for a decade and a half, she found the "nonchalance of London" incomprehensible.[13] She encountered ignorance and naiveté across the political spectrum. Her conservative friends exclaimed: "Oh, but we like Hitler!" Those in the Liberal and Labour Parties expressed a measure of hope: "Perhaps Hitler will settle down and leave the Jews alone."[14]

Chalmers Mitchell, another "premature anti-Nazi," wrote Bottome from Spain where he had retired after a career as a distinguished zoologist: "I will soon be hanged and keep you a place next mine at the lamppost," he generously offered.[15] Mitchell, like Bottome, had watched the rise of fascism while residing in Europe, in his case Spain, where he supported the Loyalist cause. Before that for thirty-two years, Mitchell had run the London Zoo. No stranger to animal behavior, he had also been a keen observer of politics. As early as 1896, he had acquired notoriety for, it seemed, unjustifiably denouncing the threat to Britain from German militarism. He wrote the London *Times* in May 1939, referring to the earlier charge, that he had never relinquished his scorn for German intentions.[16]

Bottome had made Mitchell's acquaintance in the First World War when he had pioneered the use of propaganda as a weapon of war. She had then worked for him in the Foreign Propaganda Section in the Department of

Information (later the Ministry of Information or MoI).[17] Her exposure to those first efforts at shaping opinion prepared her not only for similar work in the Second World War, but encouraged her to craft a polemical form of fiction in which she embedded her anti-Nazi message.[18] She, like her former mentor Chalmers Mitchell, had no illusions about fascism and shared with him the continental view of it. Europeans "in the winter of 1935 to 1936" were "distraught" over the successes of the dictators, she wrote years later.[19] In Britain, on the contrary, Bottome recoiled when her compatriots, with rare exceptions, considered hostility to Nazism in 1935 at best "premature," at worst cause for alarm.[20] As an old friend admonished her: "Don't try to tell English people all about Hitler. They don't want to hear it and won't believe it until they have got to!"[21] Despite Crowther's admonition, an anti-Nazi novel in 1935 would not have enjoyed a wide readership.

"Clio Deceived"[22]

Crowther might also have considered that American opinion that year lagged even further behind Britain in comprehending the Nazi menace. In the course of the 1930s, Americans tended to look backward rather than forward. *Publishers' Weekly* charted the trend. It found in 1939 that the production of fiction dropped off since 1936 while "the field of History" had doubled in output in the past decade.[23] The trade publication further noted, "most of the ten-year increase in History" occurred between 1934 and 1938, with the heaviest production in 1936 and 1937.[24] A significant proportion of that output addressed the recent past, what *Publishers' Weekly* termed "international affairs and [...] current crises of human history."[25] For Americans in the 1930s, "international affairs" and "current crises of [...] history" meant lingering memories of the First World War. Largely ignored in the decade after it ended, the Great War riveted popular attention in the 1930s. In effect, Americans in 1935 paid closer attention to Kaiser's Germany than to Hitler's.

The cultural historian Modris Eksteins has examined the dramatic disparity in attitudes toward the war from one decade to the next. He argues that in the first post-war decade, the "nightmare and hallucination" of the trenches were "consciously repressed."[26] The effort to bury the past exacted a toll, creating a "spiritual crisis" that dominated the decade and found expression in "hedonistic and narcissistic" behavior.[27] Public consciousness finally awoke to the war with the publication in January 1929 of an explosive work of fiction: *All Quiet on the Western Front*. Readers responded by clamoring for more works on the Great War. As a result, *All Quiet* "brought on a flood of new books."[28] They were, according to Eksteins, both "quickly commissioned and quickly written."[29] Exploiting the reading public's craving, those books explained in part the rash of historical works that had perplexed *Publishers' Weekly* at the end of the decade.

But there was more to Remarque's novel than the public's rediscovery of the war. Remarque described the conflict in terms of German suffering, a version that resonated with Americans and Britons increasingly ill at ease with the harsh terms of the Treaty of Versailles. It could be said that the German novelist contributed to a revisionist approach to the war by humanizing the average German soldier. Paul Bäumer and his mates could no more be labeled "Huns" than could the confused and hapless doughboys they confronted. Eksteins made the same observation in noting the resemblance among combatants on both sides: "Paul Bäumer [...] could just as easily be a tommy, poilu, or doughboy [...]," he wrote.[30] In the same fashion, the "flood of new books" on the war downplayed or refuted the official condemnation of Germany for her role in the war. Humanizing ordinary German soldiers led not only to a changed perception of the Great War but also to a new discourse regarding German national character. Again, Eksteins observed: "Remarque's novel did a great deal to undermine the view that Germans were [...] not to be trusted [...] *All Quiet* promoted at a popular level what historical revisionism was achieving at an academic and political level: the erosion of the idea of a collective German war guilt."[31] *Publishers' Weekly* argued that the "academic and the political" had become popular in the 1930s. In fact, historians and the popular media had embraced a new interpretation of Germany that both transformed the average German soldier and absolved Germany of guilt for the war.

The American historians who contributed to the new version of the First World War and the revised portrait of its combatants addressed two questions that particularly resonated with their compatriots. Why had we entered a European conflict in the first place? The second question followed logically from the first: How could we avoid fighting in a similar conflict should one arise again? Both questions discouraged perception of Nazism as a growing menace that might once more engage America in European affairs. Germany lay at the heart of the discussion, but the former enemy now appeared maligned rather than menacing. Much of the credit for that perception went to the German Foreign Office.[32] Its money and support subsidized a barrage of publications undertaken to exonerate Germany from responsibility for the First World War. According to the historian Holger Herwig, "Clio was in fact deceived in Germany as early as 1914."[33]

The effort began with what historians have termed "the German innocence campaign," which extended well into the 1930s.[34] The German Foreign Office (*Auswartiges Amt*) conducted the campaign to undermine the basis for reparation payments, as the *New York Times* observed, and more broadly to improve Germany's image abroad.[35] The Foreign Office provided the means to undercut the Treaty of Versailles almost as soon as the allies presented it. Its well-funded War Guilt Section was charged with "refuting the [...] war guilt accusation," in particular.[36] In 1920, one year later, to give the appearance of independence, the nongovernmental Center for the Study of the Causes of the War replaced the Foreign Office's War Guilt Section, tasked with offering a new perception of Germany's conduct in the war. Neither the mission nor the Foreign Ministry as the source of funding had changed. The new center targeted "public opinion in neutral and former enemy countries."[37] British and American opinion proved especially susceptible to the German viewpoint as the former allies blamed the French for the unenforceable terms of the Treaty of Versailles.[38]

But the German government's most ambitious project to refute the terms of the treaty also proved to be the most successful, at least in the United States. A school of revisionist historians who refused to take the Treaty of Versailles at face value based much of their work on sources the German Foreign Ministry provided. From 1922 to 1929, the Ministry produced a forty-volume document collection in a series titled *Die Grosse Politik der Europaischen Kabinette (The High Politics of the European Cabinets)*.[39] The trusted foreign minister Gustav Stresemann, who more than any other German statesman contributed to the rehabilitation of Germany's image in the 1920s, admitted that "the publication was an act of self-defense."[40] Taken as a whole, the forty volumes absolved Germany, while blaming the Entente for initiating the war. Deploying an arsenal of academic methodology and documentation, Germany had taken the offensive in the war for the past. One of the collection's editors admitted to having "substantially rehabilitated [...] the old regime and, morally at least, [...] the Kaiser."[41] By the late 1920s those volumes had encouraged American historians to embrace a more positive view of Germany while blaming the Allies (the Entente) for both US participation in the war and even for the war itself.

Two of those historians did pioneering work in undermining justification for the Treaty of Versailles and curbing the impulse to punish the Germans. Sidney Bradshaw Fay and Harry Elmer Barnes encouraged their compatriots to question Germany's responsibility for the war. Fay insisted "all major European powers shared the blame for the escalation of the crisis [in 1914]."[42] Barnes went even further, alleging that in the onset of the First World War, "Germany was the victim of an Entente plot."[43] Barnes's student, C. Hartley Gratten, built on his mentor's work in absolving Germany. Gratten, in *Why We Fought*, published in 1929, "indicted British publicists and Wilson's Anglophile advisors 'for luring America into war'."[44] Liberally employing the forty volumes of German Foreign Ministry documents, Fay and Barnes, along with their students, laid the foundation for a new consensus that absolved Germany of guilt for the First World War. As *Publishers' Weekly* observed, with the outpouring of works on "recent history," that consensus was successfully transmitted to the American reading public, that is, public opinion, by the late 1930s.[45]

In 1935, the year in which Bosley Crowther argued the film version of *The Mortal Storm* should have been released, the historian Walter Millis published *Road to War: America 1914–1917*.[46] Millis announced his membership in the school of revisionist historians: "I have availed myself of Mr. Gratten's work [...] 'Why We Fought', published in 1929."[47] He then explained that his book was "devoted to criticism of [...] the Entente case," adding to absolve himself of bias, "If this gives the book an appearance of relative hostility toward the Entente, that is simply an unavoidable consequence of the subject itself [...]"[48] Published in the same month that Hitler reinstituted conscription, Millis's book seemed to warn against taking the road America had traversed two decades earlier, lured into fighting Germany by the Entente.

The Neutrality Campaign of the 1930s

By the mid-1930s a determined group of US senators had joined the revisionist historians in arguing that the nation had been duped into fighting an inappropriate enemy. But they took a new approach, captured in one short, devastating phrase. The politicians found their rallying cry in the label "merchants of death" applied to the international cabal of arms makers. Helmuth C. Englebrecht and Frank C. Hanighen supplied the phrase in the title of their 1934 bestseller *Merchants of Death*, which blamed profiteering munitions manufacturers for encouraging American participation in the war.[49] According to Englebrecht and Hanighen, Germany's alleged war guilt paled before the efforts of Dupont and Bethlehem Steel to profit from the war.

A widely read article in *Fortune* magazine popularized the Englebrecht and Hanighen thesis, charging that arms manufacturers such as Bethlehem Steel, DuPont, and their European counterparts lived by two maxims: "when there are wars prolong them, when there is peace disturb it."[50] While making passing reference to Hitler's capacity for "stirring up a new outbreak of international anarchy in Europe," the article gave more attention to the Führer's failed presidential bid in March 1932, rather than to his intentions now that he ruled Germany.[51] The reason: French, German, and Czech arms makers had all contributed to Hitler's presidential campaign. The *Fortune* article urged those "anxious for more details" on the nefarious interference of arms makers in politics and government policy to read *Merchants of Death*.[52]

The Englebrecht-Hanighen work took on a political life of its own. Republican senator Gerald P. Nye of North Dakota embraced the book's title and its accusations. Using both, he catapulted his Senate investigation of arms manufacturers into national prominence. In the mid-1930s "the

Nye hearings transformed the revisionist version of American entrance into the First World War into a popular orthodoxy."⁵³ Nye embraced the conclusion of the revisionist historians that the British government, like the munitions manufacturers, had connived to take America to war. In 1935 he joined like-minded members of the Senate to pass the first of three Neutrality Acts, known collectively as the Nye legislation, designed to ensure that the United States would never be duped into fighting Europe's battles again.⁵⁴ Nye found support for his neutrality campaign from a powerful grassroots organization, the Liberty League, founded in August 1934 to oppose the new president and his domestic program known collectively as the New Deal.⁵⁵

Well financed with chapters all over the country, the League soon acquired a new task. It sought to rally the Republican Party in preparation for the 1936 presidential contest, adding foreign policy to its agenda. As part of that effort, the League held a five-day forum in the summer of 1935 at the University of Virginia. Scholars addressed the question of "U.S.-German relations, concluding with a call for greater 'understanding' of the 'New Germany.'"⁵⁶ By 1935 the old Germany had been absolved. The new Germany, influential people now urged, should be granted tolerance as well. Contrary to Crowther's admonition, producing *The Mortal Storm* on screen would have been a hard sell in 1935 had the story been available.

American Indifference to the Jewish Question

Bosley Crowther ignored another reality of the mid-1930s. The state of German Jews, while hardly secure, would not in 1935 have provided a gripping plot for American movie audiences. Despite the numerous personal and public restrictions imposed on Jews, the Nuremberg Laws announced that year convinced many German Jews that their situation would improve.⁵⁷ They preferred to believe that they now possessed a measure of protection within the new legal framework of the so-called race laws. The laws themselves appeared to dampen a spate of escalating violence toward Jews in the spring and summer of 1935.⁵⁸

In the following year, Jews found further assurance in Germany's efforts to improve its image abroad as the country prepared for the 1936 Olympics. Many of the embarrassing and annoying restrictions directed against them were removed in preparation for the games, adding a false sense of security.⁵⁹ It did not take long for the truth to become clear. Within two years conditions for German Jews had become intolerable. On *Kristallnacht* (the Night of Broken Glass), November 9, 1938, with the organized destruction of synagogues and Jewish businesses, few could fail to perceive the new reality. By 1940 matters were truly dire. MGM released *The Mortal Storm* in between the sealing of occupied Poland's two largest ghettos, Lodz in April and Warsaw in November. Jews in those two ghettos alone faced imminent starvation in the winter of 1940–1.

Crowther did hedge his bets in one respect. By the end of his second review, the critical one, he compromised on the appropriate production date for the film: "since [*The Mortal Storm*] definitely falls into the category of propaganda, we feel its effectiveness [...] would have been greater three or five years ago."[60] The year 1937 (three years earlier) as a production date, however, was almost as unlikely as 1935.

In October 1937 President Roosevelt discovered, much to his chagrin, that the country was hardly ready for an interventionist foreign policy. Already in his second term, the president gave his first major address that touched on foreign affairs. He told a Chicago audience that Germany, Italy, and Japan were the "sick" nations of the world community; they needed to be expelled and "quarantined."[61] The president had for the first time proposed that the United States join "collective security arrangements," challenging the hitherto favored policy of neutrality and suggesting instead the need to form a coalition of allied nations opposed to Nazism and fascism.[62] The press latched onto the word "quarantine" and launched an attack on the president for undermining the official US policy of neutrality.

At the president's news conference that followed shortly after the "quarantine speech," one reporter took an aggressive tone with the president. Former Rhodes Scholar and Washington bureau chief for the *New York Herald Tribune*, Ernest K. Lindley, pressed Roosevelt with the question, "How can you be neutral if you are going to align yourself with one group of nations?"[63] The president did not have a good answer. Judge Rosenman, FDR's primary speechwriter throughout his presidency, subsequently quoted the president on the fallout from the speech. "It's a terrible thing to look over your shoulder when you are trying to lead [...] and find no one there."[64] Fearing a similar lonely position, Hollywood carefully calibrated public opinion and its potential profits from a particular production. Without the prospect of an audience, a major studio would hardly invest in an avowedly "propaganda" film in 1937.

The chronologies of movie reviewers, Bill Boehnel and Howard Barnes, were equally dubious. Boehnel, in the *New York World-Telegram*, recommended that *The Mortal Storm* should have been made in 1938. That year, despite escalating persecution, the Jewish question was largely defined as a refugee crisis. Representatives of twenty-nine nations participated in the Evian Conference, which met in the south of France in the first two weeks of July to address that crisis. The United States acted as host. All participants, including the United States, refused to permit entry of significant numbers of Jews, observing, among other excuses, that Germany's policy toward her own citizens (which now included those in Austria) constituted a domestic matter for which an international response would be inappropriate.[65]

The violence of *Kristallnacht* failed to budge Congress on the immigration question and loosen restrictions on entry visas for Jews fleeing a rapidly deteriorating situation. No politician was prepared to arouse the country over the plight of Jewish refugees. The film most likely would have found an indifferent audience, if not a resentful one, in 1938.

Boehnel's "powerful, timely thunderbolt" of 1938 would have met with indifference for other reasons. Spain dominated attention that year as the Loyalists went down to defeat. Liberal publications such as *The Nation* and *The New Republic* focused on the plight of Loyalist refugees who faced slaughter at the hand of Franco's troops. Cold and starving Spaniards pulled at the heartstrings of liberal and socially conscious Americans. Those publications were strikingly bereft of information on the plight of German, Austrian, and Czech Jews, much less condemnation of it. Typical of the attention devoted to the Spanish cause was an advertisement for the Spanish clothing drive in *The Nation* in the fall of 1938. Even Jewish entertainer Gypsy Rose Lee, who chaired the drive, proclaimed: "If I can take my clothes off for Spain so can you!" she told reluctant donors.⁶⁶ Like so many others, she was notably silent about Jewish refugees.

While committees on behalf of Spanish refugees proliferated like mushrooms after rain, even that subject failed to resonate with moviegoers. Hollywood's one production to treat the Spanish Civil War, *Blockade*, only addressed the subject reluctantly. Its confused plot sank the film at the box office.⁶⁷

Howard Barnes's criticism of *The Mortal Storm* proved similarly unrealistic. Writing in the *Chicago Tribune*, he argued for the release of the film "six months earlier," as 1939 turned to 1940 and then it "would have been enormously stirring," he insisted.⁶⁸ But Europe then waged what isolationist senator William E. Borah (R-ID), Chair of the Senate Foreign Relations Committee, dubbed the "phony war," the interval between the declaration of war in September and the launching of the blitzkrieg in April. No one that winter of 1940 could be certain how bad the war might become or even if actual fighting might be averted. People in a state of suspended animation, hoping against hope, would avoid being "stirred."

Sidney Franklin, who produced *The Mortal Storm*, recognized the consistency of criticism leveled at the film. In his unpublished autobiography, Franklin listed precisely those critics who condemned the seemingly belated release of the film along with their suggested opening dates.⁶⁹ He singled out Crowther (five, maybe three years ago), Bill Boehnel (two years ago), and Howard Barnes (six months ago) with the dates of release each had argued for. The producer expressed disgust with the lot of them: "the critics thought it was too late [...]" Even so, Franklin complained, they "can't agree on when they would have preferred to have seen it."⁷⁰ Franklin, on the other hand, drew a distinction that the critics failed to make. Whether it *should* have been made earlier, the film's producer understood that it *could* not have appeared on screen any earlier than it did. And even when it did appear, to Franklin's frustration, he did not feel that he had revealed the whole truth about Nazi Germany. He explained in his autobiography, "George Froeschel and Hans Rameau, who contributed to the script, were refugees from Germany. Had we put in what they told me, no one would have believed it."[71]

Both Franklin and his critics were frustrated in 1940. As he later told the story, he had not made the film as realistic as he had hoped to. The critics in turn only implied, perhaps not even recognizing themselves, what they really complained of. Why had *The Mortal Storm* not appeared earlier to waken us from the torpor and somnambulism of the 1930s, they really asked? They seemed to suggest that one Hollywood production could do the impossible and weaken the hold on public opinion of a decade of propaganda and subsidized scholarship designed to absolve Germany.

The "deep, deep sleep [...]," George Orwell, 1938[72]

Bottome's perception of her homeland in the 1930s could be found in a distinctive phrase that appeared in her correspondence as well as in her American lectures, starting in the middle of the decade.[73] It recurs as though she were first trying it out, then revising it as her homeland gave her increasing grounds for frustration. "England has gone Nazi in her sleep," she repeatedly warned. She pessimistically wrote her old friend Ezra Pound at the beginning of 1936, for example, "I expect we shall go Nazi in our sleep."[74] Not long thereafter she stated emphatically that England had indeed gone Nazi in her sleep. She might vary the phrase, but the meaning remained the same. She told a Boston audience in October 1938, "England is losing Freedom. Going Fascist in its sleep."[75] She used the phrase for the last time in the third and final volume of her autobiography, *The Goal*, published shortly before her death in 1963. There she wrote of what she had found nearly thirty years earlier upon returning to Britain after lengthy residence in Central Europe. "It was as though England had gone Nazi in her sleep," she bemoaned at the time.[76] The phrase had so aptly captured the moment for her that it remained in her mind decades later.

George Orwell shared Bottome's perception and her metaphor. He complained less critically, however, that England had simply gone to sleep. On his return from Spain in 1938, he walked around Trafalgar Square musing to himself that the people he observed were "all sleeping the deep,

deep sleep of England from which I sometimes fear that we shall never wake till we are jerked out of it by the roar of the bomb."[77] As Bottome's unnamed friend had warned her three years earlier, "English people never believe what they don't like until they have got to!"[78]

A young American in London at the same time as Orwell and Bottome employed the same metaphor. The second son of the US ambassador to the Court of St. James devoted his Harvard senior thesis to the question of *Why England Slept*.[79] Like the two British writers, the youthful John Kennedy captured Britain's reality on the eve of war. Rather than awaken to danger, the British political establishment sought escape in appeasement, refusing to rearm adequately as Germany so blatantly prepared to fight. Astute yet disparate observers concurred: England asleep too disturbingly captured the moment.

Criticism of the somnambulism of the 1930s also appeared in cinema. But it took Charlie Chaplin, who could finance his own films, to do it. In *The Great Dictator*, Chaplin portrayed the amnesia of the interwar period as hardly confined to Britain. His protagonist, the Little Barber, suffers a head injury while fighting in the First World War. He awakens from years of war-induced "unconsciousness" and returns to find the word "Jew" painted on the glass of what had once been the window of his shop. The Little Barber finds the effacement at first annoying until he is set upon by Dictator Hynkel's storm troopers as he tries to wipe it off. Chaplin's meaning was not lost on movie audiences of 1940 for whom a rude awakening from the 1930s began in April of 1940 with the launching of the Nazi blitzkrieg in Western Europe. No one could sleep through the German conquests in the spring of 1940, least of all Europe's Jews. Bottome, like Chaplin, not only called on the world to wake up to the Nazi menace, but each of them also chose Jewish protagonists to make the point.

The Timing Was Finally Right

The pattern of the 1920s, as Modris Eksteins described it, had repeated itself in the following decade. In the 1920s, as Eksteins argues, "The spate of official and unofficial histories [...] was largely ignored by the public."[80] In the 1930s people again repressed nightmarish scenarios too terrifying to bear. This time they cringed before the future and so retreated into the past. History began to mean more in the 1930s than it had in the previous decade. The public had ceased to deny the trenches; instead, readers began to find fascination in the Great War itself. Historians, as *Publishers' Weekly* observed, monopolized the German question and the reading public in the 1930s. Going against the grain, Bottome attempted, as Remarque had, to burst the bubble of self-delusion through the immediacy of fiction.[81]

But with that the two parted company. Remarque, wittingly or unwittingly, contributed to a calculated process of absolving Germany from guilt for the war. *All Quiet* is generally regarded as a pacifist, anti-war novel. As noted above, Remarque's emphasis on German suffering in the war aroused sympathy, not for an enemy but for a Germany now perceived as a fellow combatant, whose soldiers too were subject to the dehumanizing conditions of the trenches and the strategies of sacrifice pursued by the high command on both sides. Bottome, however, did not share that image of mutual victimhood. Like her fellow British novelist Katharine Burdekin in *Swastika Night*, published in the same year as *The Mortal Storm*, she warned of a perverse strain in German culture that once more threatened civilization.[82] Remarque's novel had constituted a publishing extravaganza, inaugurating the economic and cultural phenomenon of the modern bestseller.[83] *All Quiet* also encouraged the marriage of fiction and feature film, first launched with so much success in the United States with *The Birth of a Nation* in 1915, and confirmed in 1930 with the American film adaptation of Remarque's novel.[84] The old medium of print and the new medium of film were made for each other. Remarque reinforced the point.

Bottome benefited from Remarque's dual success. Her book proved a bestseller: ninth on *Publishers' Weekly* bestseller list for 1938, encouraging MGM's purchase of the film rights in the following year.[85] And she shared with Remarque the determination to burst the bubble of delusion, in her case the "nonchalance of London" or what Eksteins has termed "conscious repression."[86] But again Bottome parted with Remarque. As the response of film critics in 1940 revealed, *The Mortal Storm* provoked annoyance, even anger. The reaction was not surprising. Remarque after all had awakened his readers to a war safely over. Bottome instead cried wolf with the predator panting at the door.

In contrast to the critical consensus that had so troubled Sidney Franklin, the premier of *The Mortal Storm* on June 20, 1940, could not have been timelier. Bottome's creative vision converged with events and did so when it mattered most. In the preceding months Hitler's armies had overrun Denmark and Norway. His forces had occupied the Low Countries. A week before *The Mortal Storm*'s premier, his army had marched into Paris. In Bottome's film the heroine dies at the end, as had the independence of much of Europe. The all-American hero Jimmy Stewart (Martin Breitner) escapes, waiting in the wings to continue the fight, which could be said of the United States itself in June 1940.[87]

Bottome's good friend as well as her publisher, the vice-president of Little, Brown & Co., Roger Scaife, described the atmosphere in the United States the day before the premier of *The Mortal Storm*. He wrote Bottome on June 19, 1940, that the country had awakened and was indeed waiting in the wings to help:

> We are grief-stricken over here-that is all those that I know-at the tragedy which is taking place in Europe, and many of us are frantic at our apparent inability to give any real help. If England and France have been asleep with all the danger threatening on their borders, we too have been equally somnolent in not making any preparations whatever. There is, however, a sudden awakening, and if you see our papers, you will know that we are voting billions for an increase in ships, planes, etc. and that furthermore, the administration is trying to cut every possible corner to supply aid.[88]

The image of a somnolent decade had taken hold on both sides of the Atlantic. Scaife had to admit, the primary members of the Entente, so recently blamed for starting the First World War, had slept while Germany rearmed.

The reality of events had intervened, forcing the democracies to do more than yawn and stretch. It was time to leap from the bed as *The New Republic* politely, but firmly, informed its readers. Within days of Scaife's letter to Bottome, the liberal weekly editorialized with restraint, "American citizens should understand that our role in world affairs has entered a new phase."[89]

Still, uncertainty prevailed. Neither the Democrats nor the Republicans had yet to nominate a candidate for the impending presidential campaign of 1940. Britain hung by a thread. The United States faced a dire question. Should the country spare its meager military resources to save the island nation or conserve supplies for its own defense and the defense of the hemisphere?

Two days before the release of *The Mortal Storm*, on June 18, 1940, Winston Churchill, in what has become known as his "finest hour" speech, pointedly called out to "the whole world, including the United States." He warned that with a German victory, "all that we have known and cared for will sink into the abyss of a new Dark Age made more sinister and perhaps more protracted by the lights of a perverted science."[90] With near perfect timing Hollywood reinforced the prime minister's message with the release of *The Mortal Storm*. One of the film's leading characters, a renowned scientist, Dr. Victor Roth (Frank Morgan), defends "scientific truth" before a classroom of "hoodlums," that is, students in Nazi uniforms, who argue that the blood of non-Aryans differs from the blood of Aryans. "Scientific truth" confronted "the lights of a perverted science." With the premier of *The Mortal Storm* two days after Churchill's speech, "the abyss of a new Dark Age" had found embodiment in the most popular medium of American culture when it mattered most.

MGM executives had hardly planned it that way.[91] The story behind the film's production, to be told below, proved nearly as harrowing as the on-screen drama. The critics notwithstanding, the film's debut appeared to be a matter of extraordinary timing, coinciding with a growing sense of crisis in the United States as the Nazis overran Western Europe.

The Nation captured that mood of crisis at the end of July. Max Lerner, professor of Political Science, and a regular contributor to both *The Nation* and its sister publication *The New Republic*, wrote in the former of the distressing awakening that had just occurred:

> The thrust of the Nazi columns has left its trauma not only on the European consciousness but on the American as well. Look at the way in which two new phrases have established themselves in our speech- *blitzkrieg* and fifth column. We are like someone who wakes out of an anesthetic sleep in a strange room, enclosed by unfamiliar walls, and wonders whether the special shapes around him are nightmare imaginings or terrible realities. Clinging to the radio hoping against hope as we listen to the sickening bulletins, we attempt to exorcise the horror. But it will not go away [...] We shall not for a long time resolve ourselves to the [loss of the] tranquility we once owned.[92]

By the summer of 1940, the image of a world gone to sleep in the 1930s, followed by the rude awakening of that year, had become commonplace. Bottome's prescience in employing that image years before lies deep in her interwar fiction. What for most people appeared like a dreaded moment in 1940, for Bottome was already too familiar, having gestated for decades in her best fiction that preceded *The Mortal Storm*. Her story of Nazi Germany was a novel before it was a film. The origins of what appeared so strikingly on screen in 1940 must therefore be sought in Bottome's interwar fiction that by 1937 had culminated in *The Mortal Storm*.

Notes

1. Phyllis Bottome, *The Goal* (London: Faber & Faber, 1962), 275.
2. Donald Gordon, "Reader's Almanac," *The Saturday Review of Literature* (April 2, 1938), 21.
3. Advertisement in *The Saturday Review of Literature* (April 2, 1938), 21.
4. On Nugent's career, see Glenn Frankel, *The Searchers. The Making of an American Legend* (New York: Bloomsbury, 2013), 252–3.
5. Bosley Crowther, "The Screen," *New York Times*, June 21, 1940, 25.
6. Ibid.
7. Bosley Crowther, "Lost Opportunity [...]," *New York Times*, June 23, 1940, 23.

8   Ironically, Crowther ended his career as he began it: out of step with mainstream opinion. He wrote a blistering review of *Bonnie and Clyde* in 1967, one of the few critics not to praise it as a new film for a new time. The *Times* is alleged to have fired him for no longer reflecting public sentiment. See *Wikipedia* entry on Crowther, accessed May 12, 2014.

9   Bill Boehnel, "The Mortal Storm," *New York World-Telegram*, June 21, 1940, 20.

10 Howard Barnes, "The Mortal Storm," *Chicago Tribune* (June 21, 1940), 20.

11 John Mosher, "The Current Cinema. A German Story," *The New Yorker*, June 22, 1940, 62.

12 *The Goal*, 258.

13 Ibid.

14 Ibid.

15 Ibid.

16 "Chalmers Mitchell," *Wikipedia*, accessed May 5, 2014.

17 See Sir Peter Chalmers Mitchell, *My Fill of Days* (London: Faber & Faber, 1937), 278–98. Cf. Pam Hirsch, *The Constant Liberal. The Life and Work of Phyllis Bottome* (London: Quartet, 2010), 83. Hirsch states that Bottome did her war work under John Buchan (Lord Tweedsmuir) in the Foreign Propaganda Section; whereas Mitchell claims to have run that division. Bottome pays homage to Mitchell in *The Goal* without explaining the origin of their relationship.

18 See Hirsch on this point, 83.

19 Bottome, *The Goal*, 258.

20 Ibid.

21 Ibid., 259.

22 The phrase comes from Holger Herwig, "Clio Deceived: Patriotic Self-Censorship in Germany after the War," in Keith M. Wilson (ed.), *Forging the Collective Memory: Government and International Historians through Two World Wars* (Oxford and Providence: Berghahn Books, 1996), 87–127. Cited in Annika Mombauer, *The Origins of the First World War: Controversies and Consensus* (London: Pearson Education, Ltd., 2002), 69.

23 *Publishers' Weekly* (henceforth *PW*), "Currents in the Trade," January 21, 1939, 183.

24 Ibid., 184.

25 Ibid., 183.

26 Modris Eksteins, *Rites of Spring. The Great War and the Birth of the Modern Age* (Boston: Houghton Mifflin Co., 2000), 256.

27 Ibid., 256–7. Cf. Paul K. Saint-Amour, *Tense Future: Modernism, Total War, Encyclopedic Form* (Oxford: Oxford University Press, 2015). Saint-Amour argues that "a set of psychic and cultural responses to the First World War" constituted the interwar period's "anticipatory syndrome" regarding a traumatic and inevitable world conflict to dwarf the First World

War (13). Eksteins in contrast argues that the psychic energy of the 1920s was expended on repressing the past as a way of avoiding the future. Both concur on a distortion of chronology in the public sphere following the First World War. In effect, trauma imposes its own chronology. Only with "the past's resubordination to the present" can "the future be reopened," according to Saint-Amour (15). To Bottome, as with Eksteins, the future in all its horror was not so much anticipated as it was repressed to evade it, captured in her frequently used metaphor of England "having gone Nazi in her sleep."

28 Eksteins, *Rites of Spring*, p. 277.
29 Ibid.
30 Modris Eksteins, "*All Quiet on the Western Front* and the Fate of War," *Journal of Contemporary History*, vol. 15, no. 2 (April 1980), 358.
31 Ibid., 361.
32 For a detailed account of the German Foreign Office's campaign to absolve Germany of war guilt, see Mombauer, *The Origins of the First World War*, 21–118.
33 Mombauer, *The Origins of the First World War*, 22.
34 Ibid., 50.
35 "The *New York Times* suspected in May 1924 that it was no coincidence that Germany released important source material just when its reparations payments to the allies were due," Mombauer, *The Origins of the First World War*, 55, as cited in John Keiger, "France," in Keith M. Wilson (ed.), *Decisions for War, 1914* (London: University College London Press, 1995), 145.
36 Mombauer, *The Origins of the First World War*, 51.
37 Ibid., 55. See also Selig Adler, "The War Guilt Question and American Disillusionment, 1918–1928," *Journal of Modern History*, vol. 23, no. 1 (March 1951), 1–28.
38 Adler, "The War Guilt Question," 20.
39 Mombauer, *The Origins of the First World War*, 60.
40 Mombauer, *The Origins of the First World War*, 60. As cited in Keith M. Wilson, "Introduction: Governments, Historians and 'Historical Engineering,'" in Wilson (ed.), Forging Collective Memory, 11–12.
41 Mombauer, *The Origins of the First World War*, 60.
42 S.B. Fay, *The Origins of the World War* (New York: The MacMillan Co., 1929), vol. I: *Before Sarajevo. Underlying Causes of the War*; vol. II: *After Sarajevo: Immediate Causes of the War*; citation vol. I, p. v; vol. II, pp. 547–8.
43 H.E. Barnes, *The Genesis of the War: An Introduction to the Problem of War-Guilt* (New York: Alfred A. Knopf, 1926), xi. As cited in Mombauer, *The Origins of the First World War*, 87.
44 Geoffrey Smith, "Isolationism, the Devil, and the Advent of the Second World War: Variations on a Theme," *The International History Review*, vol. 4, no. 1 (February 1982), 60.

45 *PW*, "Currents in the Trade," January 21, 1939, 183.
46 Walter Millis, *Road to War: America 1914–1917* (Boston: Houghton Mifflin Co., 1935).
47 Ibid., "Preface," vii.
48 Ibid.
49 See especially Smith, "Isolationism, the Devil, and the Advent of the Second World War," 60.
50 "Arms and the Men," *Fortune*, IX, no. 3 (March 1934), 120.
51 Ibid., 126.
52 Ibid., 128.
53 Selig Adler, *The Uncertain Giant, 1921–1941. American Foreign Policy between the Wars* (New York: Houghton Mifflin Co., 1965), 164–5.
54 Smith, "Isolationism, the Devil, and the Advent of the Second World War," 63.
55 See discussion in Blanche Wiesen Cook, *Eleanor Roosevelt, vol. 2: The Defining Years, 1933–1938* (New York: Penguin Books, 1992), 335.
56 Jeff Shesol, *Supreme Power. Franklin Roosevelt vs. the Supreme Court* (New York: W.W. Norton & Co., 2010), 161.
57 Robert S. Wistrich, *Hitler and the Holocaust* (New York: The Modern Library, 2001), 54–5.
58 See Ian Kershaw, *Hitler. Hubris: 1889–1936* (New York: W.W. Norton & Co., Inc., 1999), 559–73 for a detailed analysis of escalating violence as a factor in the promulgation of the Nuremberg laws.
59 Wistrich, *Hitler and the Holocaust*, 56.
60 Crowther, "Lost Opportunity," *NYT*, June 23, 1940, 23.
61 See Davis, *FDR. Into the Storm*, 131 for full discussion of the "Quarantine Speech," pp. 130–6.
62 Ibid., 132.
63 Ibid., 135.
64 Sam I. Rosenman, *Working with Roosevelt* (New York: Harper & Brothers, 1952), 167.
65 See Wistrich, *Hitler and the Holocaust*, for discussion of the issues before the conference and the range of responses, 71–2.
66 "Advertisement for Spanish Clothing Drive/Refugee Committee," *The Nation* (September 1938), 96.
67 Released in June 1938, *Blockade* was produced independently by Walter Wanger and distributed by United Artists which meant that Wanger must have incurred considerable expense with the film. It did receive two Academy Award nominations—John Howard Lawson for Best Original Story and Werner Janssen for Best Score—but did poorly at the box office and did not therefore encourage Hollywood to make other politically engaged films in 1938.

68 Howard Barnes, "The Mortal Storm," *Chicago Tribune* (June 21, 1940), 20.
69 Franklin, "We Laughed and We Cried," 287.
70 Ibid.
71 Ibid., 289.
72 George Orwell, *Homage to Catalonia* (New York: Harcourt, Brace, World, 1952), 232.
73 See, for example, letters to be found in her archive British Library (London) (henceforth BL) Add. Mss. 88921/2/8 and 88921/3/3.
74 Phyllis Bottome to Ezra Pound, January 14, 1936. Beinecke Rare Book and Manuscript Library. Ezra Pound Papers. YCAL MSS 43, Box 5, Folder 228.
75 Press clipping dated October 11, 1938, but with name of newspaper cut off to be found in BL Add. Mss. 88921/2/8.
76 Bottome, *The Goal*, 259.
77 Orwell, *Homage to Catalonia*, 232.
78 Bottome, *The Goal*, 259.
79 For discussion of Kennedy's first book, see Barbara Leaming, *Jack Kennedy: The Education of a Statesman* (New York: W.W. Norton & Co., 2006), 104–7.
80 Eksteins, *Rites of Spring*, 291.
81 She was certainly not alone in writing anti-fascist fiction in the 1930s, but such works as Storm Jameson's *In the Second Year* (1936) and Katherine Burdekin's *Swastika Night* (1937) did not become trans-Atlantic bestsellers.
82 Katharine Burdekin, *Swastika Night* (New York: The Feminist Press, 1985).
83 See Ekstein's discussion of this phenomenon in relation to *All Quiet* in *Rites of Spring*, 275–99.
84 The film was produced by Carl Laemmle and directed by Lewis Milestone, each of whom won an Academy Award. It starred Lew Ayers as Paul Bäumer.
85 *Wikipedia*, "*Publishers' Weekly* List of Bestselling Novels in the U.S. in the 1930s," accessed May 12, 2014.
86 Eksteins, *Rites of Spring*, 291.
87 The plot of the movie reverses that of the novel: the heroine escapes across the border in the novel while Freya's lover Hans has already been murdered. This reversal will be discussed at greater length in Chapter 5.
88 Roger L. Scaife to PB, June 19, 1940, BL Add. Mss. 88921/3/3.
89 "Anonymous Editorial," *The New Republic*, vol. 102, no. 26 (June 24, 1940), 831.
90 The Churchill Centre, Winston Churchill, "Their Finest Hour," Speech to the House of Commons (June 18, 1940). http://www.winstonchurchill.org (accessed January 26, 2015).
91 For a full discussion of Hollywood's reluctance to depict Hitler and the Third Reich on screen, see two recent monographs: David Welky, *The Moguls and the Dictators* (Baltimore: Johns Hopkins University Press, 2008) and Thomas

Doherty, *Hollywood and Hitler, 1933–1939* (New York: Columbia University Press, 2013).

92 Max Lerner, "The War as Revolution, I. The Breaking of Nations," *The Nation* (July 27, 1940). See also Susan Dunn, *1940. FDR, Willkie, Lindbergh, Hitler—the Election Amid the Storm* (New Haven: Yale University Press, 2013), 67–8.

2

Novelist of War

Fictional Origins of *The Mortal Storm*

While movie critics addressed the question of why *The Mortal Storm* had "come so late," a question with a more revealing answer would have been, where and when had the novel on which it was based originated, that is, how had the story come to be written in the first place? The success Bottome enjoyed with *The Mortal Storm*, first as a bestseller and then as the (belated) film of the hour in 1940, had not come easily. The novel after all defied public attitudes in both Britain and the United States regarding Germany. Bottome, on the other hand, had been thorough in her preparation to write it, practicing with other politically engaged works through the interwar period. By the late 1930s her experience converged with the harsh reality of Nazi menace. When she came to write *The Mortal Storm*, she had long been a novelist of war; her century had proven generous to her and was about to provide again.

The First World War haunted Bottome as well as her fiction. "1914 was my war," she wrote.[1] Two of her novels, both steeped in issues of the Great War, contributed to her literary preparation for writing *The Mortal Storm*: *Old Wine* (1925)[2] and *Private Worlds* (1934)[3]. In *Old Wine* she began to probe the impact of the war on Central Europe almost as soon as the conflict ended. In *Private Worlds* her heroine is a damaged survivor who has lost three brothers and her fiancé in the conflict.

Bottome also observed the consequences of the war for Germany, watching the rise of the Nazi Party in Munich. She witnessed the Nazi regime consolidate its power while safely across the border in Austria. In writing *The Mortal Storm*, she drew on those observations and her own fiction which she had written in part, believing as early as 1929 that another European war was not "wholly unlikely."[4]

By 1929 she had also met Alfred Adler. The tenets of his Individual Psychology, Adler's version of depth psychology, are found throughout *The Mortal Storm*, as well as in other fiction she produced in the 1930s.[5] In that decade she probed deeply into her past and psyche, guided by Adler and his disciples. The Viennese psychologist emphasized the importance of birth order in the development of personality, noting how one's position in the family was not fixed, but changed with each subsequent birth. The family dynamic, according to Adler, consisted of siblings jockeying for status and attention among a growing number of competitors. The arrival of a fiancé or new spouse into the family could also disturb sibling relations and destabilize the birth order. Bottome introduced those ideas into her fiction almost as soon as she began her own Adlerian analysis. Most notably, sibling rivalry consumes the protagonists of *Private Worlds* and *The Mortal Storm*.

Adler's ideas regarding sibling rivalry provided something more. She and her husband Ernan, who was grievously wounded in the fighting, had long sought an explanation for the First World War. They found it in Adler's conception of sibling rivalry. Conflict in the family could become a dress rehearsal for war. Families, as their members mature, cannot contain their own conflicts. Gravitating to contending political and social issues, siblings justified, even intensified, their hostility to each other by adhering to opposing sides in a larger political or social conflict. That dynamic operates in *The Mortal Storm*, where political rivalry reflects sibling rivalry and emerges from it. Adler called his version of depth psychology Individual Psychology, but Bottome found in it the possibility for collective as well as individual treatment. Individual Psychology could also cure the ills of society at large, she came to believe. The idea gave her a sense of mission beyond her own treatment.

In addition to their grounding in Adlerian psychology, both *Private Worlds* and *The Mortal Storm* possess a shared literary heritage in Anglo-American fiction. With each, Bottome found inspiration from a classic work whose themes she incorporated into her own writing. She evokes *Jane Eyre* in *Private Worlds*, set in a mental hospital where the caregivers at times appear as unstable as the patients. *Uncle Tom's Cabin* had an even more profound effect. It echoes throughout *The Mortal Storm*. Both Stowe and Bottome wrote novels of hounding and persecution. Bottome singles out Charlotte Brontë and Harriet Beecher Stowe in the first volume of her autobiography for providing the most memorable literary encounters of her adolescence.[6] Their concerns motivated her own fiction.

Bottome's relationship to *Jane Eyre* and *Uncle Tom's Cabin*, however, differs. She readily acknowledged her debt to Brontë's novel in writing *Private Worlds*, explaining in her autobiography, "The sheer, secret, savage horror of Rochester's mad wife in *Jane Eyre* [...] helped to push me forward towards the study of insanity, which certainly led to my writing *Private Worlds*."[7] She makes no direct mention, on the other hand, of Stowe's novel having left an imprint on *The Mortal Storm*. Yet *Uncle Tom's Cabin* permeates that novel as well as her personal experience. She saw the American South for herself at a crucial moment in the early 1930s. In 1932, less than a year before Hitler came to power, she visited friends in Virginia, where she encountered the New World's brand of racism. She was immediately repulsed, having been an "ardent abolitionist" since adolescence, "as Harriet Beecher Stowe and [her] own instincts had made" her.[8]

She soon observed a similarly destructive prejudice take root in Nazi Germany. In 1935 she watched the events that culminated in the Nuremberg Race Laws by September of that year. Intimate relations between Jews and non-Jews were forbidden. The "shadow of law," that is, the Fugitive Slave Act, which had prompted Stowe to write *Uncle Tom's Cabin*, now loomed over German Jews in the form of laws on race designed to segregate them from non-Jews.[9] In the summer of 1935, Bottome initiated *The Mortal Storm*, her own novel of protest, written under "the shadow of law." The impending promulgation of the Nuremberg Race Laws prompted her to speak out in the voice of fiction. She was ready to write what she later termed the book "of the hour."[10]

The Mortal Storm is set on the eve of war. Like its author, the novel hovers between one war and the next. The "play" of the interwar period, as Alan Hodge and Robert Graves so aptly termed it, "was about to be called on account of rain."[11] Bottome more dramatically termed the "rain" a "mortal storm." The fictional ingredients she employed to write her most important novel of war are the subject of this chapter.

Old Wine (1925): Antisemitism in Bottome's Fiction

By the time that Bottome published *Old Wine*, she was forty-three years old and had already produced eighteen novels or novellas. Yet she called *Old Wine* her "first grown-up book" and considered it "the most carefully constructed and fully worked out of all [her] novels."[12] The work is also distinctive for Bottome's exploration of antisemitism in post-war Central Europe. Already prevalent, Judeophobia took on a new coloration and intensity after 1918. The sense of defeat and humiliation, along with deprivation, converged in resentment of the small and suffering Jewish population of the former Austro-Hungarian Empire. Showing an extraordinary sensitivity and prescience, Bottome recognized the threat that an intensified antisemitism posed to the future stability of Europe. That focus on antisemitism and its implications made *Old Wine* her first adult work of fiction. It prepared her to show the consequences of that prejudice over a decade later in *The Mortal Storm*.

Old Wine also contains Bottome's first use of Adlerian depth psychology in her fiction. That too a product of her acute observation of Viennese culture from 1920 to 1923. By the time she wrote *The Mortal Storm,* she had undergone Adlerian analysis and joined Adler's Viennese circle. Her discipleship of Adler permeates *The Mortal Storm.*

Overall, *Old Wine* reveals Bottome in a new light as a novelist. She possessed an extraordinary capacity for prediction with a finely tuned sensibility to be able to translate social conflict into the narrative of "carefully constructed and worked out" works of fiction.

In *Old Wine,* set in Vienna just after the First World War, an aristocratic family, cousins and siblings, struggles to survive in the starving capital. They must attempt to unravel the dilemmas and complexities to which Austria's straitened circumstances after 1918 subject them. At the same time the former elite compounds its own problems. The old aristocracy, with an empty sense of entitlement, is especially prone to a newly aggressive antisemitism, which added to the social tensions in the Viennese capital. That attitude, filled with the bitterness of defeat and clinging to conspiracy theories to explain the Allied victory, offered a pseudo-explanation for the losses and impoverishment. The relationship of the novel's aristocratic protagonists to the Jews, once isolated and ostracized, determines their fate in a city attempting to rise "out of her ashes."[13] As one of the cousins cynically puts it, "There are a few hundred Jews in Wien who will regulate our newfound freedom and starvation to fill their own pockets. They will survive" (*Old Wine,* henceforth OW, 9–10).

Relations in *Old Wine* between Jews and non-Jews, when not overtly hostile, are tentative and uncertain, at times based on mutual exploitation. Such relationships are limited and rarely intimate. Like Bottome herself who raised and then explored the Jewish question for the first time in her fiction, her characters are uncertain what to make of each other. "We are all obliged to associate with Jews now," one of the aristocrats ruefully observes (OW, 26).

Two characters in *Old Wine,* Dr. Carl Jeiteles, who is Jewish, and the aristocratic Eugénie Felsor have traits that suggest those of the parents of Freya Roth, the heroine of *The Mortal Storm.* In *Old Wine* the relationship of Felsor and Jeiteles remains unconsummated, but their resemblance to Professor Roth and his wife Amélie is unmistakable. Freya's mother Amélie shares with Eugénie aristocratic Austrian lineage. Bottome linked them as well in choosing similar francophone first names for each which suggest the cosmopolitan culture of the European aristocracy, linguistically bonded with its own lingua franca. The two women separate themselves from their cultural milieu. They disdain the anti-Jewish prejudice that surrounds them. Eugénie reaches out to the suffering children of Vienna, donating what remains of her family fortune to a hospital that cares for them. The young patients "are all under the shadow of tuberculosis" (OW,

30). Amélie Roth too rejects the privileges of the aristocracy. She marries into the academic and medical community of Munich, leaving behind the pampered existence of the schloss where a retinue of servants provided for its inhabitants.

When writing *Old Wine* in 1924, Bottome refrained from marrying Felsor to Jeiteles. Such a liaison might not have been believable in post-war Vienna where only a few Jews had begun to forge social and economic ties with non-Jews, at first out of necessity rather than by choice. Felsor and Jeiteles represent a tentative beginning, as though they (and their creator) have begun to explore the possibility of deeper commitment. The marriage of Amélie and Johann Roth, on the other hand, is central to *The Mortal Storm*. They would have wed, less noticed, in the turmoil in Germany during the First World War. By 1935 when the novel opens, their relationship defies the newly promulgated Nuremberg Laws, which forbade unions between "Aryans" and "non-Aryans." The laws divided husbands from wives and siblings from siblings, splitting families asunder, but not Professor Roth and his wife. Liaisons in *The Mortal Storm* are matters of protest as well as emotion.

In *Old Wine* families still enjoy the luxury of creating their own divisions. Eugénie Felsor is the sister of Franz Salvatore, who insists on "loyalty" to an ancient aristocratic "code" of conduct that excludes Jews (OW, 26,43). Eugénie denounces her brother's code, proclaiming instead "loyalty [...] to a kindred spirit" who has freed her from grief after the loss of her young son and awakened her self-worth. Her "kindred spirit" is the Jewish physician Dr. Jeiteles, she defiantly tells her brother (OW, 138–9). Professor Roth also frees Amélie from deep mourning. He nurses her back to psychological health after a first marriage to an abusive libertine named von Rohn by whom she had two sons whom Roth readily adopts. In both novels Jews are depicted as healers.

Bottome first observed serious tension between Jews and gentiles in post-war Vienna. At the time she and her husband Ernan Forbes Dennis lived in the Austrian capital. He served as a well-respected, linguistically gifted official with the British Consulate. They threw rounds of "big parties" with invitations extended to "starving artists" and the "Jewish intelligentsia."[14] But "the gaiety turned strained when [she] insisted on inviting [her] Jewish friends, who were the most intelligent people in Vienna [...] to meet Austrian aristocrats." Then she "found that [the Jews] were as displeased as the aristocrats, and themselves explained [...] that it was not the Austrian aristocracy whom they wanted to meet. There seemed walls of ice on both sides [...]," Bottome had to admit; and in the end she gave "different parties for each [...]", succumbing to the social conventions of the Austrian capital.[15] In *Old Wine*, with the characters Eugénie Felsor and Carl Jeiteles, Bottome melts the walls of ice and symbolically brings together the two otherwise antithetical groups of Viennese society, which in reality she could not invite to the same parties.

Old Wine depicts how extreme one source of the tension had become. In the case of antisemitism, it could lead to murder. Word reaches Vienna of a series of fatal attacks on Jews in Budapest. A Jewish victim is brutally murdered in a government prison by four Hungarian aristocrats. Eugénie and her brother react differently to the disturbing news. Franz disparages the significance of the crimes. He scoffs: "The best men of our time and of our country died and died in vain [...] for four and a half years [at the front]. Why therefore be 'indignant at the death of one poor little Jew [...]'" (*OW*, 134). To Franz, Jews cannot be heroes.

Eugénie answers her brother by holding up Dr. Jeiteles as an example of Jewish heroism. She insists that he is surely the equal to the heroes whom Franz labels "the best of our time." But the physician is a different kind of hero for a different time, rescuing the children of Vienna from disease and malnutrition. Franz counters with another disparagement. Jeiteles is not only unworthy of the heroes who died at the front, but he is also barely the equal of his aristocratic sister. At first, Eugénie seems to accommodate her sibling, deceptively agreeing that Jeiteles is not her equal, then she fires back, "he is my superior!" Why? He possesses "the greatest [virtue] of all," that is, "generosity of mind [...] Dr. Jeiteles trained me as a nurse, he taught me all that I know without treating me as a Princess—why should I treat him like a Jew?" (*OW*, 140).

Jeiteles gives Eugénie more than a profession. He draws her back to life after the death of her young son Rudi, she reminds her brother. She challenges Franz, "You know that I am better now, don't you? So much better that I have stopped thinking of Rudi's death" (*OW*, 143). Eugénie flings a last barb at her brother, marking her independence from his atavistic values. "I am proud he is a Jew," she defiantly tells him (*OW*, 143). Eugénie also reveals to her brother that her loyalty now lies with Dr. Jeiteles and his gift as a healer rather than with the segregated world of pre-war Austria frozen in aristocratic arrogance.

Franz in the end relents. He accepts his sister's praise of her mentor and agrees to apologize to him for his rude behavior toward him in the past. She answers, "Now that you have said—that brave thing—I shall not be afraid anymore [...] I shall not have to [...] say to myself that good Jews are the only good men" (*OW*, 143–4). In *Old Wine*, at least, sibling rivalry is resolved.

The "Jew baiting" (*OW*, 125) that initially divides Eugénie from her brother will divide Freya Roth from her two half siblings who join the Nazi Party. Olaf, the older of the two and Freya's favorite, tells her, "We must destroy the power of the Jew [...] since Jews have always been an international and provocative power detrimental to the expansion of our Nordic race" (*TMS*, 74). The spark in Eugénie to defend her Jewish mentor against her brother's demeaning attacks will become the flame of identity in Freya: "Freya sprang to her feet, her face on fire, her grey eyes sparkling. 'I know what I am!' she cried. 'It is enough for me to be a Jewess'" (*TMS*,

72). The person whom Freya defends from her brother's attack is her father. She insists, "if Father is a Jew, then I am a Jewess" (*TMS*, 71).[16] The stakes have risen in *The Mortal Storm* because antisemitism has hit home, dividing Freya from her older half siblings along the fault line of Roth vs. von Rohn. She defies her older brother in a scene charged with sibling rivalry as well as moral choice. It is also the scene in which Freya determines who she is. In defiance of her brothers, she declares her father's identity as her own.

In *Old Wine* Bottome first holds the Jewish question up to the light, examining it from different perspectives. The manipulative Jewess Elizabeth Bleileben, for example, lacks Dr. Jeiteles's "generosity of mind." She is a social climber and the embodiment of negative Jewish stereotypes. She is willing to deprive the children of Vienna of milk as part of a scheme to line her own pockets. Bottome juxtaposes Bleileben's impending fictitious marriage with an impoverished aristocrat to the emotionally honest relationship of Carl Jeiteles and Eugénie Felsor, who draw together as equal partners, working for a new Austria.

Eugénie's cousin Otto Wolkenheimb and the wealthy Jewess Bleileben, whom he does not love, are engaged. Their relationship is a sham, driven by the motive, in Otto's case to sustain aristocratic status, in Elizabeth's to attain the empty shell in post-war Vienna of such status. Phyllis Lassner has aptly termed their engagement "a mutually hostile takeover."[17] In fact the status each of them lusts for is unobtainable and certainly irrelevant in suffering and defeated Austria. Otto's estate of Trauenstein symbolizes the overblown emptiness of the old aristocracy, yet he longs to retain it, "as necessary [to him] as the air [he] breathes" (*OW*, 303). To save the estate, which he can no longer afford, Otto determines to marry the wealthy, rapacious Bleileben. "I [...] feel that I am a match for Jews!" he brags to his cousins that he can beat them at their own game (*OW*, 10). He sums up his straitened circumstances and the reason for marrying Bleileben with the statement, "If I don't marry a fortune, I go to the devil" and Trauenstein will be lost (*OW*, 299).

But Bleileben has her own terms which she lists with mounting excitement at the thought that elite status is within her grasp. "I am to be received by all your friends? I shall go when I like to Trauenstein? Your mother will accept me as a daughter-in-law? Your cousin Eugénie will be like a sister to me!" (*OW*, 345). The questions culminate with a final exclamation mark, certain as she is of her advantage over the whole impoverished Wolkenheimb clan. Hers is the shrill ecstasy of the perennial outsider. At the same time there is an air of desperation to her statements. She knows she will remain an outlier no matter what her nominal or legal status among the aristocratic Wolkenheimbs.

Otto recognizes the sham and cannot sustain it. Devastated by the suicide of his comrade and fellow aristocrat Baron Eugen Erdody, he cannot marry Elizabeth, who belongs, as he once told Eugen, to the "few hundred Jews in Wien who [...] regulate our new-found freedom and starvation to fill their own pockets" (OW, 9–10). As Eugen's suicide reveals, the old world is dead, a casualty at its own hand; and a hollow marriage will hardly be able to resurrect it. When the word of Eugen's death arrives, Otto's old servant ushers Elizabeth out into the street (OW, 374). Given time, Bottome seems to say, mutual respect between Jews and non-Jews, as in the case of Eugénie and Dr. Jeiteles, can grow and flourish while greed and exploitation, as in the case of Otto Wolkenheimb and Elizabeth Bleileben, will wither of its own accord.

Bottome similarly examines the Jewish question from changing perspectives in *The Mortal Storm*, but she does so through a single character, the wise and benevolent Professor Roth. In *The Mortal Storm* Eugénie Felsor's son Rudi, notable for "his hurrying questions" (OW, 143), is reborn as Freya's inquisitive younger brother of the same name who asserts himself and asks his father, "What is being a Jew?" (TMS, 71). Bottome subsequently told MGM, that is the central question of the novel, as it is of the world today.

Rudi has been raised a Catholic, that is, in his mother's faith; but now he begins to wonder, "Was his own country turning into his father's enemy?" (TMS, 71). Professor Roth responds to Rudi's question about what it means to be a Jew with a litany of praise for the unique and defining contributions of Jews to Western civilization. Jews, he tells his son, have "enriched every country" they have "lived in." They have "given Europe its religion, its moral law, and much of its science—perhaps even more of its genius—in art, literature, and music" (TMS, 72). He finishes his peroration to Rudi with the caveat, "I do not say that there are no bad Jews—usurers, cowards, corrupt and unjust persons—but such people are also to be found among Christians," implying that a wholly positive depiction would not be credible (TMS, 72).

Professor Roth's initial answer to Rudi is not his last word on the subject. As Nazi persecution intensifies and the risk to the Roth family increases, Johann Roth presents his Jewish heritage less benignly than he did in his initial answer to his son. The balance begins to shift when he refers to negative qualities, which he claims are also distinctive to Jews. He warns Freya not to call attention to herself at the university. What he earlier described in defining Jews at their best, he now claims when asserted too openly makes them hated. "Do not [...] go too far ahead of the others. This is a bad moment for Jews to do well in. As a people we have always made that mistake; and now we see the result! Everywhere we are hated!" (TMS, 314). "Always" and "everywhere" are the exaggerations of prejudice, as though Johann Roth has incorporated a measure of the hatred that surrounds him. In the professor's changing answer to the question "What is being a Jew?" Bottome has also captured the tightening noose of Nazi antisemitism and its baleful effects on its victims.

Unlike *The Mortal Storm*, *Old Wine* only tentatively employs Adlerian ideas. Eugénie and her brother are reconciled, not torn apart, by sibling rivalry, as they might be in one of Bottome's novels of the 1930s after she had begun an Adlerian analysis. She does, however, briefly introduce Adler himself in the novel. The psychiatrist appears as a wise and insightful figure to be sure, but with no connection to the protagonists of the novel.

He makes no more than a cameo appearance. To emphasize the brevity of his role, Adler is in a hurry and "surreptitiously looks at his watch" (*OW*, 129), while attending a meeting that consists of foreign aid workers ("all Anglo-Saxons") and Austrians, Jews and non-Jews, including Eugénie and her brother Franz. Franz is dismayed to learn that the subject of the meeting is the so-called White Terror directed against Jews in Budapest. He is also dismayed at the mix of guests which "forced two social elements [Jews and non-Jews] to meet which centuries of studied isolation had kept apart" (*OW*, 125).

Adler's presence at the meeting, though brief, is crucial. He is vigilant and informed, insisting on hard truths. As will be seen a decade later, the Adler of *Old Wine* is the model for Prof. Roth in *The Mortal Storm*. Bottome claims in her autobiography to have met Adler only in 1927; yet in *Old Wine*, published in 1925, she already appears to be familiar with his ideas. She is certainly familiar with his public persona. Her fiction belies her memoir where she generously conceded the "discovery" of Adler to Ernan, who met the depth psychologist in 1926. Pam Hirsch suggests a more complicated possibility. She writes, "Initially, [Bottome] was unimpressed and even a little disappointed by Adler."[18] Hirsch explains Bottome's negative reaction by the fact "that she liked to be the intellectual leader in their relationship and in this case, it was Ernan who had discovered Adler."[19] One could also conclude that Bottome is not completely accurate in her memoir, having met or heard Adler speak by 1924, at the time she wrote *Old Wine*.

Bottome provides a telling portrait of the depth psychologist in her Viennese novel. He cautions one of the aid workers just returned from Budapest, who accuses the whole world of "lying and looting," with particular condemnation reserved for the Austrians and Hungarians. "You paint a charming picture of the world," said Professor Adler smiling, "I don't say that it is unjust, but I think that its severity may make us all a little critical of your story" (*OW*, 126). When the aid worker rejoins, refining his condemnation, "Eighteenth century manners and third century morals—that's the Hungarians for you." Again, Adler attempts to call the remark to account. "'Why third century morals?' murmured Professor Adler to himself. 'I always thought third century morals rather good. Christianity hadn't time to wear off, or the Church sufficient power to cripple it'" (*OW*, 127). The same aid worker hesitates to read "the difficult Hungarian names" of those aristocrats accused of brutally murdering Joseph Bauer, "a

Jew [...], an educated, honest man, any man's equal, most men's superior [...]. Professor Adler took the paper from him and read them in an even, unmoved voice. They were the names of four men whom Eugénie and Franz previously knew" and had argued over regarding their worth (*OW*, 132).

As early as 1924 when Bottome wrote *Old Wine*, she had the sensitivity to perceive that in the crucible of hunger and defeat in post-war Central Europe, the "walls of ice," between Jews and non-Jews and "the centuries of studied isolation," to which Jews had been subjected could make for murderous accusations and intent. In writing her Viennese novel, Bottome had introduced antisemitism to her fiction. She already understood that with the rise of the Nazis, they were not about "to settle down and leave the Jews alone"[20] as her compatriots suggested to her in the mid-1930s.

Her prescience also extended to Adler. In her initial, fictional portrait of him, the psychiatrist defuses anger and pretense. He also steps in to deliver the painful truth by reading the names of those guilty of murder, that is, friends of some of those in his audience. He is neither deterred nor intimidated by those with every reason to vent hostility toward him.

Whether Bottome encountered Adler in the early 1920s or first met him, as she later wrote in 1927, her association with his depth psychology did not begin in earnest until 1930. In that year she and Ernan started full-time analysis with one of Adler's disciples, Leonard Seif, in Munich. Her analysis with Seif proved to be a turning point in her writing of fiction.

Adler's Individual Psychology and Bottome's Fiction

> Long before I wrote *The Mortal Storm* I had become an Adlerian student, and had received an Adlerian analysis.[21]

Bottome composed *The Mortal Storm* from the summer of 1935 to the summer of 1937. By then, she had already had considerable exposure to the Nazis. But she did not at first show the prescience regarding German fascism that later gave her notoriety in Britain. She and Ernan arrived in Munich in 1930 to undergo psychological analysis with one of Adler's disciples, "his trusted colleague" Leonard Seif, who had "started a large and active group of Individual Psychologists" in the Bavarian capital.[22] Adler, then lecturing in the United States, had recommended Seif to Bottome and her husband in his absence, "if," as he said, "we wanted to know more of his psychology."[23]

Even in 1930, just as she and Ernan had begun to work with Seif, "the shadow of Hitler and his brown shirts had already fallen over Munich, but it was still only a shadow."[24] She frequently observed Hitler and his minions sitting not far from her and the members of Seif's group in the same Munich café.[25] Bottome did not regard Hitler then as a threat to any country other than Germany. "Hitler," she remembered, "as a ruler seemed incredible before he came to power and [...] we were quite sure whatever happened to Germany, we need not to be involved."[26]

In the early 1930s her analysis with Seif rather than the emerging Nazi Party consumed her. In that process Bottome reopened the door to her adolescence. That period of her life with its first literary encounters offered inspiration for her two most successful novels of the 1930s: *Private Worlds* published in 1934 and three years later *The Mortal Storm*. Both novels appeared within a few years of her work with Seif, inspired, she later recounted, by the "long and thorough analysis" he conducted with her.[27] Bottome also acknowledged Seif's influence on other fiction that she produced in the 1930s. *Devil's Due* (1931), for example, set in the Alps about an ill-fated champion ski jumper "had an intense emotion behind it aroused by my first analysis with Seif."[28] The same was true of *Private Worlds*. When she "was completely lost" in writing it she was also "absorbed" by Seif and his group of Individual Psychologists. She wrote, "my own analysis with Seif deepened and enriched my purpose."[29] To show her gratitude she dedicated *Private Worlds*, set in a mental hospital, to Seif and his Munich circle.

Adler himself had a similar effect on her when she wrote *The Mortal Storm*. She says of the stay in Vienna when she composed the novel, starting in the summer of 1935:

> We spent all our time working on Individual Psychology, although I had already begun and continued to think out *The Mortal Storm;* and I think we saw Adler every day, sometimes to attend his lectures, often to spend the evening with him among his friends, and constantly for private talks.[30]

Bottome continued the work she had begun with Seif on the dynamics within her own family, examining the interplay and rivalry between herself and her siblings. Not surprisingly, under Adler's powerful influence when she began to write her anti-Nazi novel, she took her own family as a model for the protagonists of *The Mortal Storm*. She transposed the structure of her generation within the family to that novel. Clearly Adler reinforced the work that she had already done with Seif on sibling rivalry. As in Bottome's family, there are four von Rohn/Roth children. Freya has Bottome's place in the family. She is both an older sister to Rudi and the youngest of a group of three that includes her two older stepbrothers. But there is a difference in her fiction. Bottome had two older sisters and Freya two older stepbrothers. Nonetheless the dynamic remains similar. Emil, however, is a kind of middle child caught between Olaf and Freya in the group of three. He muses to himself, he "enjoyed making Freya's blunders public—it appeased the jealousy he always felt, at Olaf's deep affection for her. She was only a half-sister, Emile resentfully felt—Olaf should have loved Emil, his whole brother—best" (*TMS*, 46). Olaf's affection for his sister is more than repaid. She moves between hero-worship for him and the role of protector to the young Rudi. Bottome introduced another similarity between her own family and her fictional protagonists. Like Freya, she was the first to introduce a fiancé into the family when she became engaged to Ernan.

Bottome singled out her earlier work with Seif as also significant for *The Mortal Storm*. The self-knowledge she acquired while working with Adler's Munich disciple, she claimed, provided an "advantage" when writing her anti-Nazi novel.[31] Seif and Bottome shared much in common. Both came from a Protestant, clerical background, and both described their initial embrace of Adler's ideas as a conversion experience.[32] Living in Munich, Seif therefore differed from those immersed in the Viennese culture of depth psychology, whether Freudian or Adlerian. In contrast to so many of the Viennese psychologists, Seif was not Jewish but had trained as a Protestant pastor, coming originally from "Swabian peasant stock."[33] He switched to medicine and practiced psychiatry as a Freudian analyst for nine years without success. Attending a conference run by Adler changed his life, and he became a committed Adlerian analyst. He once joked with Bottome, making light of what must have been a turning point for him, "If I knew any way of being a better human being than by becoming an Individual Psychologist—be sure I would have taken it!"[34]

Bottome recounted a similar conversion experience in what she described as her first encounter with Adler. The psychologist visited her and Ernan at the school for adolescent boys they ran in Kitzbühel, Austria. "On the last evening" of his visit, they sat in a café and discussed the Great War, Bottome remembered. "As he talked, we seemed to see the naked structure of the war [...] In those hours, I ceased to think of Adler as ordinary; I knew that what I was looking at and listening to, was a great man."[35] Given the all-consuming importance of the First World War for Bottome and Ernan, "my war," she termed it, a new and compelling perspective on the conflict would more than catch their attention. Adler's explanation for the war changed their lives. They apparently became committed Adlerians overnight.

Whether working with Seif or Adler, Bottome gave herself completely to Adler's Individual Psychology. The Adlerian approach to analysis, particularly in its initial stages, entails close examination of "the malleable years," that is, the first two decades of life.[36] Bottome in fact devoted the first volume of her autobiography, *Search for a Soul*, to her childhood and adolescence, that is, precisely "the first two decades of life." "It is an Adlerian book," as she explained to her literary agent, because of its focus on her formative years.[37] It is also "an Adlerian book" because it arguably reveals what she discussed in her analysis conducted by Seif and then Adler. The first volume of her autobiography therefore provides clues regarding the Adlerian analysis that she underwent in the early and mid-1930s.

Bottome's reading as an adolescent provided inspiration for her fiction in that decade. That is one reason why her analysis first with Seif, then with Adler, devoted to exploration of that period of her life, proved to be a turning point in her writing of fiction. Analysis opened the door to her experience before adulthood when she had her first encounter with serious literature. That exposure proved critical. Bottome, it would seem, produced her best work when inspired by the fiction of others, in the case of *The Mortal Storm*, modeling her plots and characters on one novel in particular. In both of her bestsellers of the 1930s, *Private Worlds* and *The Mortal Storm*, she took inspiration from a classic work of nineteenth-century literature, *Jane Eyre* and *Uncle Tom's Cabin*, respectively, first read in adolescence. With *The Mortal Storm*, she re-imagined and contextualized *Uncle Tom's Cabin* in the twentieth-century. She is direct in indicating the literary inspiration for *Private Worlds*. Much less so in indicating the earlier novel that lay behind *The Mortal Storm*. Cited or not, *Uncle Tom's Cabin* was engrained in her thinking and embedded in the structure of her anti-Nazi novel. I will first examine *Private Worlds* and the nineteenth-century literary inspiration that encouraged her to write it. That novel proved a tentative first step in taking inspiration from a classic work of literature. In its exploration of sibling rivalry, *Private Worlds* provided part of the plot structure for *The Mortal Storm*.

Private Worlds (1934): Sibling Rivalry and the First Use of a Literary Model

Bottome's creative process in writing her 1934 bestseller *Private Worlds* suggests part of her method in composing *The Mortal Storm*. She fictionalized what she knew. She needed direct exposure to a particular locale and to certain individuals before crafting them into the setting and characters of fiction. In the case of *Private Worlds,* she began it following a visit to the Cardiff Mental Hospital, where the deputy superintendent, Dr. Muriel Northcote, had shown the facility to her and Ernan, along with Adler, who accompanied them on the visit.[38] Dr. Northcote impressed Bottome with her competence and generosity. Northcote not only "gave" her "several introductions to private hospitals, all of which [she] visited."[39] She also invited Bottome to stay with her and observe patients under her supervision.[40] Bottome's visits to the Cardiff Hospital and to other psychiatric institutions proved stimulating. She now had the setting and the protagonist, a female psychiatrist, for a novel on the subject of mental illness.

Private Worlds is indeed set in a psychiatric hospital with a female psychiatrist as the central character. But Bottome needed something more to set in motion composing the novel. She found it in the disturbing world of Charlotte Brontë, whose work she encountered in adolescence.

Dr. Northcote herself raised the question of mental illness in the context of Brontë's novel, an association that, as it turned out, had long haunted Bottome. The psychiatrist expounded on her point of view:

> You will find that mental illnesses are more explicable and far less terrifying than you think and as a matter of fact no fiction writer has as yet touched on them at all—with the exception of *Jane Eyre*, which from our point of view gives a most misleading picture of a mental condition.[41]

Charlotte Brontë's novel with "the sheer, secret, savage horror of Rochester's mad wife" had left an indelible imprint on Bottome when she first read it.[42] Her analysis with Seif, in which she explored her adolescence, it would seem, had reawakened her curiosity about the novel and its relationship to mental illness. She began to consider such disorders in Adlerian terms.[43] Her visits to psychiatric hospitals in Cardiff and elsewhere provided a context for those considerations. But the catalyst for a work on mental illness had been the haunting, yet "misleading picture" to be found in *Jane Eyre*. Bottome confirmed, *Jane Eyre* "helped to push me forward towards the study of insanity, which certainly led to my writing *Private Worlds*."[44]

In that novel, as in *The Mortal Storm*, Bottome revealed important themes in the names of her primary characters. The connection of *Private Worlds* to *Jane Eyre* is made in the first name of the novel's protagonist, Jane, and in her surname, Everest, giving her most immediately the same initials as Jane Eyre. But there is more to Bottome's choice of name for her protagonist. With the addition of the letter "i" to "Eyre," the word "eyrie" is formed, that is, the mountain nest of the eagle, suggesting "Everest" as well as another link between the two heroines. Bottome's protagonist therefore evokes Brontë's novel in both her first and second names. Literary scholars have observed additional symbolism in the name of Dr. Jane Everest. Pam Hirsch, for example, suggests:

> Jane Everest has to contend with the new superintendent of the mental hospital [...] who considers the work unsuitable for women. Her name itself indicates the scale of the mountain that she has to climb in order to achieve the professional position of a female psychiatrist.[45]

Similarly, Phyllis Lassner writes, "With so much to overcome and setting her sights so high, Jane Everest is aptly named."[46]

"Everest" for Bottome had yet another meaning. As a young woman she spent five winters in the Swiss Alps from 1903 to 1907, settling in Davos and St. Moritz, while she recovered from tuberculosis. There she met her husband Ernan Forbes Dennis, also fighting the disease. When the illness threatened her again after the First World War, Ernan took her to the Austrian Alps from 1924 to 1927 to recover. Bottome knew and loved the Alps whether Swiss or Austrian. In her second winter in St. Moritz, she recounted:

> Not finding anyone with whom I felt much at home I fell in love with the mountains [...] The silence that surrounds snow mountains is the most attentive silence in the world. There are times when you feel certain that someone has just finished speaking, or if you wait a moment—will begin.
>
> The sea cannot be quite silent, even a lake lisps against its low shore, and the sky is too far away to bring you what it has, but a mountain holds your breath, listening.[47]

This feeling for the mountains finds its place in her fiction. Starting with *Old Wine*, again in the novel *Devil's Due* (1931), and most notably in *The Mortal Storm*, antisemites lurk among those who live in town. The mountains in contrast belong to the pure of heart. In *The Mortal Storm* the mountain dwellers are the Breitners, Freya's lover Hans and his family. Decent and hardworking, they are responsible in their care of animals and accepting of human imperfection. The mountains, going back to Bottome's own experience with tuberculosis, are a place of healing. Freya can be safe with Hans's family. She can give birth to their child and recover, preparing to escape to Austria. By the end of *The Mortal Storm*, Freya has joined the Breitners at least temporarily, as a person of the mountains. That Jane Everest bears the name of the greatest mountain of all suggests her goodness and towering strength in the world of Bottome's fiction.

Another interpretation of her surname arises from the fact that Dr. Everest at first appears to be aloof, safe from emotional risk in her close friendship with a married colleague. She looks down on the emotions of others from a great height and with good reason. She tells the wife of the colleague with whom she has a "safe" relationship.

> The man I was engaged to was shot for cowardice in the War. I was nineteen and he was twenty. There was an attack, and he ran away. My brother was his Colonel. I haven't been in love since then [...] It was twelve years ago.
>
> (*PW*, 41)

In private, she gives vent to the emotion of her loss. "'I've been in love once!' she said fiercely into the pillow. 'Ah, god—not again!'" (*PW*, 46). The war piles other tragedies on her. In a series of losses reminiscent of Vera Brittain, Jane loses first her youngest brother.

> Killed that first winter at Festubert. The second had been trapped and drowned in a submarine. Bertram, the eldest, the core of Jane's heart, had been blown off the hard surface of the earth. Her parents had not long survived his death.
>
> (*PW*, 46)

Such tragedies explain the emotional aloofness of the novel's protagonist. Like Vera Brittain, Jane Everest too carries a geographic place name for her surname, linking her in yet another way to the author of *Testament of Youth* who lost the three young men closest to her: her brother, her fiancé, and their best friend.

Buried within the story of Jane's losses in the war is an even deeper tragedy. The eldest of her three brothers, Bertram, "the core of Jane's young heart," is also the commanding officer who orders the execution of her fiancé after he flees with his men under fire. "Bertram had trusted her enough to send her Michael's last letter" (*PW*, 47). His generosity does not include finding extenuating circumstances in his future brother-in-law's seeming cowardice, despite his having previously shown courage under fire.

Bottome transposed the same plot line to *The Mortal Storm*. Freya's favorite of her two older brothers, her hero and self-proclaimed Siegfried, is Olaf. And like the Siegfried of legend, Olaf is capable of betraying those closest to him. As noted above, his bond with Freya makes the younger brother Emil continually jealous "at Olaf's deep affection for" their only sister (*TMS*, 46). Emil is not alone in his jealousy regarding Freya. Freya's lover Hans, a Communist, is ambushed as he tries to ski to Austria, following the Reichstag fire, which put all Communists in Germany at risk for arrest. Freya subsequently learns that Olaf had ordered Fritz Maburg, one of her would-be suitors, to shoot Hans (*TMS*, 195, 209). Fritz's father tells Freya's mother what happened: "Fritz shot the fellow himself you know, Amélie! Although Olaf—as his superior officer—gave the order" (*TMS*, 209).

In both novels the revered older brother orders the execution of his sister's fiancé. Those events are turning points in each. Jane Everest explains that the consequence of her fiancé's seeming cowardice under fire "made a psychiatrist of me [...] I had an idea even then that it wasn't just his fault [...] now I'm sure of it. It was worth finding out" (*PW*, 41). Hans's death motivates Freya in a similar fashion. It encourages her to quit Germany to pursue her career in medical research. She is able to leave her child by Hans with his family; there is nothing to hold her back and so she escapes to Austria on her way to pursue a medical career in America.

Bottome used the same plot line in both novels to reveal a critical tenet of Adlerian psychology through fictional narrative, that of sibling rivalry. (See Chapter 3 for further discussion of sibling rivalry in *The Mortal Storm*.) With the betrothal of a favored younger sister, the once worshipful and malleable sibling will have a new ally in the family and a new place within it. She will turn her attention to the object of her love and affection, even new object of hero-worship. From the point of view of the displaced older brother, the younger sister threatens to abandon him, diminishing his power and status within the family. The arrival of the fiancé, in Adlerian terms, has another consequence. It disturbs the birth order, removing the one previously first in the eyes of the younger sister from his pedestal. The formerly revered older brother harbors his own equally strong feelings and will not share his sister with a rival. In each instance, the murder is "ordered" by the brother in his capacity as superior officer, a role that hides the deeper psychological truth behind the command.

In both *Private Worlds* and *The Mortal Storm*, events that lie buried in the psychology of sibling rivalry in the end liberate the female protagonists to fulfill roles that Adler argued women were particularly suited to. Both Jane Everest and Freya Roth, after the loss of their respective fiancés, re-make themselves as healers and medical practitioners. Having been so grievously wounded themselves, they are ready, Bottome seems to say, to heal others.

She had earlier made the same point in *Old Wine*. Dr. Jeiteles, the healer in Eugénie Felsor's life, rescues her from grief over the death of her young son Rudi. She tells her antisemitic brother Franz, the committed aristocrat, "You know that I am better now, don't you? So much better that I have stopped thinking of Rudi's death" (*OW*, 143). She recounts the moment of her liberation from mourning. "One day [Dr. Jeiteles] asked me to sing to the ward songs I had only sung to Rudi" (*OW*, 143). Reluctant at first, she found that by sharing her music with other children "the weight of [her] grief had gone" (*OW*, 143). Jeiteles's generosity toward Eugénie in training her as a nurse had brought out her own capacity to share. In helping to heal others, she healed herself.

Events in *The Mortal Storm* do not simply replicate those in *Private Worlds*, or even *Old Wine*. The murder of Jane's fiancé occurs in the guise of military protocol as punishment for cowardice under fire. In *The Mortal Storm* another level of sibling rivalry motivates the perpetrators.[48] Fritz and Olaf are ardent Nazis and Hans is just as determined a Communist. Olaf, it would seem, orders his subordinate to shoot an escaping enemy. In fact, the rivalry among siblings is therefore as much political as it is relational within the family. Bottome therefore portrays the competition between political antagonists and the socioeconomic systems they advocate as sibling rivalry in yet another guise.

When Freya asks her father, "You do like communists better than Nazis, don't you?" Professor Roth equates the two: "My affections have not been stirred to any depth of passion by either of these parties" (*TMS*, 136). Freya's mother makes the same point: "If you choose to call one savage a 'Nazi' and the other a 'Communist', it is all the same to me!" (*TMS*, 197). In the 1920s Communists and Nazis had fought each other in the streets of Germany, competing for the same working-class votes. Olaf orders the death of Hans to deprive his sister of her lover for whom he harbors unacceptable jealousy. At the same time, he destroys a political rival. Adler would ascribe a single explanation for both motivations. Sibling rivalry, whether political or familial, operates in both instances.

There is yet another level of meaning to Adler's concept of sibling rivalry. Its conflicts can turn family life into a battlefield; the family itself can provide a dress rehearsal for war. Freud too searched for the origin of war, specifically the First World War, in his version of depth psychology, positing an innate human death wish. Adler seems to say that war begins "at home," within one's own House of Being, to use Bottome's image from *Private Worlds*.[49] In effect, he argues, one's House of Being harbors the ingredients that fuel war itself. Bottome suggests as much in *The Mortal Storm*, which recounts another hurricane of destruction, destroying the Roth's "House of Being" both from within and without. By the end of the novel, Freya's older brothers, Emil and Olaf, in either siding with their sister in Emil's case or against her in Olaf's, also make conflicting political choices. Olaf remains an ardent Nazi, and Emil walks away from the party. The brothers are already at war with each other. Emotional conflict haunts both novels, unleashing social madness. In *Private Worlds* the madness is the Great War, and in *The Mortal Storm* it is the fast-encroaching perversion of German fascism. The first was long over. At the time that Bottome wrote, the second loomed in all its horrific fury.

Bottome used madness in both a clinical and metaphorical sense in *Private Worlds*. Metaphorically, it was the "hurricane" in the form of the Great War that could overturn one's "House of Being." The clinical madness that afflicts Rochester's tormented wife, as Brontë recounted it, had haunted Bottome for years. Echoes of Brontë's "savage horror" can be seen in the two "mad women" of *Private Worlds*. Sally, the wife of Jane's close friend Alec Macgregor, suffers a nervous breakdown that originates in what Adler would label an "inferiority complex."[50] She is jealous of Jane's professional competence and identity. She also feels threatened by Jane's closeness to her husband based on shared professional responsibilities. Through psychiatric intervention she recovers and is restored to health and to her marriage.

The second "mad woman" in *Private Worlds* is the sister of Charles Drummond, the disdainful supervisor who ultimately admits to his love for Jane. Drummond bears the burden of responsibility for a malevolent and destructive sibling named Myra, who has murdered her husband and nearly destroys the Macgregors' marriage. Myra, in the end, beyond redemption, destroys herself. Jane descends from the heights of emotional aloofness and agrees to marry Charles, admitting that she has fallen in love for the second time in her life. Madness is cured or punished in *Private Worlds*. Bottome tamed the "savage horror" of *Jane Eyre* through the process of exploring madness in a twentieth-century clinical setting.

The dynamic between *The Mortal Storm* and its nineteenth-century inspiration operated very differently. In writing her anti-Nazi novel, Bottome had no need to exorcise a private demon that had long haunted her. Instead, she sought to arouse the conscience of her society and ring out a moral warning, she went so far as to say, "to the whole universe." She also saw herself as a truth-teller on the order of Harriet Beecher Stowe, Ivan Turgenev, or Emile Zola. With *The Mortal Storm* the stakes were much higher than they had been with *Private Worlds*. And the work of fiction that could serve as both exemplar and paradigm for a twentieth-century novel of emancipation was readily at hand.

Bottome, as noted, had earlier taken inspiration from Charlotte Brontë's novel and paid homage to it in the name of the heroine of *Private Worlds*. She then went on to write a very different novel from *Jane Eyre*. In *The Mortal Storm* she followed *Uncle Tom's Cabin* far more closely in both characters and plot than she had with the Brontë classic. *The Mortal Storm* was unique among Bottome's many works of fiction, but then its intimate relationship with another author's work was also unique for Bottome. She sought not only to evoke Stowe's novel, but to replicate Stowe's role as a socially engaged novelist. She sought to repeat with *The Mortal Storm* the monumental significance of *Uncle Tom's Cabin*. By the early 1930s the Nazis and the American South had converged in her mind and in her experience.

Bottome and the American South: Exposure to Racism

Bottome interrupted her work with Seif to visit the United States in 1931–2. She took advantage of the time in the United States to make an extended visit of two months to friends who now resided in Norfolk, Virginia. She saw the South for the first time. The region left an indelible impression. She later wrote of that encounter:

> This was the first time I had visited the American South, and its attitude towards its fellow-citizens horrified and depressed me. I could not understand how such socially enchanting people as Virginians could think and act with such insensate cruelty.[51]

In Virginia, Bottome stayed with her good friends, the artist Maida McCord and her husband George Roper. She found relief from Southern prejudice in their company. "George and Maida were both Northerners, so I only felt *the deep shadow* of the color neurosis outside their home" (italics mine).[52] Bottome's use of the phrase, "the deep shadow of the color neurosis," bears resemblance to a similar phrase that Harriet Beecher Stowe used more than once in *Uncle Tom's Cabin* to refer to the cruelties of slavery, the most extreme form of "color neurosis." For example, "oh my country! These things are done under the shadow of thy laws!" (*Uncle Tom's Cabin*, henceforth *UTC*, 349). The similarity in Bottome's phrasing to Stowe's suggests that the visit to Virginia recalled her reading of Stowe's novel (if she did not re-read it), which at first encounter in her adolescence had moved her so deeply and made her a lifelong Abolitionist.[53] She must have had occasion more than once to recall *Uncle Tom's Cabin* on that visit to Virginia in 1932.

Bottome had even earlier used the phrase "under the shadow" in *Old Wine*, where the impoverished children of Vienna "are all under the shadow of tuberculosis" (*OW*, 30). She herself had existed under the shadow of that disease for three decades. The illness also figures in *Uncle Tom's Cabin*, taking the life of the novel's saint-like heroine, Eva St. Clare (*UTC*, 235, 247–51). Bottome may therefore have recalled Stowe's novel in writing *Old Wine* or it had lingered in her mind since adolescence. She also employed the image of a menacing shadow to describe the presence of the Nazis in the Bavarian capital: "the shadow of Hitler and his brown shirts had already fallen over Munich" when she and Ernan arrived.[54] Although her use of the phrase regarding the South (and elsewhere) could be interpreted as coincidence, the context was the same for both Stowe and Bottome, namely, the "insensate cruelty" of racial persecution. That she repeatedly used the phrase under circumstances of threat and menace suggests her intentional employment of it. She took a harrowing image from Stowe and applied it to war-ravaged Vienna, Nazi Germany, and the American South. The image also captured the continued threat of the disease that killed her sister, her best friend, and haunted both Ernan and herself.[55] The versatility of the phrase and its ominous character provided a historically and politically potent connection between Stowe's novel and *The Mortal Storm*, already in gestation in the early 1930s.

The encounter with the South reinforced a connection to Stowe in other ways. On the visit to Virginia, Bottome had the unique experience of memorializing her paternal grandmother whom she deeply admired. She wrote of her, "my grandmother [...] was the most enthralling—thrilled and thrilling—Christian it has ever been my lot to meet."[56]

Her good works abounded. Margaret Bottome founded a philanthropic organization, the King's Daughters. She wrote inspirational pieces for twenty-five years in the *Ladies' Home Journal* under the title "Heart to Heart Talks." She proved to be an enthralling public speaker, devoting herself to practical topics inspired by broad religious values. In many ways Bottome followed in her footsteps. According to Pam Hirsch, "she modeled her own character on" Margaret Bottome.[57]

In Virginia, Bottome could see first-hand her grandmother's work on behalf of "Southern Negroes." She proudly wrote:

> A hospital for babies had been built in Norfolk by the King's Daughters' Society, as a memorial to their founder my grandmother, Margaret Bottome, where no color-bar existed [...]. I never enjoyed speaking for anything more than I enjoyed speaking for this hospital; and once more voicing, for my grandmother, her passionate conviction that every living creature must share the inalienable rights of Man.[58]

In her portrait of her grandmother,[59] she emphasized her grandmother's work on behalf of "the Negro race":

> She certainly did much at a time when hardly anyone else did anything to rouse a better feeling in the South towards the Negro race. One of her great friends was Amanda Smith, an African Church Missionary bishop.[60]

Margaret Bottome's friend Amanda Smith, a former slave herself, who found her own "second emancipation" through literacy, worked tirelessly as a preacher and temperance advocate.[61] Smith could educate her friend with first-hand accounts of slavery which Margaret Bottome surely passed on to her granddaughter.

In addition to her close working friendship with someone who had known bondage, Margaret Bottome had direct contact with the abolitionist movement, if she did not participate in it herself. Just as *Uncle Tom's Cabin* began to appear in serial form, almost immediately attracting broad public attention, she encountered Stowe's brother who had become an activist in the movement. At the time that her first child William, Bottome's father, was born in 1851, the family resided in Brooklyn, New York. Margaret Bottome's husband Francis, a Methodist pastor from Derbyshire, England, preached in the borough's Sands Street Church.[62] Not far away stood the Pilgrim Church. Since 1847 Stowe's older brother Henry Ward Beecher had preached there. The denunciation of slavery became the centerpiece of his ministry. Beecher galvanized the community by regularly "holding mock 'auctions' of female slaves to raise money from parishioners to purchase their freedom."[63] He also sheltered runaways. The Bottomes could not help but witness the "performance ministry" of the bold abolitionist clergy such as Beecher, who surrounded them in the city of New York. It would be surprising if they did not join them in the work of the movement.

Margaret Bottome continued to be a presence in her granddaughter's life until her death in 1906 when Bottome was twenty-four. She could pass on to her Amanda Smith's narratives of oppression as well as recount her own exposure to outspoken clergy committed to emancipation. Her granddaughter thus inherited a moral charge to speak out on behalf of the voiceless and victimized.

Bottome's single visit to Virginia belied her deep associations with the region. Through her grandmother and her grandmother's friend and professional associate, Amanda Smith, she had a connection as far back as the slave-holding South. Her grandmother had undoubtedly heard Stowe's own brother preach on the evils of slavery. But Bottome's visit to Virginia in 1932 proved significant, occurring at an impressionable moment. She had only recently begun exploration of her childhood and adolescence with Seif. At the same time, she encountered American racism, she had just begun to observe the Nazis. She wrote of Munich before Hitler came to power, "Our

Jewish friends alone knew that the terror [of the Nazis] was a reality."⁶⁴ Bottome was uniquely placed in the early 1930s to draw a parallel between Nazism and the "color neurosis" of the American South, both finding embodiment under the "shadow of law."

Under the Shadow of Law: The Nuremberg Laws and the Fugitive Slave Act

Bottome left Munich for Vienna in 1935 so that she and Ernan could devote themselves to Adlerian analysis with Adler himself. From that vantage point she followed the escalating violence directed against German Jews in the spring and summer of that year, precisely when she began to write *The Mortal Storm*. Joseph Goebbels, Minister of Propaganda and soon-to-be head of the German film industry, as well contributed to the violence, encouraging it through the many communication outlets at his disposal. His role in the escalating violence bears particular significance. He later watched balefully the success of Bottome's novel and the film based on it. Goebbels could not help but recognize *The Mortal Storm* as an attack on his carefully nurtured race laws.⁶⁵

The campaign that Goebbels waged against the Jews in 1935 contained denunciations of *Rassenschande* or racial defilement from "interracial intercourse" as its core message.⁶⁶ Goebbels simply embraced an idea that had emerged from German right-wing thought in the late nineteenth century. The country's defeat in the First World War provided an accelerant, encouraging anger and bitterness that found expression in a revitalized and newly pernicious antisemitism of the sort that Bottome witnessed in Vienna at the same time. The concept of racial defilement was reborn, now with lurid accounts of its consequences. For example, Arthur Dinter's 1918 bestseller *Sin against the Blood* (*Die Sunde wider das Blut*) recounted how an Aryan woman paid a terrible price for an affair with a Jewish man. Though she left him and married a true German, she had already been permanently defiled, a condition she passed on to her offspring. Instead of giving birth to children who possessed Aryan features, her offspring all bore those that were stereotypically Jewish. According to the historian George Mosse, the book was "not pornographic, [yet] sold in the hundred thousands," unaided by content that could be described as "prurient."⁶⁷ By the third year of Nazi rule, Goebbels and other members of the Nazi elite began to consider ways of prohibiting racial defilement in the Third Reich.

With the start of 1935, Goebbels, along with Julius Streicher, editor of the semi-pornographic *Der Stürmer,* renewed the idea of *Rassenschande,* as a legal concept.⁶⁸ He and Goebbels took up a campaign to denounce relationships between Jews and non-Jews as poisonous for German racial purity. Streicher used the pages of *Der Stürmer* to purvey "endless stories of 'racial defilement.'"[69] At an outdoor rally in Hamburg, for example, he told his audience that "when one girl gave birth to a baby nine months after marrying a Jew [...] 'what lay there in the crib, comrades?! A little ape!'"[70]

Goebbels avoided the incitement to violence and perversion that clung to Streicher's reputation, but he was no less dangerous in his restraint. In controlling the media of the Third Reich, he hoped to own the message as well. Supported by Hitler, Goebbels broke Streicher's short-lived monopoly of the intensified antisemitic campaign of 1935.[71] His newspaper *Der Angriff* soon began to resemble *Der Stürmer* in its own brand of brutal rhetoric.[72]

The campaign widened beyond the press. On May 21 the army formally "banned 'mixed marriages' between German soldiers and non-Aryan women."[73] Thus encouraged, Goebbels stepped up the anti-Jewish violence and denunciations of racial defilement in his own *Gau* of Berlin. There and elsewhere in Germany, Marriage Registry Offices became battlegrounds. The S.A. or brown shirts, renowned for their thuggery, picketed and refused to allow so-called mixed-race couples to enter. Registry Offices themselves joined the campaign. They reported such unions when they occurred to the Gestapo. According to Goebbels's biographer Peter Longerich, the Minister of Propaganda used his speeches at party meetings in Berlin "to fuel" a "pogrom atmosphere" in the capital.[74] Under such heated conditions Jewish businesses even in the best part of the city became a target. On July 15 high-end Jewish shops on the posh Kurfurstendamm were vandalized.[75] Abroad the press labeled the violence "the Kurfurstendamm riots," suggesting that violence stalked even the most affluent part of the German capital.[76]

The violence put Goebbels himself on the defensive. Hjalmar Schacht, Minister of Economics and President of the Reichsbank, argued that the economy remained too fragile to permit such disorders to continue.[77] Persistent attacks on Jews might lead to Germany's economic isolation if boycotts were instituted abroad. Hardly a desirable outcome, Schacht observed, with the winter Olympics less than a year away. There was much at stake. Germany was due to host not only the winter but also summer Olympics. The economics minister therefore advocated "regulating antisemitic activity through legislation."[78] Even many radicals in the Nazi Party who watched the violence of the spring and summer of 1935 with approval acknowledged Schacht's point. They would support his compromise if the legislation were harsh enough.[79]

Bottome could not help but be aware of the escalating violence against Jews as it occurred. She still had many contacts in Munich. Members of Seif's circle wrote of the latest horrors. Ironically, laws prohibiting "racial defilement" posed a threat to Adler himself. Ostensibly to avoid the worst of Austrian antisemitism, Adler had converted to Christianity the year before.[80] Were the Nazis to take over Austria, as they repeatedly threatened, Adler's decades-long marriage to his Russian-Jewish wife Raisa would come under scrutiny. At the very least, Adler's conversion had made his own a "mixed marriage." The psychologist must have watched the agitation in Germany with growing concern.

The race laws promulgated at the Nazi Party Congress in September provided a legislative compromise between those only too willing to encourage, if not ignore, street violence and those who feared the consequences of such violence but were nonetheless determined to isolate the Jews from German life. The new legal order, however limited in its provisions, changed the character of existence in Germany for Jews and non-Jews alike. Intermarriage, even "sexual relations between Jews and 'Aryans,'" became illegal.[81] The open intimidation, which Schacht had argued undermined Germany's reputation and her economy, gave way to the "shadow of law," which Goebbels now embraced, co-opting it for his own administrative domain. Having done so much to encourage adoption of the race laws, Goebbels soon began vigorously applying them by "'purging' culture," part of his administrative preview in the Third Reich.[82] The remaining "non-Aryans" still working in the press, theater, cinema, and all other areas of cultural life were expelled. Selfish and acquisitive, an adept and vicious infighter, the minister of propaganda jealously guarded his bureaucratic realm which he now made a show place for the Nuremberg Laws. He turned particular attention to cinema to make sure that those who produced its content should be "Aryan." Goebbels became the face of the new race laws in cinema as well as other areas of German culture. That role, some argued at the time (see Chapter 8), ultimately pitted him against the studio that produced *The Mortal Storm*. He must have recognized that film as an attack on his carefully nurtured race laws.[83] By 1940 the question loomed, whose image of the Jew would prevail in cinema, if not beyond the silver screen.

Bottome's concern regarding the Nuremberg Laws provided her with yet another link to Stowe. Like the American novelist, she now fictionized the notion of the family vulnerable to a brutal legal regime. Legality gone awry permeates both *The Mortal Storm* and *Uncle Tom's Cabin*. The Fugitive Slave Act, under whose shadow Stowe wrote, and the Nuremberg Laws that haunted Bottome share a common outcome. In addition to the threat both posed to the integrity of family life, they added new categories of individuals liable to punishment. Those who harbored runaway slaves or assisted in their escape faced federal prosecution under the Fugitive Slave Act. Non-Jews in a relationship with someone defined as a Jew by the terms of the Nuremberg Laws faced public humiliation and incarceration.

At the same time both sets of laws intensified fear in those already vulnerable. With the passage of the Fugitive Slave Act, panic "set in in northern black communities," sending hundreds to Canada where "British authorities [...] refused to extradite fugitive slaves."[84] A similar situation arose with the passage of the Nuremberg Laws. Case law from the prosecution of "race defilers" burgeoned.⁸⁵ Germans were expected to police the sexual activity of their neighbors and to report unlawful relationships.⁸⁶ Panic set in within the Jewish community now under scrutiny by neighbors as well as the Gestapo. Some couples committed suicide. Jewish emigration, which had declined in 1934, rose once more.

Bottome, like Stowe, wrote to arouse the social conscience of her readers as the circle of those at risk widened and persecution intensified.⁸⁷ The nineteenth-century abolitionist saw her audience as the "Christian and humane people actually recommending the remanding of escaped fugitives into slavery" (*UTC*, 374). She would turn her readers against complicity with the Fugitive Slave Act, if she could, by "exhibiting" slavery "in a *living dramatic reality*" (*UTC*, 374). But Stowe did something more. The novel quickly crossed the Atlantic where "Great Britain" found itself "in the grip of Tom Mania." The author traveled there and was lionized. Slavery was illegal in Britain, but Stowe quickly became the recipient of significant donations for the anti-slavery cause in the United States.⁸⁸

Bottome too found her greatest success on the other side of the Atlantic. She first saw her readership in an England that, as she repeats, had "gone Nazi in its sleep." And like Stowe, she very quickly sought a trans-Atlantic audience, hoping to use her novel to arouse the Americans, whom she believed the Nazis would threaten soon enough and whose help the British would so desperately need. *Uncle Tom's Cabin* provided her with a guide in writing her own novel condemning a brutal regime. It could also be said to have provided her with an example of a trans-Atlantic novel of protest.

Uncle Tom's Cabin and *The Mortal Storm*: Transatlantic Novels of Protest on the Eve of War

Stowe and Bottome

Within three years of returning to Europe following her visit to the American South, Bottome watched the events that led to the Nuremberg Race Laws at close hand, from just across the border in Austria. She wrote *The Mortal Storm* in part to protest those laws that erected new "walls of ice" between Jews and "Aryans," of the sort that she had observed in Vienna fifteen years earlier. In *The Mortal Storm* when Fritz Maberg proposes to Freya he tries to convince her that the Nuremberg Laws won't deter their marriage: "We talked the whole Jew question out with our commander at the fortress. It turns out he had a Jewish grandmother himself!" (*TMS*, 277). Fritz is not correct. According to the Nuremberg Laws, descent from a Jewish grandmother imposed *Mischling* status, an ambiguous, but suspect state at the time that the laws were promulgated.

Just as Stowe wrote to protest the Fugitive Slave Act of 1850, Bottome turned to fiction to protest the injection of racism into the German legal system. In her plot and characters, she took inspiration from Stowe, hoping that *The Mortal Storm* would prove as influential in denouncing antisemitism as *Uncle Tom's Cabin* had in denouncing slavery. Stowe's portrait of a society at war with its own values reemerges in Bottome's portrait of a society at war with those whom she depicts as having supplied its values (*TMS*, 72). And both were trans-Atlantic novels of protest that did far better on one side of the Atlantic than on the other. *Uncle Tom's Cabin*, while selling well in America, in England outsold the American edition and became the publishing phenomenon of the century.[89] *The Mortal Storm*, certainly a bestseller in England, by 1938 belonged to the United States, where it exceeded British sales in print and was adapted to the screen by Hollywood.

One reason for its success among American readers arose precisely from the echoes of *Uncle Tom's Cabin* that abound in *The Mortal Storm*. Bottome's novel fit into mainstream American culture in the 1930s where versions of Stowe's novel had long been a staple of the entertainment industry, particularly cinema. D.W. Griffith had in fact produced *The Birth of a Nation*, "one of the highest-grossing movies of the era," precisely with *Uncle Tom's Cabin* in mind.[90] The historian David S. Reynolds terms it "the most powerful anti-Tom work in history by appropriating several of Stowe's images and reversing them."[91] Similarly he notes, "*Gone With the Wind* [...] was like many southern novels [and films based on them] written largely in reply to Stowe."[92]

Uncle Tom's Cabin permeated American culture well into the twentieth-century, inspiring works for or against it, depending on the writer's or producer's attitude to race. Bottome herself wrote one of the most ardent defenses of Stowe in fiction. But she did something more. With *The Mortal Storm* she joined the analogy with the Civil War that permeated American culture in the late 1930s as a substitute discourse for open discussion of the Nazi threat. On screen it stood alone with its depiction of the fate of German Jews. But in its themes, plot, and characters, it consoled with a sense of the familiar. *Uncle Tom's Cabin* lies embedded in *The Mortal Storm*.

Borders

Both *Uncle Tom's Cabin* and *The Mortal Storm* are novels of hounding and escape that culminate in the crossing of a border to safety, to Canada in Stowe's novel, to Austria as a way station to America in Bottome's. Their heroines must reach a border and cross it or succumb to circumstances, they have been warned, that will be intolerable. In each novel the heroine hears the warning, learning suddenly of impending disaster or imminent danger. Eliza overhears her master Mr. Shelby reveal to his wife that the slave trader to whom they are in debt "fancied the child [now] this wretch owns [him]," Eliza's little Harry (*UTC*, 30–1). When Rudi informs his older sister Freya that Professor Roth has died in a concentration camp, he also informs her: "Someone telephoned [...] He said 'Our sister had better visit someone outside Munich' [...] There was an official letter too [...] to say you couldn't go any more to the university or take your degree" (*TMS*, 321). Both women quickly recognize that flight is their only option. In Freya's case to save herself, in Eliza's to save her son.

But Eliza's situation is far more precarious than Freya's. Her vulnerability is shown in her having few if any direct sources of information about her existence which is in the hands of others. Hearsay, rumor, and the chance opportunity at the right moment to eavesdrop provide the signals she needs to survive. Freya's information is not only direct and official, but the message carries a portent. Rudi thinks it is Emil who called with the warning, a harbinger that he will ultimately place loyalty to his sister above fealty to the Nazis. Nonetheless the result is the same for both women. They either seize their right to exist or abandon it to the slave trade in Eliza's case or to the Nazis in Freya's.

Further similarities between Freya and Eliza exist. They have both enjoyed a privileged, even pampered upbringing but necessity elicits toughness and courage each had never needed to show before. For example, "Eliza has been brought up by her mistress, from girlhood, as a petted and indulged favorite" (*UTC*, 11). Similarly, Freya, the only daughter in a family with three sons and the only one endowed with the scientific talent of her father, is the "indulged favorite." Her father proudly tells her, "It has sometimes occurred to me, my daughter, that you have the makings of a scientist" (*UTC*, 132). Each has a sense of entitlement and in Freya's case of the potential for achievement. Neither will accept the role of passive victim.

Both Freya and Eliza must make life-altering, even life-threatening, decisions on their way to safety. Freya's escape is not nearly so harrowing as Eliza's, leaping from ice floe to ice floe with Harry in her arms. Yet their passage to safety is comparable in other ways. Each woman reaches her destination in stages. Eliza finds shelter in a Quaker settlement before crossing into Canada, and Freya escapes to the mountains with her baby not in her arms but inside her. She spends several months at the Wetterstein farm of her lover Hans's family. Unlike Eliza who will never part with Harry, Freya leaves behind her baby by Hans to be raised in his family. She will go on not only to fulfill her own scientific talent but also to continue her father's work in America, beyond the reach of the Nazis. For Eliza, Canada is what America is for Freya.

Eliza is able to abandon her identity as an African American slave upon crossing the Canadian border, but she will remain bound by the shackles of the nineteenth century's constraints on women. Freya, on the other hand, as a German-Jewish refugee of talent, by the fifth decade of the twentieth-century, can expect to find the doors of a career in medicine open to her in the United States.

While Canada is a permanent refuge for Eliza, Austria as a way-station is only temporary for Freya. At the time Bottome wrote, Austria was fast disappearing as an option for escape. Hitler's regime and the Austrian Nazis pressured Vienna to join with Germany in an *Anschluss* or merger that had been expressly forbidden by the Treaty of Versailles. To Fascists on both sides of the border, the boundary was only temporary and artificial. At best, once in Austria, Freya would find a short-lived refuge and a respite, not a haven. Nazism was on the move and its adherents saw borders as mere impediments soon to disappear.

Ulrich von Maberg, whose son Fritz shoots and kills Freya's lover Hans Breitner, flippantly tells Freya's mother Amélie:

> They shot him not only without orders—but it appears that he was actually over the border, a yard or two only—but of course they dragged the body back to our side—and who cares for the Austrian border line anyhow? I beg your pardon, Amélie—I'd forgotten you were an Austrian by birth.
>
> (*TMS*, 209)

By the time that Bottome's novel was published in the United States (April 1938), the *Anschluss* had occurred three weeks earlier, creating a major refugee crisis with Austrian Jews desperate to flee. For Jews in Vienna humiliation and confiscation of property became the norm. Bottome later wrote of the *Anschluss* that the sad Vienna of 1920 "never prepared [her] for what" she "was to see in 1938 [...] when Hitler took Vienna under his harrow."[93] She described the winter of 1938 as "the darkest of [her] life [...] Czecho-Slovakia and Austria were being slowly strangled, before Hitler swallowed them."[94]

With the takeover of Austria, the Nazis had erased a European border for the first time, and as Bottome suggested in *The Mortal Storm*, it would not be the last: all European borders were at risk. She also suggested something more in equating the vulnerability of borders with the new politics. The Nazis not only disdained borders, at the same time they disdained human life on either side of the divide. Hans was murdered not only outside the chain of command, but his body was simply dragged across a border that his killers no longer recognized. Europe under the Nazis would cease to provide a haven for anyone they opposed, nor would they respect the law or tradition that made sanctuary possible.[95]

The Canadian border, in contrast, maintained its integrity in the nineteenth century as a marker for the British Empire. At the same time that boundary carried a deeper political meaning. Canada took on new importance with the Fugitive Slave Act of 1850. By the terms of the federal law, northern strongholds of anti-slavery sentiment could no longer guarantee protection to runaways, not even to their free black population already in residence.[96] British authorities, on the other hand, refused to comply with the American law on the mandatory return of fugitive slaves. By 1850 British law forbad both the slave trade and slavery.

The sanctuary that Canada afforded therefore provided Stowe with ironic symbolism. The Canadian border held a strong historical association that dated from the American Revolution, creating yet another symbolic as well as political divide between the two countries. Many Canadians by the 1850s were only a generation or two removed from those who had remained loyal to the king and relinquishing property and livelihood fled from the new republic. Stowe's message: blacks found freedom in the once-oppressive British Empire against which we had rebelled for the sake of values we ourselves now betrayed. The former Loyalists provided sanctuary to African Americans escaping from their oppressors to the South.

Bottome's novel in its narrative of escape resembles Stowe's in carrying a political message embedded in the idea of border. In Europe, *The Mortal Storm* revealed no real barrier, whether forged by law or historical tradition, existed any longer because as Ulrich von Maberg noted of the Austrian border, as far as the Nazis were concerned, "who cares for [it] anyhow?" Nonetheless, despite the odds against them, both Eliza and Freya manage to cross the borders standing between them and escape. They also share an important trait that is crucial to the social protest that motivates each novel: both Freya and Eliza are of mixed race.

Mixed-Race Characters

For Stowe and Bottome mixed-race characters are crucial to the narrative and its message. Such characters function in several ways. They provide, for example, "a transition to empathy" for a broad readership imbued with racial prejudice in the one case and antisemitism in the other. Rachel Ablow, in an essay titled "Victorian Feeling," says of *Uncle Tom's Cabin* that Stowe "elaborated a wide variety of sentimental tropes" that included "the recognizability of enslaved people as family members and Christians," providing "a transition to empathy."[97] Ablow neglects to mention, however, that most sympathetic characters in *Uncle Tom's Cabin* may be slaves, but they are also of "mixed" race. In other words, are Stowe's characters white with Negro blood or Negroes with white blood? In addition to their possession of other familiar qualities (family membership and Christian faith), empathy from the reader may depend on the answer to those two questions.

In *Uncle Tom's Cabin* the characters who are fully black embody some of the most demeaning stereotypes held by whites about African Americans. Stowe describes Uncle Tom himself as possessing "the soft, impressible nature of his kindly race, ever yearning toward the simple and childlike [...]" (*UTC*, 124). Those with white blood, on the other hand, claim virtue and intelligence superior even to their white overlords. Cassy, for example, one of the mixed-race protagonists of *Uncle Tome's Cabin*, possesses "that peculiar air of refinement, that softness of voice and manner which seems in many cases to be a particular gift to women" of mixed race (*UTC*, 11). What is the source of such superiority? Is it the white blood or an alchemical mixture of African American and white?[98] Uncle Tom's owner, Augustine St. Clare, referring to the slave revolt in Haiti argues that the majority heritage is separate and most telling.

> There are plenty among them who have only enough of the African to give a sort of tropical warmth and fervor to our calculating firmness and foresight. If ever the San Domingo hour comes, Anglo-Saxon blood will lead on the day. Sons of white fathers, with all our haughty feelings burning in their veins will not always be bought and sold and traded. They will rise and raise with them their mother's race.
>
> (*UTC*, 228)

For St. Clare, if there is a slave revolt in the American South such as occurred in Haiti, the leadership will only come from those with "Anglo-Saxon blood" because those who possess "tropical warmth and fervor" alone lack the requisite "firmness and foresight" of the "white fathers." He appears to assume such traits are discrete, unmodified by miscegenation.

Both writers are clear about the source of majority heritage in their mixed-race characters. Stowe's mixed-race characters inherit "Anglo-Saxon blood" through the father, as Augustine St. Clare notes. The Southern social system condoned racial mixing if it did not encourage it. In the South white slave-owners commonly had black mistresses. Liaisons between white women and black men were far less common and subject for the man in the relationship to the "lynch law" of the South. Freya, on the other hand, inherits majority status through her mother. Although it is her father who is Jewish, the Nuremberg Laws hold she is Jewish no matter which parent claims that identity. She herself proclaims, "If Father is a Jew, then I am a Jewess" (*TMS*, 71). Unlike Stowe's characters, she belongs to the majority culture through her mother, but the results are the same. Mixed lineage, whether racial or ethnic, according to Stowe and Bottome, generates strength of character and giftedness that results in the best of both sides rather than a dilution of talent or diminishment of vigor.

The source of giftedness nonetheless remains ambiguous for Stowe's characters. In contrast, Bottome is clear that Freya as a scientist is her father's daughter. She possesses extraordinary scientific talent not shared by her older von Rohn stepbrothers. In fact, she is so gifted as a scientist that her Nobel Prize-winning father is moved to warn her to dampen her brilliance while at the university lest she attract undue attention from Nazi students and administrators jealous of her talent (*TMS*, 314). Similarly, in the mixed-race character of Cassy, Stowe has crafted a regal figure of poise and cunning. Cassy's daughter Eliza proves no less striking and able. She escapes by leaping from ice floe to ice floe with her son in her arms, performing one of the most harrowing feats in American literature.

Mixed-race/ mixed-ethnicity characters play multiple roles in both novels. In their superiority they defy demeaning stereotypes and extoll the virtues of assimilation. They condemn isolation and ostracism in their very person. They prove that the "walls of ice" that Bottome had observed between Jews and non-Jews in post-war Vienna can and do melt. Such characters encourage empathy with the persecuted and embody condemnation of legal systems gone awry that have turned into instruments of coercion, trading fairness for persecution. Mixed characters become the primary instruments of protest through fiction in both *Uncle Tom's Cabin* and *The Mortal Storm*.

Aristocrats

Aristocratic status is crucial to both novels where inheritance or lineage does not preclude or even determine membership in the elite. For Stowe and Bottome moral conduct and intellect confer elite status, particularly striking in the mother–daughter heroines who dominate each novel. The mother in each of them is an aristocrat, although in the case of Stowe's heroine Cassy her status is obscured by race. The same is true of her daughter Eliza who numbers among the "quadroon and mulatto women" of the South (*UTC*, 11).

Freya presents a similar mixed heritage. As the daughter of an Austrian aristocrat and a German Jew, she is a *mischling*, of mixed race, by the terms of the Nuremberg Laws. But Bottome adds a twist. It could be said that Freya is twice over or purely aristocratic.[99] As a Jew her father belongs to the moral and intellectual aristocracy of Europe, Bottome argues in the novel (*TMS*, 72). The name "Freya Roth" is no oxymoron, as the Nazis would have it. Each name reinforces the other, proclaiming aristocratic lineage from both sides of her family. Similarly, Eliza is the daughter of a plantation owner, a Southern aristocrat, who never fulfilled his promise to marry her mother. She and Freya may be "mixed," but they just as surely belong to the aristocracy of their respective cultures.

Cassy is the aristocratic, mixed-race mother of *Uncle Tom's Cabin*. She has been educated in a convent and is fluent in French. With a white father, she is able to pass as a "Creole Spanish lady" (*UTC*, 358). Even her owner Simon Legree is unnerved by the daunting combination of her "refinement" and independence. He has title to her but he does not possess her. It is sooner she who wields possession of Legree "for Cassy had an influence over him from which he could not free himself" (*UTC*, 313).

Amélie von Trattenbach Roth also unnerves those close to her with her aristocratic aloofness and self-possession. Freya especially could find her mother at times unnerving: "It was her mother that Freya most feared—her mother who was the aristocrat who had such perfect manners—who did not wholly belong to her father and to herself" (*TMS*, 60). As with Stowe's heroine Cassy, Amélie allows others to make a claim on her only because she permits it. Each is independent and self-sustaining in a society that barely tolerates such conduct in women, certainly not in African American women. And each pays a terrible price. Cassy disdainfully co-habits with the sadistic Simon Legree. With strength of mind and independence of will, she contrives her escape from him. But her escape is merely physical. She has already left in spirit because she never submitted to his attempt to destroy her independence or compromised her contempt for him.

The same is true of Amélie Roth. Forced by convention and family into marriage with the libertine and alcoholic von Rohn, who succumbs to venereal disease, she is able to find a warm and loving relationship with Johann Roth. She gives her love freely to him while still retaining that air of aristocratic independence that so unnerved her daughter and caught her husband's attention. Not only does Amélie escape from a relationship that harbored the abuse that Cassy endures under Legree, but for both women independence lies first in internal liberation before, in Amélie's case, finding refuge in a second marriage and a loving relationship.

Externally, there is still enough to threaten her. She is disdainful of the Nazi assault on the family from the Nuremberg Laws and contemptuous of the regime's claim to interfere in her marriage. Professor Roth proudly tells Freya, "The Nazis have requested your mother to leave me [per the terms of the Nuremberg Laws]. She is not forced—but she is warned; if she refuses, she will be suspect, and, must live under their displeasure. Perhaps I need not tell you that she *did* refuse!" (*TMS*, 252). While Professor Roth is proud of his wife's response, both he and Freya know that it comes as no surprise. Johann Roth's reaffirming "I need not tell you" captures the unflinching certainty of her independence. Such independence also made her a feminist.

Feminists[100]

Amélie Roth's contempt for the regime is not only a hallmark of her independence; it contributes to what defines her as a woman. Both Stowe and Bottome have filled their fiction with determined strong-willed women who share with their creators a commitment to their identity as women. Stowe came from a family and culture where feminism found its clearest expression in the suffrage movement. Her sister, Isabella Beecher Hooker, for example, joined Susan B. Anthony and Elizabeth Cady Stanton in forming the radical wing of the movement.[101] Stowe herself held back from the radicals, but supported the cause of women's suffrage. Her female characters in *Uncle Tom's Cabin* prove far more competent, intelligent, and resourceful than the male characters in the novel. Elizabeth Fekete Trubey observes that the white women of the novel, that is, such characters as Mrs. Shelby, Mrs. Bird, Eva St. Clare, and, I would add, Ophelia St. Clare ("Miss Vermont"), "are exemplars to men, teaching them that religion-fueled empathy [...] demands one abhor slavery."[102] At the same time, Stowe's novel can be read as a feminist tract as much as an anti-slavery appeal.

Similarly, *The Mortal Storm* condemns sexism nearly as strongly as it condemns Nazi brutality and antisemitism. Both novels amply confirm that just as causes cohere so too do their opposite: multiple victimizations.[103] Feminism divides the Roth/von Rohn family as surely as the Nuremberg Laws. Freya as a woman and a Jewess is doubly victimized and must fight on two fronts. She appeals to her mother, "are the boys [her brothers] always to do what they like and have what they wish, and I—simply because I am a girl have no such rights—no such freedom!" (*TMS*, 61). Her brother Emil says disdainfully (and with seeming impunity), "A girl in the family always makes trouble" (*TMS*, 75). His older brother Olaf is the committed Nazi and the ideologue of the two von Rohn sons. Olaf's comment on the subject chills his mother's heart:

> "[...] we Nazis do not believe in men's professions for women—there will be, if no women doctors, at least far fewer, under our regime [...]" Amélie Roth sat down and stared straight before her, with blank, unseeing eyes. "Her future too"—she said in a low voice.
>
> (*TMS*, 91)

In other words, Freya is to suffer the same indignities and constraints as her mother's generation.

Instead, Amélie is determined, Bottome suggests, to give her daughter the opportunity to go into medicine that the mother and aunt of Jane Everest made possible for her, defending Jane's independence within an old-fashioned family, and paying for her medical education in secret (*PW*, 45–6).

It is the generation of the mothers that make emancipation possible in Bottome's novels and Stowe's bestseller. Having lived the life of a more traditional woman, Amélie Roth is the bearer of the feminist message in *The Mortal Storm*. She tells her sons, rising to her feet, and "looking incredibly tall and terrifying [...] 'I thought we had escaped from the world where women were at a man's mercy—considered only as his tools or his toys'" (*TMS*, 199). She proclaims of her own home, "let there be one roof in this land under which a woman has the same rights as a man and knows herself to be equally valued" (*TMS*, 61).

The heroines of Stowe and Bottome extend their determination to emancipate beyond their own daughters. Those women reveal themselves in the way they treat their servants, to be discussed in greater detail below. Stowe imparts a feminist message when she recounts the collusion between female servants and their mistresses in *Uncle Tom's Cabin*. Mrs. Emily Shelby, for example, conspires with her kitchen slave Chloe against her husband Mr. Shelby, who is hopelessly inept with money. His insolvency leads to the sale of Eliza's son Henry and Uncle Tom, setting in train the plot of the novel. Stowe juxtaposes his confusion over finance to his wife's good sense regarding money. Shelby tells her, "Once get business running wrong there does seem to be no end to it [...] these cofounded notes coming due [...] dunning letters and dunning messages—all scamper and hurry-scurry" (*UTC*, 215). Mrs. Shelby in contrast knows what to do:

> It does seem to me, *my dear* [italics mine], that something might be done to straighten matters. Suppose we sell off all the horses and sell one of your farms, and pay up square?
> "O, ridiculous, Emily! You are the finest woman in Kentucky, but still you haven't sense to know that you don't understand business; women never do, and never can!"
>
> (*UTC*, 215)

Mrs. Shelby proves him wrong. In a conspiracy of women, she arranges with her cook Chloe to rent out the skills of another slave who she has trained as a confectioner. The money the girl earns at $4/week will help redeem Chloe's husband Tom and contribute to returning the Shelby estate to solvency. In suggesting a remedy to her husband, Mrs. Shelby adds emphasis to her statement by interjecting "my dear," as in "it does seem to me, *my dear*, that something might be done to straighten matters." Through such language of endearment, the women of the South "wield emotional influence" over their spouses.[104]

There is a similar highly charged exchange in *The Mortal Storm* between Amélie and her husband that bears a notable resemblance to the Shelby's discussion of money in *Uncle Tom's Cabin*. Freya complains to her parents about her lack of rights and freedom as "a girl" in comparison to her brothers. Her mother intervenes: "'it would not be fair' her mother agreed. '*Dearest* [italics mine],' she added her eyes fixed entreatingly on her husband's face, 'let us be fair to the last!' Freya had never heard her mother use the word 'Dearest' to her father before, and it startled her very much" (*TMS*, 61). Both writers use the same words of pleading, not to say under the same circumstances, of desperation: "dearest," "my dear." In one instance, "to straighten matters" out includes the lives of loyal slaves. In the other to "be fair to the last" includes the very life of Amélie's daughter. The women who plead demonstrate their own vulnerability, even helplessness, before their husbands. Yet both know how to employ the English language to manipulate, "wielding," as Elizabeth Ferekete Trubey observes, "emotional influence" over them to get what they want. Bottome's Amélie Roth in pleading for her daughter's future is painfully like Emily Shelby, who pleads for her slaves. With mitigating endearments, they address issues of social as well as personal importance. Both novelists imply, however, that even strong and treasured women must tread carefully because at times they too are no better than servants themselves.

Servants

The characters of Bottome and Stowe reveal themselves in the way they treat their servants. In *Uncle Tom's Cabin* Marie St. Clare, for example, whose guilt-ridden and repentant husband Augustine had purchased Tom, insists on a harsh regime toward her slaves. She is the center of her own world and sees the behavior of others only in relation to herself. The result is baleful for those at her mercy. St. Clare regards her slaves as unreliable and untrustworthy. They must be subjected to stern discipline if they are to work at all. For Marie St. Clare such discipline amounts to unbridled cruelty. She proclaims, "Now, there's no way with servants [...] but to *put them down* and keep them down [...] you must make them *know their place*," she insists with a measure of studied euphemisms (*UTC*, 149). She reveals the truth of what she intends when she states that to maintain discipline, slaves should be sent to "places to be flogged" (*UTC*, 149).

In the mistreatment of servants, St. Clare has her match in Amélie Roth's cousins, the von Mabergs. The von Mabergs, father and son, so entwined with the von Trattenbachs by marriage and cousinage, suffer unrequited love for Amélie and her daughter. Both Ulrich and Fritz, respectively, have been spurned by Amélie and her daughter Freya. The Mabergs could hardly be compatible with the Roth family. They are only too willing to welcome the Nazis, finding nothing offensive in their aggressive brand of antisemitism. Ulrich von Maberg unthinkingly says to Amélie Roth of the Nazis, "today they made a good impression on me—a very good impression indeed" (*TMS*, 208). Ulrich corrects himself, returning to the subject of the Nazis and their would-be victims with the placating qualification: "look out for the Jews, your husband and his family excepted." But he adds, revealing his true sentiments, the Jews are "not a race I care to see battening—like leeches—on our good German blood!" (*TMS*, 213).

In his conversation with Amélie, again showing complete incomprehension regarding her values, Ulrich reminisces about the good old days when he could "flog" a servant with impunity (*TMS*, 207). Bottome employs the same word that Stowe attaches to Marie St. Clare, who insists that there should be places where unruly slaves can be "flogged." For both Stowe and Bottome, the willingness to "flog" another is the ultimate marker of moral indecency. As in the Old South, in Nazi Germany racism and abuse go hand in hand. Brutality, it seems, is gender neutral under a system as toxic as that to be found in both places.

Ulrich's wife, the Countess Hermine von Maberg, more subtly terrorizes her servants while hopelessly exploiting them. In *The Mortal Storm* the victim, not the victimizer, is named Marie/Maria. She is the servant of the Countess von Maberg, mother of Fritz and Sophie. Sophie will marry Freya's revered brother Olaf. Bottome describes the servant's encounter with the countess with all its vulnerability and exploitation. Maria steps into her mistress's bedroom as though entering a circle of hell.

> Maria knocked at the door, bringing in a heavy silver tray, which she laid with desperate care upon a small *Biedermeier* table, beside the *Grafin*'s tapestried chair. The room filled with the delicious aroma of immaculately made coffee. A plate of Brotchen containing a pate de foie gras and kavier was placed on one side of a dish of whipped-cream and upon the other plate of petit fours. The *Grafin*'s eyes rested upon the tray with austere vigilance. She touched the delicate porcelain cups, to see if they were warmed. Nothing had been overlooked.
>
> Maria stood nervously, her eyes fixed in an agony of suspense upon those of her mistress. The *Grafin* nodded her head with grave satisfaction.
>
> "It is well, Maria," she observed with the solemnity of a Divine Power conferring the final sentence after death. The instant relief upon Maria's face indicated her escape into Paradise. "It is well! You may go! [...]"
>
> Maria retired murmuring her gratitude. She had nothing to be grateful for, since the *Grafin* paid her the lowest possible wages and exacted the hardest amount of work from her, nevertheless the utterances of the *Grafin* to her servants seldom failed to inspire gratitude.
>
> (*TMS*, 228–9)

The Countess von Maberg rules with an iron hand over a kingdom of *Biedermeier* furniture and petit fours. She is the Simon Legree of the boudoir. For Maria, the terror lasts from her knock on the door to her exit from the presence of her mistress. In contrast, Ulrich von Maberg remembers Amélie von Trattenbach, who spurned him in their youth, "would always wait—or turn aside—for a servant with a tray [...]" (*TMS*, 205). Her consideration for others places her in a different moral universe from that of the von Mabergs. At the same time both Stowe and Bottome allow that a person can escape from one moral universe to another. Redemption is possible.

Redemption

In each novel one character is dissuaded from evil and turned to the path of righteousness. Tom Loker is redeemed in *Uncle Tom's Cabin*, though he was one of Eliza's more determined pursuers. Badly wounded in a skirmish with members of the underground railway, he is nursed back to health by abolitionist Quakers. They bring him to a state of moral health as well:

> Tom arose from his bed a somewhat sadder and wiser man; and in place of slavecatching, betook himself to live in one of the new settlements [where blacks and whites reside]. He always spoke reverently of the Quakers.
> (*UTC*, 324)

Stowe also notes of Loker that he had "lain three weeks at the Quaker dwelling, sick with a rheumatic fever, which set in, in company with his other afflictions" (*UTC*, 324). Those afflictions might not necessarily have been those of the body. Just as his fever burned itself out so did his capacity to oppress others. In the character of Tom Loker, Stowe not only reveals that redemption is possible, but also suggests that slaveholding is an infection that has inflamed individuals as well as the body politick. Tom wisely removes himself from the contagion by residing in one of the "new settlements" for people of both races (*UTC*, 324).

Stowe literally names Loker as a character willing to change. In doing so, she draws on the growing collection of myth and legend, a product of the European Romantic Movement, at first largely German, which emphasized folk culture imbued with pre-Christian Germanic and Norse myth. "Loki" or "Lokki" is the trickster and changeling among the Norse gods who slips from one place to another, from one role to another. Tom Loker is a changeling of a sort, transformed from slaveholder to abolitionist, slipping from one world into another. Not only does he prove that redemption is possible, but Stowe also demonstrates his role with a mythological association, a narrative strategy that Bottome too will employ with Freya and her brother Olaf.

Like Stowe, Bottome allows that a cure from the fever of political infection is possible, revealing the possibility in the fate of Freya's two older stepbrothers, Olaf and Emil. One is saved, and one is lost. Emil allows his feelings for his sister to override his loyalty to the Nazis, in the end placing family ahead of ideology. At first, he shares his brother's commitment to the Nazis. Olaf announces to the family, "Emil and I have accepted the rule of our leader" (*TMS*, 69). And Emil like his brother demands that Freya reject her Communist lover. In the end it is Emil who renounces. He rejects the Nazi Party and its uncompromising tenets. He also jeopardizes his own safety and what status he still possesses in the party to accompany Freya on skis across the Austrian border to safety. Olaf, on the other hand, remains, as Bottome explains, "nearly honest a man," but "nearly" does not suffice for integrity (*TMS*, 348). When Olaf visits Freya at the Wetterstein farm in the mountains he "did not kiss her good-bye. He had not once touched her, but suddenly he stooped down, and kissed her child. Then he turned quickly away and swung off out of sight without looking back" (*TMS*, 348). Olaf, unlike his brother, cannot be saved.

Olaf's gestures of rejection, refusing to kiss Freya or to look back at her, appear calculated to hurt the sister who once adored him. But the loss will be his. He skis away to return to his bride Sophie von Maberg, whose failings mount. Emil reveals contemptuously, she cheats at bridge. He ascribes her deficits to a lack of "pluck" (*TMS*, 129). But Sophie's conduct harbors even worse. She informed her future sister-in-law Freya that one of the bridesmaids had complained that Freya's presence would make the nuptials a "Jewish wedding." Freya refuses to withdraw from the ceremony, and Sophie exacts revenge. "Freya found that the chief bridesmaid's name had been given as Fraulein Freya Trattenbach too late to be rectified," rather than Freya Roth (*TMS*, 273–5, 289). Olaf has found a spouse worthy of him: she is as vengeful as he is.

Sophie also connives at a far worse deed than forcing Freya's Jewish surname from the wedding program. She and her mother, the countess, form an unholy alliance of destruction to exclude Freya from the Maberg family and alienate her from Olaf once and for all. Sophie and the countess reveal to Freya, almost as a slip, that Olaf ordered Fritz to shoot Hans. A stunned Freya escapes the wedding festivities in the von Maberg schloss when Emil drives her back to Munich. But the bad news does not end there. As they get ready to leave, Emile shocks her yet again. Professor Roth has been arrested, he tells her. Freya begins to realize that she can no longer remain in Germany (*TMS*, 291–5).

Sophie and her mother intend to unhinge Freya, if not destroy her. In doing so Sophie excludes her most formidable rival for Olaf's affection. She and Freya will not bond as sisters-in-law or in any other way. In an Adlerian sense, Sophie has removed a sibling rival. But Freya is not so easily dealt with. She after all bears the name of a Norse goddess. Her name invokes the goddess of love and beauty who impels romance but remains aloof from it. In the course of the novel three men seek Freya's hand. In the end she skis to Austria single and romantically unencumbered, as her goddess namesake would have it. But her name in Norse mythology also suggests something more. After battle half the souls of the dead go to the terrible Odin, god of war, and half are saved and go to Freya. In Norse mythology the division between siblings can extend into eternity.

Both Stowe and Bottome allow souls to choose for themselves. Individuals have the power to determine which side they are on. Both writers deviate from mythology, making redemption possible. Olaf reveals that truth in telling Fritz Maberg, "'I once told Freya how I wanted to be for Germany—a second Siegfried; and I have not forgotten her answer [...]' 'But Siegfried is supposed to be a hero and behaved like a cheat [...] she begged me to model myself on some other—more real hero'" (*TMS*, 269). Freya had predicted the truth of her beloved older brother even before adulthood: that he would fulfill the destiny suggested in the name of his chosen hero and make the wrong choice at every turn.

Olaf failed to find another role model among the gods. He remained loyal to his first choice, the flawed hero Siegfried. And like the Siegfried of legend, he betrayed the one closest to him. Olaf turns his back on Freya, returns to the Third Reich and a shallow, vengeful wife whose bridge scores cannot be trusted. Emil makes the opposite choice. He skis in the other direction toward Austria to help his sister escape. He is the Tom Loker of *The Mortal Storm*, who is cured of the fever and contagion of Nazism, in the end refusing submission to "the rule of our leader."

Both novelists assure that redemption is possible even in the midst of evil. Redemption for Tom Loker means rejecting his former way of life even if, as he admits, he cannot completely embrace the alternative. The Quakers "wanted to convert me but couldn't come it exactly," he admits (*UTC*, 324). As with Loki the trickster, the door is always open to change. In Emil's case loyalty to his family and love for his sister prove stronger than a belief system that disdained family ties and would destroy them. Emil, like his brother, has chosen for himself. He will go to Freya, and Olaf to Odin where war awaits him.

Emil harbors doubts about his choice of "the leader" from the beginning. While still a Nazi, he confides to Freya, "I've always wanted what you've had—after all you are the old man's flesh and blood child—and I'm not. Freya, even though he's a Jew—I wish I *were* his child!" (*TMS*, 129). Emil would rather belong to a family than a party. He differs from Olaf in another respect. His name in its German form, Emil, recalls the French version, Emile, as in Emile Zola. Why would Bottome employ such a name for a young German and seemingly committed Nazi, writing as she was in 1937? The answer to the source of Emil's name lies in Bottome's adolescence lived back in the 1890s. In that period of her life, she embraced the cause of Alfred Dreyfus. Bottome in her youth had been a Dreyfusard and therefore gave her character an association that recalled the most famous instance of antisemitism in recent memory. With the death of Dreyfus in 1936, the case sprang to life again precisely when Bottome was writing *The Mortal Storm*.

Bottome as Dreyfusard

Bottome's exposure to the Dreyfus case provides yet another clue to the origins of *The Mortal Storm*. The Jewish question had entered her life as early as her adolescence with the sharpness of conflict almost as intense as the one that raged in France. Shortly after her family's return to Britain in 1896, following their six-year stay in America, Bottome fell under the sway of her French teacher in the local Grammar School in Bournemouth. She wrote of Mlle. Mellie Darius, "I loved her very dearly and would I think have given up anything I had to her, except the freedom of my will."[105] Darius recognized her pupil's talent. She deftly encouraged the emerging adolescent to accept her own sexuality without challenging her loyalty to her father's clerical calling. Her influence proved all the greater for being judicious and restrained. Bottome described it in the following way:

> All she taught me swept over my parched life like the waters of the Nile over the barren Egyptian desert. She taught me the essence of French literature. She took away from me, with her Latin matter-of-course attitude towards sex, half my fears. She gave me courage and taught me to believe in my own abilities. She laughed me out of many morbid imaginings. She had no religion; but she respected mine [...] the clear force of her precise and factual mind cut its way through my unreal church life, and helped to set me on my feet as a human being in a physical universe [...].[106]

Into this heady mix of French literature and Latin sensibility, there poured the scandal of a French officer accused of selling military secrets to the Germans. Every aspect of the Dreyfus case resonated with painful associations for the French. Dreyfus was Jewish and for the past forty or fifty years Paris had witnessed a new economic phenomenon in its midst: the emergence of wealthy Jewish families with status and property acquired in a matter of decades. Their rise and near assimilation, to some, appeared uncanny.[107] Dreyfus himself came from a prosperous Jewish family, but he came from Alsace that is one of the "lost" provinces acquired by Germany as a result of the French defeat in the Franco-Prussian War of 1870–1. As a Jew and an Alsatian, Dreyfus presented the specter of questionable loyalty twice over. The French regarded Alsace as "too German" and the Jews, some fulminated, were more loyal to their own "international enterprise" than to France.[108] It was hard to know which association was worse: the German taint that came with Dreyfus's Alsatian origins. Or was it simply that Dreyfus was a Jew?

"The shadow of law" hung over Dreyfus in the form of trumped-up charges and the proceedings of a kangaroo court. His second trial in 1898 occurred thanks to the efforts of the novelist Emile Zola. Bottome could observe that the truth-tellers were paradoxically also, like Stowe and Turgenev, the great critic of Russian serfdom, and now Emile Zola, the writers of fiction. Zola's letter to the Parisian newspaper *L'Aurore* with the ringing repetition of the words, "*J'accuse*," had forced the French general staff to conduct a second trial with Dreyfus as defendant. The Dreyfus case became a scandal at a heady and impressionable period in Bottome's life. It provided, in the form of victimization and blatant injustice, her first exposure to the Jewish question, which was to be one of the most significant issues in her creative life after the First World War.

She recounts the striking impression the Dreyfus case made on her. Curiously missing is any mention of the antisemitism which underlay the accusations against the French officer. Bottome indirectly broaches the subject when she compares Dreyfus's trial in its "dishonesty" to that of Jesus Christ. Both, after all, were crucified Jews.

The trial prompted her to disagree with Mlle. Darius, not only for the first time but with vigor. She had otherwise served as a willing vessel into which her French teacher had poured culture and values, it seems, to overflowing. Bottome now protested. She joined the Dreyfusards. She defied Mlle. Darius, who counted among the anti-Dreyfusards. She raised her own barricades. In fact, she describes her reaction to the trial as an ongoing argument with her French teacher. "We had one chief point of difference [...] Neither of us could give way to the other and restate our passionate convictions."[109]

At the core of their disagreement lay the question of who was willing to lie rather than tell the truth of the situation. For Mlle. Darius, Dreyfus could rot on Devil's Island rather than stain the honor of France by allowing an accusation of treason against a French officer (other than Dreyfus) and claiming that the army of the Republic had conducted sham judicial proceedings. Bottome had previously admired Mlle. Darius precisely for her straightforward and matter of fact honesty: her "Latin matter-of-course attitude toward sex" and "precise and factual mind" that cut its way through her pupil's "unreal church life." Mlle. Darius betrayed her own essence in the matter of Dreyfus. It was too much for her young pupil who discovered, like Zola, she would have to side with the truth as she saw it no matter what the consequences.

The implications of the Dreyfus case continued to haunt her long after the exoneration of the accused. Residing in Vienna in the early 1920s, she once more encountered the pernicious force of European antisemitism. In writing *Old Wine*, she explored the danger it posed to European stability, reappearing with renewed vigor so soon after the First World War. The relevance of the Dreyfus case itself emerged again in the 1930s. Hollywood made the connection for her. In 1937, as Bottome was finishing *The Mortal Storm*, Warner Brothers released the film *Emile Zola*, starring Paul Muni as Zola. While the deft viewer had to watch attentively to catch a single reference in the film to Dreyfus's Jewish identity, much was made of Zola's role as the author of the manifesto titled "*J'accuse*," which forced a second trial for Dreyfus.

Not long after the release of the Warner Brothers film, events prompted Bottome to employ Zola's signature phrase. In March 1938 when the Nazis in a surprise move took over Austria, Bottome denounced the indifferent response of her own government. She titled her statement "I accuse." In no uncertain terms, similar to those that Zola had used thirty-six years earlier, she accused the British establishment, starting with the Archbishop of Canterbury, of abandoning the Jews of Austria to their fate under the

Nazi heel. British printers refused to set the short essay in type. It did not appear until *The New Republic* published it in December 1938, thanks to the intervention of her friend, the novelist and socialist Upton Sinclair.

The end of the 1930s, which saw Nazism on the march, made Zola's defense of Dreyfus more relevant than ever. The redeemed truth-teller in *The Mortal Storm* is Emil von Rohn, whose name invokes Zola and thereby honors the novelist-hero of the Dreyfusards. Emil, true to his name, reveals his deepest emotions (the truth about himself) to Freya and labels their sister-in-law Sophie what she is, a cheat, lacking character and spirit. The truth-tellers—Emil and Freya—pair up and he assists her to escape to America. The self-deceivers—Olaf and Sophie—link in marriage.

On to America

For Bottome, *The Mortal Storm* constituted a cause. She sought to arouse her compatriots to the threat before them lest they too suffer the fate of Europe's Jews. She also hoped to alert the Americans before they suffered the malady of inadvertence that had so disturbed her when she encountered it in Britain. But her intentions toward the Americans were not limited to altruism. Britain would need the Americans to defeat the Germans, just as she had in the Great War. Like *Uncle Tom's Cabin*, *The Mortal Storm* would have to be a trans-Atlantic phenomenon. Stowe had taken her novel to Britain, visiting there herself three times in the 1850s to enlist the support of British abolitionists for the American anti-slavery cause.[110] But unlike Stowe, Bottome had twentieth-century entertainment technology at her disposal. She knew that for the novel's ultimate success on the other side of the Atlantic, Hollywood held the key. The great majority of Americans were sooner moviegoers than readers of fiction. No novel, moreover, could reach the eighty million who went to the movies each week. The most effective medium for her message lay with a major studio, preferably the one that the late Irving Thalbeg had put at the forefront of Hollywood, namely, MGM. Bottome sent her novel there in 1937, almost as soon as Faber & Faber published it in Britain. The studio rejected it within months of submission. Upon revising the text for American readers and more particularly for MGM, she determined to try again. Republished in the United States just weeks after the *Anschluss*, Bottome's novel had only grown in timeliness. From the spring of 1938 onward, *The Mortal Storm* became an American phenomenon.

Bottome left for the United States the third week in September 1938, ostensibly to conduct another lecture tour of the States "from end to end [...] in hope of stemming the rising tide of antisemitism."[111] In fact her primary purpose was to convince MGM, or barring that another major Hollywood studio, to produce *The Mortal Storm*.

Notes

1. Bottome, *The Goal*, 219.
2. Phyllis Bottome, foreword by Phyllis Lassner and Marilyn Hoder-Salmon *Old Wine* (Evanston: Northwestern University Press, 1925/1998). Henceforth *OW* followed by page number in the text. All references to *The Mortal Storm* (henceforth *TMS*, followed by page number in text) are taken from Phyllis Bottome, forward by Phyllis Lassner and Marilyn Hoder-Salmon (Evanston: Northwestern University Press, 1998).
3. Phyllis Bottome, *Private Worlds* (London: Penguin Books, Ltd., 1937). Henceforth *PW* followed by page number in the text.
4. Bottome, *The Goal*, 162.
5. See especially *Devil's Due* (1931) and *Danger Signal* (1939), where Adler's system of ideas known as Individual Psychology is prominent.
6. Phyllis Bottome, *Search for a Soul* (New York: Reynal & Hitchcock, 1948), 148 and 219.
7. Ibid., 148.
8. Ibid., 219.
9. Harriet Beecher Stowe, *Uncle Tom's Cabin* (New York: Dover Publications, Inc., 2005), 9 and 374. Henceforth *UTC* followed by page number in the text.
10. Phyllis Bottome, *The Challenge* (New York: Harcourt, Brace & Co., 1953), 397. For discussion of the influence of American race laws on the drafting of the Nuremberg Laws, see Isabel Wilkerson, *Caste. The Origins of Our Discontents* (New York: Random House, 2020), 78–88.
11. Robert Graves and Alan Hodge, *The Long Week-End. A Social History of Great Britain, 1918–1939* (London: Faber & Faber, 1940), 423.
12. Bottome, *The Goal*, 128 and 109.
13. Ibid., 73.
14. Ibid., 70.
15. Ibid., 87.
16. Freya becomes a Jew by choice. Jewish tradition in the diaspora holds that Jewish identity is passed from the mother. The Nuremberg Laws, however, would impose on Freya the status of *Mischling* of the First Degree whether she claimed Jewish identity or not. See Wistrich, *Hitler and the Holocaust*, 53.
17. Phyllis Lassner, "'Objects to Possess or Discard': The Representation of Jews and Women by British Women Novelists of the 1920s," in Billie Mellman (ed.), *Borderlines. Genders and Identities in War and Peace* (New York: Routledge, 1998), 255.
18. Hirsch, *The Constant Liberal*, 153.
19. Ibid.
20. Bottome, *The Goal*, 258.
21. Ibid., 128.
22. Ibid., 105 and 162.

23 Ibid., 162.
24 Ibid., 163.
25 Ibid., 192 and 194.
26 Ibid., 195.
27 Ibid., 166.
28 Ibid., 181.
29 Ibid., 190–1.
30 Ibid., 250.
31 Ibid., 128.
32 Ibid., 166.
33 Ibid.
34 Ibid., 165.
35 Ibid., 139–40.
36 Letter to her literary agent Ann Watkins as cited in Hirsch, *The Constant Liberal*, 344.
37 Quoted in Hirsch, *The Constant Liberal*, 344.
38 Bottome, *The Goal*, 190 and 263.
39 Ibid., 190.
40 Ibid.
41 Bottome, *The Goal*, 190.
42 Bottome, *Search for a Soul*, 149.
43 Bottome, *The Goal*, 191.
44 Bottome, *Search for a Soul*, 148.
45 Hirsch, *The Constant Liberal*, 187.
46 Phyllis Lassner, "'On the Point of a Journey': Storm Jameson, Phyllis Bottome and the Novel of Women's Political Psychology," in Antony Shuttlesworth (ed.), *And in Our Time. Vision, Revision and British Writing of the 1930s* (Lewisburg: Bucknell University Press, 2003), 126.
47 Bottome, *The Challenge*, 169.
48 With Adler, the personal and the political readily merge, each explaining the other. According to Adler, basic sibling rivalry underlay the origins of the First World War. That idea attracted Bottome the first time she claims to have met him when his explanation for the First World War encouraged her to see him as "a great man" (see Bottome, *The Goal*, 139–40).
49 In musing on her losses in the war, Jane Everest refers to her family as her "House of Being" and the war itself as a destructive "hurricane" that overturned it (*PW*, 46).
50 Sally's breakdown, brought on by her fears for her identity and place in her husband's life, curiously anticipates Jean Rhys's 1966 novel, *Wide Sargasso Sea*, which suggests that Rochester's wife descended into madness from mistreatment at his hands which included incarceration in the attic of their house.

51 Bottome, *The Goal*, 177.
52 Ibid.
53 Bottome, *Search for a Soul*, 219.
54 Bottome, *The Goal*, 162.
55 Tuberculosis links Bottome to *Uncle Tom's Cabin* in yet another way. Her account of the death of her best friend of nineteen years, Lislie Brock in *The Goal* (99–106) bears a distinctive resemblance to Stowe's account of Eva St. Clare's death in *Uncle Tom's Cabin* (*UTC*, 247–51). Both died from tuberculosis. Bottome nursed Lislie with the help of the perfect nurse. "I have known many good nurses, but none to touch Maria Theresa" (Bottome, *The Goal*, 103). "Eva's aunt, Miss Ophelia, day and night performed the duties of a nurse [...] with such perfect adroitness [...] with such perfect sense of time [...] such exact accuracy" (*UTC*, 247). Employing the liberty of fiction, Stowe describes a Christian aura surrounding Eva's deathbed: "she was so beautiful [an] air of innocence and peace [...] seemed to breathe around her" (*UTC*, 248). Despite the secular attitudes that she and Lislie shared, Bottome uncharacteristically refers to the "beautiful soul" of her friend and her last twelve hours as "inconceivably beautiful." She describes the end in the following way: "I sat beside Lislie, her hand in mine, an extraordinary sense of boundless love passed from her heart into mine and seemed to fill the room [...] It was as if we were wrapt together in an endless unbroken peace" (Bottome, *The Goal*, 105). Bottome's account of her friend's death, which occurred in 1923, constitutes a unique chapter within her three-volume autobiography. Its revelations of her deepest and most private emotions along with its spiritual emphasis occur as an unexpected deviation from the otherwise largely dispassionate narration. Its resemblance to the deathbed scene in *Uncle Tom's Cabin* suggests at least Bottome's familiarity with it. Bottome may have also used Stowe's account as a model, acquiring license to reveal her own deep emotions and break through her usual reserve.
56 Phyllis Bottome, *From the Life* (London: Faber & Faber, 1944), 83.
57 Hirsch, *The Constant Liberal*, 1.
58 Bottome, *The Goal*, 177.
59 The others include Alfred Adler, Max Beerbohm, Ezra Pound, Sara Delano Roosevelt, Ivor Novello, and Victoria Drummond.
60 Bottome, *From the Life*, 95.
61 See accounts in Amanda Smith, *Autobiography* (no publisher given, 1893).
62 Bottome, *From the Life*, 84–5.
63 Eric Foner, *Gateway to Freedom: The Hidden History of the Underground Railway* (New York: W.W. Norton, 2015), 117.
64 Bottome, *The Goal*, 190.
65 Goebbels would have relied on the extensive reports that the German consul in Los Angeles, Georg Gyssling, sent to him, starting in 1936. Those reports were lost in the spring of 1945 when an American incendiary raid made a direct hit on the Ministry of Propaganda. This information was supplied by an archivist in the Political Archive of the German Foreign Office in Berlin in conversation with the author.

66 The phrase "interracial intercourse" belongs to George L. Mosse, *The Crisis of German Ideology. Intellectual Origins of the Third Reich* (New York: Schocken Books, 1981), 142.
67 Ibid.
68 Ian Kershaw, *Hitler. Hubris, 1889–1936* (New York: W.E. Norton & Co., 1990), 560.
69 Ibid.
70 Richard J. Evans, *The Third Reich in Power* (London: Penguin Books, 2005), 541.
71 Peter Longerich, *Goebbels. A Biography*, Alan Bance, Jeremy Noakes, and Lelley Sharpe, trans. (New York: Random House, 2015), 303. Ian Kershaw makes the same point in *Hitler. Hubris*, 560–3. Streicher, who had been "at the forefront" by mid-summer gave way to Goebbels.
72 Kershaw, *Hitler. Hubris*, 560.
73 Evans, *The Third Reich in Power*, 542.
74 Longerich, *Goebbels. A Biography*, 303.
75 Kershaw, *Hitler. Hubris*, 562.
76 Longerich, *Goebbels. A Biography*, 304.
77 Wistrich, *Hitler and the Holocaust*, 51–3.
78 Ibid., 52–3; Kershaw, *Hitler. Hubris*, 564.
79 Kershaw, *Hitler. Hubris*, 563.
80 The actual circumstances of Adler's conversion remain obscure. To Bottome's dismay, Raisa, Adler's wife, insisted that she cut as much as one-fifth of the authorized biography that she had completed by 1939. That material must have contained discussion of Adler's conversion. See Raisa Adler's correspondence with PB in BL Add. Mss. 88921/3/1.
81 Kershaw, *Hitler. Hubris*, 568; Evans, *The Third Reich in Power*, 550–1.
82 See Goebbels, *Diaries*, September 15, 1935, as cited in Ralf Georg Reuth, *Goebbels* (New York: Harcourt, Brace & Co., 1993), 206 for an account of the cultural purging.
83 Unfortunately, Goebbels's immediate response to *The Mortal Storm* and the other so-called anti-fascist films released by American studios in the summer of 1940 is not available. Entries in his diary for the summer of that year appear to be lost.
84 Foner, *Gateway to Freedom*, 134, 137.
85 Evans, *The Third Reich in Power*, 551.
86 Ibid., 552–4.
87 Contemporaries recognized UTC as "fictional propaganda." See *The Westminster Review* (July 1852) and *The Monthly Review* (October 1856). The latter defends the novel as propaganda that succeeds.
88 For discussion of Stowe in Great Britain, see David S. Reynolds, *Mightier Than the Sword. Uncle Tom's Cabin and the Battle for America* (New York: W.W. Norton, 2011), 131–2.

89 Although often passed from hand to hand so that US readership and sales figures diverge, "*UTC* [...] sold more copies in Britain than in the United States," according to Patrick Brentlinger, "Race and the Victorian Novel," in Diedre David (ed.), *The Cambridge Companion to the Victorian Novel* (Cambridge: Cambridge University Press, 2000), 135. According to Kate Flint, "Since ten different transatlantic editions of [... *UTC*] were produced within two weeks and forty within a year, it is hard to be exact about figures, but, including colonial sales, around 1,500,000 copies were sold to the British market" in Diedre David, *The Cambridge Companion to the Victorian Novel*, 28. Simon Eliot in "The business of Victorian Publishing" compares *UTC* as a publishing phenomenon to the *Bible*, noting that between 1848 and 1850, 2.1 million copies of *The New Testament* and 2.4 million copies of the *Bible* were produced in Britain; David, *Cambridge Companion*, 57.

90 Reynolds, *Mightier Than the Sword*, 225.

91 Ibid., 222.

92 Ibid., 253.

93 Bottome, *The Goal*, 73.

94 Ibid., 272.

95 Ibid.

96 Foner, *Gateway to Freedom*, 7–9.

97 Rachel Ablow, "Victorian Feelings," in Diedre David (ed.), *The Cambridge Companion to the Victorian Novel*, 203.

98 See discussion among Stowe's slave-owner characters as they ponder the same questions, *UTC*, 227–9.

99 See my "Phyllis Bottome's *The Mortal Storm*: Film and Controversy," in *The Space Between: Literature and Culture, 1914–1945*, vol. 6, no. 1 (2010), 40–1.

100 For further discussion of feminism in *The Mortal Storm*, see Judy Suh's *Fascism and Anti-Fascism in Twentieth-Century British Fiction* (Basingstoke: Palgrave Macmillan, 2009), 79–81.

101 For a fictionalized, but accurate portrait of Hooker and Stowe, see Patricia O'Brien, *Harriet and Isabella* (New York: Simon and Schuster, 2008). The novel also contains a portrait of their abolitionist brother known to Bottome's grandparents.

102 Elizabeth Ferekete Trubey, "Success Is Sympathy": *Uncle Tom's Cabin* and the Woman Reader in Janet Badia and Jennifer Phegley (eds.), *Reading Women. Literary Figures and Cultural Icons from the Victorian Age to the Present* (Toronto: University of Toronto Press, 2005), 53–76, 58.

103 See Nadia Valman, *The Jewess in British Nineteenth Century Literary Culture* (Cambridge: Cambridge University Press, 2007) and Catherine Hall, "Missionary Stories: Gendering Ethnicity in England in the 1830s and 1840s," in Catherine Hall, *White, Male and Middle Class: Explorations in Feminism and History* (Cambridge: Polity Press, 1992), 214 for the linkage between the Jewish and woman questions to the cause of abolition. Valman notes that abolitionists as well as the campaigners for Jewish emancipation and women's

rights employed the same argumentative strategies (p. 8). Louis and Rosamund Billington link the emergence of "mid-nineteenth century feminism" to "the earlier anti-slavery movement" in "'A Burning Zeal for Righteousness': Women in the British Anti-Slavery Movement, 1820–1860," in Jane Rendall (ed.), *Equal or Different: Women's Politics 1800–1914* (Oxford: Basil Blackwell, 1987), 82. See also Gisela Bock, who links racism and sexism in the Third Reich in "Racism and Sexism in Nazi Germany: Motherhood, Compulsory Sterilization, and the State," *Signs*, vol. 8, no. 3. Women and Violence (Spring 1983), 400–21.

104 Ibid., 62. Trubey observes, "Stowe offers a number of potential measures by which women can facilitate the end of slavery, ranging from wielding emotional influence over their husbands to limited domestic civil disobedience."

105 Bottome, *Search for a Soul*, 240.

106 Ibid.

107 For an account of the rise and near assimilation of wealthy Jewish families in Paris in the last quarter of the nineteenth century, see Edmund de Waal, *The Hare with Amber Eyes. A Family's Century of Art and Loss* (New York: Farrar, Straus, & Giroux, 2010).

108 For a gendered approach to the Dreyfus case, see Erin Carlson, *Double Agents: Espionage, Literature, and Liminal Citizens* (New York: Columbia University Press, 2013). See also Robert Harris, *An Officer and a Spy* (New York: Vintage Books, 2014), which vividly captures French society in the 1890s and the sources of Dreyfus's outsider status.

109 Bottome, *Search for a Soul*, 240.

110 F. J. Klingsberg, "Harriet Beecher Stowe and Social Reform in England," *American Historical Review*, vol. 43 (1938), 542–52: 547.

111 Bottome to the Bishop of Chichester (September 19, 1938). BL Add Mss. 10308/3/3.

3

Selling *The Mortal Storm* to Hollywood

The Politics of Hollywood

Bottome had much to do before she could sell the movie rights to *The Mortal Storm*. The studios preferred proven winners. From 1937 to 1939 Hollywood on average purchased half the works of fiction on *Publishers' Weekly* annual top ten bestseller list.[1] Given its controversial topic of Nazi persecution of Europe's Jews, *The Mortal Storm*, in order to satisfy a major studio, would do well to top the bestseller lists, preferably for an extended period. But before that could happen, Bottome had to revise the British edition of 1937 to satisfy American political sensibilities and taste. For example, on the American side of the Atlantic, a red scare hung over national politics and threatened Hollywood for much of the decade. The Communist Hans Breitner would have to modify his politics. Bottome also had to satisfy wary American reviewers and the public that the novel harbored no propaganda for war.

And then there was Hollywood itself. Bottome recognized that greater emphasis on Freya might make the novel more attractive to the industry where the studios favored vehicles obviously suited to showcase female stars. The last novel that she sold to Hollywood, *Private Worlds*, had focused on the protagonist Jane Everest. On screen, Claudette Colbert had turned that role in 1934 into an Academy Award-nominated performance.

The moguls themselves posed a problem. They were a conservative lot, she believed, lacking in daring as well as imagination. Nor did she have faith in their judgment, sound or otherwise. She complained to her supervisor, the head of the Ministry of Information (MoI), Duff Cooper, "[…] there is the ragged edge of folly to the studios […]"[2] On the other hand, she admitted in her "American Notes," "Hollywood double crosses you first, but [is] tender to you afterwards. If you give them value [...] they'll see you get money later. They want something for nothing, but they have a heart."[3] Should the studios show reluctance, it would be particularly helpful to engage a powerful voice, a figure with influence behind the scenes in Hollywood, who could advocate on her behalf and argue for the crucial timeliness of the novel.

This chapter will explain how Bottome accomplished all those tasks, transforming *The Mortal Storm* into fiction palatable to American readers and acquiring a backer with influence among the moguls or at least someone who possessed influence with an individual they were inclined to heed. It will explain why MGM, Hollywood's most successful studio in 1939, the producer of *The Wizard of Oz* and distributor of *Gone with the Wind*, agreed to make a black-and-white anti-Nazi film that focused on the persecuted group the moguls so reluctantly acknowledged as their own.

The "false optimism which lies deep in the Anglo-Saxon race"[4]

Bottome arrived in the United States in the first week of October 1938 with a sense of mission to sway American opinion in favor of Britain and to arouse awareness of the threat to Europe's Jews. To bring *The Mortal Storm* to the screen would accomplish both. She was determined to sell the rights of the novel to Hollywood at the same time that she fulfilled the terms of her contract with the Colston Leigh lecture bureau.[5] The success of *The Mortal Storm* filled her with optimism that she could readily make the sale to Hollywood. She had done so with *Private Worlds*, and *The Mortal Storm* had outsold that earlier novel, also attracting far more attention. She told her fellow Adlerian, Commander Locker-Lampson, that her anti-Nazi novel had enabled her "to impress ... a far wider public" than any of her previous works of fiction.[6] Since early April the novel had figured prominently on bestseller lists with no other fictional competitor set in Nazi Germany to rival it. That achievement, along with the status it afforded her, convinced Bottome that she could accomplish still more for the causes she championed. Just before leaving England, she buoyantly told the Bishop of Chichester that she intended "to lecture from end to end of [the U.S.] in hopes of stemming the rising tide of anti-Semitism."[7] She traveled across the Atlantic also believing that she had a staunch ally with unique influence whose support could advance all her most cherished causes, perhaps even expedite the sale of *The Mortal Storm*. The ally Bottome thought she could count on was the renowned journalist, Dorothy Thompson.

Dorothy Thompson

Bottome and Thompson had known each other since they first met in Vienna in the early 1920s. In recounting those days in *Old Wine*, Bottome had included Thompson as the aspiring journalist Carol Hunter, just learning her trade.[8] The two had then collaborated on a novel titled *The Depths of Prosperity* published in 1924.[9] They maintained their friendship through the 1930s. On Bottome's visits to the United States in those years, she occasionally stayed with Thompson and her husband, Sinclair (Hal) Lewis, when in New York.[10] She and Lewis shared the craft of fiction, and Bottome sought his advice on her work.[11] Thompson even considered that if something were to happen to her and Lewis, their son Michael could be given over to Bottome and Ernan to be raised "in a cultivated atmosphere."[12]

By 1938, Thompson was long past the apprenticeship Bottome had observed in Vienna. She held a unique place in American journalism. Through her column "On the Record," which appeared three times per week in the *New York Herald Tribune*, she became "the leading American voice in the war against fascism."[13] Thompson was a self-described "friend of Britain," and like Bottome expended time and money to aid Jewish refugees from Hitler.[14] She shared with Bottome disdain for Charles Lindbergh, whom both regarded as a dangerous voice for fascism. From the fall of 1939 to 1941, Thompson wrote fourteen columns denouncing the aviator.[15]

Bottome and her husband met with Thompson in the fall of 1938 shortly after arriving in the United States. She recounted to her friend and political ally Julian Lucas that "Thompson is entirely with us and working on our lines."[16] Bottome went even further. She claimed by the summer of 1939 to have "an unpublished partnership" with Thompson and that they "worked together in support of democracy."[17]

Thompson did appear for a time to be working closely with Bottome. On the night of November 9–10, 1938, known as *Kristallnacht* or Night of Broken Glass, the Nazis attacked Jews and Jews-owned property. Twenty thousand Jews were marched on foot to concentration camps and 100 died in the violence. Thompson joined thirty-five other writers calling on President Roosevelt to institute an economic boycott of Germany to protest the antisemitic atrocities.[18] The document sent to the president stated in part, "We ... no longer have any right to remain silent ... it is deeply immoral for the American people to continue to have economic relations with a country that avowedly uses mass murder to solve its economic problems."[19] Rumor had it, Dorothy Thompson "may have been the actual author of the missive."[20]

Thompson had seized the initiative as the American voice of anti-Nazi protest. Bottome had done the same in Britain. Shortly after the *Anschluss* in March, the author of *The Mortal Storm* had condemned the country's establishment for ignoring the tragedy that now befell Austrian Jews. Unlike Thompson at the time of *Kristallnacht*, Bottome stood alone. Her essay of protest titled "I Accuse" recounted that "200,000 Jews in Vienna are being systematically pillaged and tortured [...] 600,000 half Jews [...] are in danger of being deprived of their livelihood [...]." The political and clerical leadership of Britain chose silence, she charged, preferring to "hand England over to the Dictators in order to save their skins and their pockets."[21] No British publication would touch the essay. Thompson's husband, Sinclair Lewis, indirectly assisted Bottome in getting it into print. He introduced her to his fellow novelist and Yale man, Upton Sinclair, who urged *The New Republic* to take it.[22] The essay appeared in the issue for December 28, 1938.[23]

Bottome and Ernan had "escaped the avalanche in Vienna by three days," leaving just before the German invasion.[24] Safely across the border in Italy, she wrote a select number of "American friends," among them Thompson and Sinclair Lewis. She recounted the ordeal for Austrian Jews.

> The state of things in Vienna is past belief ... The insults to the Jews are so inhuman and so studied it is no wonder the pick of them find it too outrageous to live ... The suicides have begun ... all these people have received what amounts to a sentence of death.
> (PB to American friends, March 19, 1938)

Thompson quickly responded with an article that appeared in the respected journal *Foreign Affairs*, titled "Refugees: A World Problem."[25] More accurately, it could have been titled "Jewish Refugees: A Proposed Solution." Thompson called for the creation of an umbrella organization to assist Jewish emigration and resettlement. Bottome, in the letter to Thompson and others of March 19, had suggested something similar, proposing that she and Hal work with her so "that a colony of reputable Jews may be allowed to enter America and that" they "work for the establishment of such a quota." Thompson in her essay did not call for something as controversial as a quota for entry into the United States. But Bottome's suggestion and harrowing account of Nazi-occupied Vienna may have encouraged her to shift the emphasis of the piece at the last minute and insert material on Jewish flight and rescue from the now-expanded Third Reich.

The essay attracted a good deal of attention. Oswald Harrison Villard, one of the regular columnists for *The Nation*, maintained that Thompson's "article in the April issue of *Foreign Affairs* ... moved President Roosevelt" to convene the Evian Conference on refugees, held in France.[26] Devoted to the European refugee crisis that followed mounting Nazi atrocities, the conference met in July. If Villard's assertion was correct, the "unpublished partnership" between Thompson and Bottome had initially proven effective.

The Mortal Storm and *Kristallnacht*

The very increase in Nazi aggression in 1938, while demoralizing to those who had warned of the Nazi threat all along, also fueled Bottome's optimism that an aroused public opinion might awaken the studios to the timeliness of *The Mortal Storm*. *Kristallnacht* indeed forced papers all over the country for the first time to condemn Germany outright. The *Buffalo Courier-Express* called the violence and destruction a "lynching." The *St. Paul Dispatch* "a throwback to barbarity," and the *Syracuse Post-Standard* announced, "humanity stands aghast and ashamed" before the "brutality."[27]

Kristallnacht or the November pogrom proved a turning point for the leading liberal publications as well. *The New Republic*, for example, "turned openly hostile toward Germany after the November pogrom ...."[28] Its sister publication, *The Nation*, observed, "the November outrages ... [have] aroused anti-Nazi feeling in this country to a new pitch of intensity."[29] That "new pitch of intensity" encouraged interest in the brutal aspects of the Nazi regime which did not go unsatisfied. "[...] forty accredited foreign correspondents in Germany" provided the American public with regular sources of information.[30] Their readership grew overnight.

Bottome's novel addressed Nazi brutality on a personal level. In *The Mortal Storm*, she described the conditions for the inmates in Nazi concentration camps. Her depiction of their ominous brutality added to the immediate relevance of the novel. At the same time, she revealed the Nazis' murderous intent toward the Jews. Bottome could argue to the studios, by 1938, *The Mortal Storm* stood at the cutting edge of public concern about Hitler's regime. She charts the hounding of Professor Roth through references to the Nazis' new criminal justice system. Before his arrest the scientist knows of the camps only through rumor. He tells Freya, "These concentration camps are starting up everywhere and the tales of what goes on in them are terrible" (*TMS*, 250). After his arrest, with her brother Emil's help, Freya is granted permission to visit her father. Now he knows the camps from the inside. Arriving at the camp where her father is incarcerated, Freya cringes, "The very air smelt of [...] fear [...] Once she heard a shrill scream of terror but the complete silence that took its place was more frightening than the scream" (*TMS*, 308). Freya finds her father "thin as a specter" (*TMS*, 309). He warns her with his usual sense of irony, to prepare for the worst. "I am a very dangerous criminal," he confesses. "I have sinned so gravely against the Fatherland that but for my stepsons, and my former reputation, I should have been already shot! Or beheaded!" He adds, "I want you to realize [...] the probabilities that lie ahead" (*TMS*, 316). As for his work, he tells her, you "will go on with it," both reassuring and insisting (*TMS*, 316). Not long after Freya's visit to her father, Rudi breaks the terrible news to her, "in a shaking voice [...] 'He's dead' [...] 'Then they killed him,' Freya whispered half to herself and half to Rudi" (*TMS*, 320).

End to Optimism

At the end of 1938 Bottome went with Ernan to Hollywood to sell *The Mortal Storm*. She believed that despite their aversion to acknowledging the German threat for much of the decade, the studios would still bid for it. The book-buying public had embraced it. Hitler's recent aggression, particularly the events of *Kristallnacht*, had made *The Mortal Storm* timelier than ever. Nor was the novel itself any longer outside mainstream opinion. It expressed views, she could argue, shared by leading American newspapers as well as by "Dorothy Thompson (Mrs. Sinclair Lewis)," her "intimate friend, who has great influence as the chief *Herald Tribune* columnist."[31]

In Hollywood, she was able to have "long private talks" with four studio heads.[32] But the discussions did not go as she expected. She found no studio willing to commit to production of the novel. The director George Stevens, for example, wanted to purchase it; but George Schaefer, the head of RKO, "definitely afraid [to] commit us to any picture that is propaganda against anything." Schaefer insisted the studio confine its productions to "Americanism."[33]

By way of contrast, she compared the negotiations with the moguls to the long conversations she conducted with academics on the same trip to California. She recounted to her old friend Admiral Drax "the thought margin between these two [groups] is, as you can imagine, pretty steep."[34] One presumes she gave the intellectual advantage to the academics. The moguls, after all, had failed to grasp the import of *The Mortal Storm* even under the current circumstances of renewed Nazi aggression. That failure must have been all the more distressing to Bottome, given the amount of effort she had expended to make the novel palatable to both American readers and Hollywood. She told her friend Stephen Potter, Lecturer in English Literature at the University of London, "the whole Chamberlain trouble is caused by a [...] false optimism which lies deep in the Anglo-Saxon race." The moguls were equally naïve, she added.[35] Her own false optimism ended with the year. Nor did Thompson in the end prove supportive. Consumed by her journalistic responsibilities, she had no interest in expending the effort to promote her British friend's novel with the studios. "I always think of this winter [1938–9] as [...] the darkest of my life," Bottome later wrote.[36]

The Red Scare of the 1930s

> Martin Dies, the one-man Gestapo from Texas ....
> (Frida Kirchway, *The Nation*, December 16, 1939)

In *The Mortal Storm*, Bottome juxtaposes the caring, manly, and unpretentious mountain dweller, Hans Breitner, to Freya's stepbrothers and would-be fiancé Fritz Maberg—so unlike Hans, all quickly lured into the Nazi Party. When Freya falls in love with Hans, she thinks it appropriate to join him as a member of the Communist Party. To take such a momentous political (and romantic) step, she seeks her father's permission. "Father, would you mind if I joined the Communists," she asks Professor Roth with seeming casualness (*TMS*, 134). He answers with his own questions. There is nothing casual about them.

> "Are police spies an incentive to brotherhood? Do executions spell peace? Can we punish our brothers without open trials? Is peace to be procured from a propaganda that hides our own faults, and reveals those of others? ..." Freya hung her head—that was the worst of her father—if you ask him a question at all, he usually answered by asking half a dozen other questions which you were not particularly anxious to see brought up. "You do like Communists better than Nazis, don't you?" She demanded defensively. "My affections have not been stirred to any depth of passion by either of these parties," he answered.
> (*TMS*, 134 & 136)

In the British edition, the scientist's evenhandedness in condemning Nazis and Communists contrasts with Hans Breitner's perorations. Freya's lover presents a different, altogether positive version of Soviet Communism in contrast to the harsh images that hang in the air between Professor Roth (Toller in the British edition) and his daughter in their conversation on the subject. Modifying Hans Breitner constituted the biggest change to a single character that Bottome made for the American edition of *The Mortal Storm* and with good reason. A red scare emerged in American politics almost as soon as Roosevelt diplomatically recognized the Soviet Union in December 1933. The red baiters quickly found two targets: Hollywood and the Roosevelt administration itself. In *The Mortal Storm*, Hans remains a Communist; but Bottome modified the harsh, determined idealism of his ideology, endowing it with sobriety and dulling its edge in the edition for American readers.

The ingredients of the American red scare were not lost on Bottome. She spent more time in the United States in the 1930s than at any other period of her life, except for the eight years of her childhood in the 1890s. Between 1931 and 1940, she made four extended visits, lecturing all over the country on each trip. She and Ernan had even considered the possibility of "settling in America" on their second visit in 1934.[37] The possibility arose again with "new urgency of purpose [...] four years later in 1938" when they "thought [...] that England was going Nazi in its sleep under Chamberlain." At that time they "prepared naturalization papers ... and became potentially American citizens [...]."[38]

As their plans to immigrate to the United States grew more serious so too did American red baiting. Some of the fiercest attacks against the administration began with Roosevelt's reelection campaign in 1936. The ultra-conservative and well-financed Liberty League, founded to defeat Roosevelt, denounced the New Deal, claiming the administration was riven with Communists.[39] The political mainstream made similar charges. Samuel Rosenman, Roosevelt's close friend and longtime speech writer, remembered of the 1936 campaign, "Republican leaders" and "the right wing of the Democratic party [...] charged that the New Deal [...] was the forerunner of communism, if not communism itself."[40]

The charges against the administration began to come from another quarter as Bottome prepared to sell the novel to Hollywood. In May1938 the crudely ambitious Martin Dies (D-TX) acquired the chairmanship of the newly established House Un-American Activities Committee (HUAC). Many thought that Dies's mandate consisted of investigating Fascist penetration and influence in American life. Dies did not share that view. He believed that investigation of another brand of subversive would sooner advance his political career which included presidential ambitions. In November 1938 the "cold-eyed, unscrupulous, ruthlessly ambitious Texas Democrat" announced "his determination to rid the government of such subverters as Harry Hopkins, Harold Ickes, Frances Perkins and other 'Communists and fellow travelers,'" that is, the most prominent members of Roosevelt's administration.[41] Dies also set his sights on Hollywood, presumably another hot bed of Communism and one sure to generate even more publicity for his investigations. Under the circumstances the studios would take a dim view of a novel soft on Communism in addition to "luring the country into war" against Nazi Germany.

The moguls watched the red baiting warily. Communism indeed existed in the studios, certainly among left-wing writers. As a group, writers were relative newcomers to the studio system, flocking to Hollywood, starting in 1929, enticed by the new technology of sound and the salaries the movie business offered. The studios certainly needed the writers. The industry's profitability in hard times required the moguls to rely on independent-minded, often left-leaning script writers who provided the dialogue for the "talkies."

The British writer R.C. Sherriff, author of the renowned play *Journey's End* (1929), set in the trenches of the Western front, has described the sudden importance of writers to the Hollywood studio system:

> Talking pictures were in their infancy, and script writers were hard to come by. The old-time writers employed to supply captions for silent films were rarely any good at dialogue. The way was wide open for a generation of younger writers, with golden opportunities for those who could master the new technique for the talking film.[42]

Sherriff was among those who did. He subsequently contributed to scripts at Universal and MGM.

The newcomers quickly showed their independence from the moguls and their iron-fisted control of studio system. In April 1933 they formed the Script Writers' Guild (SWG), which the studio heads refused to recognize or bargain with. To strengthen their fledgling union, the script writers attempted to align with the New York Dramatists Guild.[43] Their timing was impeccable. They began negotiating with the playwrights in the midst of the 1936 presidential campaign, filled with right-wing accusations of Communist influence in the Roosevelt administration and ominously in the entertainment industry as well. The moguls saw an opportunity to rein in the unruly writers. They "raised shrill cries of warning that the writers were trying to subject Hollywood to the domination of New York Communists."[44]

Bottome stepped into the American political maelstrom with *The Mortal Storm*, containing a protagonist who was a Communist. First and foremost, she would have to address the character of Hans Breitner. Advice on revision could come from several quarters. Among her American friends, Dorothy Thompson and Roger Scaife stood out. Scaife was her editor at Little, Brown & Co. In the 1930s he and Bottome drew personally and professionally close. She came to rely on his judgment.[45] Scaife, as a fiction editor with a major publisher, would have Hollywood contacts and know the mood of the studios. Uniquely connected to politics and liberal journalism, Thompson could provide Bottome with the larger picture of the mood of the country. It remains to compare the British and American versions of the novel to discern what changes Bottome made to sell *The Mortal Storm* on the other side of the Atlantic.

British Version/American Version[46]

He's a von Rohn—but I'm only a little Jewess! Freya speaking of her older brother Olaf and herself

(*TMS*, 1937, 127)

He's a von Rohn—but I'm only a Jewess!

(*TMS*, 1938, 103)

Sometime between completing the British edition of *The Mortal Storm* in the summer of 1937 and fleeing Austria the following spring just days before the *Anschluss*, Bottome revised the novel for her American publisher Little, Brown & Co.[47] At the same time, she began to work intensely on the biography of Adler that his family had commissioned her to write. As part of that project, she and Ernan went to Vienna in the spring and "visited all [Adler's] old haunts and took notes from anybody whom [they] could find who had any connection with Adler and his family."[48] However constrained by lack of time, working on two projects simultaneously, she modified the manuscript of the novel with a clear sense of purpose and attention to detail. She deleted and added chapters.⁴⁹ She removed almost three pages of text which contained Hans Breitner's passionate defense of Communism. Other changes were minor. Often no more than a phrase added, or a word deleted. The changes nonetheless sharpened the text and refined both her purpose and her characters. Overall, Freya emerges more sharply and fully developed. The self-demeaning "little Jewess" of the British edition has become defiantly in the American edition "a Jewess." Hans Breitner, on the other hand, has become ideologically diluted and diminished in his political motivation from one edition to the other.

Toller into Roth

The most obvious change from the British edition to the American consisted of changing the surnames of the protagonists. The Toller family became the Roths, as though Bottome intended to emphasize the Jewish identity of her characters. The name Toller would not necessarily carry Jewish associations for American readers, although the sentence, "His name discloses his Jewish stigma," said of Professor Toller/Roth occurs in both versions (*TMS*, 1937, 110; *TMS*, 1938, 90).

In using the name Toller in the British edition, Bottome invoked the famous German-Jewish playwright of the interwar period, Ernst Toller.⁵⁰ Like Charlotte Brontë and Harriet Beecher Stowe, Toller was another writer to whom Bottome owed a debt of inspiration. In his best-selling autobiography of 1933, *I Was a German,* Toller wrote of his identity as both a German and a Jew.⁵¹ He stated that a Jew is "a member of a great race who had never bowed their heads to their persecutors, who had preferred death to dishonor."⁵² Bottome's Professor Toller/Roth provides a similar answer to his son Rudi's question, "What is being a Jew?": "to be a Jew," he intones, "is ... to be strong with a strength that has outlived persecution" (*TMS*, 1938, 71/72). Like Ernst Toller, Bottome places survival in the face of persecution at the forefront of Jewish identity.

But the Jews, according to Toller, had done more than survive persecution. Their prophets had provided civilization with a lasting gift in "calling the world to righteousness" and "exalting the wretched and oppressed then and for all time."⁵³ Bottome gave Professor Toller/Roth his own version of "a call to righteousness." The Jews, he tells his son, have "given Europe its religion; its moral law; and much of its science-perhaps even more of its genius-in art, literature and music" (*TMS*, 1938, 72). For both Bottome and Ernst Toller, the Jews are the people who have "outlived" or disdained their persecutors to provide the religious and moral foundation of Western civilization, that is, the "call to righteousness for all time."

By the time Bottome wrote *The Mortal Storm*, Toller's question of Jewish identity, which he posed in his autobiography, had taken on new urgency because of the Nuremberg Laws. Bottome used her version of Toller's answer with its emphasis on Jewish contributions to civilization to preempt the Nazi definition of Jewishness in terms of lineage, that is, "blood," as it occurs in Goebbels's race laws.

But invoking Toller also had its drawbacks for Bottome. He was precisely the sort of unruly leftist the studios found difficult to contend with. Working for MGM as a script writer, Toller belonged to the leftist Hollywood Anti-Nazi League. Founded in 1936, the organization attempted to pressure the studios to make politically engaged films critical of the Third Reich. The organization was anathema to the moguls. Toller was also active in the Federal Theater Project, subsequently subjected to congressional investigation on the grounds that Communists had penetrated the organization.[54] Toller's very association with it encouraged that conclusion.[55]

Toller's leftist credentials pre-dated the 1930s and were unique, certainly by the standards of American radicalism. He had been a leading member of the Independent German Social Democratic Party and briefly the head of the Bavarian Soviet Socialist Republic or "Red Republic" in Munich in May 1919. For those activities he spent five years in a Bavarian prison. Afterward, until the Nazis came to power, he remained an international literary celebrity, living in Weimar Germany. In using Toller's name for her protagonists, Bottome referenced not only Toller's two decades of opposition to the Nazis, but she also suggested the tolerant, humanistic strain in German culture that was now forced to live in exile, like Ernst Toller himself.

Unfortunately for Bottome, Toller's name carried another association. His brief sojourn in Hollywood did not go well. He worked for MGM from February 1937 until sometime in the summer of 1938. None of his scripts was produced. While Louis B. Mayer offered to renew his contract in 1938, the mogul refused to guarantee that Toller's subsequent scripts, like the previous ones, would be produced either. Toller left Hollywood thoroughly disillusioned.[56] Bottome apparently recognized the wisdom of renaming the Toller family for the American edition. Dropping a name that had negative associations for the studios, MGM in particular, was part of her strategy to remove provocative leftist references from the novel or at least to blunt their effect. In doing so she replicated the accommodation of Toller himself. On his North American lecture tour of 1936–7, the playwright removed all Marxist terms from the lectures that he had recently delivered in Britain.[57]

Hans Breitner

In the British version of the novel, Hans explains how he and his brother came to join the Communist Party: "We're Communists ... We kept Russian prisoners to help us after the war was over—and when they went back, they went back into the revolution—and wrote to us" (*TMS*, 1937, 15).

Bottome rewrote that passage for the American edition. Little, Brown & Co. liked the new version so much that it figured in the novel's pre-publication publicity. Ann Ford of the publisher's Publicity Department circulated the revised passage:

> The government sent Russian prisoners up here to us, as farm workers—and told us they were our enemies. We soon found this to be a lie! No farmer ever had better friends! They worked for us—and with us—as hard as we worked ourselves.[58]

Hans suggests in the British edition that Russian prisoners who subsequently joined the Bolshevik Revolution persuaded him and his brother to become Communists. In the publicity statement, the Breitners simply find solidarity with the Russians in hard work, rather than in radical ideology.

In the British edition, Hans defends Stalin's dictatorship as limited by the control of the party and the people. "In Russia," he tells Freya, "Stalin's dictatorship has its limits—he moves with the Party and cannot act without their consent, and behind the Party stand the people and a secret ballot" (*TMS*, 1937, 25). Stalin's Russia is so attractive to Hans that he and his brother Karl "would go to Russia tomorrow and start a fresh life" (*TMS*, 1937, 25). All that stops them is the age of their mother who is too old for "such a change."

Bottome excised the above passage from the American edition. Her explanation for American readers why Hans should be attracted to Communism contains no mention of his desire to leave Germany for a "dictatorship" with "a secret ballot." Instead, Hans tells Freya that as a Communist he is dedicated to a war on "selfishness." He explains, "People call Communists 'Reds' as if they were by nature violent; but that is not our ideal—our ideal is only to attack selfishness" (*TMS*, 1938, 34). Hans's anodyne version of Communism excludes violence and idealizes generosity. It contains nothing to discomfit readers uneasy about alleged Communist penetration into American life.

Bottome also removed negative references to the United States from the debates between Hans and Freya. In challenging Hans's picture of Stalin's benign regime, she notes that the United States too fails to live up to its ideals. "Russians aren't free ... I don't believe there's such a thing as freedom anywhere in the world! In America perhaps—but even there they ill-treat negroes!" (*TMS*, 1937, 16). Bottome in the British edition recalled her visit to "the American South" in 1932 when she first saw its "attitude towards its Negro fellow-citizens" which had so "horrified and depressed" her.[59] The passage in the novel with its reference to "ill-treating negroes" is absent from the American edition. Similarly, she excised Hans's condemnation of American capitalism, in league with militarism and willing to suppress the truth. In the British edition, he tells Freya, "America [is] where big trusts still stamp out truth—there is still danger that all may go wrong again—sink back into militarism and the support of death" (*TMS*, 1937, 23). Ironically, Hans's comment, while seemingly Marxist in its inspiration, could also recall the American isolationists who only recently denounced the "merchants of death" who, they charged, had lured America into war for their own profit. Hans's condemnation of American capitalism did not appear in Little, Brown & Co.'s version of the novel.

Freya too lost her ideological edge of the British edition. She tells Hans, defending her beloved older brother Olaf,

> He wants to make Germany great again. He wants to see her take her place in the world as the greatest of the European powers. We Germans are the heart and soul of Europe! ... "If we are," Hans said, ... "we need make no fuss about it ...."
>
> (*TMS*, 1937, 25)

That passage too is excised from the American edition, and Hans's unpretentious wisdom regarding German greatness is lost as well. Freya becomes more ideologically consistent: anti-Nazi and drawn only to the politics of her lover, and not those of her fascist brother.

Freya

Bottome expanded the portrait of Freya while she shortened the perorations of Hans for the American edition. She did so largely in the three chapters at the beginning of the novel that she added to the American edition. As Phyllis Lassner and Marilyn Hoder-Salmon have observed, those chapters "significantly deepened the feminist and anti-Nazi themes" of *The Mortal Storm* (*TMS*, "Foreword," xv). The new chapters also do something else. Even before Freya encounters Hans and is consumed by her relationship with him, Bottome presents her as a distinct individual, giving her greater clarity as one of the protagonists of the novel. She emerges in the new chapters, for example, as an individual of genuine scientific talent, worthy to be her father's heir in medical research. Worried nonetheless about her examination results, she tells her mother,

> "if I do well, they'll all say: 'What else could you expect from Johann Roth's daughter?' and if I do badly, and who knows if I haven't done badly after all," — Freya's voice shook,—"then they'll be sure to say: 'Think of her father's daughter coming such a crash!.'"
>
> (*TMS*, 7)

After Freya wins a prestigious award for her exam results, her father warns her not to tell her brothers, "since they both belong to the Nazi Party, and they might feel uneasy at your having success that seems to violate one of their [anti-feminist] principles" (*TMS*, 14). That issue is joined when Olaf chides her for giving insufficient help to their mother.

> You might have helped her this morning, instead of dashing off for that lecture of yours; a girl should behave like a girl sometimes [...] Freya had a temptation as sharp as Saint Anthony's [...] to reveal to Olaf that she had won the Grant for anatomy.
>
> (TMS, 19)

In expanding and deepening the portrait of Freya by giving her enviable scientific talent, Bottome evoked the characterization of Jane Everest in *Private Worlds*, where the protagonist is a successful clinician as well as researcher. In modifying Freya, she also addressed the interests of the studios as well as those of the novel. Particularly at MGM, as noted, feature films tended to be vehicles for female stars. Bottome designed the American edition, starting with the opening scenes, to attract a studio buyer who could then cast a prominent actress in the role of Freya.

Freya's sharpened scientific identity does something more. It allows her to become more assertive and a feminist, as Lassner and Hoder-Salmon observe (*TMS*, "Foreword," xv). She is less comfortable in a traditional role, more determined and forward. It might be said that she is now less European and more American. She acquires a new persona in the first three chapters, just as Hans does in becoming a Communist without ideology, relinquishing the role of committed defender of Stalin, who allegedly sits at the head of a benevolent and qualified dictatorship. Freya, in contrast, as a budding scientist has a clear source for her motivations. She has just won a "Stipendiary Grant for Anatomy and Physics" and will go to the United States to conduct research at the Rockefeller Institute after completing her final exams (*TMS*, 11). In other words, she has been "Americanized" both in her personality and in finding the place where her future lies.

On other levels Freya emerges with new clarity. In the third of the new chapters, she stands before a mirror, seeing "the eyes [...] of a fighter who would not retreat easily or give from mere good nature. The girl looking back at her from the long looking-glass possessed a power that Freya had never used" (*TMS*, 18). The "power that Freya had never used" was that of a woman. She had yet to explore its potential because the "passionate aim to succeed as a doctor ... had ... crowded out" the "aim of succeeding as woman ..." (*TMS*, 19). "There was a magic in this new Freya ..., " revealing that the scientist in her had made way for her role as a woman, or at least agreed to share pride of place with it (*TMS*, 1938, 18).

Her self-contemplation is soon disturbed. Olaf jerks her back to the new reality when he observes admiringly, "You don't look as if you had a drop of Jewish blood in you, thank goodness" (*TMS*, 1938, 19). For Olaf, the beauty of the magical new Freya lies in the absence of Semitic features. His comment opens a divide between him and his half-sister that will only widen in the novel. Of the multiple possibilities Freya discerns in the mirror—woman, doctor, fighter—the latter will crowd out the others as she is forced to confront the Nazi that her favorite brother has become.

Professor Roth also undergoes a change from one edition to the other, that is, the elevation of his status as a scientist. In the British edition his professional renown lies with his reputation as "the greatest living expert on T.B." (*TMS*, 1937, 20) Bottome opens the American edition with the news that his stature has been confirmed yet again "in the past year." Freya's father has magnified his reputation by winning "the Nobel prize for Medical Research" (*TMS*, 1938, 3). As with Freya's "magical" new image, Bottome immediately juxtaposes a personal triumph to the menacing new political reality. Having just revealed Professor Roth's international accolade, she informs the reader that in the past year too, "the boys had come to talk of nothing but Hitler" (*TMS*, 1938, 3). The boys include Freya's two older von Rohn stepbrothers, her mother's offspring by a previous marriage, as well as her younger brother Rudi. Rudi, like Freya, is the offspring of Amélie Roth's second marriage, the one to Professor Roth. They are both therefore half Jewish. Bottome emphasizes Freya's place among her siblings in the new introductory chapters. In doing so she introduces Adler's conception of family dynamics where birth order and sibling relationships were fundamental.

Adlerian Themes

Freya "had no sisters to borrow [clothes] from" (*TMS*, 1938, 4).

Freya's place at the center of a family with no other daughters to challenge her role is made clear from the start. Her elder half-brother Olaf reminds her, "you are the only daughter in the house" (*TMS*, 1938, 19). Indeed, Freya encounters the occasional inconvenience of that position as she tries to find what to wear for her other stepbrother's birthday party that evening, with no one "to borrow from" (*TMS*, 1938, 4).

Freya's place was unique among her three siblings. She had the best of both worlds. As the only daughter, she enjoyed the status of an eldest with no big sisters to challenge her. Yet she was also a coddled younger sibling. She could look up to her older brother Olaf and regard him as a hero. At the same time her scientific talent added luster to her already special place in the family. Professor Roth reminds her of her unusual status in that regard. Her other stepbrother, Emil, he tells her, "has not won a Grant for Anatomy, though of course that may still be in store for us," he generously observes (*TMS*, 1938, 15). Emil, for Freya, is the lessor of her two older brothers. He is an annoyance, yet Freya must admit, "life would lose half its savor if [she] lost Emil to quarrel with" (*TMS*, 1938, 22).

Olaf holds a different place in her world. He is the revered older brother with whom she always agrees and trusts implicitly. "Not to save his life would Olaf ever give her away or break his word to her," she was certain (*TMS*, 1938, 20). But as the scene reflected in the mirror reveals, Freya will come to relinquish that certitude as reality shows the mirror opposite of what she has always believed. Only when she falls in love outside the family will she realize that Emil, not Olaf, is the one she can trust; and, for her, he assumes the place in the family constellation once occupied by Olaf.

Bottome used material in the new chapters to foretell the dramatic upheaval in Freya's life. The British edition opens with Freya sneaking out early on the morning of her twentieth birthday to go skiing in the mountains "alone into the starlet, splintering cold January dawn" (*TMS*, 1937, 7). The American edition opens with a different birthday, that of Emil, who is about to turn twenty-one. At the party in his honor, Professor Roth sings Freya's favorite song, *Der Tod und das Madchen* (*Death and the Maiden*), with her older stepbrother Olaf accompanying him on the piano, playing with his "almost savage precision" (*TMS*, 1938, 22). With the same "savage precision," Olaf will order that Hans be shot just as he is escaping across the Austrian border.

Olaf's determination to slay Hans is motivated, as Adler would explain, on several levels. Hans threatens his relationship to Freya which formed deep in their childhood. In that sense Olaf's order is an act of revenge against a rival for seemingly stealing his sister's undivided attention. In loving Hans, Freya, from Olaf's perspective, has brought a surrogate sibling into the family to challenge his status as her hero as well as her older brother. He therefore orders Hans's removal by execution.

But there is another source of Olaf's hostility. As Adler suggested, familial divisions can present themselves as political conflicts. Freya's love for Hans, a Communist, to her older siblings amounts to a political betrayal. To Olaf, who never outgrew his childhood role, and it seems is doomed to continue it into adulthood, Freya's behavior cuts even deeper. She has betrayed him, as noted, for a new object of affection, even worship. But she has also betrayed him for a political enemy. Olaf's need for revenge against those he perceives as threats or rivals will turn, as Adler might predict, deadly. By the same token, Olaf's observation regarding Freya that she does not "look as if" she "had a drop of Jewish blood in" her "thank goodness!" carries its own ominous implications (*TMS*, 19).

It will be remembered (Chapter 2) that Bottome had earlier used the same plot in *Private Worlds*. Jane Everest's revered older brother Bertram, as the commanding officer of her fiancé Michael, orders the execution of his would-be brother-in-law for desertion under fire, that is, for cowardice. The author makes clear that Bertram did not so much stick to regulations for the sake of morale as slay a rival for his sister's affection. Bottome conveys the basic Adlerian concept of sibling rivalry through the same plot line in both novels. But in *The Mortal Storm*, with Olaf ordering that Hans be shot, sibling rivalry posed new threats because it had acquired dangerous political implications.

The political message too was steeped in Adlerian psychology. She told a friend that her novel set in Germany along with her public lectures conveyed the same Adlerian prescription.[60] To outgrow childish patterns of behavior and reach adulthood, the individual had to make moral choices and set goals based on a forthright examination of past behavior. Only by acknowledging and assessing current circumstances could one hope to function as an adult. The same was true for societies as well as individuals. To Bottome, self-deluding denial and unwarranted optimism (the "false optimism which lies deep in the Anglo-Saxon race") were used to justify appeasement in Britain and isolationism in the United States. Such behavior in the late 1930s portended self-destruction because, as she had warned since her return to England in 1936, the dictators intended war. To her immense frustration, her message, whether couched in fiction or offered directly in public lectures on Adler's psychology, elicited the same response. Americans resented what they perceived not as a truthful account of the threat before them. They instead condemned her for purveying propaganda to lure them into another European war.

Was It Propaganda?

Propaganda has taken so many strange and terrible meanings ....[61]
(*Duff Cooper, Minister of Information, British wartime cabinet*)
Propaganda becomes ineffective the moment we are aware of it.[62]
(Joseph Goebbels, Minister of Propaganda and Information, the Third Reich)

The question of propaganda loomed over the novel and could impede its acceptance by the American public. The sentiments of the 1930s remained. Americans resented being told how to interpret Europe's conflicts, particularly from the point of view of their former allies. An anti-Nazi novel by a British author in 1938 could not help but arouse suspicion as to the real purpose behind it.

The same concerns troubled Hollywood in 1938. In July of that year, the International Alliance of Theatrical Stage Employees (IATSE) met in Cleveland and "declared its opposition to the inclusion of propaganda in any film whether in the name of entertainment or otherwise."[63] The union, which was open to theater projectionists as well as most technical personnel in the studios, then went a step further, declaring that "it will not be responsible for the handling of propaganda films by its members"[64] The matter had turned serious, according to *The Nation*, because the union had declared its intention to stand behind those projectionists who refused to show films deemed propaganda. The sticking point was propaganda, however that might be interpreted.

The same issue imperiled the public lectures Bottome gave through the fall of 1938.[65] Her audiences were dubious as to her motives. The hostility was not quite so overt or intense as it would be two years later when Britain was already at war and desperately sought US assistance.[66] In the fall of 1938, the British policy of appeasement, at least some believed, might still placate the Führer. But by early 1940 circumstances had changed. Britain's need for American aid was no secret. Bottome wrote Duff Cooper for whom she then worked covertly:[67]

> From our first batch of lectures in the Middle West, we discovered that the fear of propaganda, heightened naturally by Nazi agents and perhaps equally naturally from the fear of being dragged into the war has practically made any statement of our case suspicious and liable to be taken very antagonistically. We therefore made up our minds to stick to our [subject of Adlerian] psychology and except when directly questioned, not even to give our own reasons for entering into the war.[68]

In 1938, Bottome and her husband had still been able to conduct extensive question-and-answer sessions after each lecture, touching on "the whole political situation in Europe."[69] In 1940 such give and take with her American audiences was no longer possible. Cooper sympathized with her, bemoaning the difference that two years had made. "The word propaganda has taken on so many strange and terrible meanings in the United States that people are now overanxious to avoid it."[70]

Two years earlier when the charge of propaganda had first dogged her public lectures and her newly published novel, Bottome rushed to her own defense. She wrote an essay titled "What Is Propaganda?"[71] The manuscript bore the phrase "published in California in 1938," but no publisher was indicated nor has one come to light. The essay nonetheless conveys her view of propaganda's "strange and terrible meanings," in the words of Duff Cooper.

Bottome maintained that she had no ulterior motive when she lectured publicly; she simply told the truth. She took offense at the accusations leveled at her; but they would not deter her, arguing "the antidote to Propaganda is not silence; it is the truth" (1). And that, she insisted, is what she offered. Yet those who charged her with using propaganda, Bottome argued, only sought to prevent her from speaking out. "A new and very dangerous desire to stop people saying what they have reason to think is true, lies hidden beneath the mask of protecting the public from what is falsely termed 'Propaganda'" (1). She and others like her who know and understand what is happening in Europe are being muzzled. She decried a situation where "the very people who have been in a position to estimate the facts of the Dictatorships, since they have either lived in those lands or so close to them as to get firsthand evidence of what takes place there [...] are those to whom we are now asked not to allow a hearing" (2). When that happens, Bottome argued, "The purposes of Dictatorship will have been accomplished, the courage and responsibility of the individual, having been first misled, can now be destroyed" (2). This was Bottome's point based on Adlerian premises: ignorance and self-delusion propelled appeasement and isolationism. Only an informed individual could act responsibly, she insisted. Instead, she repeatedly encountered the charge that as a citizen of "one of the European democracies, she had 'been sent over [...] to drag America into war'" (5).

Bottome recognized that the hostility to her attempts to tell the truth had serious implications for her mission to sell *The Mortal Storm* to Hollywood. She closed her essay on propaganda with the bitter complaint, "Keep on hitting at the Jews; and encourage the Hollywood studios to give the public pap, sweetened with indecency while keeping off what's going to do them in, until it gets strong enough to do it!" (8).

In 1938 events could justify her frustration as well as the indignation of her audiences. Europe had yet to go to war. Bottome's point, however, was that because the Dictators intended to fight, war between them and the Western democracies was inevitable. The essay, if not actually ever printed, does reveal how Bottome defended herself in the press and in her lectures. She held that expertise and experience trumped baser motives she might be charged with. At the least, she was no war monger, she insisted. She urged recognition of the very real and present danger before the West. Preparation for conflict, she maintained, was the only reasonable response to that threat.

Two years later Ernan weighed in on the propaganda controversy, by then moot once MGM had released *The Mortal Storm*. He enthusiastically wrote a friend, "'Mortal Storm' as a film is doing better work for our cause in America than any other form of propaganda which has been devised."[72] Had the film (and Ernan's statement) been made two years earlier when fear of propaganda for war was at its height, his words would have shocked some and confirmed the worst fears of others. The same could be said of Bottome's reaction to the film version of her novel. She wrote delightedly to her supervisor Sir Frederick Whyte, the head of the American Division in the Ministry of Information, "I hear from the USA and Canada how tremendously it is helping to strengthen and deepen the war spirit in both countries."[73] Bottome could always claim, rousing "the war spirit" was a far cry from "dragging America into war." She merely sought to awaken a willingness to support a worthy cause, and her method was to relate the truth of the European situation to her American audiences as she saw it. She neither embellished nor exaggerated in her lectures, she argued. She simply conveyed the reality of the threat. It was no fault of hers if the benighted insisted on calling her efforts propaganda.

The Critics

The critics were not so generous. They did not share Bottome's explanation of what motivated her. They scrutinized the novel, asking was it a "form of propaganda" like her lectures? Or simply literature? Or something of both? If it was propaganda, then propaganda for what? None of the American critics observed that Bottome's novel also fit among a group of writers in Britain who had already begun to address her concerns. For example, Eric Ambler's *Background to Danger* (1937) contains stories of imperiled Jews. Pamela Frankau would in the following year publish a novel of Jewish rescue, *The Devil We Know* (1939). Helen MacInnes produced *Above Suspicion* in 1941 where one of the protagonists confronts a Nazi spy and asks, "But what about Lebensraum for Jews?"[74] At the heart of the matter for American critics was the question Bottome herself admitted hung over her work: Was she helping to drag the country into war?

Three publications whose verdict was crucial to the novel's success in 1938 addressed Bottome's purpose in writing it. Speaking for the *New York Times*, Jane Spence Southern complained that "[i]t is hard to endure the rhetoric that gets into so much of the dialogue." She nonetheless offered qualified praise, "Despite speakers who call for the lecture platform [...] the story gets across with astonishing force." One character transcended the rhetoric, she offered. "Professor Roth ... stands before us almost as if in the flesh."[75] His wisdom and humanity apparently redeemed the message-ridden novel for the *New York Times* critic.

The left-leaning *New Republic* offered a similar judgment that allowed for the novel's message, while praising its effectiveness as a work of fiction. The weekly's anonymous critic wrote that even if "the characters" were "somewhat typed," the novel "remained convincing in background and emotion."[76]

The *Saturday Review*, the bellwether of American literary culture, allowed that Bottome had reconciled the contradictions of message-driven fiction. "Mrs. Bottome [sic] has written not a tract but a rapidly moving story [...] the characters who became involved in National Socialism are more impressive than any preaching could possibly be."[77]

Bottome could be satisfied with the reviews of influential American critics. Just days before the novel's launch on April 4, three politically and culturally influential publications had absolved her of message mongering and, the bête noir of American public opinion, propaganda. The critic for the *New York Times* summed up the consensus. "The astounding force" of "the story" outweighed the novel's didacticism of "the lecture platform."[78]

None of the reviewers noticed, or at least remarked, that Bottome had revised the novel for publication in the United States. Had they done so, they might have modified their judgment regarding her intentions, observing how politically astute she was in the presentation of her characters for an American audience. But Bottome ran the critical gauntlet unscathed, avoiding the charge of propagandizing for war. With the publication of *The Mortal Storm* in the United States, she cleared several hurdles at once. Neither wary American readers nor cautious Hollywood moguls, she thought, need shy away from a timely novel that offered engaging characters, including a sober, Communist, whose idealism is tempered by restraint and realism. More than any other character, given the red scare that hung over American politics in the 1930s, Hans Breitner could sink what Ernan subsequently called the most effective "form of propaganda ... for our cause." In condemning Nazism, Bottome did not provide in Hans an apologist for Marxism. What she wrote of Professor Roth could be said of Bottome herself. When Freya anxiously queries her father, "You do like Communists better than Nazis, don't you?" He answers, "My affections have not been stirred to any depth of passion by either of these parties" (*TMS*, 1938, 134 and 136).

At the height of its popularity sales of the novel reached 65,000.[79] By the time Bottome began her lecture tour in the fall of 1938, however, *The Mortal Storm* had ceased to be a bestseller. The novel nonetheless continued to sell steadily through 1938, helped by continuing critical comment.[80] For example, in September 1938, five-and-a-half months after the novel's release, the *New York Herald Tribune*'s "Books Supplement" showcased *The Mortal Storm* and A.J. Cronin's *The Citadel*, along with Charles Nordoff and J.H. Hall's *The Dark River*, in its section "What America Is Reading."[81] Such attention made Bottome a sought-after speaker before women's clubs, psychological organizations, and especially synagogues and Jewish organizations. The Jewish-American press lauded *The Mortal Storm*.[82] She learned that Professor Roth's answer to Rudi's question, "What is being Jewish?" became a staple in Bar Mitzvah speeches across the country.[83] Her growing fame in the Jewish community earned her an invitation to speak at the largest synagogue in Canada, only recently erected, Holy Blossom Temple in Toronto, where Rabbi Maurice N. Eisendrath presided as Chief Rabbi.

Rabbi Maurice N. Eisendrath

The rabbis are all my friends on account of my anti-Nazi attitude ....
(PB to Duff Cooper, February 4, 1940)[84]

Of all the rabbis with whom Bottome claimed a friendship, Rabbi Eisendrath stood out. She found in him a figure of influence who could employ moral suasion, dispensing a measure of guilt, to nudge the moguls forward to gamble on producing a film that dramatized the plight of Europe's Jews.

The subject was not a comfortable one for the Jewish community. Nor was it comfortable for the religious leadership of that community. The case of Hollywood is instructive. References to Jews and Jewish culture, having appeared with such promise in the first "talkie," *The Jazz Singer*, had all but disappeared from the screen since 1927 when Warner Brothers released the film. The screen writer Ben Hecht observed somewhat hyperbolically in 1944, "The greatest single Jewish phenomenon in our country in the last twenty years has been the almost complete disappearance of the Jew from American fiction, stage, radio, and movies."[85] Patricia Erens refined Hecht's chronology. She writes that at least "for most of the thirties, the Jew as a recognizable character practically disappears from the screen."[86]

The moguls made sure of that. As antisemitism increased with the onset of the Great Depression, they did not want cinema to be seen as "Jewish."[87] By the end of the decade, the Jewish community as a whole sought to attract as little attention to itself as possible. Its members for the most part felt the same way about the plight of Europe's Jews. A notable example of Jewish self-effacement occurred when a vacancy arose on the Supreme Court. In January 1939 on the verge of appointing Felix Frankfurter to the seat of the late Benjamin Cardozo, the president received a delegation of Jewish leaders that included Arthur Hays Sulzberger, who had taken over management of the *New York Times* four years earlier. They advised the president not to appoint Frankfurter, lest "in the present world situation [the appointment] inflame antisemitic passions."[88] Roosevelt thought the argument "cowardly" and put Frankfurter on the court.[89]

Rabbi Eisendrath was an exception to such "cowardice." He was also an exception in joining the small number on both sides of the Atlantic who, from the beginning, warned of the Nazi menace. He recalled in one of his sermons that he had been in Berlin in 1933, just when the newly appointed American ambassador, William E. Dodd, arrived. Roosevelt, according to Eisendrath, "had specifically instructed" Dodd "to seek some manner of amelioration" to the "merciless persecution" of the Jews.[90] Alas, Eisendrath bemoaned, Dodd found no allies in the Jewish community itself, either in Germany or in America. He further recounted to his congregation:

> To our everlasting shame, the first of the many appeasers who Ambassador Dodd proceeded to stumble across ... were from among our own number; ... who, instead, of vowing war to the death against the foe who from its very beginning had declared a battle of extermination against our people and our faith, naively believed that by stroking the tiger's skin they could soften its wrath if not toward their people as a whole then at least toward their privileged and supposedly protected selves.[91]

Eisendrath's prescience was remarkable. He gave that sermon on December 7 as Japanese planes prepared to bomb Pearl Harbor, an event that would end US neutrality once and for all. The Holocaust, the "battle of extermination against our people and our faith," had begun as soon as Germany invaded the Soviet Union five months earlier.[92] There had been almost no official recognition of the slaughter at the time that Eisendrath spoke, with the exception of statements by Churchill on August 24, 1941, in which he referred to "a crime without a name" being committed by the Germans on the Eastern Front.[93] Eisendrath's sermon, like Churchill's passing references, was among the few acknowledgments of the frightful events unfolding in the borderlands of the Soviet Union.

Bottome came to know Rabbi Eisendrath three years earlier in the winter of 1938–9, precisely the period in which she sought to sell *The Mortal Storm* to Hollywood. Acquaintance with him offered her a unique opportunity. As he told her, "I know Rabbi Edgar Magnin of Los Angeles exceedingly well and he is on the most intimate terms with the people in Hollywood."[94] Eisendrath had aptly characterized his fellow rabbi. Neil Gabler, author of a collective biography of the moguls, called Edgar Magnin "the closest thing ... Hollywood Jews ... had to a spiritual advisor."[95] More significantly, Rabbi Magnin was "especially close to Louis Mayer" of MGM.[96] Eisendrath too possessed a connection to the movie business. He told Bottome, "A number of the men in my congregation are very closely identified with the motion picture industry."[97] By that he meant that his congregants included the owners of theater chains throughout the United States and Canada.[98]

Eisendrath and Magnin had much more in common. Both had graduated from the Hebrew Union College in Cincinnati, Magnin a few years before Eisendrath matriculated.[99] They followed similar career paths: a short stint with a small, isolated congregation followed by a call to a large metropolitan area, Los Angeles in the case of Rabbi Magnin, Toronto in the case of Rabbi Eisendrath, where each built a landmark synagogue. Rabbi Magnin's Wilshire Boulevard Temple could seat 1,500 congregants and nearly always did. Magnin's services were so popular that the Hollywood Bowl could not compete. It ceased to offer Friday night concerts, losing out to Magnin's popularity.[100] Holy Blossom Temple in Toronto had a capacity of 1,200. It too was nearly always full.

Rabbi Eisendrath's gamble had paid off. He moved Holy Blossom from the center of Toronto to an underpopulated suburban location at the same time that he constructed a significantly larger house of worship.[101] Almost as soon as the temple doors opened, the *Bulletin* proudly announced, "1200 worshippers" had filled "every cranny of our Temple."[102] No other house of worship of that size was built in Canada during the Depression. Eisendrath was able to construct the magnificent new temple thanks to donations from the men of the congregation "very closely identified with the motion picture industry."[103] Both Magnin and Eisendrath had enriched their respective temple building funds from the largesse of the movie industry. Magnin could claim that in his case he had acquired even more from the movie industry. The head of the Art Department at Warner Brothers studio had drawn the stately murals that covered the walls of the Wilshire Boulevard Temple.[104]

When Rabbi Eisendrath wrote his Los Angeles colleague he did so not as a supplicant, but as someone whose stature equaled that of Magnin's. The two men diverged over only one issue: the most important one facing world Jewry in 1938, namely, the Nazi threat to the Jews. Magnin belonged to "the appeasers ... among our own number."[105] He urged restraint and caution regarding the plight of Europe's Jews. Eisendrath did not. When he wrote Magnin about *The Mortal Storm*, "this searching anti-Nazi story," he termed it, he could not resist expressing "amazement" at the moguls' reluctance to purchase it.[106] He explained that Bottome was "trying to interest motion picture people in filming" her novel, adding "I am amazed that it is necessary for her to do this as I should think that they would be pleading with her for the rights so to do."[107] Eisendrath knew only too well why the moguls failed "to plead" with Bottome for the rights to her novel. Since 1933, as Bottome herself noted, no "straight forward anti-Nazi film, depicting the plight of Europe's Jews, produced by a major studio had appeared on screen."[108]

Eisendrath himself had already used the novel to good effect. He made it the centerpiece of the programming to inaugurate the newly constructed Holy Blossom Temple.[109] He invited Bottome to speak at the temple in late November 1938 to participate in that inaugural program. She was to conduct the first Forum in the new building. The lectures, talks, and sermons in November–January 1938–9, part of that celebration, similarly contributed to the rabbi's advocacy on behalf of Europe's Jews and a whole range of related causes. He used the *bima* and the educational outreach of the synagogue to espouse an interventionist foreign policy. Earlier in the fall he had given a sermon condemning the dismemberment of Czechoslovakia at Munich.[110] All the inaugural events addressed the current political situation in Europe. Rabbi Eisendrath devoted his own inaugural presentation to *The Mortal Storm*. Bottome's presence made a unique contribution to that event,

The weekly temple *Bulletin* announced the rabbi's forthcoming sermon with a synopsis of what he intended to say:

> This Sunday morning, November 27th, Rabbi Eisendrath will take as his theme the widely read and much discussed book, "The Mortal Storm," by Phyllis Bottome, who is to be the first of our Forum lecturers. This book reflects in a most intimate and personal way precisely what is happening not so much to the Jews in Germany as to the human soul in the "mortal storm" that is raging in the land. It conveys, as no press headlines can possibly do, the tragedy through which the spirit of mankind is passing in this dark hour. We are particularly certain that all of our members, together with their family and friends, will be particularly interested in Rabbi Eisendrath's interpretation of "The Mortal Storm."[111]

A reprint of the sermon has not come to light, but the announcement itself is revealing. Eisendrath's subsequent advocacy for Bottome's novel was no one-time event because it served his own political purposes. Nor was it a polite response to her request to assist in selling it to a studio. Nor was it even a sudden change of heart motivated by worsening conditions for Jews at the end of the 1930s. Eisendrath, on the contrary, had watched the Nazis warily since 1933, if not earlier. He had long spoken out about the menace they posed to Jews in particular. His call to bring Bottome's novel to the screen was all the more forceful because he understood that it embodied precisely the message that he believed had to be conveyed to the American public on the eve of war.

The novel also conveyed a universal message that transcended immediate events, as Eisendrath told his congregation. "This book reflects ... what is happening not so much to the Jews in Germany as to the human soul in the 'mortal storm' ...."[112] The moguls would feel safer with that reading. Eisendrath's sermon offered reluctant studio heads a more comfortable perspective from which to treat an otherwise-controversial work of fiction. He also insisted on the relevance of the novel to large numbers of non-Jews who flocked to his sermons. In fact, the beginning and ending of the film that MGM ultimately produced referred to "mankind" at the mercy of a mortal storm. The film employed other universal themes, expressing the "tragedy through which the spirit of mankind is passing ...." Rabbi Eisendrath shared the moguls' impulse to emphasize universal themes. But unlike them he harbored no fear addressing Jewish suffering under the Nazis as well.

Eisendrath regarded Holy Blossom Temple as both a space for Jewish ritual and an interfaith house of worship. Unlike Magnin, he conducted no Friday night services. His Saturday services were part of his intent to make Holy Blossom into "a bastion of classical Reform Judaism."[113] On Sundays, when Christians often outnumbered Jews, he preached sermons with an interdenominational, often secular message devoted to current affairs.[114] A universalist interpretation of *The Mortal Storm* addressed the interests of his expanded congregation. It also served the interests of the moguls. Eisendrath suggested a way to assuage Hollywood's anxiety over propaganda for war. He understood the moguls' concern that their product should have a universal appeal and not appear as a one-sided advocate for a cause. Eisendrath could show the moguls how to balance advocacy for the particular while generating universal appeal. He himself had made a profession of it. He was a founding member of the Canadian Council of Christian and Jews.[115] By the late 1930s he had become a faith leader in the Toronto community as a whole, but a leader who refused to be silent about the Nazis.

The day after Eisendrath's sermon on *The Mortal Storm*, Bottome gave a lecture titled "Love and Marriage" in which she introduced Adler's teaching on those subjects. As was the format with her lectures, Bottome used the question period that followed the formal presentation to discuss "European politics from A to Z."[116] The talk was a great success as Rabbi Eisendrath subsequently wrote her, "It would be impossible to convey to you the fervid words of commendation which I still hear on every hand regarding your memorable address."[117]

Bottome's sending Eisendrath a copy of the manuscript of the talk initiated their correspondence regarding *The Mortal Storm*. After thanking her for her "generosity" in providing the copy, he asked, "Is there anything that I can do to help you" in the "possibility that your novel may be filmed?" He offered to contact Rabbi Magnin on her behalf.[118] Ernan quickly replied for his wife, requesting "an introduction … so that we could meet him during the next few weeks while Los Angeles is our headquarters."[119]

Rabbi Eisendrath replied with equal alacrity. He wrote Ernan, "I most assuredly will do my very utmost to help secure the necessary influence to have 'Mortal Storm' filmed … Consequently, I am writing to Rabbi Magnin." He added, making two critical points: "I do hope that you will go immediately together with your wife, to see him and discuss the matter with him as I do believe he can be most helpful." Eisendrath recognized that it would take personal persuasion to win Magnin to their cause. He then insisted, "I know of nothing that would be more important than to have this story brought … to the attention of the American masses." Rabbi Eisendrath urged haste in capturing the moment to produce a film that could finally move public opinion after a near decade of Hollywood's inertia.[120]

On the same day he wrote his fellow rabbi. True to his word, Eisendrath advocated forcefully for *The Mortal Storm*. "Dear Magnin," he began, addressing his colleague as an equal. He termed Bottome "a magnificent spirit;" but more to the point, he called "her message … a most challenging and timely one," which "she is trying to interest the motion picture people in filming." As in his sermon on *The Mortal Storm*, Eisendrath argued for its universal appeal. He was also careful to refer to the novel as "anti-Nazi material," avoiding the dreaded phrase "anti-Nazi propaganda." "I know of no recent piece of literature," he told Magnin, "that quite aside from its value as anti-Nazi material, is at the same time a more moving and thrilling story, or one which would make a more popular and exciting scenario." Eisendrath ended with flattery, "I hope … that you will use the great influence that you have with the motion picture people to interest them in this project."

Two phrases stood out in Eisendrath's letter to Magnin. The "message" of *The Mortal Storm* was both "challenging and timely." And the production of the movie version constituted a "very vital matter." He closed, noting that he would be watching developments as a mark of his commitment to a film version of *The Mortal Storm*. Implied was his concern for Hollywood's reluctance to make an anti-Nazi film. "Please let us hear from you," he nudged Magnin, "as to whether they have been to see you and whether there is anything that you can do in this very vital matter."[121] In effect, Rabbi Eisendrath told his colleague, he would be watching what transpired with Bottome's novel as well as what role Magnin might play with the studios.

Bottome and her husband indeed called on Rabbi Magnin. She spoke at his temple just as she had at Holy Blossom. She apparently came to know him to the extent that she subsequently called him "a real friend." She wrote Adler's son-in-law about him that Rabbi Magnin is "the head of the Liberal Jewish Colony, who is one of the best and most enlightened people I know and a real friend."[122] Whether true or not, Magnin had apparently convinced her of his commitment to her cause. Bottome in turn believed that she had won him over. Both probably came away pleased. Magnin's greatest skill lay in his powers of reassurance, according to Gabler, while Bottome believed in her powers of persuasion.[123] Her ability to conduct lengthy question-and-answer sessions after each public lecture would confirm her in that skill. Rabbi Eisendrath had shown his gifts in bringing together in concert two individuals with incompatible convictions. With the sale of *The Mortal Storm* safely behind her, she wrote her friend in Toronto with gratitude, "Your kind letter to Rabbi Magnin did us great service."[124] Eisendrath had done even more. He put Magnin on notice that he would be watching the subsequent fate of Bottome's novel over which they both knew Magnin had some influence. Within weeks of Rabbi Eisendrath's letter to his colleague, Bottome had indeed begun "to unloosen" MGM.

"Unloosening MGM"

I am in the midst of a sale of 'Mortal Storm' to M-G-M.[125]

(PB to Maida McCord)

Only at the last minute of our stay here did MGM decide to make the picture.[126]

(PB to Rabbi Eisendrath)

Hollywood insiders also contributed to the sale of Bottome's novel. David Welky names "MGM's Victor Saville, a British born, virulently anti-Nazi director" as the one who convinced Louis B. Mayer "to buy the rights to Phyllis Bottome's blockbuster novel about Nazism's devastating effect on a German family."[127] According to Louella Parsons, who had inside sources at MGM, Kenneth MacKenna, a story editor at the studio and an "enthusiastic" advocate for *The Mortal Storm*, "worked out a story treatment" for the novel. MacKenna, Parsons revealed, had "found a way to adapt [the] story of Nazi Germany" that others wanted to shy away from.[128] Bottome added another Hollywood insider to those who assisted in the purchase. She thanked the independent producer Walter Wanger, who had brought *Private Worlds* to the screen. "We have a feeling that you are largely responsible for our having placed successfully 'M.S.' [...]," she wrote Wanger.[129]

Eisendrath, on the other hand, as a rabbi and outsider without a financial stake in the matter could play the formidable card of guilt before the man who enjoyed unique access to Mayer. In the same letter to Rabbi Magnin in which he introduced Bottome and her husband, he also wrote, "they are both seeking to the utmost of their ability to rescue many of their cherished friends from the Hell that Austria has become."[130] His message: the hellish plight of Europe's Jews could no longer be ignored, and Bottome's novel offered Hollywood the opportunity to speak out before the widest audience possible. The loaded subtext: even the "appeasers ... among our number" must now do something.

Bottome had wanted to sell the novel to MGM all along. She told her friend and editor at Little, Brown & Co., Roger Scaife, that she had offered the novel to the studio even before it was published in the United States. "My only disappointment is that we could not have had the film two years earlier, but it took that amount of time to unloosen M-G-M."[131] Bottome had raised the same question that the critics posed regarding the just-released film: Why had it not been made earlier? She laid the blame on MGM, but in fairness it must again be said that not until *Kristallnacht* in November 1938 was the public mood receptive to acknowledging Nazi atrocities toward the Jews. The tipping point was reached with Nazi street violence so intense that Roosevelt recognized that he could then recall the American ambassador for consultations without a public outcry. *The Nation* noted at the time, "the November outrages" had "caused a semi-rupture in relations" between the United States and Nazi Germany anyway.[132]

Even before those events, according to film historian Bernard Dick, "as early as March" of 1938, "the book was synopsized for Louis B. Mayer,"[133] Bottome had sent the studio a copy on the eve of its American publication. Nothing came of that initial attempt, as she told Scaife. Dick, however, raises a critical point, namely, how the cautious studio head Louis B. Mayer evolved in his perception of Bottome's novel.

Mayer's understanding of the novel would have come first through Helen Corbaley of the MGM Story Department, known around the studio as "Mayer's Scheherazade."[134] Each night she consumed an extraordinary number of publications and recounted the content to her boss each morning. In the case of *The Mortal Storm*, Corbaley either misunderstood Bottome's intent in writing the novel or she provided a synopsis that would placate Mayer and make possible a production that she, at that precarious time believed, belonged on the screen. Corbaley portrayed the Nazis as no more than a backdrop to the intense human drama in the plot. She reassuringly described the novel in a way that would counter Mayer's reservations.

> The author has not taken sides on the question of Nazism ... this is not a book of propaganda, but a fair picture of the situation in Nazi Germany. Miss Bottome is not trying to prove anything.[135]

Like Rabbi Eisendrath, who euphemistically referred to the novel as "challenging," Helen Corbaley had absolved it of the dreaded charge of propaganda and other tendentious sins.

Unaware of her ally in Mayer's inner circle, Bottome despaired that she would ever be able "to unloosen" her first choice among the studios. The "double-crossing" industry, as she termed it in her unpublished "American Notes," had yet to show it had "a heart."[136]

Shortly before Corbaley made a second synopsis of *The Mortal Storm*, in January 1939 Bottome and her husband took up residence in the Garden of Allah Hotel, on the doorstep of the studios. Her optimism at the prospect of the sale of the novel which she had shared with Rabbi Eisendrath back in November had not panned out. Eisendrath referred to that earlier optimism when he wrote her, "I was exceedingly interested in the suggestion that there is a possibility that your novel may be filmed."[137] Instead, the sale had yet to occur; she lay in bed recuperating from exhaustion and a severe attack of pleurisy contracted after conducting a grueling lecture schedule "in more than thirty cities."[138] The indifference of the studios must have compounded her ill-health, and she had temporarily withdrawn from public lectures to recover.[139]

By early March she was ready to return to the fight, preparing once more to besiege the studios. She recounted the situation to her friend Stephen Potter, a lecturer in English Literature at the University of London. Potter already had a reputation as a wit and raconteur. After the war he would become a highly successful producer for the BBC.[140] She shared with him her contempt for the movie industry in its current state.[141] The studio heads, "the very men who are going to suffer most from their cowardice are too timid to present their cause through the most perfect medium the world has ever had, and which is entirely in their own power to use." As a result, she lamented, "not one of the big picture studios has yet dared to put on a straight-forward anti-Nazi film." She despaired in March 1939 that any of them ever would. She had little hope for the soon-to-be-released *Confessions of a Nazi Spy*, calling it "the usual truth-distorted film work ...."

Bottome might have tempered her litany of contempt had she known how soon MGM would "unloosen" and agree to purchase *The Mortal Storm*. Several factors converged. Within a week of her letter to Potter, what remained of Czechoslovakia fell to the Nazis and with it the demise of Chamberlain's policy of appeasement. The release of even a "truth-distorted film" by Warner Brothers, MGM's biggest rival, had to act as goad for the studio to answer in kind. And there was another factor. Mayer numbered among those, who, as Bottome claimed, "are going to suffer most from their cowardice." The words are ambiguous. Did Bottome refer to the pangs of guilt they might suffer or to their vulnerability as Jews in the event of Nazi victories?[142] Rabbi Eisendrath through Magnin had attempted to inject a sense of guilt into the moguls' considerations, but fear at their own vulnerabilities may have also driven Mayer and other moguls to reconsider their non-engagement as the situation in Europe worsened.

It was all a matter of timing. What could not happen in 1937 or 1938 had changed by 1939. One of the most knowledgeable observers of that evolution was Frank Nugent, who for four years wrote film criticism for the *New York Times* before turning to Hollywood as a scriptwriter in 1940. Nugent made the point that starting in 1939 a change had come over Hollywood. The studios that year acquired a newfound political realism. "Hollywood has begun to wave the flag. It has discovered America."[143] He added, "It is an interesting discovery for the film industry to have made just when the world is tuning the war drums."[144] At last, it seemed, "we have [...] an astonishing picture of Hollywood no longer shunning propaganda and [...] dealing charitably with foreign nations."[145] With the last phrase, Nugent referred to the motion picture industry's Production Code which mandated that no country's history or culture could be mocked or criticized.

Nugent attributed Hollywood's newfound willingness to produce Sinclair Lewis's "It Can't Happen Here," Warners' "Confessions," Chaplin's "The Dictators," as *The Great Dictator* was then known, and the long shelved "Personal History" (to be filmed subsequently by Hitchcock as "Foreign Correspondent") to the industry's loss of German and Italian markets.[146] He also named the Munich Agreement of 1938 as a factor. Just as significantly, the month before, in March 1939, Hitler had taken over the rest of Czechoslovakia. Those developments, he wrote, "may account for Hollywood's change of heart."[147]

Nugent did not mention one other factor in Hollywood's evolution. In March 1939 Will Hays, president of the Motion Picture Producers and Distributors Association (MPPDA), had informed the moguls that a broader range of films could now receive censorship approval. There would no longer be objection to films that "dealt with issues of war and peace."[148] Such coded language opened the door to productions about Nazi Germany should the studios care to address the subject that had been taboo since Hitler came to power.

Closing the Deal

Even with the convergence of so many portentous events, the controversial subject matter of the novel still gave the studios qualms to make the purchase. The process of negotiations proved especially harrowing as Bottome prepared to close the deal. The adage, success has many fathers, failure only one, applies to the sale of *The Mortal Storm*. Had the sale not gone through, the agent Bottome relied on to represent her with the studios,

William Dozier, would have borne the brunt of the blame. Dozier had begun work in the Story Department at MGM, rising to the position of its director. He was a recent addition to the Literary Department of the Beverly Hills agency of Berg-Allenberg, subcontracted to Bottome's literary agent Ann Watkins in New York.[149] Against the advice of those who urged her to use a more experienced, better-known agent, Bottome insisted on Dozier, then only thirty-two. She told Ann Watkins, "I am very satisfied with Bill Dozier and like him very much ... but I think he will have to have a certain amount of guidance both from you and from me."[150]

Dozier had taken over negotiations from Ann Watkins in early March. Watkins had grown frustrated with Metro's reluctance to close the deal and told Dozier "in view of diminishing sales" of *The Mortal Storm* they "should close at once ... for best price ... with $15,000 as a goal ...."[151] Dozier answered her with a more optimistic possibility. "Information gleaned last night leads me believe Metro will go above fifteen thousand. Instead holding out for twenty-five and Bottome agrees." He added that he had "put the screws on Metro" that morning.[152]

Dozier's optimism was premature. A month later the negotiations had stalled. By then representatives of other studios had joined Metro in the discussions and were competing for the rights to the novel. Yet the sale did not seem any closer. Bottome told Ann Watkins, "[T]he studios are turning up a lot of old stuff and want to talk it over."[153] On the same day she told her dear friend the artist Maida McCord in Norfolk that she faced the opposite difficulty: "the studios have leapt up with fresh problems."[154] "Fresh problems" had replaced "old stuff," but an obstacle was still an obstacle.

Whether the problems were new or old, the studios' objections within days appeared insurmountable. Bottome panicked. She vented her frustrations on Watkins and Dozier, threatening to fire both. Dozier bore the brunt of her wrath: "[...] in view of the fact that [...] the general situation has worsened from hour to hour, I have decided to withdraw "M.S." from your office." She added one last caveat that allowed the negotiations to remain with Dozier, "unless you ... sell the picture rights for at least $25,000 ... by 6:00 tomorrow evening ... April 10th, I shall consider myself free to deal with them myself."[155] Dozier in the end justified Bottome's trust in him. He managed to sell the rights to *The Mortal Storm* to Metro by Bottome's deadline and at her price. The *Hollywood Reporter* confirmed, "MGM Purchases 'Storm' After Wild Bidding Spree."[156] To Dozier, it must have seemed wilder than ever.

By April 15, with the harrowing "hour by hour" negotiations behind her, Bottome thanked Wanger for his help in the process and informed him that "MGM want me to work on 'Mortal Storm' with them in two weeks' time."[157] Not only would Bottome be involved in the production, but the studio, her first choice, intended to move quickly to get it to the screen. Louella Parsons confirmed that Metro wanted to release it as quickly as possible. "Phyllis Bottome's 'The Mortal Storm' ... is such a topical subject dealing as it does with Nazism that M-G-M bosses are eager to lose no time in filming it."[158] She also confirmed the film had sold for the generous sum of $25,000. Bottome wrote Rabbi Eisendrath that she could not ask for a better production team. She believed the picture would "be beautifully done for the producers are Mr. Sidney Franklin and Mrs. Claudine West who were responsible for 'Good Earth,' 'Zola,' [sic] and 'Good-bye Mr. Chips.'"[159]

Bottome could not have asked for more. She would work with one of MGM's best production teams, and MGM intended to move quickly. Under the circumstances it was easy to forget that the negotiations had been long and hard with repeated objections from the studios because of the difficulty in "finding a way to treat the story," according to Louella Parsons. Behind the scenes the film still had enemies. Rabbi Magnin, for one, warned Victor Saville, subsequently brought on as producer, to avoid controversy in making it.[160] But for now Bottome could believe the film would do as she hoped and contribute to "war propaganda in America" and to "the war spirit in Canada," as she subsequently told her boss, Sir Frederick Whyte, director of the American Division in the MoI.[161]

She described her intentions differently to Rabbi Eisendrath to whom she wrote of her high-minded purpose, "I was not seeking a great price because what I really wanted was to give the true story of the effect upon the world of this hideous new creed."[162] Like Rabbi Magnin, Bottome was adept at presenting herself appropriately to a particular audience. She would soon, she believed, have the opportunity to make the presentation to the biggest audience of all, the American moviegoing public. For now, she could again indulge in a sense of optimism. Only time would tell if it would be justified or once more prove to be the "false" variety she claimed innate to the "Anglo-Saxon race."

Notes

1. *Publishers' Weekly* list of best-selling novels in the United States in the 1930s. http://en.wikipedia.org.accessed, June 25, 2014.
2. PB to Duff Cooper, February 4, 1940. BL Add. Mss. 88921/3/3.
3. PB, "American Notes," no date. BL Add. Mss. 88921/4/7.
4. PB to Stephen Potter. March 9, 1939. BL Add. Mss. 88921/ 3/2.
5. For the terms of that contract, see BL Add. Mss. 88921/4/10.
6. PB to Locker Lampson; December 12, 1938. BL Add. Mss. 88921/3/1.
7. PB to Bishop of Chichester; September 19, 1938. BL Add. Mss. 88921/2/2.
8. *Old Wine*, "Foreword," by Lassner and Hoder Salmon, x.

9   William Holt (ed.), Dorothy Thompson and RoseWilder Lane, *Forty Years of Friendship. Letters, 1921–1960* (Columbus and London: University of Missouri Press, 1991), 26.
10 Hirsch, *The Constant Liberal*, 175.
11 Bottome, *The Goal*, 236.
12 Dorothy Thompson to Letitia Irwin, January 26, 1930, cited in Marion K. Sanders, *Dorothy Thompson. A Legend in Her Time* (New York: Avon books, 1974), 161.
13 Peter Kurth, *American Cassandra. The Life of Dorothy Thompson* (Boston: Little, Brown & Co., 1990), 219.
14 See Kurth, *American Cassandra*, 335; for her assistance to Jewish refugees, see Kurth, *American Cassandra*, 275–81. Ernan to Mrs. Burns; February 20, 1939 "We are responsible for 20 Jewish refugee families." BL Add. Mss. 88921/3/2.
15 Kurth, *American Cassandra*, 312.
16 PB to Julian Lucas; December 12, 1938. BL Add. Mss. 88921/2/1.
17 PB to Arthur Salter; July 19, 1939. BL Add. Mss. 88921/2/1.
18 Davis, *FDR. Into the Storm, 1937–1940*, 365.
19 Ibid.
20 Ibid., 366.
21 BL Add. Mss. 88921/3/1. Typed copy of "I Accuse."
22 Hirsch, *The Constant Liberal*, 236.
23 If Bottome believed that Lewis and Thompson might also assist in the sale of *The Mortal Storm* to Hollywood, she was to be disappointed. There is no record that either played a role in Bottome's negotiations with the studios. Bottome, with seeming naiveté, subsequently engineered a break between herself and Thompson. She wrote a portrait of the journalist to be included in the collection of essays titled *From the Life* (Faber & Faber, 1943). Bottome suggested that Thompson had encouraged her husband's drinking problem. Worse, she stated that she lacked "the power to attend to life itself" (cited in Sanders, *A Legend in Her Time*, 292). After seeing an advance copy of the essay, Thompson demanded that it be withdrawn and ceased all relations with Bottome. (See Kurth, *American Cassandra*, 506 and Sanders, *A Legend in Her Time*, 292–3 for further discussion of this episode).
24 PB to Frank and Esther Adams; March 19, 1938. BL Add. Mss. 88921/3/1.
25 Dorothy Thompson, *Foreign Affairs*, vol. 16, no. 3 (April 1938), 375–87. See also Kurth, *American Cassandra*, 280 for discussion of this essay. I would like to thank Phyllis Lassner for bringing it to my attention.
26 Oswald Harrison Villard, "Issues and Men," *The Nation* (July 1938), 226. Cf. Davis, *Into the Storm*, 196. Davis attributes the idea for the Evian Conference to Under Secretary of State Sumner Welles, who proposed it to the president in March 1938. Welles could have acquired the idea from Thompson, learning of her essay in advance of publication.
27 All citations from Davis, *FDR. Into the Storm, 1937–1940*, 365.

28 Michaela Hoenicke Moore, *Know Your Enemy. The American Debate on Nazism, 1933–1945* (Cambridge: Cambridge University Press, 2010), 67.
29 *The Nation*, February 25, 1939, 219.
30 Moore, *Know Your Enemy*, 43.
31 PB to Robert Vansittart, September 9, 1939. BL Add. Mss. 78848.
32 PB to Admiral Sir Reginald Drax. No date. BL 88921/3/3. See also Hirsch, 248 where she suggests the date of the meeting may have been December 27, 1938.
33 I owe this quotation from the George Stevens papers, held in the Margaret Herrick Library, to Steven Carr, who generously supplied it.
34 PB to Admiral Drax, December 12, 1938. BL Add. Mss. 88921/3/3.
35 PB to Stephen Potter; March 9, 1939. BL Add. Mss. 88921/2/2.
36 Bottome, *The Goal*, 272.
37 Ibid., 236.
38 Ibid.
39 See Blanche Wiesen Cook, *Eleanor Roosevelt*, vol. 2, *The Defining Years, 1933–1938* (New York: Penguin Books, 2000), 335.
40 Rosenman, *Working with Roosevelt*, 110.
41 Davis, *FDR. Into the Storm, 1937–1940*, 360. Also, Robert E. Sherwood, *Roosevelt and Hopkins. An Intimate History* (New York: Enigma Books, 2008), 81.
42 R. C. Sherriff, *No Leading Lady* (London: Victor Gollancz, Ltd., 1968), 242.
43 Otto Friedrich, *City of Nets. A Portrait of Hollywood in the 1940s* (New York: Harper & Row, 1986), 73.
44 Ibid.
45 See their correspondence in BL Add. Mss. 88921/ 4/1. On September 16, 1946, she wrote Scaife: "I have long had the feeling that you and I stood and fell together at Little, Brown."
46 The two versions, to be cited in the text, will be distinguished by year of publication: the British in 1937 and the American in 1938. British edition: Phyllis Bottome, *The Mortal Storm* (London: Faber & Faber, Ltd., 1937).
47 See Bottome, *The Goal*, 287–8.
48 Ibid., 287.
49 The deleted chapters consisted most often of redundant material that did not advance the narrative or that contained material that Bottome incorporated into the three chapters added to the beginning of the American edition to be discussed above.
50 For the best account of Toller's life and work, see the following on which I draw for my discussion of this section: Martha Gustavson Marks. "Ernst Toller. His Fight against Fascism" (University of Wisconsin-Madison, Ph.D., 1980).
51 Ernst Toller, *I Was a German. The Autobiography of a Revolutionary*, Edward Crankshaw, trans. (New York: Paragon House, 1991), 284–5.

52 Ibid., 285.
53 Ibid.
54 Chaplin too contributed to the Federal Theater Project. Toller's play *No More Peace!*, with lyrics by W. H. Auden, was produced in 1937 and 1938 by the Federal Theater Project. In it a barber named Cain is appointed the dictator of the Kingdom of Dunkelstein, the play may therefore have inspired the plot of Chaplin's *The Great Dictator*. For further discussion of *No More Peace!*, see Richard Dove, *He Was a German* (London: Libris, 1990), 224–34. See also Ernst Toller, *No More Peace! A Thoughtful Comedy*, Edward Crankshaw, trans. (New York: Farrar & Rinehart, Inc., 1937).
55 Dove, *He Was a German*, 234.
56 Kurt Pinthus, "Life of Ernst Toller," *Books Abroad*, vol. 14, no. 1 (Winter 1939–40), 3. Within a year of leaving Hollywood, Toller had taken his own life, hanging himself in a New York hotel room.
57 Dove, *He Was a German*, 231.
58 BL Add. Mss. 88921/3. "An excerpt from 'The Mortal Storm' by Phyllis Bottome to be published on April 4 by Little Brown & Co., Boston. March 2, 1938. From Ann Ford, Publicity Department; Little, Brown & Co." Cf. *TMS*, 1938, 30. The text changed yet again when it went into print: Hans tells Freya: "We're Communists ... does that frighten you? We kept Russian prisoners to help us during the war. They wrote to us when it was over; and we liked what we heard of it." All that Bottome has removed from the British edition is the prisoners' writing back about revolution.
59 Bottome, *The Goal*, 177.
60 PB to Duff Cooper; February 4, 1940. BL Add. Mss. 88921/3/3. "'The Life of Adler' [published in the spring of 1939] is beginning to do its work over here in a small way. 'Mortal Storm' has prepared its spreading."
61 Duff Cooper to PB; February 21, 1940. BL Add. Mss.88921/3/3.
62 Joseph Goebbels as cited in Susan Tegel, *Nazis and the Cinema* (London: Continuum Books, 2008), 19.
63 *The Nation*, July 9, 1938, 39. The same article noted that I.A. T.S.E. was "notorious for its reactionary bureaucracy."
64 *The Nation*, July 9, 1939, 39.
65 See BL Add. Mss. 88921/4/10 for her nationwide lecture schedule and specific lecture titles on Adlerian psychology and contemporary literature, 1938–40.
66 PB to Duff Cooper; February 4, 1940. BL Add. Mss. 88921/3/3.
67 See Hirsch, *The Constant Liberal*, for an account of Bottome's recruitment by the MoI (Ministry of Information) for propaganda work as a British lecturer in the United States, 243–4.
68 PB to Duff Cooper; February 4, 1940. BL Add. Mss. 88921/3/3.
69 See PB to Julian Lucas; December 12, 1938. BL Add. Mss. 88921/3/1.
70 PB to Duff Cooper; February 21, 1940. BL Add. Mss. 8891/3/3.

71 PB, "What Is Propaganda?" no date of publication. BL Add. Mss. 88921/2/1. Page numbers cited in parentheses in the text are from this unpublished pamphlet.
72 Ernan Forbes Dennis to J. J. Llewellin: July 30, 1940. BL Add. Mss. 88921/3/3. Llewellin was Parliamentary Secretary in the Ministry of Aircraft Production.
73 PB to Sir Frederick Whyte; August 29, 1940. BL Add. Mss. 88921/4/7.
74 For more on British culture in the 1930s, see Part II of Elizabeth Maslin, *Life in the Writings of Storm Jameson* (Evanston: Northwestern University Press, 2014); Steve Ellis, *British Writers and the Approach of World War II* (Cambridge: Cambridge Univ. Press, 2015); Richard Overy, *The Morbid Age: Britain and the Crisis of Civilization* (London: Penguin, 2010); John Baxendale and Chris Pawling, *Narrating the Thirties. A Decade in the Making* (London: Macmillan, 1996).
75 Jane Spence Southern, "Terror in Munich," *New York Times*, 94.
76 *The New Republic*, March 30, 1938, 23.
77 *Saturday Review*, April 4, 1938, 36.
78 Jane Spence Southern, "Terror in Munich," *New York Times*, 94.
79 PB to Robert Vansittart; September 9, 1939. BL Add. Mss. 78848.
80 PB to F.L. Lucas; December 12, 1938. BL. Add. Mss. 88921/3/1.
81 *New Your Herald Tribune*, "Book Supplement," September 18, 1938. See clipping in BL Add. Mss. 78856.
82 See, for example, clippings from *The Seattle-Jewish Transcript, The Texas Jewish Press, The Young Judaean, The Jewish Outlook* in BL PB Mss. 78856 for such laudatory reviews.
83 PB to Sidney Franklin; February 7, 1940, University of Southern California Cinematic Arts Library. MGM File on *The Mortal Storm* (henceforth USC/MGM).
84 PB to Duff Cooper, February 4, 1940. BL. Add. Mss. 88921/3/3.
85 Ben Hecht, *A Guide for the Bedevilled* (New York: Chas. Scribner & Sons, Inc., 1944), 207.
86 Patricia Erens, *The Jew in American Cinema* (Bloomington: Indiana University Press, 1984), 135.
87 See Leonard Dinnerstein, *Anti-Semitism in America* (Oxford: Oxford University Press, 1994), 105–49 and Steven Carr, *Hollywood and Anti-Semitism. A Cultural History Up to World War II* (Cambridge: Cambridge University Press, 2001), 60–93.
88 Davis, *FDR. Into the Storm, 1937–1940*, 391.
89 Ibid.
90 Rabbi Eisendrath, "Berlin Diaries," *Holy Blossom Pulpit*, vol. 2, no. 3 (December 7, 1941), 6.
91 Ibid.

92 See Christopher R. Browning, *Nazi Policy, Jewish Workers, German Killers* (Cambridge: Cambridge University Press, 2000), 26–33. See also Browning's *The Path to Genocide. Essays on Launching the Final Solution* (Cambridge: Cambridge University Press, 1992), 86–121 for discussion on the onset of the Holocaust.
93 Wistrich, *Hitler and the Holocaust*, 206.
94 Rabbi Eisendrath to PB; February 14, 1939. BL Add. Mss. 88921/3/2. All correspondence between the two can be found in this file.
95 Neil Gabler, *An Empire of Their Own. How the Jews Invented Hollywood* (New York: Random House, Inc., 1988), 267.
96 Ibid., 281.
97 Rabbi Eisendrath to PB; February 14, 1939. BL Add. Mss. 89921/2/2.
98 Michael Cole and Howard Roger, archivists, Holy Blossom Temple to the author, personal communication of August 20, 2013.
99 Gabler, 268. For biographical information on Rabbi Eisendrath, see "The Lost and Found Sermons of Rabbi Maurice Eisendrath," http://eisendrathsermons.blogspot.ca/p/about-rabbi-eisendrath.html. Henceforth eisendrathsermons.blogspot.
100 Gabler, *An Empire of Their Own*, 266.
101 eisendrathsermons.blogspot.
102 "Sunday Morning Service," "Holy Blossom," *Bulletin*, vol. xiv, no. 12 (November 24, 1938).
103 Rabbi Eisendrath to PB, February 14, 1939. BL Add. Mss. 89921/2/2.
104 Gabler, *An Empire of Their Own*, 283.
105 See Felicia Herman, "Hollywood, Nazism, and the Jews, 1933–1944," *American Jewish History* (March 2001), 90 for an account of Magnin's involvement in keeping Jews and Jewish issues off the screen through the 1930s.
106 Rabbi Eisendrath to Rabbi Magnin; February 28, 1939. BL Add. Mss. 88921/2/2.
107 Ibid.
108 The phrase, "straight-forward anti-Nazi film" occurs in a letter she wrote Stephen Potter, March 9, 1939. BL Add. Mss. 88921/3/3.
109 For the entire program, see "Holy Blossom Forum," "Holy Blossom," *Bulletin*, vol. xiv, no.12 (November 24, 1938).
110 Rabbi Eisendrath, "Czechoslovakia: A Nation Crucified. What Now?" Holy Blossom Temple Bulletin, vol. 12, no. 12 (November 24, 1938).
111 "Holy Blossom" *Bulletin*, vol. xiv, no. 12; November 24, 1938.
112 Ibid.
113 eisendrathsermons.blogspot.
114 Ibid.
115 Ibid.

116 PB to Com. Locker-Lampson; December 12, 1938. BL Add. Mss. 88921/3/1.
117 Rabbi Eisendrath to PB, February 14, 1939. BL Add. Mss. 88921/2/2.
118 Ibid.
119 Ernan Forbes Dennis to Rabbi Eisendrath; February 21, 1939. BL Add. Mss. 88921/2/2.
120 Rabbi Eisendrath to Ernan Forbes Dennis; February 28, 1939. BL Add. Mss. 88921/2/2.
121 Rabbi Eisendrath to Rabbi Magnin; February 28, 1939. BL Add. Mss. 88921/3/2.
122 PB to Henry H. Starr; October 11, 1940. BL Add. Mss. 88921/2/2.
123 Gabler, *An Empire of Their Own*, 280–2.
124 PB to Rabbi Eisendrath; May 20, 1939. BL Add. Mss. 88921/3/2.
125 PB to Maida McCord; April 5, 1939. BL Add. Mss. 88921/3/2.
126 PB to Rabbi Eisendrath; May 20, 1939, BL Add. Mss. 88921/3/2.
127 Welky, *The Moguls and the Dictators*, 201.
128 "Louella Parsons in Hollywood," *Lexington Kentucky Herald*; March 29, 1939. BL Add. Mss. 88921/5/7. Press Cuttings. America.1930s.
129 PB to Walter Wanger; April 15, 1939. BL Add. Mss. 88921/3/2.
130 Rabbi Eisendrath to Rabbi Magnin; February 28, 1939. BL Add. Mss. 88921/3/2.
131 PB to Roger Scaife; August 12, 1940. BL Add. Mss. 88921/3/3.
132 *The Nation*, February 25, 1939, 219.
133 Bernard F. Dick, *The Star-Spangled Screen. The American World War II Film* (Lexington: University of Kentucky Press, 1985), 69.
134 Scott Eyman, *The Lion of Hollywood. The Life and Legend of Louis B. Mayer* (New York: Simon & Schuster, 2005), 138 and 199. Eyman refers to Corbaley as Kate. In the material that I examined in the Academy's Margaret Herrick Library, she is indicated as Helen.
135 Helen Corbaley, "Comment on *The Mortal Storm*," Los Angeles. Margaret Herrick Library of the Academy of Motion Picture Arts and Sciences.
136 PB, "American Notes," no date, BL Add. Mss. 88921/4/7.
137 Rabbi Eisendrath to PB; February 14, 1939. BL Add. Mss. 88921/2/2.
138 PB to Julian Lucas; December 12, 1938. BL Add. Mss. 88921/3/1.
139 See Ernan's letters for January 21–February 1, 1939, for negotiations with Colston Leigh, the owner of the lecture bureau for which Bottome spoke. Leigh took a dim view of her illness, insisting that she resume her arduous schedule as soon as possible. BL Add. Mss. 88921/5/5.
140 "Mr. Stephen Potter." *Times* [London, England] December 3, 1969: 13. *The Times Digital Archive*. Web. July 18, 2016.
141 PB to Stephen Potter; March 9, 1939. BL Add. Mss. 88921/2/2.

142 Some moguls took the latter point seriously. Sam Goldwyn prepared to escape to Mexico in the event of Nazi victories and possible American collaboration with the Third Reich. See PBS American Masters portrait of Goldwyn.
143 Frank Nugent, "Hollywood Waves the Flag," *The Nation*, April 8, 1939, 398.
144 Ibid.
145 Ibid., 399.
146 On Hitchcock's subsequent filming of Foreign Correspondent, see Taylor, "Secret Movie Censors," *The Nation*, July 9, 1938, 39.
147 Frank Nugent, "Hollywood Waves the Flag," 399.
148 M. Todd Bennett, *One World, Big Screen. Hollywood, the Allies, and World War II* (Chapel Hill: University of North Carolina Press, 2012), 40.
149 William Dozier to PB; March 9, 1939. BL Add. Mss. 88921/5/5; See also Hirsch, *The Constant Liberal*, footnote 47, 397.
150 PB to Ann Watkins; April 5, 1939. BL Add. Mss. 88921/4/10.
151 Watkins to Dozier; March 9, 1939. BL Add. Mss. 88921/5/5.
152 Dozier to PB; March 9, 1939, BL 88921/4/10.
153 PB to Ann Watkins; April 5, 1939. BL Add. Mss. 88921/4/10.
154 PB to Maida Mc Cord; April 5, 1939. 88921/3/2.
155 PB to Wm. Dozier; April 9, 1939. BL Add. Mss. 88921/4/10.
156 *Hollywood Reporter*; April 11, 1939, 1.
157 PB to Wm. Wanger; April 15, 1939. BL Add. Mss. 88921/3/2.
158 *Salt Lake City Desert News*-no date. Press Cuttings. America. 1930s. BL Add. Mss. 88921/5/7.
159 Bottome mistakenly attributed the Warner Brothers production of *Zola* with its mention of the Dreyfus case to Franklin and West.
160 Welky, 204: Dr. Edgar Magnin to Victor Saville, May 29, 1940, USC/MGM.
161 PB to Sir Frederick Whyte; August 28, 1940. BL Add. Mss. 88921/2/8.
162 PB to Rabbi Eisendrath; May 20, 1939. BL Add. Mss. 88921/3/2.

4

In Production, 1939

Introduction: The Reversals of 1939

Louella Parsons had captured the atmosphere at MGM when she reported, "MGM bosses are eager to lose no time filming *The Mortal Storm*."[1] The mood of the studio, if not the whole country, had turned exigent. The first three months of the year had proven disturbing. The president raised the specter of war in his State of the Union address when he warned that "all around us are threats of new aggression," adding ominously, we "cannot [...] let pass, without effective protest, [such] acts of aggression against sister nations."[2] As if to confirm the threat, in mid-March the Nazis took over all of Czechoslovakia, abnegating the Munich Pact and incorporating the rest of the country into the Reich.

More particularly in Hollywood, MGM confronted its cinematic rival, Warner Brothers, about to release the provocative *Confessions of a Nazi Spy*. While the studio's first film to dramatize the Nazi menace, it also typified Warner Brothers' approach to controversial issues. The film embodied gritty realism based on an actual FBI agent's memoir about thwarting a Nazi spy ring in New York. It may have broken new ground in subject matter; but in another sense, it was simply a crime drama for which the studio was well known.

MGM, too, prepared to make a film about the Nazis as far as possible consonant with its traditional approach and style. *The Mortal Storm* provided the studio with the opportunity to produce a drama centered on family. In that way reminiscent of the studio's preference for stories depicting a tight-knit family group bound by ties of blood and experience, whether light-hearted or dramatic. But not quite. What its rival Warner Brothers ignored in *Confessions of a Nazi Spy*, namely, Nazi antisemitism, stood at the center of *The Mortal Storm*. MGM's first foray into depicting the Nazi menace could prove far more provocative than Warner's spy drama set on American soil.

Uncertain but determined, the studio took an unusual step. It engaged the author of the novel as a consultant and advisor, violating the usual practice of making free use of a work once the purchase agreement had been signed.[3] Within days of acquiring the rights to *The Mortal Storm* on April 10, Sidney Franklin and Claudine West, producer and lead scriptwriter, sat down with Bottome, seeking guidance in the studio's first attempt to realize the Nazis on screen.

For Bottome, being asked to join the production after so many months of finding herself snubbed, must have offered a measure of consolation. Beyond providing her personal vindication, the discussion revealed that the author had given considerable thought to filming the novel. She wanted the studio to get it right. She intended the film to portray the truth of the Nazi menace in Europe and to warn Americans that the threat loomed over them as well. She spoke at length on the suitability of particular individuals for which parts and which scenes from the novel had to be retained and given prominence on screen.

West too moved quickly. She had completed the first full version of the script by mid-July. The studio was so anxious to release the film that it began shooting snow scenes in high summer while West worked. When it became difficult to obtain permission to film in a national park the studio's front office approved a venue abroad. Just as West completed the script, a crew filmed the snow scenes in Switzerland required by the production. In August émigré writers who had fled Germany or Austria provided additional hard-hitting scenes, depicting Nazi brutality in a concentration camp. The production would certainly be completed by the end of the year.

It was not to be. The onset of war in Europe on September 1 changed the political climate in the United States overnight. The official American policy of neutrality, seemingly theoretical at the time that it was initiated in the mid-1930s, acquired new significance as a means to keep the country out of actual conflict that had just begun. Hollywood almost immediately began to rethink its newfound activism. By mid-September the studios had halted production on all so-called war pictures in which Germany had clearly been the villain. Will Hays, who had charge of public relations for the movie industry as head of the Motion Picture Producers and Distributors Association (MPPDA), confirmed that "anti-Nazi films" would now be denied the seal of approval from the industry's Production Code Administration.[4] Without that seal, studios that distributed such films would receive stiff fines. The new policy began on September 15, 1939, and lasted until January 1940 when the studio heads deemed the political climate no longer hostile to reminders of war from Hollywood. But at least temporarily, Hays withdrew the encouragement that he had offered the moguls back in March "to deal with issues of war and peace."[5] The studios might still deal with peace; they could no longer remind their audiences of war. For MGM that meant reconsideration of the rush to complete filming

The Mortal Storm. The studio had four months, from mid-September to the resumption of the film's production on February 7, 1940, in which to reevaluate the picture it had been so keen to make in the spring and summer of 1939.

The adaptation of Bottome's novel presented danger on two fronts. It unequivocally condemned the Nazis. In the original script, the film also raised the specter of the moguls' use of the media in defense of the Jews. Those who ran MGM, Louis B. Mayer especially, developed reservations and now determined to obfuscate the film's original message. As a result, the screen version of Bottome's novel differed from what it might have been once production resumed in 1940. But the work conducted on the production in 1939 nonetheless contributed to the final version. The earlier version must be examined to understand the film that MGM released in 1940. That version raised the question of what *The Mortal Storm* might have been had work on it continued uninterrupted with the original sense of urgency driving production. Certainly, a very different film would have been released on the eve of the attempted annihilation of Europe's Jews. By using the word "Jew," the film would have contained a direct warning of that impending disaster. Instead, Mayer called for "indirection." He insisted that the persecuted of *The Mortal Storm* be referred to as "non-Aryans." The film still managed to play a striking political role in the year of its release. *The Mortal Storm* advocated intervention, urging symbolically that the United States should come to the aid of those opposed to the Nazis. Yet the production could have been so much more, calling the Nazis to account for their antisemitism and warning of the Holocaust to come.

Safe Choices

Even with MGM's initial concern to complete production of *The Mortal Storm* without delay, the studio intended to exercise its usual caution where potential controversy threatened. Mayer was about to make a picture that addressed persecution of Europe's Jews, yet he had been active for a decade in Hollywood's effort to keep the Jewish question off the screen. The fate of Europe's Jews permeated the novel he had just purchased. The head of MGM therefore chose carefully among the nine production teams located on the floor below his suite of offices in the studio's newly built Thalberg Building.[6]

The choice was important for another reason. As the studio photographer Karl Struss observed, "MGM was a producer's studio."[7] The MGM producer, Pandro Berman, made the same point. He compared the role of producer and director at the time that MGM made *The Mortal Storm*:

The business of Hollywood in the 30s and 40s was a producer's business. [At MGM] we usually put the director on a movie after we had developed the screenplay [...] the directors in those days [...] were mostly employees [...] on 40-week contracts [...] months of labor on a movie were generally behind us before one of our contract directors took charge.[8]

Frank Capra resented MGM's division of labor. He fumed, the Culver City studio, "absolutely thought [I] was nuts [because] I believed in one man, one film [and] the director should be that man."[9] In the case of *The Mortal Storm*, Mayer ultimately found himself forced to employ both approaches to moviemaking. But first he turned to the studio's "producer system."[10] The problem at MGM was that while producers ruled the studio sound stages, few at MGM were competent to make *The Mortal Storm*.

Eight of the nine had obvious drawbacks in terms of inexperience beyond the lighter, musical fare MGM was known for. Edwin Knopf, for example, was more a writer of light entertainment. Sam Zimbalist had never produced a serious film of the import of *The Mortal Storm*. Larry Weingarten produced comedies. Carey Wilson had succeeded as a writer of *Mutiny on the Bounty* in 1935 but had little experience as a producer since then. Pandro Berman produced the Astaire/Rogers films. Arthur Freed, a lyricist, Joe Pasternak, and Jack Cummings all produced musicals for the studio. That left Franklin, who had earned plaudits for his work on *Good-bye Mr. Chips*, as close a film to *The Mortal Storm* as any MGM had produced in the past decade.

Franklin stood out in other respects. Trained by Thalberg, he would emphasize romance over politics. Though Jewish, he belonged to the Hollywood circle of devout Christian Scientists and seemed to have relinquished any claim to Jewish identity or the need to defend it.[11] He therefore seemed the most appropriate among potential MGM producers, likely to avoid controversy and make the film with the delicacy and tact he had shown in *Good-bye Mr. Chips*, a production he had overseen with intelligence and insight.

Franklin was safe for other reasons. Mayer believed that he could control him. Since September 1936 when Franklin's mentor Irving Thalberg died, he lacked a protector within the cutthroat world of MGM run by Mayer and eight other members of the Executive Committee who surrounded him.[12] Franklin had to satisfy men like Sam Katz and Eddie Mannix, who together held the purse strings at MGM. Of Katz, it was said that he was "a master double-crossing son of a bitch."[13] Of Mannix, it was said, "He wasn't Hollywood tough, he was Jersey tough—authentic [...] he could put a bullet through your ass."[14] A far cry from the refined and dignified Thalberg. Franklin, who served as one of the ushers at Thalberg's funeral, had no choice after 1936 but to show himself a studio loyalist and that meant bowing to the will of Mayer and his circle.

Claudine West, Franklin's partner on his production team and his lead scriptwriter, appeared to be another safe choice. She was no left-wing writer of the sort that abounded in Hollywood during the "Communist heyday from 1936–1946," when the Screen Writers' Guild not only welcomed Communists but encouraged party membership.[15] West did not go in search of causes. She signed nothing at a time when anti-Fascist petitions and manifestos proliferated in the Hollywood studios like mushrooms after rain. Her restrained and retiring demeanor gave no cause for alarm. Greer Garson characterized her as "extremely shy and self-effacing."[16] True, she was British and subsequently had brothers in the RAF.[17] In *Good-bye Mr. Chips* she slipped in a critical reference to German militarism.[18] If, as Franklin insisted, the script belonged to her, then she was most likely the author of that pointed ant-German pointed remark. For West, such a reference, written in 1938, stood out in an otherwise seemingly apolitical career.

West could be recommended for another reason. Neither Mayer nor anyone else at MGM would have reason to believe that she had any Jewish connections. In fact, she did. Her late stepfather was Jewish, and the issue of the identity of that much-loved member of the family mattered. After West's death her mother raised the question of Jewish identity with Franklin. Querying him about his own sense of Jewishness, she wrote, "Will you think it impertinent if I ask you if you are of Jewish descent? Someone said you are. I hope you are. My dearly loved Husband was, and I have never known a Christian man yet worth to tie his shoes."[19] Honoring her stepfather's memory, West contributed to Jewish charities in southern California.[20]

Like Bottome, West's own family resembled the birth order of the Roth offspring. Of the scriptwriter's five siblings, the youngest, Mervyn, was the son of her mother and her stepfather Ernest Goldsmid-Abrahams. West's relationship to Mervyn mirrored Freya's to Rudi, the youngest Roth offspring in *The Mortal Storm*, who is half Jewish with a Christian mother and a Jewish father. West therefore had a deeper connection to Bottome's novel than Mayer could have imagined. Unbeknownst to the studio head, the otherwise shy and retiring scriptwriter had more reason to identify with *The Mortal Storm* than with any other work she adapted to the screen. She also had first-hand knowledge of how rapidly the terrain had shifted for Europe's Jews. Traveling in Europe in 1938, she had witnessed the vulnerability of families like hers, if the Nuremberg Laws were applied to them.

But the Nazis targeted more than the Jews. They had other victims as well. Starting in 1934 the regime outlawed homosexuality. The Rohm purge in June of that year had been directed against homosexuals in the SA, or so-called Brown Shirts. At the same time those accused of homosexuality were arrested from all over Germany and began to crowd the barracks of the recently constructed Dachau concentration camp.

West might have watched those developments with unease. Some evidence exists that she had a committed relationship with another woman. She not only kept the relationship discreet in Hollywood. She also maintained it as a secret from her own family. After she died Franklin explained to her mother, living in England, that "a certain individual had arranged matters in the end."[21] He said no more than that, but the individual in question was most likely Dr. Blanche Slagerman, a prominent obstetrician and gynecologist in Los Angeles who was the primary beneficiary of West's estate.[22] Both women were single, with West claiming to be a widow. Her will, however, makes no mention of beneficiaries from a spouse's family; and no record of West's marriage has come to light.[23] It was plausible that she and Slagerman had a relationship that would certainly have undermined Slagerman's professional standing given her medical specialty had knowledge of a relationship with another woman become known. West arguably therefore bore a personal connection to the two most persecuted groups in the Third Reich of the 1930s: Jews and homosexuals. Remarkable for her "perfect syntax and great gentleness," fellow scriptwriter Salka Viertel recalled, West unexpectedly but with good reason defended her script of The Mortal Storm with tensile strength.[24]

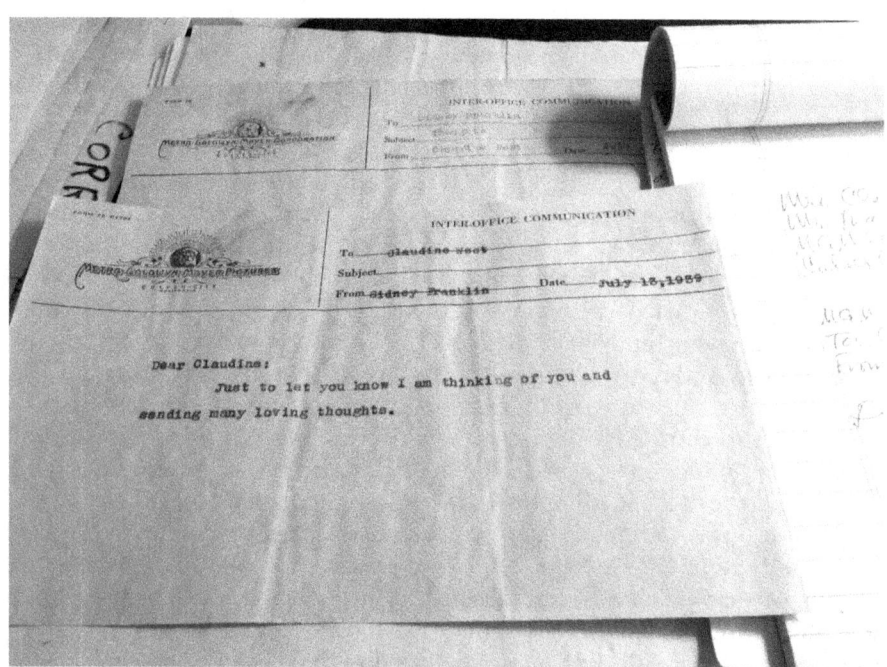

Figure 1 Example of West's affection for Franklin and the basis for their close working relationship. Credit: SAF, with kind permission of Victoria Franklin-Dillon.

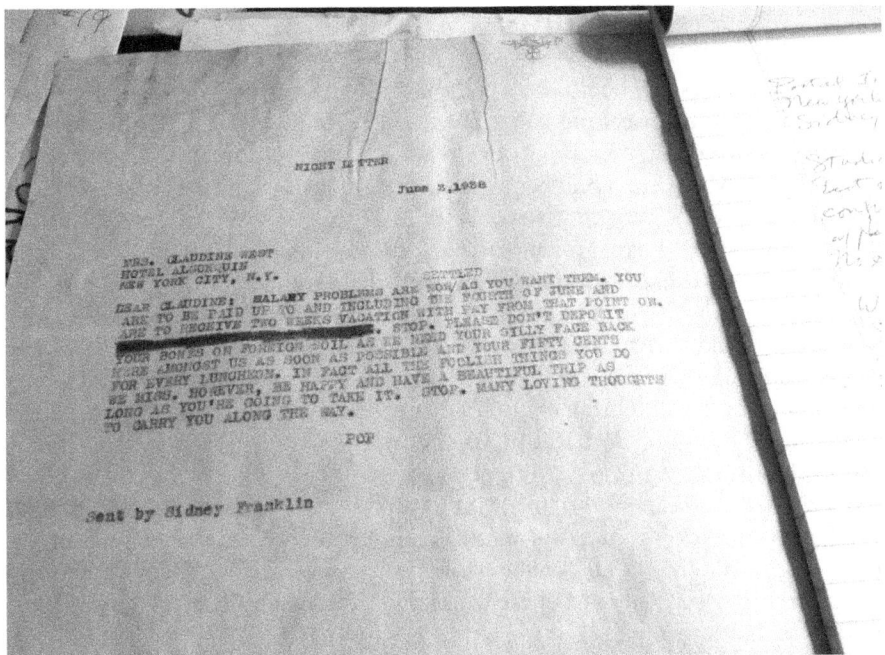

Figure 2 Franklin to West as she prepares to leave for several weeks in Europe, June 3, 1938. Her affection for him was clearly reciprocated. Credit: SAF, with kind permission of Victoria Franklin-Dillon.

She and Franklin had a close working relationship. He relied on her, as he said, "to write his scripts." They also had an abiding friendship. In letters to him, she called him "Pop," and "Cherished Pop." In 1938, she signed a letter from London, "Good-bye. Good-bye. Good-bye, Mr. Chips," referring to their just completed script, finished in eleven weeks.[25] That name, like the others, suggested that she saw Franklin as a warm and paternal figure. He told her as she left for the trip to Europe:

> Please don't deposit your bones on foreign soil as we need your silly face amongst us as soon as possible and your 50 cents for every luncheon. In fact, all the foolish things you do we miss. However, be happy and have a beautiful trip.[26]

She had started out on trial from the department that provided synopses of stories for possible purchase by the studio. She became Franklin's production partner, a relationship that only one film, *The Mortal Storm*, ever tested.

Consulting with Bottome

Within four days of the studio's purchase of the novel, West and Franklin met with Bottome, seeking her advice on how to bring it to the screen. Kenneth MacKenna, a story editor at MGM and a close friend of Franklin, joined them. MacKenna had been especially anxious that the studio purchase Bottome's novel. According to Louella Parsons, he was an "enthusiastic" advocate for *The Mortal Storm*, and had already "worked out [an acceptable] treatment" for the adaptation of the novel to the screen (See chapter 3). MacKenna had a personal interest in the story. Though he took his mother's Scotch-Irish maiden name, he was also of Prussian-Jewish origin, evident in his given name of Leo Mielziner. His grandfather was a famous Reform rabbi connected to Hebrew Union College, the institution that had prepared both Rabbi Magnin and Rabbi Eisendrath for the rabbinate. The initial preproduction meeting regarding *The Mortal Storm* therefore consisted of individuals, Franklin, West, and MacKenna, with a personal connection to the Jewish question that Bottome insisted was the key to the novel and the film to be made from it. If Mayer wanted the issue treated gingerly or to shy away from it altogether, his choices for the production team might not have been so safe after all.

The film was not the normal fare for West and Franklin. True, they had never collaborated on a production so politically charged until they worked together on *Good-bye Mr. Chips*, which had political undertones regarding German militarism as well as war guilt. For the most part, West had joined Franklin on adaptations of the classics or bestsellers such as *The Good Earth* or the period costume drama *Marie Antoinette*. In 1938 she described at length to Franklin how she would adapt Clare Booth Luce's play *The Women* to the screen, a project they never undertook.[27] Other work intervened. In that year she urged a reluctant Franklin to produce James Hilton's bestseller *Good-bye Mr. Chips*. *The Mortal Storm* in 1939 would take their collaboration in the direction of the timely and the political for only the second time. With *Good-bye Mr. Chips* scheduled for release at the end of July, West and Franklin began to work on the adaptation of Bottome's novel.

The Mortal Storm was no ordinary work for Bottome either. She had more at stake with that novel than with any other of the more than twenty that she had previously written. With none of the others had she fought so hard for a major studio to bring it to the screen. Transferred to "the most perfect medium the world has ever known," *The Mortal Storm*, from Bottome's perspective, was supposed to awaken America to the threat of war and the needs of Britain in the event of European conflict.[28] She also intended to place the plight of Europe's Jews as dramatically as possible before the American public. As she told her old friend Professor Potter, it would be the first "straight-forward anti-Nazi film" from "a big picture studio" ever made.[29]

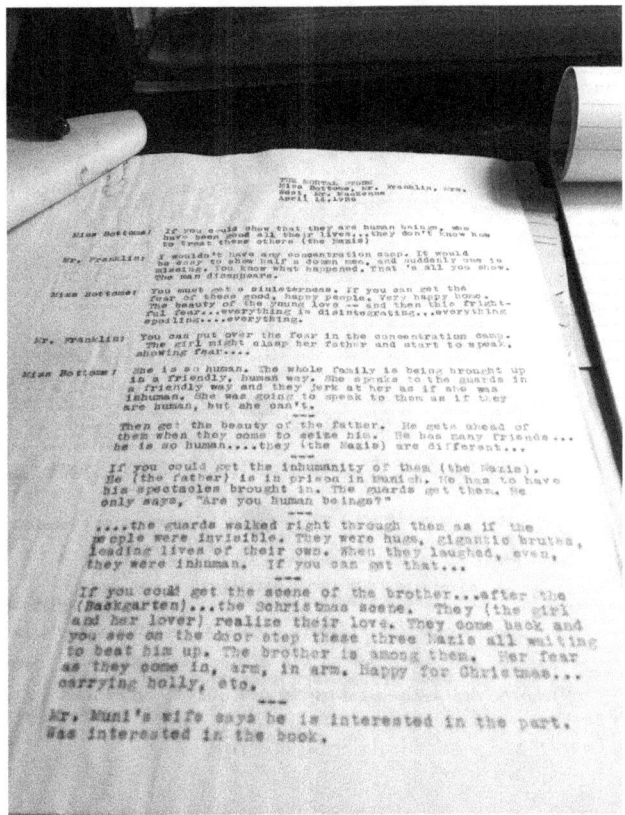

Figure 3 Summary of Bottome's meeting with Franklin's production team held within days of the novel's purchase by MGM. Credit: SAF, with kind permission of Victoria Franklin-Dillon.

West had her own emerging agenda. Between 1938 and 1943, starting with *Good-bye Mr. Chips*, she made a major contribution to forging the heroic, stalwart, high-minded image of Britain that pervaded American cinema in those years. She was every bit as much a propagandist as Bottome, employing *The Mortal Storm*, along with other films of that period, on behalf of intervention and subsequently Britain's war effort. Bottome's story of Jewish oppression cried out for joining the struggle against Hitler. Nor was the cause of Britain lost in the production about the Nazi hounding of the Jews. The Roth family, like the British in 1940, stood alone and vulnerable before the Nazis. West therefore attempted to capture Bottome's many layered message, urging the cause of intervention and aid to Britain along with the striking depiction of the threat that loomed before Europe's Jews.

She possessed a critical set of skills for the adaptation of the novel to the screen. Her forte lay in perceiving the underlying thread of a work of fiction

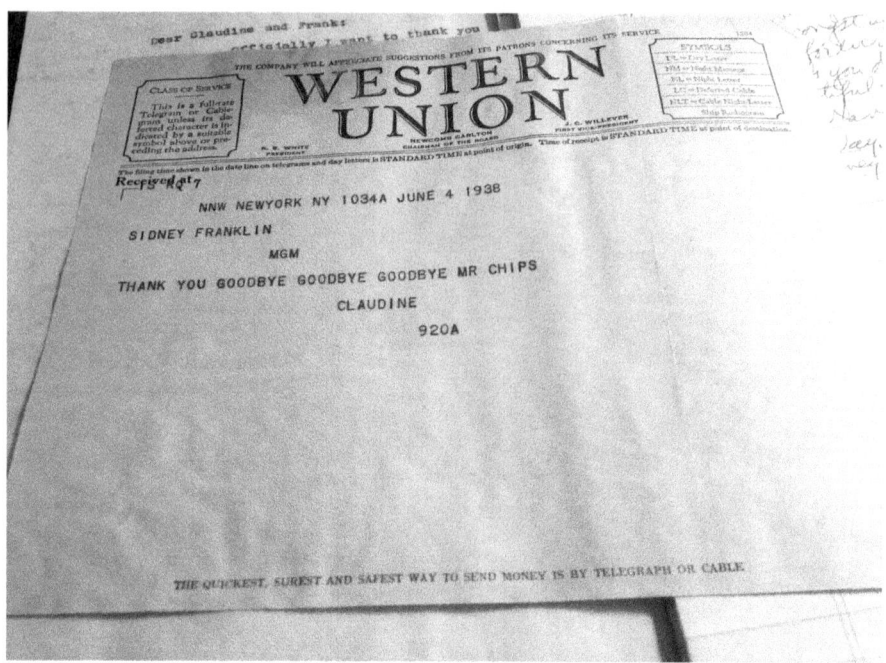

Figure 4 West advocated making *Good-bye Mr. Chips*, which Franklin at first opposed. Her farewell alludes to their script for the film they had just completed, June 4, 1938. Credit: SAF, with kind permission of Victoria Franklin-Dillon.

and retaining it within the constraints of a film script. She knew how to compress the time frame of a novel and turn narration into dialogue. West did not produce original work herself. Her shy, effacing manner carried over into her writing. She submerged herself in the creativity of others. An exception was *Mrs. Miniver*, which Franklin attributes almost exclusively to West.[30] Jan Struthers's novel provided so little in the way of plot or character development that West could be said to have begun the script from scratch. But that film was the exception.

West had honed the skills she required for scriptwriting well before she came to Hollywood. After sound came in, as Thalberg used to say, "the story is king," in the making of a picture. In the 1930s the stories, at least at MGM, primarily came from the bestseller lists. West was among the most talented at encrypting the original story in the adaptation for the screen. She had in fact been trained as a codebreaker in the First World War.[31] That experience served her well in Hollywood. Her tenacity with a script and insight into how to adapt from one medium to another, that is, to encode a work of fiction into a script, along with her powers of concentration, to which Franklin attested, all recall her employment in decryption.[32]

Codebreaking left another discernible trace on her work in Hollywood. She used a pencil in making script changes and writing instructional notes to herself and others in the margins of scripts. She was hardly alone in doing that, but the lowly pencil provided a link between her occupation in wartime and her work in Hollywood. Her use of a pencil offers something more. It permits following her emendations to the evolving script of *The Mortal Storm*. The script copies that bear her name in the Margaret Herrick Library contain her penciled corrections as she literally tried one version on top of another to gain front office approval for retention of the Jewish question in the film. Those penciled modifications and substitutions in her distinctive handwriting reveal her numerous attempts to address studio objections to the explicit depiction of Nazi persecution of German Jews. Despite what proved to be a lost cause, she sought to retain as many of those scenes and references as possible.

Penelope Fitzgerald, in her account of the work of the great codebreaker Dilthy Knox, explained why a former codebreaker like West would use a pencil and what that might symbolize for her in the insecure and uncertain world of the Hollywood studios. Fitzgerald said of codebreakers generally, "The codebreaker writes any probable solutions […] in pencil […] Ink is for certainties."[33] West found few certainties in adapting *The Mortal Storm* to the screen. By 1939, she wielded a pencil on behalf of a script with integrity that the studio was determined to censor. She tried again and again to craft a formula of encryption that MGM's front office would accept, yet at the same time retain the novel's essential message. Like a codebreaker she penciled in possible solutions to controversial scenes, attempting to satisfy Mayer and those who surrounded him. Until the final scenes were shot, only a month before the film's release in June 1940, she continued to make penciled changes to the script in search of a solution to retain the Jewish question on screen.

Bottome shared with West previous wartime experience. Like her fellow writer, she had worked for the British government in the First World War. In Bottome's case she trained as a specialist in the burgeoning field of wartime propaganda under the diplomat and novelist John Buchan, Lord Tweedsmuir. In other words, she worked for the Ministry of Information in two wars.[34] The experience with Buchan and his deputy Chalmers Mitchell taught her much. She learned that popular, accessible entertainment provided the most effective propaganda.

Buchan inculcated other lessons that Bottome took to heart. He insisted that visual imagery would also succeed as propaganda whether as photographs or painting, but the new medium of film would be the most powerful of all.[35] Buchan imparted another truth as he saw it. Propaganda constituted a higher calling, not a mendacious or deceitful ploy to sway opinion. Buchan's wife explained her husband's sense of mission in the production of propaganda: "It was highly necessary that Great Britain should put her case imaginatively and intelligently to other countries and explain the greatness of her war effort."[36] In this context, by "greatness," Lady Tweedsmuir meant the moral superiority of Britain in its fight against German militarism capable of atrocities on a hitherto unknown scale.

Bottome regarded *The Mortal Storm* as part of the same high-minded mission with war against Germany looming again. Britain's cause was moral as well as magnanimous. She believed that Britain would stand with the victims of Nazism, offering shelter to refugees from all over Europe. Both she and West carried into the Second World War the sense of mission and commitment to a righteous cause imparted to them by the First World War. After 1914 they had fought a brutal enemy notable for committing atrocities against civilians and combatants alike, from the use of poison gas on the battlefield to the aerial bombardment of major cities. The military capabilities of Germany in 1939 dwarfed those of the Kaiser in 1914. But at least Buchan had been right. Film could be a magic bullet in Britain's arsenal, and both Bottome and West had access to it.

Nor had British leadership, as Bottome and West knew it, changed from one war to the next. Churchill himself embodied that continuity. He had insisted on a codebreaking operation in the First World War and overseen the establishment of a unit devoted to decryption within the Admiralty which he then administered.[37] Churchill had in addition endowed that work with an ethical standard. Codebreaking did not constitute an intrusion into private communications, he argued; rather, it provided insights into the mind of the enemy, that is, the Germans.[38] John Buchan had similarly insisted on a moral standard in propaganda. It provided a message of significance rather than a means of purveying mere deception.

West and Bottome thus shared formative experiences in the First World War. Each possessed deeply held convictions originating with revered mentors in previous wartime service. For much of the discussion that took place only days after the studio bought the rights to the novel, West sat silent while Bottome held forth. One can already imagine a kind of silent partnership between the two compatriots. That made Franklin the odd man out.

Bottome, West, Franklin, and MacKenna gathered in a conference room at the MGM studio in mid-April 1939. A studio stenographer was present. Bottome opened the discussion, beginning with the character of Professor Roth.[39] She insisted to her MGM hosts that the success of the film depended on getting his depiction right. Victor Roth, she explained, embodied the intellect and values of the renowned depth psychologist Alfred Adler, who had inspired her to write *The Mortal Storm* in the first place. He "was the person in her mind when she wrote the book [...] He had extraordinary wisdom and strength [...] You have to have someone who is very learned to give the effect of a very learned man [to play him]." Bottome weighed the pros and cons of as many as six actors for the role of Professor Roth.

Showing her familiarity with the possible male actors appropriate for the film, she listed Paul Muni, Spencer Tracy, George Arliss, Charles Boyer, Paul Lucas, and Robert Donat as potential leads. She maintained that all could play the part with the possible exception of Tracy. She rejected him on the grounds that "while a very good actor, [he] is too Western. He couldn't do it." By "too Western" she probably meant too American.

Franklin, on the other hand, expressed concern over the audience reaction to suffering on the part of the actor who played Professor Roth. He preferred Paul Muni because, he argued, "you can suffer with him terrifically." Muni may also have come to mind because he had recently played Zola in Warners' *The Life of Emile Zola*, which had addressed the Dreyfus case. Muni was himself Jewish and had trained in the Yiddish theater.

The issue of suffering was much on Franklin's mind in the course of the discussion. It clearly made him uncomfortable. He objected to Charles Boyer, for example, because "the women resent it if you make him suffer." Instead of emphasizing the suffering of the protagonists, Franklin argued for developing the romantic potential of the story over depicting the victimization and brutality that also figured in the novel. He explained, "Taking the girl [...] it's easy to follow that [...] but if you take the father's story you would have to develop more [to make it comprehensible]." By that Franklin meant depiction of Nazi abuse directed toward the Jewish professor. He preferred a conventionally melodramatic script to one that emphasized the oppressive treatment of Freya's father. The latter approach, he could imagine, would be unlikely to receive the studio's approval anyway.

Franklin's preference for restraint in adapting the novel arose from the fact that he was to produce a film on a controversial subject under the auspices of a cautious studio whose head took an ambivalent attitude to his own Jewishness.[40] In the 1930s Mayer had discouraged the presence of distinctly Jewish characters on screen. As though that issue were not enough, the producer had another concern. To maintain his status and influence at MGM, Franklin could not afford to arouse controversy. Discussions with Bottome, though cordial, proved a harbinger of the conflicts that would subsequently dog the production and Franklin himself. The author urged harsh depiction of the Nazis, emphasizing at the same time the central role of Professor Roth, the focus of the most brutal Nazi persecution in the novel. Franklin, on the other hand, preferred merely to suggest brutality through the disappearance of a character or sounds off screen rather than to depict lurid details. He urged emphasis instead on the safer, romantic themes, writing in his autobiography, "There was a beautiful love story in 'The Mortal Storm.'"[41] Franklin, if only for his own job security, hoped to construct the adaptation around that aspect of the novel.

Bottome, in contrast, insisted that the Nazis should be portrayed in all their brutishness and intimidation. "If you could get the inhumanity of them ...," she said. She also advised, "you must get the sinisterness [...] good happy people [...] and then this frightful fear [...] everything is disintegrating [...] everything." The concentration camp scenes of the novel, she insisted, were crucial to show the Nazis as they really are. She explained, "the guards" are "huge, gigantic brutes" who regard Freya when she comes to visit her father "as if she was inhuman." Bottome peppered her comments with the words "inhuman" and "inhumanity" to emphasize how the film's villains should appear and conduct themselves.

Franklin conceptualized the film differently. He intended to avoid cinematic statements whether visual or verbal that brought to the fore what Bottome considered so decisive for the adaptation of her novel to the screen. At the most he would convey through subtext, communicating by implication and indirection rather than depict the Nazi cruelty Bottome considered critical for the film's message. Franklin countered her:

> I wouldn't have any concentration camp. It would be easy to show half a dozen men, and suddenly one is missing. You know what happened. That's all you show. The man disappears.

In their polite, understated discussion, Bottome and Franklin were poles apart. His preference for a romantic adaptation with as little controversy as possible meant downplaying the very issues about the Nazis that Bottome considered essential for the on-screen version of her novel. Franklin instead advocated for an MGM production of *The Mortal Storm*, that is, a film that hinted rather than depicted and that emphasized romantic elements over political references. Franklin, after all, had been nurtured in the business by Thalberg, who had once insisted no background music in an MGM production could be played in a minor key. The sound itself was to reflect the upbeat mood of the studio's productions. Bottome, on the other hand, wanted to stretch the boundaries of the studio to capture the spirit of her novel and the political gravity of the moment.

The memorandum of the discussion described West as sitting quietly. In fact, no comments are attributed to her in the document. She must nonetheless have listened closely because she subsequently embraced several of Bottome's suggestions. For example, Bottome said of Freya, "She's got to have a child," emphasizing the importance of the child out of wedlock she has by Hans, the peasant Communist in the novel. Story editor Kenneth MacKenna observed that "it would be hopeful [if] someday everything will be all right in Germany [and] someday she's going to get the child back." MacKenna wanted to balance Nazi brutishness with a hopeful future. He, like Bottome, in essence argued that Germany's future lay with children of mixed ethnic and class heritage for whom traditional social boundaries and Nazi racial concepts held no meaning, certainly no grounds for persecution. The discussion then turned to "whether or not the girl should leave the baby with the peasant family. In this case you would have to have a good actress for the peasant grandmother. Miss Bottome mentioned Irene Iseiva (played in *You Can't Take It with You*)."

West took the last comments to heart and made "the peasant grandmother" a major player in the script. In contrast to the film, the character of Frau Breitner had been a minor figure in the novel at best. In fact, the character of Frau Breitner in *The Mortal Storm*, as West wrote her, presages the formidable Lady Beldon in *Mrs. Miniver*, another West creation.[42] Both figures stand out for their role in blessing a youthful marriage; Lady Beldon somewhat more reluctantly than Frau Breitner until Kay Miniver calls her bluff. The studio, however, dropped all mention of a child out of wedlock in *The Mortal Storm* as incompatible with the Production Code; but West's indelible version of Frau Breitner, strong and distinctive, played by the redoubtable Maria Ouspenskaia, remained.

In West's script, Freya and the Breitners, mother and son, bond. Frau Breitner is delighted at the emerging love between her son (now named Martin and played by Jimmy Stewart) and the sophisticated girl from the town whose father is a professor and whose mother is descended from the aristocracy. She blesses their union when her son and Freya drink from Martin's wedding cup in what Franklin subsequently called the "marriage in the mountains," one of his favorite scenes in the production.[43] It was precisely the kind of romantic emphasis that he had hoped to see in the film.

The scene, however, in contrast to Franklin's preference, also carries political meaning. It suggests that "the only possibility for a democratic German future lay in marrying political resistance to the acceptance and integration of cultural [and religious] difference."[44] Freya's child by Hans in the novel bore the same message of a better future if traditionally incompatible class and religious identities could be wedded together to make a new Germany.

The message is as much American as German. Class barriers, as in America, evaporate on the mountain where traditional obstacles present no impediment to the couple's love for each other. A peasant can marry or have a child with an aristocrat endowed with all the sophistication of the town. Romance also triumphs over religious differences. Freya and Martin can wed themselves in West's script without the sanction of religion. Knowing the studio would never permit Freya to have a child out of wedlock West provided a scene that is both traditional and defiant. Frau Breitner blesses more than the couple in the mountain wedding scene. Freya and Martin consummate their love for each other in a non-traditional, that is, non-religious ceremony that legitimizes their relationship. At the same time their very relationship defies Nazi ideology which imperils a future Germany that integrates all its people and their talents.

West took Bottome's advice regarding another relationship in the novel: that between Rudi and his father. But she changed the emphasis entirely, attempting through the boy's love for his father to address the Jewish question in Nazi Germany outright. Bottome had explained to the production team the importance of a "father-son" scene. She emphasized how affecting a conversation between Rudi and his wise professorial father would be, recommending how it should transpire:

> One scene would be between the father and younger son [...] when his father is told of [the death of] the girl's lover, it suddenly occurs to him, "Father, they couldn't kill you [could they?]" An extraordinary insecurity comes over the child. He believes his father is all powerful. This scene has moved most people.

West, however, had another scene in mind to move her audience. She took for the "father-son" scene the one in the novel between Rudi and his father where the boy asks, "What is being a Jew?" followed by his father's answer, a paean to Jewish contributions to civilization. It proved to be the most controversial scene in the script that West drafted, and the one she fought hardest for, writing and rewriting it. In 1940, had it remained in the film, the scene would have been the most significant, confronting the Jewish question in Nazi Germany head-on.

For Bottome more than a particular scene or scenes was at stake. More even than an emphasis on a romantic plot as opposed to one filled with suffering. She made it clear to her MGM hosts precisely what the picture had to be.

> If you could only make the thing the way it feels [...] it's about an attack on all that's good and decent. They're wolves. Hitler is out to kill two things—family life and all religion. He is ready to destroy both. "The Mortal Storm" is a message to the whole world. This is the thing we want to feel we're working for.

As part of that "message to the whole world," Bottome sought to convey that Hitler intended to destroy the most cherished values of civilization embodied in religion and love of family. Franklin and no doubt Mayer and those around him preferred a romantic vehicle albeit set within the context of Nazi Germany and portraying uncomfortable episodes of persecution and intimidation by indirection, even better, suggested off screen. And MGM had no problem with a script centered on family life, a staple of its productions for a decade. But religion in *The Mortal Storm* meant Jewishness, a taboo subject for the studios in the 1930s. West deftly handled it in the "marriage in the mountains" scene where Frau Breitner expresses the hope that the village priest will soon marry them, then Freya, part Jewish, and Martin, presumably Catholic, wed themselves, avoiding the entanglements of organized religion altogether.

The conversation with the production team held immense significance for Bottome. That the studio sought to work with her implied that she could win it over to her point of view on how to adapt the novel to the screen. She placed great value on her powers of persuasion. The question-and-answer sessions at the end of her public lectures on literature, Adlerian psychology, or whatever topic were designed to slip in politics and allow for attempts to persuade her audiences of the righteousness of British policy.[45]

There may have been subsequent consultations following the initial discussions in mid-April 1939, although no further accounts of meetings

Figure 5 Summary of Bottome's meeting with Franklin's production team (final page). Credit: SAF, with kind permission of Victoria Franklin-Dillon.

between Bottome and the production team are to be found in Franklin's papers. Bottome remained available to MGM until her departure for England in May. She left for her homeland, believing that the film would be finished before she returned to the American lecture circuit on behalf of the Ministry of Information in the following year. She also left, believing, mistakenly, that her recommendations had prevailed. West went to work on the script, and negotiations over the right to film snow scenes in the mountainous terrain of one of the national parks began in earnest.

Making Haste to Film Mountain Scenery

During Bottome's discussion with her MGM hosts, "she spoke about her long residence in Germany and Austria." In doing so she not only emphasized her own expertise, but she also conveyed a sense of the terrain of the novel. She wanted the film to capture its Central European mountain venues and alpine scenery. Bottome had written in the second volume of her autobiography how she had fallen in love with the mountains while convalescing from tuberculosis before the First World War in Swiss sanatoriums devoted to treating patients with the disease. More specifically, she wrote in the third volume, "I have never been able to describe any place or the life in it with the same intensity as I have described [the mountain terrain of] Tirol in [...] 'The Mortal Storm.'"[46]

Mountain venues suggested something more for Bottome than mere scenery. In her fiction of the 1930s, the mountains of Central Europe acquired political significance. They remained pure and undefiled while fascism took hold in urban areas located on the flat terrain below. In *Devil's Due* (1932), for example, the narrator falls in love with a free spirit, a daredevil ski jumper. She liberates his emotions and encourages his escape from a stifling marriage. Their whole relationship occurs in an alpine setting, that is, a place of romance and emotional authenticity. After her death in a ski competition, he returns to his previous relationship with a woman who sits with him in a restaurant, her back to the mountains, making snide comments about Jews. Bottome paints a similar contrast between the mountains and the town below, that is, Munich, in *The Mortal Storm*. Mountain scenery had to figure in the screen adaptation. West and Franklin took her insistence to heart.

West herself had early exposure to the Swiss Alps, having attended boarding school in Switzerland.[47] She knew the terrain and, as will be clear, the geography of Central Europe. In her adaptation of the novel, Freya bonds with Martin on the slopes. They ski in intertwining patterns, symbolic of their growing affection for each other as the two descend from the Breitner farm to the chalet where they will confront the Nazis directly. Their final encounter with the same contingent of Brown Shirts which ends so disastrously occurs on level ground. As in Bottome's previous fiction of the decade, the mountains belong to lovers, while below is the domain of the Nazis.

In May 1939 Franklin began to seek permission from the National Park Service to film on Mt. Rainier or in another national park with similar terrain and snow conditions in summer. Among Franklin's papers there is extensive correspondence regarding lodging and travel for a large party of cast and crew. Franklin expected to remain in snow country for at least two weeks of filming. The overall expenses would have been significant for that duration and the number of individuals involved.[48] The studio's willingness to subsidize such expensive location shooting revealed the importance of the film to MGM in 1939 and the priority accorded it in the summer of that year.

To Franklin's surprise his requests to the Park Service for a permit went unanswered. The Department of Interior appeared to have little interest in expediting MGM's anxious petitions to film under what amounted to deteriorating alpine conditions. The problem lay with the secretary of interior himself. Harold Ickes was experiencing his own difficulties. A member of FDR's inner circle, he was considered one of the strongest

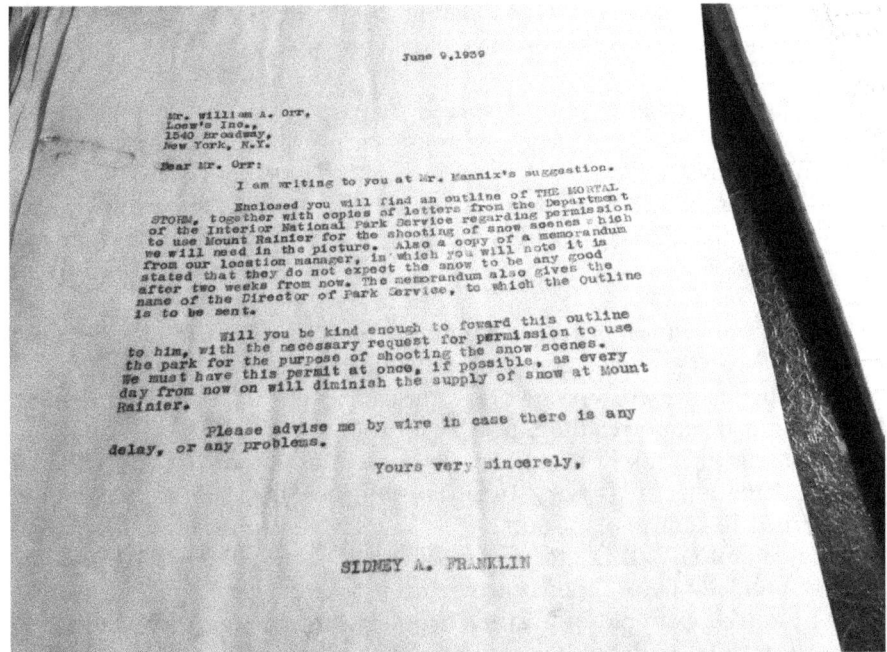

Figure 6 Franklin seeks permission to shoot snow scenes on Mt. Rainier. Credit: SAF, with kind permission of Victoria Franklin-Dillon

proponents of the movie industry in an administration that challenged the moguls' vertical control of that industry. In October 1938, for example, he had visited Los Angeles. The moguls regarded him as an ally in their struggle with an increasingly aggressive Justice Department. They literally wined and dined him, treating him to lunch at Twentieth-Century Fox where he sat between Darryl Zanuck and Louis B. Mayer.[49]

Half a year later, Ickes's own vulnerabilities within the administration became clear. The impediment for MGM to film in the mountains originated with the president himself. As FDR prepared for a third term, he undermined the power of those in the Democratic Party who might be his rivals in a future contest.[50] Ickes fell victim to the purge of the president's allies in 1939, suffering a loss of responsibility within the bureaucracy that spring. He then sought to tighten his hold on the Interior Department. Just as Sidney Franklin importuned the Park Service, Ickes was engaged in purging it of "too many incompetent people."[51] In the summer of 1939, the Park Service was in a state of turmoil. Worse, Ickes himself had become angry and churlish, stymied by the president who continued to confide in him but had limited the secretary's reach within the government. When Ickes belatedly replied to MGM, he expressed his own frustrations by imposing petty restrictions on the movie company regarding filming in a national park.

Franklin grew desperate. On June 9 he turned to William A. Orr, who worked for Loew's Inc., MGM's parent company located in New York, regarding the situation that threatened delay in production.

> Sending you tonight air mail special delivery [...] copy of [outline of] script "The Mortal Storm" with instructions to obtain permission from the Director National Park Service [...] to shoot snow scenes at Mt. Rainier. As snow will remain less than two weeks important we get immediate action on this. Mr. Mannix suggests someone fly to Washington to expedite.[52]

The communication is noteworthy for several reasons. In 1939, Franklin had both MGM's parent company and the front office behind him and backing the picture. Also noteworthy, the financial watchdog over the film, Eddie Mannix, supported the expensive location shooting at high altitudes in a national park. Franklin's concern for the security of the script also figured in his calculations at a trying time. He told Orr that the outline should be returned to him just as soon as "it had served its purpose."[53] If script material fell into hostile hands, the studio could receive premature, possibly adverse publicity before the controversial film even went into production. MGM had the example of Warner Brothers in that regard. Warners had imposed strict security on the script and the production of *Confessions of a Nazi Spy* after receiving death threats during filming. Jack Warner himself received threats at the time of the film's release.

Despite Franklin's plea for immediate approval, it took eleven more days to obtain permission from Ickes, who only on June 20 granted MGM the right to shoot on Mt. Rainier, intervening on behalf of the Park Service. But he imposed conditions. MGM had to make

> a donation to the national park trust of $100 per day of actual shooting [...] and post a $1000 bond against actual damage. Advises [...] no artificial settings nor structures to be erected [...] in park and no principals used in actual shooting of skiing scenes in park.[54]

The conditions, while hardly onerous, seemed like a gratuitous obstacle in place of ready assistance for a film that carried warnings similar to those in the president's State of the Union address. But the real problem lay in the delay that had arisen. By the time that a production crew reached Mt. Rainier, Franklin had already realized, the snow would have melted. He would have no freedom to make the shots he might want. He sought another venue.

The Perilous Terrain of Switzerland

> All references to 'Brown Shirts' in the list of shots to be made by Mr. Locke [in Switzerland] will be eliminated.
> (Claudine West, June 15, 1939)[55]

Five days before permission came from Ickes to allow a film crew on Mt. Rainier, an MGM employee, Eric Locke, shooting scenes in Switzerland for another film, offered his assistance.[56] Franklin consulted with West about the Swiss option where there was "snow good for skiing throughout July."[57] West knew the terrain, having gone to school in Switzerland, but she recognized the perils of shooting *The Mortal Storm*, just across the border with Bavaria, that part of Germany where the novel takes place. She had traveled in Europe only the year before which gave her insight into the extent of Nazi influence on the continent.[58] West now took over, making arrangements for the location shooting in Switzerland. She imposed certain conditions of her own on the filming. She insisted that "all reference to Brown Shirts in the list of shots to be made by Mr. Locke will be eliminated."[59] West presumably had several concerns. She did not want Swiss Nazi sympathizers to get wind of work on Bottome's anti-Nazi novel and interfere with the production or stir up the kind of trouble that Warners had recently experienced in making *Confessions of a Nazi Spy*. She insisted that the studio send Locke neither a copy of the script when completed nor even the preliminary outline that had been used in negotiations with the National Park Service. Neither document could leave the country. She recognized that the very phrase "Brown Shirts," that is, the Nazi paramilitary organization known formally as the *Sturm abteilung* or S.A. and renowned for its thuggery, would arouse suspicion among pro-Nazis regarding the film's treatment of Hitler's regime. She ordered the term removed from all instructions. West instead offered a "draft of the List of Costumes, containing a description of the characters" that would be sent to Locke to guide him in filming. She was thus careful to avoid any hint of the film's anti-Nazi sentiments.[60]

Locke told the studio that he could provide snow and meadow scenes as well as a "girl ski champion" at a cost of $10,500.[61] By June 26 Franklin had made his decision to take the Swiss option. He wrote a detailed communication to Locke regarding precisely the shots that he wanted. By the end of the week he had thanked Orr for his assistance with the Department of Interior, explaining that the melting snow on Mt. Rainier precluded that location. Instead, "Mr. Locke could get these scenes in Switzerland, and it was arranged for him to do so."[62] By July 1 all was in order, including Mannix's permission to release the sum required by Locke to film in the Swiss Alps. Chas. Chic, the liaison to Mannix, told Franklin, "I had a talk with Mr. Mannix. He questioned a few items but okayed the expenditure and I have cabled Locke" to go ahead.[63]

Using a camera mounted on a sleigh, Locke shot the snow scenes for *The Mortal Storm* from July 14 to 31. The film canisters were sent back to the United States in their own rooms on luxury liners such as the *Normandie* and the *Queen Mary*. A representative from MGM's New York office met the ships at the dock to collect the studio's freight which was then transported by train to Los Angeles prior to the short ride to Culver City.

MGM, which calculated salary costs down to the penny, in the summer of 1939 generously proved willing to fund remote location shooting for *The Mortal Storm*, whether on Mt. Rainier or in the Swiss Alps.[64] The sum of $10,500 for filming in Switzerland, not originally budgeted, plus considerable transportation costs for the raw film footage, confirmed both the studio's commitment to the production and that the production at this point belonged to Franklin.

Not only did MGM go to considerable expense in the summer of 1939 to expedite production of *The Mortal Storm*, the studio lauded the script that West had completed so efficiently. Within weeks of completion in mid-July, her work circulated among studio executives who raised no objections to it. In hiring the émigré writers Hans Rameau and George Froeschel in August, the front office sought even more vivid scenes of Nazi brutality. Liberal use of the word "Jew" throughout the script, it seemed, had yet to attract attention. Franklin, for example, wrote West in September about the enthusiastic response the script had elicited. He described a visit to the office of Sam Katz, a member of Mayer's inner circle and the head of musical production at MGM. "Just returned from Sam Katz's office. Nicky Neyfak [Nicholas Nayfack, nephew of Joseph Schenck, who chaired Loew's Inc.

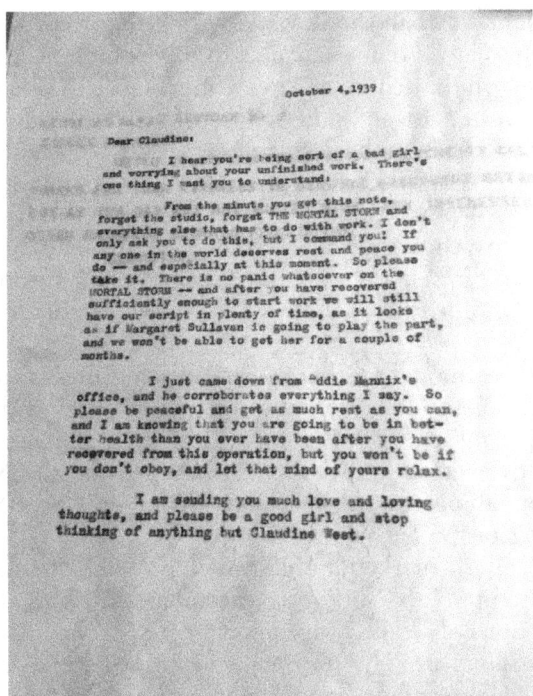

Figure 7 West is hospitalized. Franklin insists she rest and forget *The Mortal Storm*, October 4, 1939. Credit: SAF, with kind permission of Victoria Franklin-Dillon.

and ran the studio's New York office. Nayfack headed the MGM Business Office in Culver City] was there. Told me he read *The Mortal Storm* and was simply crazy about it. Said some of the scenes were wonderful. Thought this would please you. Love, POP."[65] The week before, Hays had issued the ban on war-themed pictures. MGM must have regarded it as a temporary annoyance. West continued refining the script, which still belonged to her, into the fall.

Was *Professor Mamlock* a Model for *The Mortal Storm*?

While West completed the script in late spring and early summer of 1939, she had Bottome's novel to draw on as well as the guidance that Bottome herself had offered the production team in April. But another source existed that arguably expedited her efficient completion of the script, guiding its organization and plot. Bottome had emphasized Professor Roth more than any other character in the novel, advising that the success of the film depended on who played that particular role. The fact that "the gist" of the novel for Bottome amounted to the Jews' contribution to Western civilization made Professor Roth, who embodied those gifts as well as proclaimed them, pivotal to the film. She emphasized to her MGM colleagues that she had continually borne her revered mentor Alfred Adler "in mind" when crafting the character of Professor Roth. Since 1927, Bottome had been a proponent of Adler's depth psychology. She and her husband had pursued analysis either with Adler himself or with one of his pupils through the 1930s. For Bottome, *The Mortal Storm* served as a kind of paean to the recently deceased Adler.

West had another model for the revered Jewish professor readily at hand. The hero of the Soviet film, *Professor Mamlock*, released the year before, which closely resembled *The Mortal Storm* in its plot, centered around an accomplished Jewish surgeon/scientist hounded by the Nazis. The film proved to be something of a cause-célèbre in 1939–40, precisely when West composed the script for *The Mortal Storm*.

Professor Mamlock marked a milestone for Soviet cinema in the United States. It opened in New York on November 7, 1938, the twenty-first anniversary of the Bolshevik coup d'état and just two days, as it turned out, before *Kristallnacht*. The film enjoyed immediate success, its release coinciding with heightened American awareness of Nazi atrocities as a result of *Kristallnacht*, the Night of Broken Glass.[66] The Soviet production seemed to confirm an emerging consensus in the United States regarding the need to condemn Nazi aggression, whether it occurred abroad or within our own borders as subversion or propaganda.[67] The film also attracted unusually large audiences for a foreign import. In its first run *Professor Mamlock* played "in 103 cinemas [...] in the greater New York area alone."[68]

Frank Nugent, in his third year as movie critic for the *New York Times*, saw an opportunity in that success. He took advantage of the film's popularity to lodge a complaint regarding the studios' unwillingness to depict Nazi persecution of the Jews. He described Hollywood's timidity as a failure "to grasp the nettle of the social film." By that he meant that Hollywood cared more about its bottom line than about moral or social responsibility. He wrote, "That long overdue indictment of Nazi persecution of the Jews has arrived at last. As we might have expected, it comes from Russia which is beyond Hollywood's anxiety about the foreign [i.e., German] market." Unfortunately, it took a state-subsidized Soviet production to condemn the Nazis outright. Shame on Hollywood, Nugent insisted.[69]

The movie capital had its own answer to critics like Nugent. While it did not have an anti-Nazi film ready for immediate release, it could still demonstratively show its support for the Soviet production. In early 1939 *Professor Mamlock* received the Production Code Administration's seal of approval. The theater chains of the major studios could show it without incurring substantial fines from the industry's Motion Picture Producers and Distributors Association (MPPDA). "The film had therefore crossed over into the American mainstream," film historian Thomas Doherty observed.[70] The motion picture industry's approval for an explicitly anti-Nazi production that depicted the plight of Europe's Jews had an additional meaning. Hollywood, it seemed, was now willing to acknowledge the possibility of using the movies against the Nazis and in defense of the Jews, even if it had begun to do so with a Soviet surrogate.

Professor Mamlock, whether it was Hollywood's intention or not, could play yet another role. Bearing the PCA seal of approval, the film could serve as a trial balloon. Would the moviegoing public pay to see such a film or not? Unfortunately, state censorship boards proved to be a harsher critic than the public. As a result, the film was constantly in the news for the controversies that it generated. Ohio, for instance, banned the film as did Rhode Island.[71] More disturbing for the moguls was the reason Chicago banned it. The film consisted of "purely Jewish and Communist propaganda against Germany," stated the city's Censorship Board.[72] The word "propaganda" disconcerted the moguls. Even worse, the city's elders had appeared to conflate Jewishness with Communism, an association studio heads were loath to encourage. MGM took note of the controversies. It had to. The content of *The Mortal Storm* bore a strong similarity to that of *Professor Mamlock*.

Similarities between the two films are indeed notable. For example, both open with a landmark event in the history of Nazi Germany. *Professor Mamlock* begins on the day of the Reichstag fire, February 27, 1933, which led to the new regime's arrest of German Communists and the outlawing of the party. Soviet audiences and leftists abroad would immediately recognize the significance of the Reichstag's destruction. It resulted in the liquidation of the German Communist Party within months of Hitler's coming to power. At the same time the opening set the terms of the film to follow. Communists and Nazis are at daggers drawn. The rest of the film is devoted to conflict between good and evil, that is, Communists vs. the minions of Hitler. A simultaneous battle will be fought for the allegiance of Professor Mamlock, who ultimately realizes that the scientific and medical truths that he reveres can only flourish under the mantle of Communist ideology.

The Mortal Storm too begins with a distinctive historical moment and uses it in a similar fashion: to establish the themes to follow. The MGM production opens a month earlier than *Professor Mamlock*, that is, on January 30, 1933, the day that President von Hindenburg appointed Adolf Hitler Chancellor of Germany. At that very moment in *The Mortal Storm*, Professor Roth enters his classroom to discover a gala celebration in honor of his sixtieth birthday. He was therefore born in 1873 and has thus lived as long as the Jews had enjoyed full emancipation in Germany. That evening, with the formal announcement and celebration of Hitler's appointment, two views, as in *Professor Mamlock*, are set on a collision course in a scene that occurs around the Roth's dining room table. Professor Roth's humanistic values and adherence to scientific truth will now confront the pseudo-science of Nazi racial theories and Hitler's determination to undo sixty years of Jewish emancipation in Germany.

The protagonist of each film recalls the other. Beyond being Jewish, Professors Roth and Mamlock resemble each other in their professional competence and successful personal relationships. They are both revered scientists regarded with affection by students and colleagues alike. Both show uncompromising courage before Nazi persecution. Their fates are similar. In each film fanatical Nazi students confront a revered professor. Professor Mamlock is paraded through the streets of Berlin with the word "Jude" emblazoned on his surgical gown. Professor Roth, in a scene absent from the novel, confronts a hostile classroom of uniformed students who stalk out when he insists that blood does not differ by race. He then looks out the classroom window to see the humanistic and scientific ideas he treasures being consigned to the flames as books are burned in the courtyard below. The high culture of poetry and science is targeted in the person of Jewish authors. Fritz Maberg (Robert Young) shouts, "Heinrich Heine [poet and Christian convert from Judaism], we burn you!" "Albert Einstein, we burn you!" Books and their authors converge ominously as both, from Maberg's words, appear to be thrown into the flames together.

The protagonist of each film has vibrant offspring who, like their fathers, model defiance and symbolize the continuity of their parents' values into the next generation. Young Rolf Mamlock, a medical student, is also a committed Communist who joins "the People's Front."[73] He convinces his father that Koch and Pasteur are insufficient as scientific models. Even a pure scientist, he insists, must add Marx and Lenin to the list. Freya, while not the promising medical student on screen that she is in the novel, shows consistent defiance in confrontations with the Nazis and in her own way is the bearer of scientific truth. When Professor Roth's manuscript is confiscated and impounded Freya refuses to leave Germany without it. She is determined to carry her father's work with her and protect his legacy which includes, in addition to the results of his research, a commitment to scientific truth no matter what the cost.

Aside from similarity in content, both films could claim authenticity from the contributions of anti-Nazi émigrés. *Professor Mamlock*, made by Lenfilms, was largely the work of German and Austrian émigrés who had sought refuge in the Soviet Union, having learned of Nazi atrocities at first hand. Frederich Wolf, who wrote the original play on which the film *Professor Mamlock* was based, left Germany for the Soviet Union in 1933, hoping to see the work adapted for the screen there. Wolf himself did contribute to the Soviet production[74] Another émigré, the Austrian Herbert Rapaport, who co-directed the film, had worked with G.W. Pabst from 1928 to 1932 before a stint in Hollywood. He immigrated to the Soviet Union in

1936.[75] Both Wolf and Rapaport were Jewish exiles from their respective homelands.

The same was true of two contributors to *The Mortal Storm*. Like Rapaport, George Froeschel and Hans Rameau had worked in Weimar cinema. They also had direct exposure to the Nazis. Rameau had been a successful scriptwriter who left Germany in 1933. He wrote under the pseudonym of Ellis Anderson to protect relatives who remained in the Third Reich. Froeschel, similarly, came to the United States. from Austria in 1936, a refugee from the harsh antisemitism there. Franklin signed him for MGM in April 1939, anticipating that his expertise would be useful for *The Mortal Storm* (see "We Laughed and We Cried," 289). Since arriving in Hollywood, he had been unemployed and had even been contemplating suicide when Franklin offered him a short-term contract to contribute to the adaptation of Bottome's novel. In August both Rameau and Froeschel were brought in, along with John Goulder, to write scenes set in a concentration camp after Professor Roth is arrested.

They provided material distinctively different from the rest of the film. Their scripts, also found in the Margaret Herrick Library along with West's, contain acts of brutality and torture to which Professor Roth was to be subjected as a prisoner. Almost none of those scenes remained in the final version of the film. The film did, however, in the camp scenes retain the distinctive quality of German Expressionist cinema from the Weimar era. The harsh atmosphere and utter bleakness of the camp, if not the lurid scenes of brutality, remain. The émigrés prevailed at least with their insistence that depiction of the Nazis required the noir world of post-First World War German cinema.[76] Franklin, on the other hand, lost on the issue of dispensing with a camp scene altogether. Over his objections, Professor Roth is made to suffer, but not to the degree the émigré writers had written into their scripts.

MGM's ambivalence about the film, even reluctance to make it by 1940, is written all over the finished product. Professor Roth wears the letter "J" on the sleeve of his prison uniform. The single letter, an abbreviation for Jew or Jude, symbolizes both the studio's reluctance to reveal the obvious, namely Professor Roth's Jewish identity—Professor Roth is labeled "non-Aryan" in the film—as well as the studio's insistence to expurgate the portrayal of what he is subjected to in the camp. As released, the film still contains a bleak German Expressionist core, that is, the concentration camp scenes, which are different in look and content from the scenes that precede and follow them. Wolf and Rapaport had had far more control over accuracy and authenticity in the Soviet film. The quintessential MGM character actor, Frank Morgan as Professor Roth, set the tone of understatement for the American depiction of Nazi Germany.

Bottome herself never mentioned Wolf's play nor the Soviet film made from it in her autobiography or extant correspondence. Written in 1933 and originally titled *Dr. Mamlock's Way Out,* the play had its German language premier in Zurich in 1935.[77] That same year Bottome, as she writes in her autobiography, "began and continued to think out *The Mortal Storm* [...] seeing Adler every day."[78] Then living in Vienna, she could have learned of Wolf's play, acquiring from it at least some of the plot structure of *The Mortal Storm*, what Franklin would have called "the architecture," for her own anti-Nazi work of fiction. The Nuremberg Laws, then much discussed, would also encourage an answer which Bottome provides in the form of the Roth's interfaith marriage. She placed an Adler-like character, as it turned out so similar to Mamlock in Jewish identity and scientific achievement, at the center of the novel. The strong feminist Freya represented the novelist's own views about the place of women in society as well as Adler's belief that women were particularly well suited to medicine. She figured as the heir to her father's, that is, Adler's values in the next generation, just as Rolf Mamlock did in the Soviet version of Wolf's play. Bottome, however, as noted earlier, had ample preparation to write *The Mortal Storm*. Her abolitionist heritage, work in wartime propaganda, and post-First World War fiction all contributed to the novel's composition. Adler alone could serve as the model for Professor Roth without the example of the protagonist of Wolf's play. West, on the other hand, in the opening scene of the cinematic adaptation, arguably drew on the film version of *Professor Mamlock* with its clear historical moment to both initiate and determine the drama to follow.

The hold on the production of "war pictures" in the fall of 1939 gave MGM executives time to reconsider their initial enthusiasm for Bottome's novel. They could also address the resemblance of *The Mortal Storm* to *Professor Mamlock,* which received both MPPDA approval and notoriety among censorship boards around the country. As David Welky has observed, "Hollywood Jews" suffered from "never complete confidence" in opposing the dictatorships.[79] The resemblance of *The Mortal Storm* to a controversial anti-Nazi film from the Soviet Union, employing the word "Jew" and extolling Communist values, could hardly console the studio. With almost perfect timing, the opportunity to expunge portions of West's script arose. Franklin's most valuable collaborator fell seriously ill. By October 1939 West had been hospitalized and was forced to withdraw temporarily from the production or at least diminish her involvement with it.

Claudine West Falls Ill

West apparently succumbed to a serious lung ailment that required both surgery and a lengthy hospital stay. The illness was never named in her correspondence with Franklin, though it was probably cancer. She fell ill again while she was at work on *The White Cliffs of Dover* in 1943. She signed her will on February 24 and left the set on February 27 never to return.[80] She died on April 12.[81] Despite formal suspension of production of *The Mortal Storm*, West insisted on continuing to modify the script even though hospitalized and in considerable discomfort. Franklin failed to convince her "to forget 'The Mortal Storm' and everything else that has to do with work."[82] He reassured her, "There is no panic whatsoever on M.S.—and after you have recovered sufficiently enough to work, we will have our script in plenty of time, as it looks as if Margaret Sullavan is going to play the role [of Freya] and we won't be able to get her for a couple of months."[83] Franklin made no mention of the suspension of "war pictures" as cause for the delay. The moguls apparently regarded the matter as no more than a political ploy on Will Hays's part. They would soon be back in production of such films once the public recovered from the shock of the renewal of war in Europe.

Franklin punctuated his efforts to convince her to rest with a final argument: "I just came down from Eddie Mannix's office, and he corroborates everything I say [about the importance of recovery]."[84] Franklin could not invoke a higher authority, with the exception of Mayer himself. Filled with a sense of mission regarding the film, West ignored the good advice to rest. And at least into early fall, the studio supported her original version of the script which she honed from a hospital bed.

West provided Franklin an example of her capacity for work even under the most adverse circumstances. She told him, "under the influence of hypodermics, I wrote the changes in 'M.S.' to the ski train [scene] [...] If an emergency should arise tell me and I can do all changes in two or three days [...]."[85] She did admit, "there seems no part of my wretched torso that is not involved and if it's not one pain, it's another. And the medicines nauseate."[86]

West imparted a powerful feminist message to the scene on the ski train despite her physical discomfort when she wrote. There emerges in that scene and the one preceding it in the chalet, where the schoolteacher Mr. Werner is set upon by Nazi thugs, the feminist theme that Bottome endowed the novel with and that West carried over into the script. West deftly inserted Freya's feminism—that is, her determined sense of independence in a society that took male dominance for granted. Although no longer the successful medical student of the novel with a profession of her own, on-screen Freya nonetheless stands up to Nazi sexism. In the chalet scene when she defends Martin for his refusal to join the Nazi Party, her fiancé Fritz Maberg injects the woman question into the film, telling her "Keep out of this, Freya. This is no women's business." In the next scene, on the ski train, Fritz and Freya discuss the altercation in the chalet that culminates in the Brown Shirts' beating of Mr. Warner. She had rushed to join Martin in helping the bruised and shaken school teacher. Fritz tells her, "It doesn't become a woman to mix in public affairs [...] women don't know anything about politics." The scene ends with Freya quietly but firmly telling him, "I don't think I shall ever be heart and soul with your convictions."[87]

Despite West's determination and Herculean effort, by December she had to withdraw temporarily from the production to recuperate from a mortal illness at least for a time held at bay.[88] Her absence made it easier for the studio to intervene with a script change that diminished the film's power and distorted Bottome's intention in the first place. "Non-Aryan" had replaced "Jew" in the working script circulated on February 7, 1940, the day that production on *The Mortal Storm* resumed. Bottome learned of the change on that very day and immediately wrote Sidney Franklin, complaining about the substitution and urging him to reinstate the word "Jew."[89] The battle within MGM over which version of *The Mortal Storm* would reach the screen had begun.

Notes

1. *Salt Lake City Desert News* (no date). America Clipping File. 1930s BL Add. Mss. 88921/5/7.
2. Kenneth Davis, *FDR, Into the Storm*, 387–8.
3. See for example Bottome's contract for the sale of rights to *Private Worlds* to Paramount in BL Mss. 78861 for the relinquishment of her authorial rights to a Hollywood studio.
4. Michael E. Birdwell, *Celluloid Soldiers. The Warner Bros. Campaign against Nazism* (New York and London: New York University Press, 1999), 78.
5. Todd Bennett, *One World, Big Screen*, 40.
6. Scott Eyman, *Lion of Hollywood*, 239.
7. Jeanine Basinger and Sam Wasson, *Hollywood. The Oral History* (New York: HarperCollins Publishers, 2022), 186.
8. Ibid., 296.
9. Ibid., 304.
10. Ibid.
11. Conversation between the author and Tory Franklin-Dillon, great niece of Sidney Franklin.
12. Scott Eyman, *Lion of Hollywood*, 245.
13. Ibid., 245.
14. Screenwriter Millard Kaufman to Scott Eyman, cited in *Lion of Hollywood*, 130–1.
15. See Larry Ceplair and Steven England, *The Inquisition in Hollywood. Politics in the Film Community*, 1930–1960 (Berkeley: University of California Press, 1983), 47–82 (quotation, p. 51).

16 SAF, Box 24, Greer Garson to West's stepbrother Mervyn Lambert, January 8, 1950.
17 "Claudine West," *The Times*, April 13, 1943. It should be noted that the entry was more than an obituary. It was a front-page story in Britain's premier daily newspaper. West enjoyed fame in Britain for her contribution to the script of *Mrs. Miniver* as well as other films depicting the country in wartime.
18 Franklin insisted to his biographer Kevin Brownlow that despite several claimants such as the playwright R. C. Sherrif, West alone was responsible for the script. Email to the author of August 8, 2014, from Kevin Brownlow.
19 SAF, Box 24, Mrs. Lambert to Sidney Franklin, September 24, 1943.
20 See for example U.S. Jewish Welfare Board. War correspondence–Claudine West, National Jewish Welfare Board, Army-Navy Division Records, 1–180. American-Jewish Historical Society, New York. Ancestry.com Operations, Inc. 2012.
21 Sidney Franklin to Mrs. Lambert; July 15, 1943, SAF, Box 23.
22 See "Last Will and Testament of Claudine West," Probated January 8, 1945, in Superior Court, County of Los Angeles, State of California.
23 West came to the United States in 1920 with the name Ivy Godber. She subsequently took the name West as her married name, becoming Mrs. West, but an official record of the marriage in the United States has not come to light in the places that she would most likely have married, the state of California for example or New York to which she frequently traveled to catch the latest plays. There is no record of her marriage in New Jersey. She had close friends in Princeton with whom she stayed on those trips East.
24 Salka Viertel, *The Kindness of Strangers* (New York: Holt, Rinehart, & Winston, 1969), 183.
25 Claudine West to Sidney Franklin; June 3, 1938, SAF Box 19, Sack 17; see footnote 31, below.
26 Sidney Franklin to Claudine West; June 2, 1938, SAF Box 19, Sack 17.
27 See West's Letter to Franklin June 1, 1938, in SAF, Box 19, Sack 17.
28 PB to Professor Steven Potter, March 9, 1939. BL Add. Mss. 88921/2/2.
29 Ibid.
30 Sidney Franklin told his biographer Kevin Brownlow of West's contribution, "She did the writing, and I was good on construction. […] We did the script of *Goodbye Mr. Chips* in eleven weeks. She did *Random* [*Harvest*] and *Mrs. Miniver* with me-we had others too." Kevin Brownlow to author, August 16, 2014. Cf. Mark Harris's account of the writing of *Mrs. Miniver* in *Five Came Back. A Story of Hollywood and the Second World War* (New York: The Penguin Press, 2014), 120, 122.
31 West's obituary in *The Times* stated that "During World War I, she was a code expert with the British Admiralty." "Claudine West," April 13, 1943, 1.
32 For an account of the skills required of codebreakers at the British Admiralty in the First World War, see National Archives (NA) (London). Code and Cypher Personnel Report. No date. HW3/35. W524.

33 Penelope Fitzgerald, *The Knox Brothers* (London: Counterpoint, 1977), 134.
34 Bottome joined Buchan in what was at first known as the Department of Information. By 1917, Lloyd George elevated the department to the level of Ministry, because of what came to be perceived as its growing significance.
35 On the use of the visual for effective propaganda, see Susan Tweedsmuir, *John Buchan by His Wife and Friends* (London: Hodder & Stoughton, Ltd.,1947), 82 and 87.
36 *John Buchan by His Wife and Friends*, 82. Buchan's wife observed that those in her husband's circle all embraced that patriotic view of propaganda.
37 Churchill's memorandum on codebreaking, "in order to know the enemy," is cited in W. F. Clarke, unpublished memoir, 1951. NA (London) HW3/3W524. That memorandum led to the establishment of Britain's codebreaking operation of the First World War in the Admiralty's Room 40 where Dilthy Knox played a major role.
38 Clarke, unpublished memoir, discusses Churchill's motivations in establishing the operation in Room 40.
39 The account that follows of the April 14, 1939, discussions held at the MGM studios is taken from the memorandum of the studio note-taker to be found in SAF, Box 23. It is not a verbatim transcription but a summary with occasional direct quotations. All references, citations, and quotations of that discussion are from that memorandum.
40 On Mayer's ambivalence regarding his Jewish identity, see Neal Gabler, *An Empire of Their Own*, 147–50, 167–9, 283–5, and Scott Eyman, *Lion of Hollywood*, 342–3.
41 Sidney Franklin, unpublished autobiography, "We Laughed and We Cried," 286.
42 Email to the author from Kevin Brownlow, August 16, 2014, confirming that West was the primary author of the script of *Mrs. Miniver* according to Sidney Franklin.
43 Franklin, "We Laughed and We Cried," 286.
44 Phyllis Lassner and Alexis Pogorelskin, "An Anti-Nazi Special Relationship: British Writing, Hollywood Filmmaking, and *The Mortal Storm* (1940)," in Nathan Abrams (ed.), *Hidden in Plain Sight. Jews and Jewishness in British film, Television, and Popular Culture* (Evanston: Northwestern University Press, 2016), 63.
45 PB to Duff Cooper, February 4, 1940. BL Add. Mss. 88921/3/3.
46 *The Goal*, 163.
47 Obituary for Claudine West, "Born in Nottingham," *The Nottingham Evening Post*, April 13, 1943, 3.
48 The extensive exchange of communications regarding shooting ski scenes in mountain terrain in the United States can be found in SAF, Box 16.
49 *The Secret Diary of Harold L. Ickes*, vol. II. Harold L. Ickes, *The Inside Struggle, 1936–1939* (New York: Simon & Schuster, 1954), 490, entry for October 22, 1938.

50 Ibid. See entries for April 1939, vol. II, for more on the upheavals in the administration as FDR prepared to run for a third term and sought to diminish the status of potential rivals, one of whom was Ickes. See especially entries for April 23, 1939, and April 29, 1939, 618–25.

51 Ickes, *Diary*, II, March 5, 1939, 585. Ickes purged the Park Service right after he lost responsibility for government buildings in the capital. Such a responsibility had allowed him to provide the Lincoln Memorial for Marian Anderson's famous concert in April 1939. Ickes had won plaudits for that decision. FDR had summarily removed Ickes's control over such venues and the opportunity to use them for his own ends in future.

52 Sidney Franklin to William A. Orr, June 9, 1939, SAF, Box 16.

53 Franklin to William A. Orr, June 9, 1939, SAF, Box 16.

54 William A. Orr to Sidney Franklin, June 20, 1939, SAF, Box 16. By the summer of 1940, Ickes had become far more supportive of war-themed films, showing them in the evening at his Maryland retreat. See the unpublished version of his diary for August 1940 in the Manuscript Division of the Library of Congress.

55 Memo from Sidney Franklin to Chas J. Chic at MGM. Subject: Mortal Storm, June 15, 1939. "Confirming telephone conversation between Mrs. West and yourself," SAF, Box 16.

56 The account that follows of shooting scenes for *The Mortal Storm* in Switzerland is confirmed by correspondence in Franklin's papers: SAF, Box 16. According to Hervé Dumont, Frank Borzage's biographer (Borzage took over the production from Franklin in early March 1940), "the ski runs and sequences at Karwendel Pass" were "filmed [...] in Sun Valley, ID [...] and above Salt Lake City, UT. Olympic champions John Litchfield and Beth Crookes doubled for Stewart and Sullavan. Jack Arnold from the special effects department designed a vehicle on three sliders that allowed them to follow the skiers very rapidly without the camera shaking." See *Frank Borzage. The Life and Times of a Hollywood Romantic* (London: McFarland & Co., Inc, Publishers, 2006), 287–8. If Dumont is correct, Borzage duplicated the filming that Franklin oversaw in Switzerland in July 1939, thereby putting his stamp on the film to claim full credit for the production. Or, possibly, Dumont acquired a garbled version of the making of the film. It seems unlikely that MGM would duplicate the considerable expenses of the year before to re-film snow scenes near Sun Valley and Salt Lake unless Borzage insisted on it. Dumont's account replicates the version to be found in Franklin's memos and correspondence for the summer of 1939 down to the use of Olympic skiers and a way to keep the camera steady while shooting on snow.

57 Eric Locke to L. B. Mayer at MGM, June 15, 1939, SAF, Box 16.

58 See correspondence with Franklin regarding that trip. She promised to hurry back and "mitigate my murderous pace across Europe," if he were to direct *Good-bye Mr. Chips* which West was urging him to do. "Good-bye, good-bye, good-bye Mr. Chips," she told him in a farewell telegram, one last time urging him to produce Hilton's bestseller. Claudine West to Sidney Franklin, June 1, 1938, SAF, Box 19, Sack 17.

59 Sidney Franklin to L. B. Mayer and Chas. J. Chic, June 15, 1939, SAF, Box 16.
60 Ibid.
61 Ibid., June 25, 1939.
62 Sidney Franklin to Wm. A. Orr, June 30, 1939, SAF, Box 16.
63 Chas J. Chic to Sidney Franklin, July I, 1939, SAF, Box 16.
64 For MGM's approach to salaries, see financial spread sheets in SAF, Box 5.
65 Sidney Franklin to Claudine West, September 22, 1939, SAF, Box 19.
66 See Doherty's account of the film's unprecedented popularity for a Soviet import in *Hollywood and Hitler*, 193.
67 Jeremy Hicks, *First Films of the Holocaust. Soviet Cinema and the Genocide of the Jews, 1938–1946* (Pittsburgh: Pittsburgh University Press, 2012), 18.
68 Ibid.
69 Frank S. Nugent, "Russia Grasps a Nettle," *New York Times*, November 13, 1938, 26. All quotations in this paragraph are from this article.
70 Doherty, *Hollywood and Hitler*, 193.
71 Annette Insdorf, *Indelible Shadows. Films and the Holocaust* (3rd edition) (Cambridge: Cambridge University Press, 2003), 155.
72 Ibid.
73 Ibid.
74 Hicks, *First Films of the Holocaust*, 25.
75 See Olga Gershenson, *The Phantom Holocaust. Jewish Cinema and Jewish Catastrophe* (New Brunswick: Rutgers University Press, 2013), 14 and 18; Jeremy Hicks, 23–4 for Rapaport's career. Note: Gershensohn, who seems to have done the most work on Rapaport, uses the spelling that I have adopted. Hicks and Doherty spell the name Rappaport.
76 On this point see Anton Kaes, *Shell Shock Cinema. Weimar Culture and the Wounds of War* (Princeton: Princeton University Press, 2009).
77 Insdorf, *Indelible Shadows*, 155.
78 *The Goal*, 250.
79 Welky, *The Moguls and the Dictators*, 2.
80 "Last Will and Testament of Claudine West," Superior Court, County of Los Angeles, State of California, Probated January 8, 1945.
81 "Claudine West," *The Times*, April 13, 1943, 1 and "Claudine West," *Los Angeles Times*, April 12, 1943, 16.
82 Sidney Franklin to Claudine West, October 4, 1939, SAF, Box 19.
83 Ibid.
84 Ibid.
85 Claudine West to Sidney Franklin from the California Hospital, November 9, 1939, SAF, Box 19.

86 Ibid.
87 Copyright Script for *The Mortal Storm*, submitted June 25, 1940, Moving Image Research Center, U.S. Library of Congress, reel 2, p. 16.
88 The last full script West submitted before shooting began, based on her original version completed in July, included the concentration camp scenes contributed by émigré writers and is dated December 11, 1939.
89 MGM Collection (USC Cinematic Arts Library), "The Mortal Storm," Folder 2 (Box128). Bottome to Franklin, February 7, 1940. I am grateful to Edward Comstock, Senior Librarian of the collection for a copy of the letter.

5

In Production, 1940

Which *Mortal Storm*?

As originally conceived in 1939, *The Mortal Storm* could be seen as Hollywood's, certainly MGM's, declaration of war on Nazi Germany. After a decade of almost no Jews on screen, the most prominent studio in Hollywood prepared to show Jewish characters standing up to the Nazis. West had produced a manuscript unlike any other she had written for Franklin, nor would she ever write another like it again.

The politics of the Jewish question in contemporary Germany framed the story. West made the plight of the Jews clear from the very beginning. At the celebration for Professor Roth's sixtieth birthday where family and friends learn of Hitler's appointment as Chancellor, Mrs. Roth asks in alarm, "And what of his antisemitic propaganda? Hasn't he threatened to kill all the Jews?"[1] With a single line, West warned that Europe's Jews faced annihilation. Had the line remained, *The Mortal Storm* would have called on the country to respond to the threat of mass murder that confronted the Jewish communities of Europe.

But the head of MGM began to hesitate over his rashness in rushing into production with such a potentially controversial work. The studios had arguably sent *Professor Mamlock* into distribution, blessing it with the PCA seal of approval to test the public's response to the image of persecuted Jews on screen. The result had been mixed. The film did well at the box office for a Soviet import, but censorship boards across the country banned it, in Chicago, *horrible dictum*, conflating Jews with Communism. The solution for Mayer was to make *The Mortal Storm Judenrein*, that is remove the word "Jew," if not the Jews themselves from the film, just as he, had helped to make Hollywood productions free of Jews on screen for a decade. Director Sidney Lumet, who got his start in Yiddish theater, summed up how successful earlier efforts to expunge the Jews from the screen had been.

"I know this sounds crazy, but I don't remember hearing the word 'Jew' in any movie before *The Great Dictator* [1940], American movie."[2]

Ambivalence regarding the "Jewish" decision weighed heavily on Mayer in 1940. Europe's Jews were at risk but would overt support for them provoke a backlash and even jeopardize the security of American Jews? The debate on this issue roiled the American-Jewish community.[3] In the end, the head of MGM opted for caution. According to Scott Eyman, "From Mayer's point of view, Nazism was a legalized pogrom, and he had no desire to inadvertently foment one in America. Caution was the watchword."[4]

Caution, however, had become more difficult in the second half of the 1930s. Mayer and other moguls had watched the rise of political pressure groups among studio employees that agitated for Hollywood to oppose the Nazis openly.[5] No less than Irving Thalberg and Jack Warner had joined the largest and most vocal of those groups, the Hollywood Anti-Nazi League (HANL), founded in 1936.[6] They did so, Mayer could imagine, more for show than out of conviction, because they were the same studio heads who had worked with the Los Angeles Jewish Community Committee (LAJCC) and its Motion Picture Committee behind the scenes to keep Jewish characters and issues off the screen in the 1930s.[7] Now Mayer himself, with the production of *The Mortal Storm*, could open the door to the Jewish question far wider than Jack and Harry Warner had dared with *The Life of Emile Zola* three years earlier with its fleeting reference to the Dreyfus case.

The head of MGM had nearly a year to ponder treatment of Bottome's novel. Even before the studio's purchase of it, his trusted synopsis writer Helen Corbaley, known at MGM as his "Scheherazade," had offered him an elided warning to accompany her praise of the novel.[8] "If a picture is made on this controversial subject, the book is recommended for aside from the politics involved, it is a great story."[9] "A great story" was one thing, but controversy and politics, he believed, had no place in the movies, least of all his own. Yet how to make *The Mortal Storm* without them?

Mayer's ambivalence could be seen in his attitude to one scene in particular. What Claudine West called the "father-son scene," and Mayer's assistant Al Block called more pointedly the "Jewish scene." It was significantly abbreviated in the first week of shooting (early February 1940), then quickly reinstated in its expanded form, possibly because of protest on the set.[10]

Helen Corbaley had anticipated trouble over the scene, for the most part taken directly from the novel. Recognizing its significance, she provided Mayer with a detailed synopsis of that very scene. She characterized it as "dramatic-passionate." Finally, she utilized her most powerful argument to calm Mayer's predictable anxieties. Corbaley informed her boss, the scene was "very MGM."

To no avail. Mayer still agonized over it. His inability to come to a final decision on whether to include it or not forced the production scheduled to be completed on March 24, to drag into April, then May, even though the "father-son" or "Jewish scene" had been budgeted for one day of shooting.[11] The MGM still of Prof. Roth's study (unavailable for reproduction) taken on May 14 shows that the set was exactly as it was on the first day of shooting, revealing that the "father-son" scene remained under consideration to the very end of production.

The script was continually modified, and retakes made in that three-and-a-half-month period to placate Mayer's deep uncertainty about allowing a discussion of Jewish identity in *The Mortal Storm*. Another measure of Mayer's ambivalence, if not that of the whole front office, is the very condition of the stills, showing the set of Professor's Roth's study. To this day they stand out among the hundreds of photos taken at the time of production. They are worn, torn, and bent as though the photographic paper had been held up to the wind. Clearly the photos had been passed back and forth among several hands, as Mayer and his cohort debated whether to retain the "father-son scene" or not.

Confusion among the Censors

Mayer was not alone in uncertainty about what the screen could accommodate as 1939 turned to 1940. Joseph I. Breen, the powerful head of the PCA, for example, had his own concerns. What were the limits of censorship if the Nazis launched all-out war in the spring of 1940? Between them, Breen and Mayer held the fate of *The Mortal Storm* in their hands. The film could not be released and go into distribution without the seal of approval of Breen's censorship board: the PCA. And Mayer himself was uncertain as to just what film he would make.

Like Mayer, Breen had reached a turning point with the resumption of the production of war pictures at the end of 1939. In Mayer's case he could simply accept the script in hand and produce an anti-Nazi film that addressed the Jewish question with integrity. Or, he could tamper with what he already had in the way of a shooting script, provided by Franklin's production team, that is, Claudine West. Breen had at least two options as well. He could return to the Production Code's ban on speaking ill of other countries. Or, he could continue a policy initiated in the spring of 1939, permitting political engagement in Hollywood productions.

Breen had wavered over censorship policy for months. He confided in his opposite number in Britain, J. Brooke-Wilkinson, Secretary of the British Board of Censors, that "the general situation throughout the nation is quite confusing. There is an unsettled feeling in the air everywhere and this has had its effect on our industry here in Hollywood."[12] The situation did not improve by the fall of 1939 when the making of war pictures was suspended during what was dubbed the "phony war," that is, the months without fighting before Hitler launched the blitzkrieg in April 1940.

Breen's uncertainty regarding the film industry as a whole mirrored his evolution concerning another issue crucial to *The Mortal Storm*. The head of the PCA had undergone a sea change only a few years earlier on the Jewish question. At the beginning of the 1930s, his letters had been peppered with antisemitic outbursts against the Jewish studio heads.[13] After 1934, he became an outspoken opponent of antisemitism.[14] By the end of the decade, although he had not joined HANL, he could be seen attending events that the anti-Nazi organization sponsored. With *The Mortal Storm* about to go into production, Breen appeared to have resolved his political uncertainties regarding both Jews and Nazis. He determined to resume the liberal policy of the spring and summer of 1939. MGM could complete the adaptation of Bottome's novel, and other studios continue with production on temporarily suspended war pictures.

Breen's newfound certainty was never clearer than in his response to Mayer's submission of the first full shooting script for *The Mortal Storm* dated December 11, 1939. Largely West's original script of July, it also contained graphic scenes written by the émigré writers Ellis Anderson (Hans Rameau) and George Froeschel, who in August had deepened its anti-Nazi message with vivid details of Professor Roth's mistreatment in a concentration camp based on their first-hand knowledge of life under the Nazis. That last script of 1939 contained the full father-son scene with the word "Jew" used amply throughout. Breen informed the head of MGM: "We have read the temporary complete script dated December 11, 1939 for your proposed picture THE MORTAL STORM and are happy to report that it meets the basic requirements of the Production Code."[15] Breen had resolved what had months earlier been "confusing" and "unsettled," as he told J. Brooke-Wilkinson, and resulted in the suspension of "war pictures." He now permitted the most radical of anti-Nazi films to go forward. The question remained, would Mayer?

Dismantling the "Father-Son" Scene: The Fate of Jewish Identity in *The Mortal Storm*

Mayer's uncertainty over how to adapt Bottome's novel to the screen could be seen most starkly in the struggle over whether to employ the word "Jew" or not. One alternative to "Jew," that is, the term "non-Aryan," was readily at hand, straight from the Nuremberg Laws, which lent authenticity, it could be argued, in the Nazi context. But for a general audience, the term could serve another purpose, obfuscating the "religious difference" among the characters.[16] The "Jewish question" which so unnerved Mayer could be submerged for an American audience in the use of the unfamiliar "non-Aryan."

"Non-Aryan" in fact figured in all the scripts, starting with West's first draft of July 1939. A distinction in meaning, however, existed between "non-Aryan" and "Jew" in the versions of the script of that year developed before shooting began. In the 1939 scripts, the term "non-Aryan" is spoken with irony, even disdain, by those who do not sympathize with the new regime and regard the word as a shibboleth to distinguish between those who support the Nazis and those who do not. Nazis, on the other hand, employ "non-Aryan," without irony, as though it were the proper designation for a group held in contempt. "Jew" is uttered disdainfully, if they use the term at all.

In the ski train scene, for example, following the beating of Mr. Werner, Fritz and Freya argue over what has just transpired. Fritz is angry because Freya had joined their longtime friend Martin Breitner in rushing to aid the victim. He tells her:

It doesn't become women to mix in public affairs, if I may say so.
Freya, it's particularly unwise for you.
"Why," she asks.
Well, because of your father, for one thing.

She looks spitefully at him. "My father. Oh, you mean he's non-Aryan."[17] In using the term, Freya expresses contempt for Fritz rather than confirming the questionable status of her father.

The exchange between Fritz and Freya remained in the final shooting script but because by then the word "Jew" had been excised from the script, "non-Aryan" no longer possessed the irony nor the contempt it had carried earlier when spoken by an opponent of the regime like Freya. Margaret Sullavan, as Freya, however, manages to invest the term with a measure of both.

Similarly, in the 1939 scripts, Freya's older half-brother Otto (Olaf in the novel) shows his Nazi correctness in his use of the term. He explains to their mother why he and his brother Erich (Emil in the novel) wear their brown shirt uniforms at home. "We have to face facts. You know very well how wild feeling runs nowadays against all non-Aryans!"[18] Otto, like Fritz, refers to the Jewish identity of Professor Roth. If the brothers are to reside in their stepfather's household, they feel compelled to display their Nazi allegiance in their clothing and in their terminology, making the Jewish scientist an object of scorn.

In West's 1939 scripts, the father-son scene is juxtaposed to such exchanges where the politically correct use of "non-Aryan" among Nazis has replaced the word "Jew." In contrast, the scene in which Professor Roth tells Rudi to take pride in being a Jew requires that very word. The boy could hardly take pride and show defiance in being non-Aryan, even if the hyphenated word did not connote diminished status. What Mayer's assistant had dubbed "the Jewish scene," indeed required the word "Jew." Much was at stake in the film's terminology. Were the Jews in the film to be an independent, self-identified people, justly proud of their heritage and contributions or instead bear an inherently negative label, artificial, in which they could take no pride, one with legal consequences, disdainfully imposed by a hostile regime. In effect, would the film mirror the larger reality of Nazi Germany, or not?

West modified the father-son scene in the novel where Rudi asks, "What is being a Jew" (*TMS* 1938, 72) to show how vulnerable the Jews in Germany had become. She added a new dramatic purpose to Rudi's discussion with his father, beyond the question of Jewish identity. Freya has just broken her engagement to Fritz when Rudi rushes in, interrupting their painful silence. He hands his sister a questionnaire. Emblazoned at the top are the words "Proof of Aryan Descent." His school requires his parents to complete and return it the next day. Freya glances at it, then glares at Fritz. "I think this is something Father should see. I'll go with you," she says to Rudi.[19] If not fully Aryan, the questionnaire demands that the family provide "percentage of Jewish blood" the boy possesses. Rudi explains to his father, "We had a new teacher-who told us all about Jews-about having Nordic blood."[20] Such questionnaires as the one Rudi presents to his father were required by the new race laws of 1935. Bottome did not directly mention the Nuremberg Laws in the novel. West, in contrast, with the school questionnaire, brought the race laws into the script, perhaps under the influence of the émigré writers Rameau and Froeschel.

Professor Roth defies the new legal system. The measure of Jewish identity, he explains to his son, lies not in blood, but in achievement. In West's script he has an additional charge. He must reconcile Rudi to an identity he did not know he possessed. The boy had believed that the family was Catholic, like his mother. The professor tells Rudi, "I'm proud to belong to the race that has given Europe its religion; its moral law; and much of its science-perhaps even more of its genius-in art, literature and music."

West then added prominent examples to Bottome's list of achievements. "Mendelson was a Jew, and Rubenstein-the great English statesman Disraeli was a Jew and so was our poet Heine who wrote Lorelei."[21] West changed the names of renowned Jews with each resubmission of the script as though a new combination of great men might be acceptable to the studio. Every change required consideration by the MGM front office and then Breen's PCA. The delays, one can surmise, bought more time to argue for the scene's place in the film.

West also altered Rudi's response to the discovery of his Jewish identity which comes with harassment, even stoning by his schoolmates. In West's original script, that of July 18, 1939, the boy says to his father with the news of his real identity, "I won't be a Jew-I won't-I won't." This response had evolved by the spring of 1940 to become Rudi's expression of pride to be what his father is.[22] In West's initial scripts, Rudi's rejection of his Jewish identity prompted Professor Roth to extol it. Rudi's immediate acceptance of it in the later scripts diminishes Professor Roth's need to defend it. Less had become more regarding Jewish identity by 1940.

The studio nonetheless rejected every version of the father-son scene that West submitted that spring. She provided as many as ten, attempting to find a formula of Jewish achievement that the studio's front office would accept. The modifications stand out on the page. They are always in West's precise, codebreaker's penciled handwriting. By May 9 the original scene, which in West's initial draft of July 1939 had come to eight pages, consisted of no more than Rudi's query, "I'm not Jewish, am I, Father?" Gone are the boy's accounts of being bullied at school or Professor Roth's paean to Jewish achievement. Instead, only the book burning earlier in the film remains to turn Jewish achievement upside down, using Jews as examples of decadence and corruption, giving the Nazis the last word on Jewish contributions to Western culture. Fritz Maberg tosses Heine's poetry into the flames for its "poisonous sentimentality," along with Einstein's "false and pretentious theory."

On May 13 what little remained of the conversation between Rudi and his father was dropped entirely.[23] The excision required "two sets of retakes [on] May 11th and 13th."[24] It had taken ten months, from July 1939 to May 1940, to determine the fate of the father-son scene where "Rudi and the Professor discuss [the] Jewish situation."[25] Franklin had been optimistic to budget one day of shooting for it.

According to Gene Reynolds, who played Rudi, the controversy over the father-son scene caused confusion on the set. He never knew from one day to the next in what form Frank Borzage, the director, would be required to shoot it, that is, whether he as Rudi would be a Jew or non-Aryan, pleased or angry at the discovery. Reynolds was disgusted with the decision to drop the scene altogether.[26]

Adding to the frustration, the studio had appeared to remain committed to the scene if the right formula could be found to satisfy the underlying anxieties of the front office. For example, by late February with the scene reinstated a major change in casting had occurred. The little-known Miss Anderson (first name never mentioned), whose hair it seemed was not right for the part, originally played the role of Mrs. Roth and a boy of eight named Scotty Beckett played Rudi.[27] Stills show much of the film shot with them in February.[28] Abruptly, at the end of that month, Irene Rich and Gene Reynolds replaced them. Rich, well-known from radio, not only possessed an arresting, emotionally laden voice, in appearance she presented an aristocratic, almost regal quality. She received a four-week contract with a starting date of February 24, 1940.[29]

The potential impact of the scene should not be underestimated. The wise and courtly Frank Morgan would have not only broken the decade's long barrier (at least at MGM) to the depiction of Jews on screen. But West's scene went even further. Jewish contributions and achievements, Professor Roth explains, were foundational to Western civilization. With that scene, Hollywood would have defined the place of Jews in European and by extension American culture. The message transcended the limits of the screen, merging with the political context of 1940. To use Frank Nugent's phrase, MGM could not have "grasped the nettle of the social film" more tightly had it retained the word "Jew" in *The Mortal Storm*.[30] Gene Reynolds also provided a new tone and character to the film. Certainly no child, he possessed the voice of a sixteen-year-old breaking into manhood. He stood nearly as tall as Professor Roth and could look him in the eye.

In the "father-son" scene, before the casting change, Professor Roth took Beckett's chin and gave it a reassuring, affectionate squeeze, saying appropriately, "Chin-up, son," after the boy reveals the racial questionnaire and the bullying at school that accompanied it. With Gene Reynolds in the part, the scene acquires a newfound seriousness. Rudi is undergoing a painful rite of passage into manhood. Professor Roth talks man to man with his son. He neither blunts nor obfuscates the situation. The change in casting therefore had its greatest impact with the "father-son" scene.

The change in casting raised another issue. The very actors who would have played the scene brought another dimension of meaning to it. Frank Morgan (Francis Wupperman) and Gene Reynolds (Blumenthal) were the Jewish members of the cast. They would therefore have been conducting a discussion of their own heritage. Some would see them endowing the scene with authenticity. On the other hand, those hostile to the film would have another reason to condemn its message. Jews used the screen for their own ends, went the charge. Mayer wavered, but in the end decided that controversy was not "very MGM," to use Helen Corbaley's phrase, after all. The scene had to go. For *The Mortal Storm*, dropping the father-son scene with the word "Jew" at its core meant a profound change for the film. Other excisions had to follow. Amélie Roth would no longer ask desperately, "Doesn't [Hitler] mean to kill all the Jews." Instead, she inquires with a measure of anxiety, "What about those who think differently, freely [...] those who are non-Aryan?"[31]

The Mortal Storm Judenrein

With the decision to remove the father-son scene, Mayer had decided the film would no longer present Jewish identity in terms of creativity or unique contributions to civilization. Still more had to go. The contrasting scenes in which the Nazis turned Jews into victims went as well. It was pointless to engender pity for "non-Aryan" victims with whom the audience would not identify with anyway.

Over the course of the first months of 1940, Al Block, Mayer's personal assistant, communicated the ongoing script changes to Joseph Breen for his approval. Breen, like those working on the production, therefore watched the film whittled away on an almost daily basis in early 1940. Scenes that contained the word "Jew" were cut or shortened to eliminate the word. For example, almost all of Martin's courtship of Freya after she breaks her engagement with Fritz was eliminated. Professor Roth's confrontation with Nazi students would have been harsher had the bullying of Jewish students in the classroom been retained. The concentration camp scenes that remain mitigate the brutality and humiliation to which the professor in previous scripts was subjected. Roth and other prisoners were to wear yellow arm bands with the word JUDE on them. As filmed, Professor Roth alone is shown as a prisoner in the camp. He wears a white band with the letter "J," a mere remnant of the full word in the scripts of 1939.

MGM submitted a final pre-shooting script to Breen on January 19, 1940. Almost as soon as the script received PCA approval, Mayer hesitated and began to demand changes. West went to work. On January 30, she presented a rewrite of Mrs. Roth's lines, "But what of [Hitler's] antisemitic propaganda? Didn't he intend to destroy all the Jews?" a line that went back to the original script. She modified it to read, "And of his antisemitic program-Jewish people have no reason to rejoice in his rise to power."[32]

More drastic modifications were impending. Dave Friedman, the film's Unit Chief, told Franklin in passing on February 2 that he had just "received [a] new script [of TMS] and will work on it tomorrow."[33] Friedman did not yet realize how seriously the "new script" would change the film. Most of his first memo to Franklin dealt with costume changes and music choices. Friedman soon discovered the father-son scene had been cut from eight to two pages. The word "Jew" remained, but the scene had lost its former dramatic power. While the full "father-son" scene reappeared a week later to hang on in one form or another until May, other scenes with the word "Jew" were soon cut or "non-Aryan" substituted if the scene were retained.[34]

In her original version, West, as noted, devoted several scenes to Martin's courtship of Freya. Those scenes too became victims of Mayer's heavy hand because the Jewish question had figured in them. For example, in one of them, Martin and Freya attend a performance of Offenbach's *Tales of Hoffman* that is summarily interrupted. An official approaches the podium, stops the conductor, then whispers to him. The conductor turns and informs the audience,

"By order of the Government, I must interrupt this rendition-It is no longer permissible to present the work of any Jewish composer!" Black uniformed SS men appear and glare at [...] the audience [...] which subsides into submission—no one dare utter a sound.³⁵

Professor Roth's confrontation with Nazi students remained but was cut considerably to excise the word "Jew." The scientist has just explained that races do not differ by blood. The SA leader Holl suddenly stands up in protest, demanding that "all those loyal to our leader walk out!" He adds ominously, "Those who remain in the class do so at their own peril!" Holl's interruption remained but the following was cut:

> As the students leave, one of the Brown shirts puts out his hand-'Not you Jew! We have no use for your kind!' He thrusts him backward—some four others hesitate, knowing the remark refers to them also-they sit down again, cowering as a group.

Substituting the word "non-Aryan" in those scenes carried its own perils. Mayer and his circle sought to confuse audiences with the term.³⁶ Overuse of the term might bring comprehension, even annoyance at its awkwardness.

The concentration camp scenes supplied by émigré writers proved especially vulnerable. The studio had begun expurgating them even in 1939 almost as soon as they were written, foreshadowing the larger excisions to come. What remained nonetheless evoked the merciless and grinding abuse of a totalitarian state. The first script to which the émigré writers contributed bore the date August 7, 1939. It expands West's original script, completed in the preceding month, with lurid scenes of brutality directed at Professor Roth. In one, the professor's stepson Erich accompanies an SA brigade leader to a camp. The brigade leader walks slowly, glaring at a group of prisoners: "old men with Jewish faces, cultivated and pale; they have a special yellow arm band with the inscription JUDE. The men bear looks of crushing despair and exhaustion."³⁷ Erich sees that one of the men pushing a lorry loaded with sand and stone up from a deep pit is his stepfather. "His face has lost none of its dignity [or] intellectual distinction." Erich rushes to save him from being crushed as the wagon nearly rolls back on him. He is thoroughly reprimanded for intervening. In an alternative version of the same scene, Erich approaches a row of prisoners chained to a wall. One turns. He sees to his shock that it is his stepfather.

Amélie Roth too is subjected to humiliation in a scene that effectively juxtaposes "Jew" to "non-Aryan," making clear the distinction. Upon entering the camp to visit her husband, she is harassed by the first official she encounters (script of 8/7/1939).

> The guard asks her,
> Amélie Roth-wife of the Jew Ludwig [sic] Roth?

- Are you Aryan?
- Yes. I am Aryan.
- ... And married to a Jew-Shame on you!
- She overhears that the "Jew Ludwig Roth" has been consigned to "the dark cell" for being "too high-headed." One guard assures another, "we'll humiliate him."

The studio also removed another theme that the émigré writers had attempted to impart to the script, namely the Nazi intent to conquer the world. The conquest of lebensraum or living space was a companion idea to the Nazis' murderous antisemitism. Only global conquest would make possible the annihilation of all Jews and therefore a world that was *Judenrein*, the ultimate Nazi goal. When Fritz Maberg refuses to lead the patrol that is sent out to arrest Freya and Martin before they can cross the Austrian border, he admits he cannot hunt down his dearest friends. He is told, "It is our goal to conquer the world ... a true Nazi [has no] place for sentimentalities."[38] The reference to world conquest remained until the script of February 2, 1940, when it was removed; unlike the "father-son" scene, it was never reinstated.

The original final scene of the film was cut too. It was to have shown storm troopers marching past the now abandoned Roth home singing, "For the world will be ours tomorrow-as Germany is today!" In 1940, references to German world conquest called out for intervention, implying that the United States had no choice but to involve itself in the European conflict, a notion still highly controversial in American political life.

But the dangerous idea that the Nazis intended world conquest was not lost from the script entirely. It remained, almost slipped in, referred to in the last verse of one of several songs in the film, which is sung in the ski chalet scene, notable for the beating of the schoolteacher Mr. Werner. The storm troopers on the order of SA brigade leader Holl join in singing the *Horst Wessel* song, the unofficial Nazi anthem originating in the Nazi-Communist brawls of the late 1920s in which a particularly brutal SA member, Horst Wessel, was killed. The song honored his memory. In the original scripts, Holl shouts over the noise of the inn,

> "German men and women ... it is our grateful duty to pay homage to our beloved leader ... let us sing our new National Anthem: the *Horst Wessel* song!! ... I don't doubt that every good German will join in this song with enthusiasm!"
> [They sing]
> Close up the ranks! Raise high our honor'd banner! The Storm Troopers march with

Calm and Steady Pace! Our comrades shot by Red-Front and Reaction, amid our ranks in spirit keep their place! (scripts of 7/18 [West's original] and 8/7/1939 [script with émigré contributions]).

Although Breen had approved use of the *Horst Wessel* song, which had served as the Nazi Party anthem before Hitler came to power, in the scripts of 12/11/1939 and 1/19/1940, Mayer excised it. He insisted that the studio Music Department write a new song. Block, Mayer's assistant, duly submitted the new lyrics to Breen on 2/20/1940; Breen approved them, sending word of that to Mayer two days later.[39]

Ironically, the new anthem with music and lyrics by studio song writers Edward Kane and Earl Brent contains far more provocative language than the *Horst Wessel* song would have provided. In the version heard on screen, just as before, Holl shouts to the crowd in the ski chalet, "I'll name a song. A song every loyal German man and woman will sing with high hearts! The glorious song of the New Germany!" That song is no longer the simple pounding march of the SA, unmistakably Nazi. The new song instead bears a striking political message in the last line: "No race on earth can keep our land from glory! We are by birth the rulers of the world.!" It was the ideology of the master race, combined with the mission to conduct world conquest and by implication to annihilate Jews worldwide. Did Mayer overlook the implications of the MGM version? Replacing the *Horst Wessel* song, Kane and Brent had produced an even more ominous anthem for the Nazis in the film to sing and one that provocatively raised the specter of intervention. Breen approved it too. The studio head and chief censor must have believed Hollywood's use of the near sacred *Horst Wessel* song would offend the Nazi regime, whereas a generic anthem would not. A pair of popular song writers had captured the essence of Nazi ideology, retaining the themes of racism and world conquest that the émigré writers had employed the year before to warn of what they knew the Nazis really intended. Little else of the émigré contributions was retained in the shooting script of 1940, except for the highly expurgated scenes of Professor Roth as the sole prisoner in the concentration camp, wearing the letter "J" on his sleeve.

With the loss of the father-son scene and other scenes containing the word "Jew," the pace of the film quickened, at times moving so rapidly that viewers could be confused by events that occur with little or no motivation. But then in substituting "non-Aryan" for "Jew," the studio intended not only to avoid controversy but to sow confusion as well.[40] Moviegoers had no time to dwell on potentially controversial issues or consider the implications of obscure references. The audience is left with coded language that obfuscates rather than reveals. For example, one of the Gestapo agents tracking Mr. Werner accosts Freya in the Breitner home and tells her, "You know your name doesn't sound very well to German ears."[41] The viewer must translate the awkward sentence to mean, "Your name sounds Jewish, and Germans don't like Jews." But the film has already moved on. Similarly, an SS officer from whom Freya tries to retrieve her father's confiscated manuscript tells her, "You belong in part to the German race [and] you have shown yourself unworthy to represent that race abroad."[42] The viewer must conclude that Freya, as half-Aryan, is also only part German. The audience must also comprehend the idea of Jewishness in all that as well as the notion that German identity constitutes a race. It was a lot to ask of the American moviegoing public, even as knowledgeable about events as many viewers were in 1940.

Basic motivations are also lost as the pace of the film intensifies. Just as Freya is deprived of Martin's courtship, Mr. Werner arrives at the Breitner farm needing to escape to Austria with no explanation why other than his refusal in the ski chalet to sing the Nazi anthem followed by a beating, apparently not punishment enough. In the scripts of 1939, the Gestapo is chasing him because he has intervened to protect his Jewish students from being stoned on the playground and facing unjustified punishments from the school administration. Dispossessed of Claudine West's original pacing, including its most graphic scenes of Nazi brutality and Jewish humiliation, *The Mortal Storm* speeds to its conclusion, as though careening downhill. The very momentum of the story could confuse as much as the "non-Aryan" identity of the film's protagonists.[43]

Possible Protest on the Set

While no direct evidence has come to light regarding open protest among cast and crew to the changes Mayer imposed through the first five months of 1940, it is possible to infer that objections arose. For the past four years, the mood in Hollywood had been decidedly anti-Nazi and pro-interventionist. Mayer's rapid re-instatement of the father-son scene on February 8 after dropping it a week earlier would suggest some sort of pushback to the first decision. At the same time (to be discussed in greater detail below) someone on the set contacted Bottome, still in Hollywood, to alert her to Mayer's excisions and went so far as to supply her with a copy of the modified script. That the father-son scene had initially been budgeted for one day of shooting yet managed to delay the production for three months would also suggest controversy. In addition, the cast itself included strong-willed individuals, some of whom had bucked the studios in the past. Personal exposure to the Jewish question encouraged neither West nor the film's star Margaret Sullavan to show compliance.

The cast, for example, already possessed some natural cohesion from previous work together. Several of the leading players had known each other for nearly a decade. For Sullavan and Stewart, it was their fourth film together. Only months earlier they had starred in *Shop Around the Corner*. Before that they worked together in *Next Time We Love* (1936) and *The Shopworn Angel* (1938). Robert Young, who played Fritz Maberg, had worked with Sullavan on *Three Comrades* and *The Shining Hour*, both released in 1938. Esther Dale, who played Marta, the Roth family cook, had known Stewart and Sullavan in Josh Logan's summer stock company, the University Players. They had performed together on Cape Cod in 1932. Stewart remembered Dale with great affection years later.[44]

Political divisions nonetheless divided the cast. Robert Stack has described Robert Young walking around the set, wringing his hands over fear of Nazi reprisals against those who participated in the film.[45] Young would have been unlikely to object to the less transparent term, "non-Aryan." All cast members would indeed face reprisals from the German government. Participants in *The Mortal Storm* were banned from travel to Germany after the film's release.[46]

Stewart and Sullavan, on the other hand, showed ample evidence of support for intervention.[47] Sullavan, in addition, had already confronted Nazi antisemitism even before making *The Mortal Storm*. She had witnessed Jewish persecution firsthand in Germany and could feel a moral imperative to protest Mayer's heavy hand on the issue. Both stars in fact had had experiences that would encourage them to perceive the film in the larger context of European upheaval in 1940.

Stewart's broader perspective came through aviation. He shared a passion for flying with Sullavan's husband, the powerful Hollywood agent and theatrical producer Leland Hayward, who managed Stewart's career. Hayward had introduced Stewart to flying in 1935, shortly after he arrived in Hollywood.[48] The star readily caught the flying bug, his boyhood hero having been Charles Lindbergh, and soon invested in Hayward's company Southwest Airlines.[49] As talk of war increased, Stewart's partnership with Hayward in aviation expanded. He invested in an idea that Hayward brought to fruition in 1940.[50] That year the Hollywood agent began to train military pilots at the Thunderbird airbase "near Phoenix" that he built in ninety days "with the cooperation and gratitude of the United States army."[51]

Stewart invested more than money in the project. He purchased and regularly flew a Stinson 105 Voyager "because the Army used that model as trainers."[52] But he did even more than prepare for combat by logging flying time. According to MGM publicity material for *The Mortal Storm*, he had recently patented a part to increase the efficiency of a plane's fuel pump, a most useful device in combat. In 1940, Stewart showed his support for the allied cause in yet another way. He organized rallies calling for aid to Britain in which other Hollywood stars participated. Stewart as both star and aviator prepared for military intervention in Europe. Hayward and his wife Margaret Sullavan partnered with him in those endeavors.

Sullavan possessed a unique attribute among cast members. She alone had had direct exposure to Nazi mistreatment of Jews in Germany. She joined the émigré writers in having witnessed Nazi conduct at first hand. If any member of the cast challenged the MGM front office on the Jewish question, it would most likely have been the film's star.[53]

In 1935, she went on her honeymoon with director William Wyler, a nephew of Carl Laemmle, the head of Universal Studios. Laemmle was one of Hollywood's most outspoken opponents of the Nazis. He offered financial support for every Jewish resident of the small town in Germany he came from, enabling them all to obtain US visas. His production of *All Quiet on the Western Front* (1930) had enraged the Nazis, who on Goebbels's orders let loose mice to create pandemonium in the theaters where it played.

When Wyler took Sullavan to meet his family and to visit his former homeland, now two years under the Nazis Sullavan saw firsthand what the new Germany had become. After visiting Wyler's hometown of Mulhausen in Alsace, the couple went to a family reunion in Munich. They stayed in a posh hotel and invited all of Wyler's relatives to a reception. The family, as Jews, feared even stepping inside such a place lest they call attention to themselves. Wyler's cousin, Walter Laemmle, explained, "A Jew stayed out of places like that."[54] Walter nervously met them in the hotel but could barely bring himself to dance with Wyler's movie star bride, telling her, "I'm Jewish [...] I feel uncomfortable."[55] Walter ended up in Dachau following *Kristallnacht* but was released when the prison became too full. He quickly emigrated. By then Wyler and Sullavan were divorced, but she had witnessed the ordeal of Jews in Germany and had heard even more about it from Wyler's cousin Walter Laemmle.

In addition to being married to the power broker Leland Hayward, Sullavan had other sources of influence with the studio. MGM had been so anxious for her to play the part of Freya that her salary dwarfed that of other cast members.[56] Franklin told Claudine West at the time she was hospitalized, "after you have recovered sufficiently enough to start work we will still have our script in plenty of time, as it looks as if Margaret Sullavan is going to play the part [of Freya], and we won't be able to get her for a couple of months."[57] MGM was determined to wait out her contract with Universal in order to have her in the role of Freya. Sullavan therefore had some room for maneuver to put pressure on the studio.

Nor was she a stranger to protest. Eddie Mannix, Mayer's "enforcer," said of her, "She was the only player who out bullied Mayer-she gave him the willies."[58] She had already shown a willingness to buck the Hollywood system. She insisted and won on the issue of the title to her 1936 film *Next Time We Love*. Universal had wanted *Next Time We Live*. She also insisted on a relatively unknown, James Stewart, to play her co-star in that film. Sullavan won on that issue as well. She lost in fighting Universal over her contract of 1933. In 1940, a court ruling forced her to make two final pictures with the studio which she had hoped to avoid.[59] She had nonetheless been willing to take on her own studio under a system in which such conduct, while not unheard of, was still potentially self-destructive.

The film that Sullavan made shortly after the release of *The Mortal Storm* provides another clue to the intensity of her political activism. *So Ends Our Night* (February 1941) can be seen as an answer to Mayer's compromises in *The Mortal Storm*. Sullavan made it with United Artists, a company founded twenty years earlier by the stars Charlie Chaplin, Mary Pickford, Douglas Fairbanks, and the producer D. W. Griffith to give players rather than studio bosses control over production. Although by 1940–41 United Artists was no longer the independent studio it had been founded to be and was suffering from significant financial losses, it harbored a tradition of independence, distinguishing it from the major studios.

In *So Ends Our Night*, Sullavan played a would-be scientist, still a student, named Ruth Holland on the run from the Nazis who hound "non-Aryan" stateless refugees like herself. Characters employ the word "Jew" in two highly charged scenes. An Austrian policeman accuses Sullavan of conniving with her friends to cheat him in a carnival game. Angry over his defeat and his losses, he prepares to arrest her, shouting, "Mind your own business, you filthy little Jew!"

The second scene invokes the Nuremberg Laws of 1935 which forbid, among other prohibitions, marriage between Jews and non-Jews. Those laws, even though never mentioned, hung over the plot of MGM's version of *The Mortal Storm*. Professor Roth, who is Jewish, and his wife, who is not, defied the intermarriage prohibitions of Goebbels's race laws. Had the "father-son" scene been retained with its questionnaire, calling for proof of Aryan descent, the issue would have been met head-on.[60]

Quite the contrary occurs in *So Ends Our Night*. In a scene reminiscent of Freya's breaking her engagement with Fritz Maberg to be discussed below, Ruth Holland's fiancé ends their engagement. He tells her in a brutal introduction, "A pity you're not dead like your father and mother." Ruth's fiancé has been labeled in the newspapers "a race profaner" for being "engaged to marry a Jewess," language taken directly from the Nuremberg Laws. "It's over," Ruth says despondently, a line straight from *The Mortal Storm*, now pronounced with resignation rather than defiance. Ruth reminds her erstwhile fiancé that they had grown up together, creating the same bond that Freya alludes to among her friends in *The Mortal Storm*. In *So Ends Our Night*, I would argue, Sullavan and others answered Mayer's compromises and carried out Bottome and West's original anti-Nazi agenda for the MGM film.

According to Sullavan's daughter, Goebbels took seriously her mother's intentions as well as her influence over Hollywood studios. He went so far as to plant spies in the Sullavan-Hayward household. She recounts that in 1943 "Otto our butler" along with his wife Elsa "were arrested as German spies ...."[61] Goebbels recognized Margaret Sullavan as an anti-Nazi crusader on and off screen. He apparently worried that she was insisting on the production of more anti-Nazi films, at the same time arguing for sharpening their message as she had apparently attempted with *The Mortal Storm* and succeeded in doing so with *So Ends Our Night*. A telling still taken behind the scenes in the production of *The Mortal Storm* (not available for reproduction) shows Sullavan, the novel in hand, lecturing to fellow cast members.

Mayer's wavering over employing the word "Jew" sowed confusion beyond the studio, evident in the publicity campaign that W. K. Ferguson, MGM's Manager of Exploitation, a section in the studio's Publicity Department, prepared for the film. Ferguson sent theater owners instructions on how to advertise the film. One possibility he suggested was to emphasize the popularity of Bottome's novel. Ferguson explained,

> Key a major part of your exploitation around the book. Its 500,000 [readers] can be multiplied into many more times that no. of theatre patrons if you promote it with all the force and power at your command.[62]

In keeping with that approach, Ferguson reissued the novel in a special edition to be sold in theater lobbies along with screenings of the film for a token price of 79 cents. The novel naturally contained ample use of the word "Jew." But Ferguson did not stop there. He provided a detailed synopsis of the film containing a reference to the father-son scene, noting "Little Rudi learns what it is to be a Jew."[63] Ferguson certainly knew the script, and he probably saw a version of the film with the word "Jew" intact. Such versions were produced only to be quickly discarded as Mayer changed his mind repeatedly over the film in the spring of 1940.

A compromise of sorts appeared to be reached only in May after more than three months of uncertainty, and possibly contention, surrounding the use of the word in the script. It occurs in one of the last scripts West submitted to Mayer. She modified the exchange between Fritz and Freya in which she breaks their engagement. The change is penciled in in West's careful, precise handwriting. That scene was to have preceded the father-son scene, now dropped. Freya tells Fritz, "You belong to this new Germany that comes between us. The new Germany that persecutes my people."[64] Freya did not refer to her people as "non-Aryans," awkward, even ludicrous. Her use of "My people" falls between "Jew" and "non-Aryan" in its explicitness. The phrase was as close to the word "Jew" as the studio was prepared to go in 1940. Freya joins the persecuted, even if they do not bear their true name. The phrase carries another meaning. It belongs to Margaret Sullavan, who was the most likely member of the cast to seek a compromise over politically charged excisions from the script. Claudine West had penciled in one last solution, and Sullavan delivered it with force and unnerving contempt for her former fiancé and what he represents, ironically played by the politically conservative Robert Young.

Jimmy Stewart has provided insight regarding Sullavan's skill in playing such a scene. In conversation with Sullavan's daughter, he described her mother's ability to merge meaning and emotion, with multiplying effect. Stewart explained, "she could do [...] moments that would hit you, maybe a look or a line or two, but they would hit like flashes or earthquakes; everybody'd sort of feel it. It's a very rare thing".[65] Sullavan's delivery of West's compromise line, "The new Germany that persecutes my people," provides an example of one of those earthquake moments in which she transcended literal meanings.

Sullavan's daughter has also revealed how strongly her mother felt about antisemitism and the Jewish question. Possessing "grave misgivings about bigotry in Greenwich," she had occasion to replay the father-son scene one more time in the late 1940s. She knew the scene well, having played it in one form or another through the spring of 1940. Her daughter has recounted the last occasion of that performance.

> One afternoon [...] a friend of mine idly quoted her mother as being greatly relieved that the owners of such and such a house had held out against the irresistible bid of a rich New York Jewish couple [...] whereupon Mother exploded [...] She sprang to her feet, her face purple with emotion. "There is one thing I will not tolerate-not in my house, not from anyone, not ever!—and that is discrimination of any kind, particularly anti-Semitism [...] the finest, most brilliant people I know are Jews, my closest friends are Jews! She gave a long, impassioned lecture that not only detailed the entire history of the Jewish race, its accomplishments and persecutions, but also lamented the incalculable loss-cultural, intellectual, and scientific—that the rest of civilization would have suffered without it."[66]

It was the last time that West's father-son scene had an audience. Played on this occasion by Freya, rather than by Rudi and his father, on a patio in Greenwich, Connecticut, rather than a sound stage in Culver City, California. But the film itself, in 1940, remained *Judenrein*.

Bottome Protests

> I would not put in Freya's mouth the word: 'Non-Aryan' instead of 'Jew' [...] I should make the Jew question utterly clear.
> (Phyllis Bottome to Sidney Franklin, February 7, 1940)[67]

Bottome received word from an unknown source that the adaptation of the novel she advocated was at risk. That communication alone suggests discontent on the set over the imposition of the non-Aryan version of the story. Whoever contacted her also managed to supply a copy of the current working script. West herself is a possibility, but on the other hand it is unlikely she would reveal the script to someone outside the studio. She guarded copies meticulously, fearing premature publicity as occurred with *Confessions of a Nazi Spy*. If West did alert Bottome, however, she could see her as a potentially effective ally, having observed her uncompromising determination in negotiating with MGM before and after the purchase of the novel. As the author of the novel, Bottome might have credibility with Mayer. She was indeed available, temporarily residing in Hollywood, and ready to fight.

Bottome did not hesitate to protest when she learned that the production, from her point of view, was going awry. Clearly upset, she wrote Franklin on February 7 in high dudgeon, just as production resumed in 1940.[68] She now knew that a new script dated February 2, a copy of which she possessed, had replaced the one approved by Breen on January 30 with the word "Jew" intact. She began disarmingly that she had only "a few suggestions," then quickly added, the "changes of omission and commission from the book are [...] considerable," suggesting that she might have more than "a few suggestions" to make. She then offered "to heighten both the drama and the clearness of the [book's] message." In other words, she again asked to be involved in the production and wanted *The Mortal Storm* on screen largely as she had written it without MGM's "changes of omission and commission." And she was prepared to tell the studio just how to do it. The script she complained of was the latest one dated February 2 that Block had submitted to Breen with the father-son scene drastically reduced from eight to two pages. The script had also begun replacing "Jew" with "non-Aryan" throughout.

Bottome insisted, "I would not put in Freya's mouth the word: 'Non-Aryan' instead of 'Jew' [...] Freya would have flung up her head and said with pride to Fritz, 'My father is a Jew!'" By the same token, she explained, that Rudi would never seek "to escape his Jewish heritage" or "begged not to be a Jew [...]" She explained the "old German Jewish families [...] had tremendous pride in being Jewish [...]"

But the father-son scene as a whole aroused her greatest concern. Rudi's question to his father, "'What is being a Jew?'" [...] is the crux of the book and the crux of the world today [...] I should make the Jew question utterly clear," she insisted to Franklin. Bottome reassured that the studio need have no fear of controversy over Professor Roth's answer to his son's query because "all over America—on radios, in schools, and in the Jewish preparation for their coming of age, Roth's speech to his son is being used. Can you not keep the *exact wording*? It is a very short speech which is the answer to Rudi's famous question: 'Father—what is [being] a Jew?'"

"Can you not keep the exact wording" is the crux of her letter to Franklin. She wanted to retain the scene between Rudi and his father from the novel, if not the longer version from West's scripts of 1939. She asked to meet "any time the following week to talk over the picture," adding "it would give [her] very great pleasure as it did before" to consult with him. She closed with the reassuring request that he tell "all those who wrote your script how really beautiful and impressive I have found it!" despite, she might have added, her profound reservations regarding it.

Bottome's praise to Franklin barely concealed her actual displeasure. She clearly knew of the last-minute modifications with the start of shooting, although she had not consulted with Franklin again nor probably even seen him since the initial discussion with him and West in April 1939. The new content had clearly caught her as well as those connected with the production by surprise.

Also frustrating, Franklin did not respond to her entreaty for a meeting. A week after her initial communication of February 7, she still had not heard from him. She wrote him again on February 13 with what must have been disconcerting news to Franklin: she possessed a copy of the shooting script. Bottome informed him that she and her husband had "gone over" the script once more. She now told him that she wanted to start over with production with herself in charge of the script. She requested substantial changes regarding what she labeled "the Time question" or chronology of the story. She recommended shifting a significant amount of the action to the period before Hitler came to power by way of contrast with Germany under the Nazis. Bottome apparently believed that she could win MGM over to her point of view, convincing the studio to modify the script with what now amounted to a radical departure from the adaptation of her novel that she herself had originally advocated. Highly unlikely, but her possession of the script and vocal complaints spelled trouble for a production already delayed and about to undergo controversial revision.

On the same day she wrote Franklin a second time, she wrote Mayer himself. She returned to her original concern about the portrayal of the Jewish question. As she had with Franklin, she assured the studio head that "the M-G-M script is a grand one." She then turned to the "whole message of the book" which she feared was being lost. Bottome believed that it was crucial that the film "not end in Defeat." She had made the same point to Franklin when she wrote in her letter of February 7 that Freya's escape from Germany at the end of the novel meant "the bird is blown in out of the storm […] the Mortal Storm of the dictatorships." In the shooting script in Bottome's possession, Freya dies, and Martin is arrested. She urged instead that Martin escape across the border with her body as a gesture toward hope for the future.

Bottome then made a casting suggestion, playing on what she believed to be Mayer's Jewish pride and sympathies. Neither the suggestion nor her understanding of the mogul's Jewish identity would have been well-received.

I believe that if Mickey Rooney does Rudi, you will not only get a marvelous box office win, but what I am sure means far more to you, as it does to me, that the world is once more shown the value of Jewish training, family life, and that David and Goliath courage, which is the hope of the world today![69]

Bottome misread Mayer in 1940. She had more accurately registered his attitude when she wrote an old friend a year earlier that the moguls, themselves Jewish and vulnerable, were "too timid to present their [own] cause."[70] Mayer lacked the courage at the heart, Bottome had delicately suggested, of his own heritage and culture.

Another hint of Bottome's relations with the cast and producers of *The Mortal Storm* comes from a communication sent to her editor at Little, Brown, Roger Scaife. In August 1940 with *The Mortal Storm* still on its first run, Little, Brown & Co. published a collection of Bottome's short stories titled *Masks and Faces*. She sent Scaife a distribution list for those connected to *The Mortal Storm*. First came "Borzage, my Director," with whom she must have been on good terms.[71] He had replaced Franklin in that capacity once shooting began, although Franklin remained as producer until early March. Those personnel changes are discussed below. Second came Claudine West, listed above any of the stars in the cast. Then followed James Stewart, Margaret Sullavan, Robt. Young, Frank Morgan, Irene Rich (Amélie Roth) in that order. Even the politically conservative Robt. Young was included. "Franklyn" came last, with his name misspelled. Both the placement of his name and its misspelling suggest her annoyance with the film's one-time producer/director. From her point of view, he had twice played a dubious role. There is no record that he answered her anxious communications of early February when she first learned of serious modifications to the script. In late April, although no longer connected with the production, he had been chosen to mollify her by showing her a version of the film that employed the word "Jew."

With the publication of *Masks and Faces* in August, Bottome was beginning to get word that MGM had duped her and released a totally different version of the film, "non-Aryan" substituted for "Jew." "Franklyn" apparently bore the brunt of her ire. Bottome felt betrayed. She had left for England in June just before the film's release, believing her influence had prevailed. As she told her dear friend in Norfolk, Virginia, Maida McCord, "I have 'Mortal Storm' changed and stiffened by my own suggestions on the verge of release."[72] She was to learn soon enough, the studio had successfully placated her, in the end ignoring her pleas about the necessity to showcase the Jewish question in the film drawn from her novel.

Bottome unfortunately never addressed in print the events surrounding the film adaptation of her most popular novel. *The Goal*, the third and final volume of her autobiography, ends with 1937 and the publication of *The Mortal Storm* in Britain. Her silence was small wonder. MGM ignored nearly all advice she generously offered. On top of that she would have to admit to her friends that she had been mistaken to believe that she could influence MGM after all. The studio was not about to rewrite the script, setting half the film in Germany before Hitler came to power. Nor would it replace the young, little-known Gene Reynolds with Mickey Rooney, already stamped with the all-American features of Andy Hardy. Freya does die in Martin's arms in Austria, both having made it, if not safely, across the border.

Bottome in the end had little chance to influence the production. The studio did not share her concern that the film reflect the book even though for her the "father-son" scene was "the gist of the novel," as she told her editor Roger Scaife.[73] To Mayer, the scene spelled both politics and controversy. Even worse, it put the dreaded Jewish question front and center in the film. Unbeknownst to Bottome, she had erred in yet another regard. She had first turned to Franklin. His responsibility for the film had diminished considerably since her consultation with him in April 1939.

Borzage and Saville Replace Franklin/The Producer's Film Belongs to the Director

The whole thing became repulsive to me [...] the set [...] was a private Germany of our own [...]. Sidney Franklin, "We Laughed and We Cried," unpublished autobiography, p. 287.

As 1939 turned to 1940, Mayer not only rethought the use of the word "Jew" in the film, he also rethought the role of Sidney Franklin, who, since the studio purchased Bottome's novel, had combined the roles of producer and director before shooting began. Up until 1940, the film was his. All that changed with the New Year. With the actual shooting about to start, Frank Borzage took over as director. Borzage was no "employee [...] on a 40-week contract" as was usually the case with directors at MGM, where producers developed the script and had charge of production.[74] *The Mortal Storm*, with the exception of the Jewish question, now belonged to its director. The studio went so far as to label the film a "Frank Borzage production," wiping out credit for nearly a year of preparatory work that belonged to Franklin. Not until Franklin left the set in early March did Victor Saville replace him as producer. By then, it would seem, Franklin's position with *The Mortal Storm* had become untenable, if that had not occurred even earlier.

Mayer might have decided to replace Franklin for several reasons. Franklin, the studio head believed, had the talents of a producer, not those of a director.

His precise, meticulous approach to such details as costumes and hairstyles had too often delayed the pictures that he had directed under Thalberg.[75] The suspension of war pictures had already delayed *The Mortal Storm* by several months. Now that shooting was about to begin, Mayer wanted the picture to be speeded up. Actors, for example, in supporting roles were contracted in February for no more than four weeks, several of them for less time than that.[76] MGM's rival studios such as Paramount and Twentieth-Century Fox were about to release their first anti-Nazi pictures. Warners' *Confessions of a Nazi Spy* had already scooped them all. Mayer therefore sought a director who, like Franklin, would emphasize romance over politics, but avoid the delaying details of production the studio would no longer tolerate.

From Mayer's point of view, several factors made Frank Borzage a reasonable replacement for Franklin. Mayer could start anew with Borzage. The director had no stake in previous conceptions of the film, nor even exposure to them. It could be said that he was untainted by discussion with Bottome and her determined insistence on the Jewish question. He had not worked with the émigré script writers whose lurid scenes had been excised. He nonetheless had had exposure to the film's subject matter, having already made two films set in Weimar Germany, *Little Man What Now* (1934) and *Three Comrades* (1938). In each one he had avoided depicting the political violence that had marred post-First World War Germany. Instead, he had emphasized the romantic story embedded in each novel that he adapted to the screen. In the case of Hans Fallada's *Little Man What Now*, Borzage's adaptation did not include the powerful Nazi figure of the novel nor even mention the rising Nazi Party. Borzage's adaptation of *Three Comrades* similarly remained remarkably apolitical, and thus untrue to Remarque's novel of Germany in the 1920s. Mayer wanted the same treatment for *The Mortal Storm*, emphasizing romance over politics. That meant avoiding, or at least obfuscating, the persecution of German Jews.

Borzage had another advantage to recommend him. He worked well with the strong-willed Margaret Sullavan. She had taken his direction and been nominated for an Academy Award for *Three Comrades*. She was likely to listen to him again. In fact, she did. The studio had another reason to satisfy her in the choice of director. It very much wanted her for the part of Freya. As Franklin told West in October of the year before, the front office was willing to wait several months for her to be available.[77] She had to make her last two films for Universal, and Hays had put war pictures on hold anyway. In that interval, Mayer decided that Borzage would direct the non-Aryan version of Bottome's novel and be the director most likely to work well with Sullavan.

Franklin remained as producer but grew increasingly uncomfortable on the set. He found that "the very sight of the swastika" unnerved him. The Nazis launched the blitzkrieg in the midst of filming *The Mortal Storm*. The visual cues of Nazism that abounded on set added to Franklin's discomfort, reminding him of Hitler's rapid conquest across Europe. He wrote nothing in his autobiography about his own diminished status with the film, that is Borzage's takeover. He instead insisted that circumstances abroad discouraged his enthusiasm for a picture that he had devoted himself to for nearly a year.

> The more terrible the war news from abroad [...] the more difficult my participation became. Every time I went on the set, it was like a private Germany of our own [...] as the production proceeded, I became increasingly disturbed. [After seeing] storm troopers [...] singing the *Horst Wessel Song*, and some of them jumped a Jewish character and beat him into insensibility, [I] went straight to Eddie Mannix and told him that [I] wanted to be relieved of *The Mortal Storm* [...].[78]

Franklin explained to Mannix that "the subject matter" made him "quite ill." He had lost his "impartiality toward the picture." As a result, his "value as a producer [was] gone."[79] Franklin completed his account of his work on *The Mortal Storm* with the statement that "the production was handed over to Victor Saville."[80] He made no mention of Borzage nor that the film's credits labeled it "a Frank Borzage production," abnegating his previous contribution altogether.

Franklin's account raises more questions than it answers. Having been at work on the picture for nearly a year, it was not the first time that he had encountered its harsh subject matter. The script had already contained worse scenes of brutality than the beating of the schoolteacher. Why then would Franklin wait until well into 1940 to drop the project?

Franklin's relationship with Claudine West may provide one explanation. The consequence of his departure had to be significant for her. She now fought alone for the word "Jew" without her production partner. Franklin was the senior member of the team with access to the front office that she presumably lacked. Her shy and retiring nature must have made the responsibility thrust upon her even more daunting. But West was determined. Her commitment to the picture was profound. Her personal connection to the story has been described. She had sharpened and modified scenes the previous fall even while recovering from major surgery. With or without Franklin, in the spring she continued to seek a formula that would satisfy the reluctant studio head to permit retaining the word "Jew." West shared Bottome's vision of the novel. Franklin, on the other hand, had never embraced the controversial elements of the picture. By leaving the production, he avoided conflict with West while preserving his relationship with her which he explained to close friends after her death had been irreplaceable.

He subsequently wrote that he left the picture when it was about "halfway through [shooting]."[81] That would be sometime in March 1940. In fact, before the first week of March, West and Franklin had each received freshly typed copies of her script changes. The arrangement changed on March 4.

On that day, West wrote the MGM driver who made the deliveries, "Copies [of the script] only to me."[82] That note of West's confirms that Franklin left the picture, as he wrote, "about halfway through," that is, early in March.

Another event coincides with his departure. He states that the singing of the *Horst Wessel Song* contributed to his decision to leave. Correspondence between Breen and the studio confirms that the new song to be sung in the inn to replace the *Horst Wessel* song had been received by the PCA on February 20, 1940, and quickly approved. The Kane/Brent song was so close to the original, Franklin might not have been able to tell the difference. He would have heard it in rehearsal or while it was being filmed in late February/early March.[83] West's note about script copies and the date of the MGM replacement song confirm the timing of Franklin's departure.

West's note, however, raises another question. With Franklin's departure why were script changes not sent to Borzage and Victor Saville? Borzage is conspicuously absent from Franklin's papers as though he and Franklin never consulted even while Franklin remained as producer. The same is true of Franklin's autobiography where he writes that when he left "the production was handed over to Victor Saville," a British film director of Jewish heritage, once again bypassing mention of Borzage.[84] Saville, however, later claimed to have taken over as director, rather than producer, and to have then set the production on track. He is reported to have told Mayer, "These boys [making the picture] haven't got the idea of the Nazis at all."[85] He further claimed that he directed "all but a week" of the film, hence he had been on set, probably starting in January 1940.[86] The claim cannot be sustained. In the MGM stills collection in the Margaret Herrick Library, there are no photos of Saville on set. Instead, Borzage is shown (unavailable for reproduction) directing nearly every major scene in the film.

Others disputed Saville's claims to have directed *The Mortal Storm*. Borzage's biographer, Hervé Dumont, attempted to verify the assertion. He interviewed Robert Stack (Otto von Rohn), Gene Reynolds (Rudi Roth), and Jimmy Stewart (Martin Breitner), all of whom agreed that Borzage, not Saville, directed the film. Stewart even put in writing for Dumont that Borzage had "directed all of the picture."[87]

Yet after he left, Franklin attempted to tie up loose ends by corresponding with Saville, not Borzage. Franklin had always had a passion for the details of production. He wrote his replacement on March 4 about one in particular:

Dear Victor [...] when she went to the Gestapo office [...] Maggie Sullivan [sic] had a white hat. I understand it looked very bad, and as long as we are retaking this, would you be kind enough to see that she gets a new hat, if you feel the same way about it after seeing the scene.[88]

The white hat was indeed replaced with a black one, but Borzage oversaw the change.

Tensions certainly existed between Franklin and Borzage, possibly outright animosity. According to Dumont, the ski scenes of the film belonged entirely to Borzage and were filmed not abroad but in the United States. He makes no mention of the filming that Franklin oversaw in Switzerland in July 1939. Instead, in April 1940, Dumont recounts, Borzage sent a production unit to film "the ski runs [...] in Sun Valley, Idaho [...] and above Salt Lake City [...] Olympic champions doubled for Stewart and Sullavan [...] A specially designed vehicle allowed them to follow the skiers [...] without the camera trembling."[89]

Dumont appeared to be unaware that Borzage duplicated Franklin's efforts in the summer of 1939 in acquiring ski scenes for the film, down to the use of Olympic skiers as doubles and a special vehicle to keep the camera steady while filming on snow. In effect, Borzage simply duplicated Franklin's work of the year before and claimed it as his own. He undertook the ski scenes within weeks of Franklin's departure. It would seem he sought to put his stamp on the finished project without acknowledging Franklin's contribution at all.

One can therefore surmise that, aside from the Jewish question, tensions existed on the set. Franklin's apparent discord with Borzage helped to propel his departure. Borzage and Saville, at least in Saville's mind, jockeyed for control and claim to the role of director. Borzage continued to battle Franklin even after he left the set, attempting to duplicate his contributions and excise his name from the credits. Franklin's name, as noted, is indeed absent from the film. West, possibly together with Sullavan, was determined to retain acknowledgment of Jewish suffering. Bottome had sent her complaint about the loss of the word "Jew" to the wrong person in writing to Franklin in February 1940, although Franklin's connection to the production was far from over even if he had been displaced. In the same way, West, even without Franklin, continued to have a say in the script.

West Manages to "Grasp the Nettle"[90]

West's continued influence on the film was remarkable on several counts. Borzage must have seen her as Franklin's "man." After all, she belonged to his production unit and had always worked with him. West, therefore, not only battled the front office, but she also confronted the new director on the production. She nonetheless had cards of her own to play. Mayer was under pressure to finish the picture to compete with his rivals who were also hard at work on their versions of Nazi Germany. Borzage was apparently willing to put his stamp on the picture, not with time-consuming modifications, but rather by simply duplicating Franklin's efforts. West's original script of 1939, along with subsequent revisions, mostly hers, provided the architecture of the film. Once shooting began, on set rivalries, whether between Saville or

Borzage or Borzage and Franklin could derail the picture. West provided continuity between the film of 1939 and the shifting versions of 1940. With dissension over the "non-Aryan" version, West was the one to provide more than continuity. She found a formula to placate all sides.

While *The Mortal Storm* remained *Judenrein*, she seized the opportunity to address the politics of intervention. As she lost again and again on the Jewish question, events abroad afforded her a chance to insert another message into the film. She turned a particular scene of Nazi brutality in the ski chalet into a heroic call for intervention. If the film could not fulfill Bottome's original purpose for it regarding antisemitism, it could still meet another need, namely condemnation of American isolationism. West remained determined to exploit *The Mortal Storm* for the sake of Hitler's victims, whether Jewish or not. That too could placate those who condemned Mayer's squeamishness over his own identity. Even with Franklin's departure, West must have retained some hold on the script.

She had originally included the scene in the ski chalet in the very first script, completed in July 1939. In that scene, the Brown Shirts call on those present to sing the *Horst Wessel* song replaced in early 1940 at Mayer's insistence with a generic Nazi anthem provided by MGM's Music Department, discussed above. The elderly schoolteacher Mr. Werner refuses to join in the singing and is beaten by the Brown Shirts who lie in wait for him outside the inn. The song, Werner's refusal to join in, and the beating never changed. Martin Breitner did. He evolved, as played by Jimmy Stewart, from a passive bystander into an engaged interventionist. With that character at least, West's rewrites, instead of watering down the scene, made it more overtly political, reflecting the dramatic turn of events in Europe from the summer of 1939 to the spring of 1940 and the onset of the blitzkrieg. In the same period, the debate over isolation vs. intervention in the United States had grown intense. By the time of the film's release in June 1940, Stewart, as Martin Breitner, played the role as a barely disguised argument for intervention against Nazi aggression.

West worked simultaneously on the scene in the ski chalet and Rudi's conversation with his father with opposite results. As one faded, the other gained clarity. In the scripts before February 1940, Martin remains an observer of the beating of Mr. Werner. There is little moral onus on him to assist the victim because the gendarmes intervene to save the schoolteacher. In effect an outside, neutral peace-keeping force is available to restore order: what Europeans had hoped to establish after the First World War but did not exist by the 1930s when the continent needed it most.

A dramatic shift occurs in the script of February 2, ironically the one that cut the father-son scene from eight pages to two. With the Jewish question about to be obscured, if not erased, West began to bring intervention into sharp relief. In the ski chalet, Martin leaves those gathered at the window to watch the beating and goes outside to help Mr. Werner to his feet. The gendarmes have intervened, but now in a gesture of significant political import, on as well as off screen, Martin also assists the injured victim.

In scripts that West submitted in the course of the spring, the gendarmes disappear, and Martin's statements become more focused regarding his determination to intervene.[91] West tried two phrases that were dropped. Martin tells Fritz, Freya's fiancé and her two stepbrothers, "I can't sit twiddling my thumbs while a lot of thugs bully an old man who's been decent to me." In another version he declares, "I can't sit swilling beer while a bunch of thugs bully an old man who's been decent to me." The final version is sharp and to the point. Martin intervenes in the inn to protect Mr. Werner. He helps the schoolteacher put on his coat after Holl had tried unsuccessfully to make him join in singing the Nazi anthem. Mr. Werner leaves to go home. Martin returns to the table and tells his companions, "That old chap's been decent to me. I can't stand by and see him bullied." When people suddenly shout the schoolteacher is being beaten Martin rushes outside to the old man's aid. He has just referred to Mr. Werner by using British slang, "old chap," West's hint that it is Britain we need to aid against Nazi aggression. Martin is joined by Freya who defies her fiancé and stepbrothers to do so. Her deed is a harbinger that she will reject Fritz in favor of Martin. Freya's gesture, in addition to binding her to Martin, also carried political meaning. The characters who reject the Nazis and do the right thing intervene.

With two sentences, "That old chap's been decent to me. I can't stand by and see him bullied," West had summed up the argument for intervention in 1940. If she could not defend the Jews, she could nonetheless urge American aid to Britain, the "old chap" who has been "decent" to us.

West's line revealed another issue. The American attitude toward Britain, largely hostile in the 1930s, had begun to change since 1939 when German aggression against both Czechoslovakia and Poland had occurred. Britain had at least defended the latter. By the time that *The Mortal Storm* opened on June 20, 1940, the country had undergone for the first time two nights of relentless bombing of her major cities. As the film played in American movie houses through the course of that summer, Britain's position grew more parlous, underscoring the symbolic significance of Stewart's lines in the ski chalet. Stewart himself made the connection between his role as Martin Breitner and the need to aid Britain in September when he took *The Mortal Storm* on the road to the isolationist Midwest, to be discussed in the next chapter.

Franklin Rejoins the Production

> JEWISH PERSECUTION impressed only 7 percent.[92]
> (From MGM survey of initial audience reaction to preview of *The Mortal Storm*)

Franklin was still not done with *The Mortal Storm*. Less than two months after he left the set, he returned to consult about the picture now nearly completed. Howard Strickling invited his opinion. Strickling, it seemed, had replaced Eddie Mannix as the monitor of the production for the front office. Mannix had kept the production moving forward, approving location shooting and providing the funds for it as had occurred in 1939 with the ski scenes shot in Switzerland. Now that the end was in sight, the production required a different kind of person in charge. Strickling, like Mannix, belonged to Mayer's inner circle, but he possessed an unusually strong personal bond with Mayer. When the studio head left his wife of forty years, for example, he stayed at first with Strickling.[93] In addition to the trust Mayer held him in, Howard Strickling played a special role at MGM. Formally Director of Publicity, he guarded MGM's image as well as the reputation of those who worked for it. Publicity at Hollywood's largest studio did not mean advertising; it meant controlling the message which at all times had to be positive. According to Scott Eyman, "Strickling was the 'Fixer.'"[94] That meant he fixed it so that no negative publicity ever attached itself to an MGM employee or, just as significantly, to a studio product with the potential for controversy. Katharine Hepburn shed a positive light on Strickling's responsibilities. She explained in an oral interview: "If you got into trouble, you called Howard Strickling. Your problem was taken care of. It was a wonderful sensation."[95]

Not surprisingly with *The Mortal Storm* so close to release, Strickling joined the production team. He also once more engaged Franklin, now inviting his opinion and sharing with him the most important issues surrounding the film. Strickling recognized Franklin's value to the production. The former producer/director for the film linked the preliminary version of 1939 to that of 1940. His eye for detail could also be invaluable. Strickling, who was new to the film, welcomed Franklin's advice. He must have also known that Franklin had always acted as a voice of restraint regarding controversial choices in the making of the film.

Franklin viewed the film on April 25.[96] Most of his recommendations concerned the concentration camp scenes about which he had long harbored reservations. He advised cutting the scene in which an inmate is beaten along with the line directed at Amélie Roth: "married to a Jew, shame on you." Franklin had never been comfortable with the depiction of antisemitism that underlay Bottome's novel. He wanted the chase scene at the end tightened. The studio readily agreed with his recommendations about the camp scenes, having already decided to dispense with brutality, probably also urged to do so by Borzage, like Franklin a romantic. The word "Jew" was being excised from the picture anyway and would go entirely by the time the father-son scene was finally dropped in the next two weeks. Franklin, therefore, offered suggestions compatible with the production as he had known it. He had at the same time in limited fashion rejoined the production team.

Strickling sought Franklin's advice again shortly before the picture was released. This time the matters under consideration were truly sensitive ones, that is, precisely the kind that Strickling would normally be responsible for. The Director of Publicity informed Franklin on June 5, two weeks before the release date for *The Mortal Storm*, that MGM had hired the Ross Federal Research Co. to conduct surveys among 300 people in nearby Pomona who were shown the recently completed film.[97] Strickling shared with Franklin sensitive information that would determine whether the studio would release the film at that time or not. The Director of Publicity trusted the film's former producer and, no doubt of some comfort to Franklin, respected the contribution that he had made to the film. Strickling, like Franklin, supported the "non-Aryan" version of the film. He emphasized that the term had indeed served its purpose, creating a certain amount of confusion among the audience. The survey findings also included the following: "27 percent considered it propaganda, 20 percent called it dangerous, 12 percent classed it as timely […] many question advisability of releasing it at this time." Ironically, as Strickling and Franklin would soon find, major critics regarded the picture as made woefully late for it to be "dangerous."

On the other hand, Strickling shared with Franklin that "In almost all reports, there is agreement that picture reveals truth about Hitlerism and conditions that may confront this nation." He provided other good news, consoling to those who had feared raising the Jewish question. The term "non-Aryan" had proven an effective substitute for "Jew." The Director of Publicity explained, "the Jewish question did not create any controversial reactions." To his delight, there were "many in the Pomona audience who did not understand entirely the family relationship or religious difference" among the protagonists. With that assurance, provided by a test audience of 300 in southern California, MGM approved release of *The Mortal Storm* on June 20, 1940.

Like the First World War codebreaker she had once been, Claudine West had tried version after version in pencil seeking a solution to the studio's encryption of Bottome's novel. It was now left to a national audience to decode the author's message. West could only hope, with more success than a small number of viewers in southern California.

Notes

1 West's original script of July 18, 1939, to be found in the Margaret Herrick Library, Department of Special Collections. Turner/MGM Scripts. Box 2176. F. 1647.

2 Interview with Lumet in the documentary *Imaginary Witness. Hollywood and the Holocaust*. Koch Lorber Films, 2009.

3   See Herman, "Hollywood, Nazism, and the Jews, 1933–1941," 91.
4   Eyman, *Lion of Hollywood*, 343.
5   See Welky, *The Moguls and the Dictators* on the phenomenon, 34–5, 37.
6   Ibid., 34.
7   Herman, "Hollywood, Nazism, and the Jews, 1933–1941," 90.
8   Eyman, *Lion of Hollywood*, 138.
9   Helen Corbaley, "Comment [on *The Mortal Storm*]," February 17, 1939, Margaret Herrick Library.
10 See Block's correspondence with PCA head Joseph I. Breen in the Margaret Herrick Library, February 9–March 4, 1940. See also the scripts for *The Mortal Storm*, Margaret Herrick Library, Department of Special Collections, February 2, 1940 and February 9, 1940; Box 2172, f. 1653, 1654. Block informed Breen of the scene's modification then full reinstatement without explanation.
11 SAF, "Mortal Storm," Bits and Extras: Rudi and Professor discuss Jewish situation, 1 Day, Box 24.
12 J. I. Breen to J. Brooke-Wilkinson, March 13, 1939. PCA File. Margaret Herrick Library.
13 See Thomas Doherty's account of Breen's antisemitism in *Hollywood's Censor. Joseph I. Breen and the Production Code Administration* (New York: Columbia University Press, 2009), 199, 204–6.
14 See Doherty, *Hollywood's Censor*, 204–6 for Breen's evolution on the Jewish question.
15 Joseph I. Breen to L. B. Mayer, January 19, 1940. PCA File. Margaret Herrick Library.
16 Howard Strickling to Sidney Franklin, June 5, 1940. SAF Collection, Box 21, 139.
17 Script of December 11, 1939. Box 2171, f. 1647, 1648. Department of Special Collections. Margaret Herrick Library.
18 Ibid.
19 Scripts of July 18 and December 16, 1939. Box 2171, f. 1648; Box 2170, f. 1645; Department of Special Collections. Margaret Herrick Library. The "father-son" scene is almost unchanged in scripts from July to December.
20 *The Mortal Storm*, Box 2171, f. 1647, Special Collections, Margaret Herrick Library.
21 See changing list of names of prominent Jews for "father-son" scene in scripts for *The Mortal Storm* dated November 3, 1939, February 7, 8, and 27, March 7, 1940. Department of Special Collections. Margaret Herrick Library.
22 Script of March 7, 1940, Box 2173, Special Collections, Margaret Herrick Library.
23 A. Block to J. I. Breen, May 13, 1940; PCA Archive: *The Mortal Storm*; Margaret Herrick Library.

24 Breen to Mayer, extending approval for the final version of the script, May 14, 1940; PCA Archive. See also West's script changes for final retakes in Special Collections. Box 2173, f. 1660. Both in Margaret Herrick Library.
25 SAF, Box 24, "Mortal Storm." Bits and Extras. One Day.
26 *Imaginary Witness: Hollywood and the Holocaust/Red Envelope Extertainment;* Koch/Lorber Films; produced and directed by Daniel Anker, 2009.
27 See Dave Friedman to Sidney Franklin, February 2, 1940. SAF Box 16, File 20 on the need for a wig for Anderson.
28 MGM Collection, Margaret Herrick Library, Production 1135. Stills Only, *The Mortal Storm*, 1940.
29 SAF, Box 21, 139.
30 Frank S. Nugent, "Russia Grasps the Nettle," *New York Times*, November 13, 1938, 23.
31 Copyright script, US Library of Congress, submitted June 25, 1940.
32 *The Mortal Storm*, 1940. Script dated January 30, 1940, Special Collections, Margaret Herrick Library.
33 Dave Friedman to Sidney Franklin, February 2, 1940. SAF, Box 16, file 20.
34 *The Mortal Storm*, 1940, Script dated February 8, 1940, in Special Collections (MGM), Margaret Herrick Library.
35 Ibid., West's original script dated July 18, 1939.
36 Howard Strickling said as much to Franklin after the picture had been made. See document on the audience survey and reaction to the film in Strickling to Sidney Franklin, June 5, 1940. SAF Box 21, 139.
37 *The Mortal Storm*, 1940. Script dated August 7, 1939, Special Collections, Margaret Herrick Library.
38 Ibid.
39 Correspondence between Mayer and Breen in the PCA Archive, "The Mortal Storm," Margaret Herrick Library.
40 Howard Strickling, who took over as the front office watchdog for the film from Eddie Mannix, made that point to Sidney Franklin, June 5, 1940. SAF, Box 21, file 139.
41 Copyright script, reel 3, p. 15; June 25, 1940.
42 Ibid.
43 Claudine West took the pacing of a script very seriously. When it seemed that she and Franklin would adapt Clare Booth Luce's successful Broadway hit *The Women,* she wrote Franklin a lengthy letter in which she argued that the key to the success of the adaptation lay in the pacing. She described how she would rigorously control the pace of the film were she to write the script for it. See SAF Box 19. Sack 17, letter of June 1, 1938.
44 US Library of Congress, Manuscript Division, Howard Teichmann Papers, Box 59, Folder 8, "Interview with Jimmy Stewart."

45 Robert Stack, *Straight Shooting* (New York: Grosset & Dunlap, 1981), 123.
46 See Hans Thompsen's correspondence with Secretary of State Cordell Hull in NARA (College Park). RG 59. 811.4061. Mortal Storm/1. Box 3809, complaining about the provocative, anti-German bias of the film. July 17, 1940.
47 Cf. Lawrence Quirk, who argues that Sullavan was non-political in *Margaret Sullavan. Child of Fate* (New York: St. Martin's Press, 1986), 112.
48 Robert Matzen, *Mission. Jimmy Stewart and the Fight for Europe* (Pittsburgh: GoodKnight Books, 2016), 64.
49 Brooke Hayward, *Haywire* (New York: Alfred A. Knopf, Inc., 1977), 69.
50 Matzen, *Mission*, 68.
51 Hayward, *Haywire*, 69.
52 Matzen, *Mission*, 65.
53 MGM Collection, Margaret Herrick Library, Production 1135. Stills Only, *The Mortal Storm*, 1940. Photos show Sullavan listening intently to Borzage's direction. Others show her offering direction advice of her own.
54 Jan Herman, *William Wyler. A Talent for Trouble* (New York: De Capo Press, 1997), 131.
55 Herman, *A Talent for Trouble*, 132.
56 See SAF, "Salaries for *The Mortal Storm*," Box 23/24, #5 and Franklin to Claudine West, October 4, 1939. SAF, Box 19, Sack 17.
57 Sidney Franklin to Claudine West, October 14, 1939. SAF, Box 19, Sack 17.
58 Quirk, *Margaret Sullavan*, 128.
59 Quirk, *Margaret Sullavan*, 114.
60 See photo in Margaret Herrick Lib. stills collection where Sullavan holds the questionnaire as Rudi looks on.
61 Hayward, *Haywire*, 89.
62 W. R. Ferguson (ed.), *The Lobby* (spring 1940), 5. Available in NARA (College Park). RG 59. 811. 4061. Mortal Storm/3. Box No. 3809.
63 Ibid.
64 Copyright script, reel 2, p. 21; June 25, 1940.
65 Quirk, *Margaret Sullavan*, 104.
66 Hayward, *Haywire*, 202.
67 Phyllis Bottome to Sidney Franklin, February 7, 1940. USC Cinematic Arts Library, The MGM Collection, "The Mortal Storm," Folder 2 (Box 128).
68 Ibid.
69 Phyllis Bottome to L. B. Mayer, February 13, 1940. SAF, Box 21, 139.
70 PB to Professor Potter, March 9, 1939. BL Add. Mss. 88921/3/3.
71 PB to Roger Scaife, August 3, 1940. BL Add. Mss. 88921/3/3.
72 PB to Maida McCord, April 4, 1940. BL Add. Mss. 88921/3/3.

73 PB to Roger Scaife, August 12, 1940. BL Add. Mss. 88921/3/3.
74 MGM producer Pandro Berman in Basinger and Wasson, *Hollywood the Oral History*, 296.
75 See Scott Eyman's discussion of this point in *The Lion of Hollywood*, 255–7.
76 See SAF for correspondence on such casting. Box 21, 139, "Mortal Storm," 1939.
77 Sidney Franklin to Claudine West, October 4, 1939. SAF Box 19, Sack 17.
78 Franklin, "We Laughed and We Cried," 286.
79 Ibid., 287.
80 Ibid.
81 Ibid., 286.
82 Note tucked into binding of script dated March 4, 1940, in Special Collections, *The Mortal Storm*, 1940, Margaret Herrick Library.
83 MGM-PCA correspondence. "Close Up the Ranks," February 17, 1940. Margaret Herrick Library, "Close Up the Ranks."
84 Franklin, "We Laughed and We Cried," 287.
85 Cited in Hervé Dumont, *Frank Borzage. The Life and Films of a Hollywood Romantic* (Jefferson, NC, and London: McFarland & Co., 2006), 298.
86 Ibid., 290.
87 Ibid., 291.
88 Sidney Franklin to Victor Saville, March 4, 1940. SAF, Box 16, File 20.
89 Dumont, *Frank Borzage*, 288.
90 The phrase comes from an article by Frank S. Nugent, "Russia Grasps a Nettle," *New York Times*, November 13, 1938, 26.
91 See scripts in the Department of Special Collections, Turner/MGM Scripts. *The Mortal Storm*. Margaret Herrick Library dated March–April 1940, Box 2173.
92 Howard Strickling to Sidney Franklin, MGM Inter-office Communication, June 5, 1940. SAF Box 21, 139.
93 Eyman, *Lion of Hollywood*, 313–14.
94 Ibid., 217.
95 Basinger and Wasson, *Hollywood. The Oral History*, 294.
96 Franklin memo, April 25, 1940. SAF, Box 21, 139.
97 Howard Strickling to Sidney Franklin, June 5, 1940. SAF, Box 21, 139.

6

June 20, 1940: Did Anyone Have Time to Go to the Movies?

The Film and the Moment

The release date for *The Mortal Storm* came on June 20, 1940, fourteen contentious months after MGM purchased the movie rights to Bottome's novel. The date proved to be extraordinary in American politics. Among other events on that crowded Thursday, a bill initiating conscription for the first time since the First World War was introduced in the House and Senate. The isolationists were sure to rise in opposition. But there was more. The president made two key appointments to his cabinet that could only suggest to the astute observer that he had begun to form the government that would serve him in time of war. Those two appointments—Henry Stimson as Secretary of War and Frank Knox as Secretary of the Navy—came as close as Roosevelt ever came to formally announcing, before the Democratic Convention in Chicago, that he intended to run for a third term. Those appointments also came as close as Roosevelt ever came to revealing to the American public his certitude that the country faced a two-ocean war that would not be long in coming. *The New Republic* had observed a month earlier, "Almost everything that has happened in the past week has been a consequence of the German victory."[1] The same held true in June.

The film enjoyed more than mere coincidence. *The Mortal Storm* provided the visual rhetoric that framed nearly every major political issue before the American public as the war in Europe intensified. Hollywood had produced a film that both reflected as well as advocated intervention in the cataclysmic events that occurred in June 1940. The film and the moment converged. Each enhanced the other.

An Auspicious Beginning to the Month for Hollywood

David Welky, in his monograph *The Moguls and the Dictators*, labels June 1940 "the pivotal month."[2] By the end of that year, only Britain precariously remained of the studios' once lucrative European market.[3] The first days of June, on the other hand, had been good to Hollywood. A Hollywood-Washington partnership formed as a result of critical legal decisions and organizational negotiations over the studios' role in the event of war. The moguls won a victory in court that encouraged the Justice Department to settle its anti-trust lawsuit on the studios' terms rather than the government's which had called for divesting the producers of their lucrative theater chains. The studios could therefore continue to monopolize production as well as exhibition.[4] They remained in control of the industry they had created.

On June 5 the government agreed to another matter in Hollywood's favor. After lengthy negotiations, the moguls, in collaboration with Washington, formed the Motion Picture Committee Cooperating for the National Defense (MPCC).[5] The MPCC would facilitate Hollywood's contribution to the war effort should the United States become a combatant. In the meantime Hollywood would support Roosevelt's interventionist foreign policy as war loomed.[6] Two victories forging a partnership between Hollywood and Washington on the eve of war made up for the studios' potential loss of all transatlantic revenue should Britain fall to the Nazis.

Barbed Neutrality

The Mortal Storm premiered in Washington, D.C. at Loew's Theater, one of the most plush and palatial in the city, not far from the White House. Ushers in uniform guided patrons over lush, red carpet to their thickly cushioned seats. A fitting venue in which to welcome the conquering Nazis, at least on screen, to the nation's capital. Not far away, almost simultaneously on Capitol Hill, the US Senate convened at noon with the Assistant Rector of the Church of the Epiphany, Duncan Fraser, giving the invocation.[7] It was to be a full day for the Senate with business conducted well into the evening. By 8:30 p.m., as Senator Bankhead (D-Alabama) noted, the agenda still remained full.[8]

In Europe, the real Nazis relentlessly tightened their grip on France. The *New York Times* reported that day: "Chancellor Hitler's battalions were reducing the Maginot Line to a military legend and battling their way through Southern France."[9] "The German flag flies over Versailles,"

Goebbels preened.[10] In Britain, the situation for the civilian population also deteriorated rapidly. On Tuesday, June 18, the Germans had begun to bomb the country's major population centers. Early on the morning of June 20, "Britain was undergoing another major air raid."[11]

In response to the extraordinary German advances, the Senate passed a military appropriation bill that day. At sea the threat was just as dire. The loss to British shipping in the Atlantic from U-boat attacks had more than doubled from May to June. The Atlantic had become a very dangerous place. No less so the Pacific. Three days earlier on June 17, the US navy had requested doubling the size of the fleet. To emphasize the point, it issued an alert that day for Pearl Harbor, also warning of the threat of Japanese sabotage to the Panama Canal.[12]

Certain to arouse even more controversy than a military appropriations bill, on June 20 Edward Burke (D-Nebraska) introduced in the Senate the first peacetime conscription act in US history.[13] Burke had regularly opposed the president's domestic policy with the exception of the Social Security Act. In an about face, he now embraced Roosevelt's foreign policy. He was joined by James Wadsworth (R-New York) in the House who introduced the conscription bill to that body. Wadsworth, more consistent in his opposition to the New Deal, had opposed the Social Security Act. The Burke-Wadsworth sponsorship of conscription, like the appointments of Republicans Stimson and Knox, all on the same day, showed the bipartisan commitment to a transformation in American foreign policy.[14]

In reality, those two measures, military appropriations and conscription, one passed and one debated, amounted to no more than desperate acts of catch up. Slightly over a month earlier, the US army had conducted the largest peacetime training exercise in its history.[15] The battlegrounds were located in Texas and Louisiana, the German army safely an ocean away. Among other field tests the high command pitted "horse cavalry against mechanized forces," the worth of one over the other in May 1940 still an open question for the US military.[16] As the war games progressed, it became painfully clear that cumbersome American equipment and antiquated strategies would be no match for the Germans. "American arrogance died during the maneuvers," wrote historian Doris Kearns Goodwin.[17]

The exercises took place simultaneously with the triumph of the blitzkrieg on what had been the terrain of the Western Front where the four-year stalemate in the First World War had occurred. Over there in 1940 had come to represent a potential nightmare for the US military if it had to face an even more formidable foe than the one of 1917–18. The woes of the American army and navy did not, however, make for political consensus. Some members of the Senate, for example, asked, did Germany represent the future of Europe? Should we accommodate the victor and strike a bargain to our advantage while we still could? The United States would dominate the Western hemisphere and Germany could control Europe and beyond. They were prepared to work in secret with the German embassy to subvert what they saw as Roosevelt's adventurist foreign policy. Other Senators posed different questions, asking whether the Nazi and American systems were antithetical and a clash between them inevitable. Should we prepare for conflict while we could still choose the time and place of engagement? Representatives of both sides, isolationists and interventionists, squared off in the US Senate on June 20.

In Congress: Isolationists vs. Interventionists

The Regional Divide

Senators from the West and Midwest figured prominently among the isolationists. The South, in contrast, backed Britain. By the fall of 1940, according to the *New York Times*, 70 percent in the South supported aid to Britain "even at the risk of war."[18] The newly elected, brash young Democratic Senator from Florida, Claude Pepper, for example, became an outspoken proponent of intervention in the summer of 1940. By the end of August, members of the Congress of American Mothers [Against War] had "hung 'Claude Benedict Arnold Pepper' in effigy from a Capitol Hill maple tree."[19] They protested his support of conscription. On June 20, Pepper cited a story that had appeared in that morning's *Washington Post,* warning of an impending Nazi takeover in Uruguay. Would that be a prelude, he asked, to Nazi penetration of all Latin America, much as Hitler's diplomacy and the German war machine had just accomplished in Europe.[20]

The issue of Nazi penetration in Latin America had aroused the southern states along the Gulf of Mexico. On the morning of June 20, the Louisiana State Legislature presented the Senate with a resolution calling on Congress "to provide [...] funds [...] to establish [...] an adequate national defense."[21]

Western states saw the matter differently. On June 20, for example, the civic leaders of Caldwell, Idaho, also sent the Senate a petition. Among them, was William Griffin, the son of a Confederate hero and a self-taught engineer, who had earned respect as a successful businessman and Chief Engineer of the Wyoming Timber Co. He often articulated the consensus in local politics and may have drafted the petition to the Senate of his fellow townsmen in Caldwell.[22] Their message arrived on the same day as the one from Louisiana and asked in contrast, "that the U.S. preserve its neutrality and keep out of war [...]."[23] Clearly, residents of the Gulf states in their proximity to Latin America believed they had more to fear from Nazi penetration in the southern hemisphere than those in the Western states.

Diplomat Hans Thomsen and the Isolationists

On the day *The Mortal Storm* was released, Senator Pepper rose in the Senate to ask, "Hans Thomsen [...] we are always hearing about Hans Thomsen [...] What is the word for Germanophiles that is comparable to Anglophiles? [...] I see enough of it here in the Senate [...]."[24] His colleague, Gerald P. Nye, the feisty Republican from North Dakota, responsible for the neutrality legislation of a few years earlier, who claimed to be the Senate's expert on propaganda, could have answered him.[25] On April 25, 1939, Nye filled seven pages of the *Congressional Record* with his denunciation of a recent publication by a British writer Sidney Rogerson, entitled "Propaganda in the Next War."[26] Nye condemned it as "plainly a handbook for British propaganda" that would lure the United States into war on the side of Britain.[27] Senator William H. King (D-Utah) countered that "to be entirely fair," we should balance condemnation of Britain by "referring to the propaganda of the Central Powers [in the First World War] which was more extensive, if not sinister and malevolent."[28] King spoke with authority on the matter. He had served on the Overman Committee in 1918, which had investigated German sedition in the United States during the war.[29] Nye too could be said to be an authority on German propaganda in the United States. He contributed to it.

The senator worked closely and in secret with the German embassy to further the isolationist cause. The embassy helped to reprint his Senate speeches and "distribute [them] by" a channel the Chargé d'Affaires Hans Thomsen would refer to only obliquely and never identify in his dispatches to Berlin. Thomsen explained his reticence to his government: "this understanding [regarding dissemination] is particularly delicate since Senator Nye, as a political opponent of the President, is under the careful observation of the secret state police here [FBI]."[30] Thomsen also referred specifically to his distributing Nye's speech on "Rogerson's book to 200,000 recipients."[31]

Thomsen's embassy responsibilities arose from his attachment to the Ninth Department of the Foreign Ministry which oversaw the ministry's efforts at foreign propaganda. With the outbreak of war in 1939, Hitler himself had provided the ministry's mission in that regard: "as long as [the Fuhrer] involved himself in European affairs, the principal task of Nazi diplomacy and propaganda remained that of keeping the United States out of the war."[32] The German leader further insisted that the embassy in Washington take over "as the controlling force behind all Nazi propaganda in America."[33] Thomsen's responsibilities had clearly expanded.

He had been posted to the Washington embassy in 1936 where his primary function seems to have been even then "very extensive propaganda activities under cover of" his diplomatic status.[34] His duties certainly increased after November 1938 when the ambassador Hans Dieckhoff was recalled following FDR's protest of *Kristallnacht*. At that time, Thomsen was promoted to Chargé d'Affairs and head of mission. He was trusted both for his loyalty to the Nazi cause and for his diplomatic competence. "A member of a distinguished Hamburg banking family," Thomsen had been "in charge of protocol" at Hitler's cabinet meetings and "served as one of the Fuhrer's interpreters."[35] In Washington, he combined diplomacy with propaganda as a trusted servant of the Reich.

Under Thomsen's direction, the German Foreign Office, through its Washington Embassy, had renewed the effort of the 1920s and 1930s to influence American opinion in Germany's favor. But there was a difference between the earlier campaign and the one conducted as a second war in Europe approached. The German innocence campaign of the interwar period, which initially fought reparations payments of 132 billion gold marks, seemed to have had almost unlimited funds at its disposal to combat anti-German sentiment.[36] In the period 1938–41, on the other hand, Thomsen had to justify his expenses down to the American penny. He therefore delighted in using the franking privileges of pro-German Congressmen such as Gerald Nye to save on postage, bragging to the ministry about his frugality.[37]

Once war began again in Europe, with the French and British declarations on September 3, 1939, the Third Reich hoped to stave off American intervention on behalf of the allies just as the Kaiser's government had tried to do in the First World War. "The specific order given to" Thomsen, from Hitler himself, called for him to keep "America [...] out of European affairs" as long as possible.[38] His barely adequate expense account limited his assignment to encourage Americans to believe that neutrality lay in their best interests. The inadequacy of funds for propaganda also reflected the Foreign Ministry's lack of illusions regarding its ability to "neutralize" the Americans indefinitely given long-term German goals of conquest. Nonetheless, Thomsen had no qualms about serious meddling in American politics. The election year 1940 provided ample opportunity.

On June 20 the Foreign Ministry received a lengthy account from Thomsen about how he intended to use the Republican convention scheduled to take place in Philadelphia at the end of the month to further German interests.[39] The Chargé d'Affaires had already been active in recruiting German allies on Capitol Hill. He informed the Foreign Ministry "[...] some fifty congressmen will be going to Philadelphia to explain our views to the delegates at the party convention." He observed that "it will be particularly effective if American politicians themselves provide enlightenment regarding our political aims."[40] He neglected to mention that the congressmen in question would also assist in choosing a nominee for their party in the upcoming presidential campaign. He had nonetheless revealed that a significant portion of the US Congress took money from the German embassy.

Thomsen paid for an advertisement in the *New York Times* on June 25 to which the leading isolationists in Congress affixed their names. The full-page spread listed the main points that subsequently went into the isolationist plank of the Republican Party platform.⁴¹ In addition to slipping German policy into American political discourse, Thomsen preened about his success at maintaining the secrecy of his efforts: "Nothing has leaked out about the assistance we rendered" to the isolationists, he proudly informed the Foreign Ministry.⁴² He had the same success at the Democratic Convention held in Chicago in mid-July, once again wielding influence among isolationist delegates in secret.⁴³

The Isolationist Cohort in the Senate

Thomsen could expect success at both conventions because isolationism attracted bipartisan support. More particularly, he had the ear of a group of Senators who not only shared his foreign policy goals, but also embraced, as would become increasingly clear, the antisemitism that underlay the Third Reich.⁴⁴ They had already engaged Charles Lindbergh, ex officio, as part of their Senate cohort. Lindbergh gave his first radio address on September 15, 1939, in the Hotel Carlton in Washington, DC, because he had gone to the capital to meet with his Senate allies. Like Hans Thomsen, in that speech and other radio addresses that followed over the course of the next two years, the aviator tried to prolong American neutrality as long as possible. Lindbergh in that first radio address also warned his listeners of the danger of propaganda, but more particularly, to note who wields it. He admonished his audience "to pay close attention to who owns the press and who influences the newspaper, the news picture [news reels] and the radio station."⁴⁵ It could be said that Lindbergh had launched his first salvo at the alleged Jewish control of the media with his inaugural radio address.

Starting in 1939 Senate isolationists had called for an investigation into the purveyors of propaganda. Such individuals and organizations were to be called to account. The interventionists stymied such an investigation by withholding funds for it. Senator Charles W. Tobey (R-New Hampshire) regularly condemned the tactic. He did so again on June 20. Senator Rush D. Holt (D-West Virginia) joined him, noting that the Chairman of the Committee to Audit and Control the Contingent Expenses of the Senate, James F. Byrnes (D-South Carolina), one of the president's most faithful allies in the Senate, had refused to release "twenty-five thousand measly dollars [...] to investigate foreign propaganda in the U.S. to involve us in war. If there is no foreign propaganda, why does he fear an investigation?" Holt challenged his seemingly stingy colleague from South Carolina.⁴⁶ The hardcore isolationists in the Senate constituted approximately 10 percent of that chamber which contained a broad spectrum of views regarding the appropriate US response to the war in Europe. But even as a minority, the isolationists could be formidable in their consistency and determination. Their strength lay in part with those who led them. One of them, Burton K. Wheeler (D-Montana), aspired to head the Democratic ticket in 1940 and believed that he stood a chance for the nomination in an open convention.[47] His bitter animosity toward Roosevelt, mutually shared, made him vulnerable, however.

Burton K. Wheeler, Leader of the Senate Isolationists

The isolationists of the 1930s had at first coalesced around Senator Gerald P. Nye's hearings on the owners of the munitions industry, the so-called merchants of death who had allegedly profited from the Great War.[48] By 1939, a purely domestic issue regarding the size of the Supreme Court had led to the emergence of Wheeler as the chief spokesman for those opposed to foreign wars. The Montana Senator two years earlier, in 1937, had bested a triumphant Roosevelt, fresh from his landslide victory for a second term. He defeated the president's effort to pack the Supreme Court. Nye himself came to defer to Wheeler. Wheeler's only other rival for leader of the isolationists was the powerful Chair of the Senate Foreign Relations Committee, William E. Borah (R-Idaho). Borah died unexpectedly of a stroke in January 1940, clearing a path for Wheeler's uncontested leadership.[49]

Wheeler and the Supreme Court

Wheeler had run for vice-president in 1924 on the Progressive ticket with Robert La Follette, but his real turn in the spotlight began when those opposed to FDR's bill to expand the Supreme Court chose him to lead the fight in the Senate against it.[50] The brevity of the fight over court packing, as the issue was known, belied its significance for pre-war politics. The battle lasted only from February to July 1937. Even so, *The New Republic* as late as 1940 called the fight "a kind of litmus paper to type a man as either 'reactionary' or 'liberal'" ever after.[51] Wheeler's opposition to the plan earned him the title of "forgotten liberal of American politics" in a profile by the progressive weekly.[52] His victory over FDR's proposed expansion of the Supreme Court made him the natural leader of the bipartisan anti-Roosevelt faction in the Senate increasingly opposed to the president's interventionist foreign policy.

Roosevelt seethed over the court defeat. FDR withdrew the bill to expand the Supreme Court when it was clear that neither house would pass it. John Nance Garner, vice-president and FDR's floor manager in the Senate, ceremoniously announced on the day the Judiciary Committee was to vote on the bill that he was going fishing, leaving for his annual angler's vacation. The president never forgave Garner for that well-timed desertion. As FDR confidant, journalist George Creel noted in his memoirs, "I do not think there is any question that Vice-President Garner's lukewarm attitude during the Court fight was eventually responsible for his elimination [from the ticket] in 1940."[53] But if Garner had simply withdrawn before a vote he could no longer control, Wheeler, on the other hand, played a decisive role in the defeat. His testimony before the Senate Judiciary Committee during which he pulled a letter from his pocket from none other than the Chief Justice himself, Charles Evans Hughes, denouncing the legislation, all but sank FDR's controversial bill on the spot. Wheeler described the scene in his memoirs:

> I have a letter by the Chief Justice of the Supreme Court, Mr. Charles Evans Hughes [...] You could have heard a comma drop in the caucus room while I read the letter aloud. It struck down one by one every point raised by Roosevelt [against the Court]. [...] the letter had a sensational effect.[54]

The proposed bill to expand the Supreme Court never even left the Judiciary Committee. It could not therefore come to a Senate vote. The president had no choice but to withdraw it in defeat.

Wheeler had lived up to his reputation. The historian of the Supreme Court under FDR, Jeff Shesol, said of the senator, "His geniality masked, just barely, a ruthlessness."[55] *The Nation* observed in 1924, at the time that Wheeler ran on the Progressive ticket, "he is [...] politically bloodthirsty [...] hard-boiled, hard-bitten, hard-fisted."[56] But there was more to Wheeler than the monochrome image that emerged from his aggressive and ambitious political conduct. He nursed his own complexities. The senator enjoyed warm relations with his wife Lulu and their six children. He and his wife figured prominently on the Washington social scene, counting among their close friends Justice Brandeis and his wife. The latter friendship belied the reputation that both Wheeler and his wife had acquired for antisemitism. Lulu Wheeler subsequently earned FBI attention for her allegiance to antisemitic causes.[57] The Montana Senator, like his wife, opposed intervention and gravitated to the side of the new Germany.

By the end of the 1930s, Wheeler had acquired another concern connected to his antisemitism. He watched Hollywood warily for its capacity to influence public opinion regarding Germany whether, as Lindbergh had cautioned in his first radio address, through the media, newsreels in particular, or feature films themselves. Wheeler sent his son John to Los Angeles to spy on the studios because of their "propaganda for war," as well as anti-German attitude. The senator had embraced a conflict with the motion picture industry. "The politically bloodthirsty" Montana Senator, as

The Nation had once dubbed him, had decided to challenge the influence of the Jewish moguls of Hollywood and their capacity to mold public opinion as the threat of war loomed again.

Wheeler and Hollywood: *Mr. Smith Goes to Washington*

The president had ample reason to regard Wheeler as a dubious Democrat of questionable loyalty to him and to the administration. Wheeler, for his part, may have feared that at some point the president would blindside him just as he had done to FDR when he pulled the letter from the Chief Justice out of his pocket as he sat before the Senate Judiciary Committee. The senator did not have long to wait for FDR's revenge. The president did not necessarily orchestrate Wheeler's humiliation, but those who could be regarded as his surrogates provided the circumstances. They made good use of the silver screen.

FDR and members of the Hollywood community had begun to warm to each other in the course of 1939. The president's newfound friends, moguls and movie stars, appeared with increasing frequency on White House guest lists.[58] The contacts paid off for both sides. The president's eldest son Jimmy found employment in MGM's New York office. The Academy of Motion Picture Arts and Sciences even bestowed on the young man the honor of presenting the Best Picture Oscar for 1938 to Frank Capra for *You Can't Take It with You*.[59] But it was Capra's next film, *Mr. Smith Goes to Washington*, that provided the real reward for FDR. The film humiliated Wheeler before the whole political establishment of the capital. Some might speculate that Roosevelt had waited patiently since the Supreme Court debacle to take his revenge on the Montana Senator. The master of the surprise attack now indeed found himself blindsided.

Capra's *Mr. Smith Goes to Washington* arguably aroused more controversy than any other American film made on the eve of the Second World War. It starred Jimmy Stewart whose career now appeared to have taken a new and serious turn, as had Hollywood itself.[60] *Mr. Smith*, it seemed, had made Wheeler its target. The senior senator from Montana proved a tempting one as the newly minted leader of the isolationist cohort in the Senate. The film depicted a cabal of corrupt senators who sought to profit from elected office, among them a figure who bore an unmistakable resemblance to Wheeler. While there is no evidence that FDR had any direct influence on the film, the result could not help but give him rueful pleasure. Knowledgeable viewers might ask, was the film about Senate corruption and Washington political operatives or did the film mock the isolationists, Senator Wheeler in particular? Did the film conflate isolationists with political corruption? Political questions abounded surrounding a mere Hollywood production.

Matters began innocently enough. Members of the National Press Club offered to arrange the premier in the film's setting. The technical advisor on the production was one of their own, Jim Preston, who "had been superintendent of the [Senate] Press gallery for thirty-five years."[61] When it came to arrangements Preston did not appear to show any more foresight than Capra in making it. The two turned out to be equally naïve regarding the film's reception by official Washington. For Capra, at first it seemed to be a dream come true to premier the film in Constitution Hall just down the hill from the US Senate where so much of the action takes place: "This would be Hollywood's most prestigious exploitation coup," he later wrote.[62] Unfortunately, far too many in the audience believed they were the ones being exploited, if not mocked.

Capra's account of the premier is nonetheless filled with incredulity at what transpired.[63] On October 17, 1939, *Mr. Smith Goes to Washington* opened in Constitution Hall, just down the street from the White House. Four thousand guests—nearly all of political Washington—attended the event. According to Capra, "the great Hall glittered with all the opulence of a new season's opening at the Met."[64] Although the president was not in attendance, James Farley, the manager of his two presidential campaigns and current Postmaster General, sat with the Cohn brothers, who ran Columbia Pictures. According to Capra, "Mr. Smith, in the film, allegedly came from Montana, so it was thought fitting that Montana's Senator Wheeler," along with his wife and "their teen-aged daughter should sit in the official box" with the filmmaker and his wife.[65]

Wheeler is reported to have stalked out part way through the film.[66] Capra disputes that, recounting that about one third of the audience left early, but not the Wheelers. Their remaining to the end may have been worse for the director and his wife than had their honored guests left prematurely.[67] Capra remembers:

> Mrs. Wheeler and her daughter withered us with hostile glances then whispered into Senator Wheeler's ear [...] The Wheeler family, having courteously stuck it out, [...] rose and huffily left our box; but not before Senator Wheeler had thrown me a polite, but curt over-the-shoulder "Good evening." He was not amused.[68]

Wheeler's reaction to the film would be echoed in an interview that Senate Majority Leader Alban Barkley (D-Kentucky) gave to the *Christian Science Monitor* a week later.

> Barkley declared the picture [...] a "grotesque distortion" of the way the Senate is run [...] It showed the senate made up of crooks, led by crooks, listening to a crook [...] He declared that Senator Burton K. Wheeler [...] felt as he did.[69]

The film had made strange bedfellows of Barkley and Wheeler, who were on opposite sides of the neutrality debate. Barkley sought to rescind the Nye legislation on neutrality while Wheeler was determined to retain it. By the time of the film premier, Wheeler was going down to defeat on the issue, no doubt adding to his distemper that evening.

The neutrality issue again pitted him against the president. Wheeler led the fight in the fall of 1939 to retain the Nye legislation of the mid-1930s designed to assure US neutrality in the event of another European war. At the same time, public opinion on foreign policy was shifting. Since September 3 with France and Britain at war with Germany, the president could count on public support to remove the restrictions on his ability to ship arms to America's former allies. The tide had turned. By the time of the gala movie premier, it was clear that Wheeler and the isolationists would fail to save the embargo against supplying belligerents in time of war.[70]

Already touchy because he faced a major defeat on the neutrality legislation, the Montana Senator had another reason to seethe in anger at the film premier. Senator Barkley had complained of a collective smear against the Senate, seemingly "made up of crooks, led by crooks […]." Wheeler, on the other hand, took personal offense at the portrayal of the corrupt politician "from a Western state" who mentored and then betrayed the young idealistic Jefferson Smith played by Jimmy Stewart. While the name of the Western state is never mentioned in the film, the credits acknowledge that the script was based on a "story by Lewis R. Foster," that is, a novel titled *The Gentleman from Montana*.[71] As Capra noted, Wheeler and his family sat with the director because of the film's Montana connection. Instead of feeling honored, Wheeler could well believe himself a target of the production.

The film revolves around the two senators from that state. Jimmy Stewart's performance as Montana Senator Jefferson Smith combined brash naïveté with the political wisdom suggested by his name. As Jefferson Smith, he was both the everyman who constitutes the foundation of American democracy and the founding father who drafted the Declaration of Independence. His name alone establishes him as the hero of the film. To further emphasize the point, Jefferson Smith, newly arrived in Washington, lingers in the capitol rotunda before a statue of Thomas Jefferson, pen in hand, with the Declaration of Independence curled at his feet.

Marc Eliot, in his biography of Stewart, suggests a Christ-like association with the character.[72] He has a surrogate father in Senator Joseph Paine, just as Jesus's "surrogate" father was named Joseph. Another character warns Smith that in fighting a powerful cohort in the Senate, he will be "crucified."[73] In fact in the twenty-three-hour filibuster that Smith conducts at the climax of the film, he reads from both the Declaration of Independence and the Bible. To trample on Smith was to attempt to crush by association iconic figures revered by the majority of Americans. Stewart executed the role brilliantly, winning critical and popular acclaim. He received an Academy

Award nomination for his performance when he was already at work on the set of *The Mortal Storm*.

The press in all regions of the country lauded the film.[74] The Spokane *Spokesman Review* stated: "For the first time the screen has become eloquent in relation to the significance of our times." The *New York Daily Mirror* commented on the film in an editorial: "There is a great movie at the Radio City Music Hall [...] *Mr. Smith Goes to Washington* [...] Let [Capra's] simple devotion to America be an example to the Browders [of the American Communist Party] and the Kuhns [of the German-American Bund]." The *Cincinnati Post* added: "The high privilege of being an American finds its best and most effective expression in *Mr. Smith Goes to Washington*." Those offended by the film clearly found themselves at odds with much of the public.

The source of Wheeler's anger lay in the character played by Claude Rains, the other Montana Senator in the film, Joseph Paine. By the film's end, Paine has indeed lived up to his surname and inflicted pain on both those who trusted him as a man of integrity and those who aligned with him as a co-conspirator. In the film Rains possessed a physical appearance that strongly suggested Wheeler. His hair completely white, wearing frameless glasses, Rains clearly had been made up to resemble the real senator from Montana. He also had another quality that evoked Wheeler. His British accent seemed out of place among down home Western and Midwestern politicians. The same was often observed of Wheeler whose strong Yankee/New England accent stood out in Butte, Montana.[75] The film's characterization of Senator Paine also included a quality that Wheeler himself made no attempt to hide. He was determined to succeed Roosevelt as president. In the film, Jim Taylor (Edward Arnold), powerful editor of the most important newspaper in the state, tells Paine, "You're the logical man from the West for the national ticket."[76] In the character of Jefferson Smith's perfidious mentor, Hollywood had satirized the senior senator from Montana, antagonizing Wheeler on his own turf.

As noted above, Wheeler had good reason for believing that FDR would seek revenge at his expense. Hollywood as well had ample cause to play politics. The studios recognized that by 1939 with the Justice Department's anti-trust lawsuit against them still pending, they would have to make "a stronger commitment to [the administration's] anti-fascist agenda" to placate the White House.[77] Embarrassing a prominent opponent of FDR could abet Hollywood's interests as well as the president's. *Mr. Smith* appeared to score on both counts. Hollywood suggested support for the president's foreign policy by apparently making the leading isolationist Burton K. Wheeler its target. When ardent Jefferson Smith, having become aware of the corruption surrounding Paine, storms into the senator's office, the most prominent photo on the wall is that of a youthful, smiling Charles Lindbergh. The message: corruption and isolationism cohere. A month before *Mr. Smith* premiered, Lindbergh had given his first isolationist radio address. His photo, so prominently displayed in Senator Paine's office, enhanced one message of the film, that is, the depiction of Senator Wheeler as Senator Paine. Lindbergh and Wheeler had recently aligned to form the isolationist cohort in the Senate.

The central placement of an enlarged photo of Lindbergh was carefully calculated. The attentive viewer can see a cut in the film just before Jefferson Smith enters Paine's office. Smith waits in the reception and then charges into Paine's private office. There is a blank screen before Smith walks past a wall of photos in Paine's office. Lindbergh's photo, the largest, crowds out all the others. Its prominence is evident as Smith both enters and leaves the office. The black screen indicates a cut and possible insertion of a new or re-done scene: in this case the wall of photos with that of Lindbergh the largest of all.

Since the imposition of serious censorship in 1934, the studios had learned how to work fast to drop or add scenes. For example, the scripts for *The Mortal Storm* in the Academy's Margaret Herrick Library show changes being shot and inserted almost up to a month before the film's release. A month separated Lindbergh's first radio address and the premier of *Mr. Smith*, time enough for a Hollywood studio to reshoot a short scene and splice it in. The politically active scriptwriter Sidney Buchman, rather than the naïve Frank Capra, in all likelihood, was responsible for adding a photo of Lindbergh to the décor of Senator Paine's office. The smiling photo captured the emerging isolationist terrain of American politics in the fall of 1939 and the aviator's newfound prominence in it.

Sidney Buchman, who wrote the script for *Mr. Smith*, had his home state of Minnesota in mind as much as Senator Paine's Montana. He embedded two versions of the Midwest in the film. Buchman came from Duluth, Minnesota, having grown up in that part of the state known for its radicalism and embrace of left-wing causes. By the time that Buchman left Duluth in 1919 after graduating from high school, he would have encountered the birth of American Communism among the Finnish American communities of the Upper Midwest.[78] Once in Hollywood, starting in 1934, to try his hand as a scriptwriter, he found ample opportunity to return to his political roots. He joined the Communist Party and the leftist Hollywood Anti-Nazi League. Capra acknowledged Buchman's membership in the Communist Party at the time that he wrote the script for *Mr. Smith*.[79]

Lindbergh, on the other hand, represented a very different tradition in Minnesota politics. Born the month before Buchman in February 1902, he came to maturity at the same time, but in the southern, conservative, agricultural part of the state. Lindbergh's hometown of Little Falls is located a two-hour drive south of Duluth. The political distance that separates the two communities is far greater.[80] The aviator embraced his father's isolationist politics from the First World War, along with the views of the conservative financiers who mentored him after he returned from Paris in 1927. By the late 1930s, Lindbergh, like Wheeler, applauded the new Germany. Jefferson

Smith, in contrast, rejects the tutelage of men like those from whom Lindbergh so readily found support. Buchman transposed to the nation's capital a dichotomy he had observed while growing up in Minnesota between conservative isolationists and left-wing internationalists. The character Jimmy Stewart played disdained what Lindbergh represented by 1939.

To Wheeler, it must have seemed that the silver screen gave radical Jews like Sidney Buchman far too much influence over the American public. But the senator had an answer. He had observed Roosevelt's use of the Commerce and Justice Departments to threaten Hollywood's monopoly of the movie industry. If the movies constituted interstate commerce, Wheeler was well placed to intervene against the industry. He had chaired the Senate's Interstate Commerce Committee (ICC) since 1935 and made it one of the most powerful committees in the Senate. Wheeler's committee, when the time was right, could investigate the economics of Hollywood as well as its inordinate influence on the American public.

Wheeler was not alone in considering legislation against Hollywood as a result of Capra's film. *The Detroit News* predicted "an early and smashing retaliation" for the film in passage "of the Neely anti-block booking bill."[81] The bill already before Congress would forbid the studios from forcing movie theaters to purchase blocks of films in order to acquire the best pictures. Both Congress and the Justice Department could conceivably join forces to divest the studios of their monopoly of the distribution and exhibition of motion pictures. Overnight, it seemed, Hollywood had become a political player with an unfair advantage that its rivals in politics were determined to curb.

According to Capra, the Washington press corps, initially enthusiastic about a political film set in the capital, like the politicians, turned against it because reporters and pundits quickly perceived the medium "as a rival opinion maker."[82] One group of journalists, Capra noted, proved the exception and almost immediately rallied to his defense. Capra praised the New York critics for their defense of him:

> Most of New York's important film critics had been invited [to the premier] as guests. Sensing an ugly scene, Frank Nugent (*Times* [soon to be replaced by Bosley Crowther]), Howard Barnes (*Herald Tribune*) [...] Bill Boehnel (*World Telegram*) slipped into our booth and set up a shock absorbing barrier. All had [just] written reviews lauding *Mr. Smith* as one of the year's most impressive films."[83]

Boehnel, for example, had called the film "a stirring patriotic document [...]."[84]

Within eight months, Barnes, Boehnel, and Crowther, Nugent's successor at the *Times,* criticized *The Mortal Storm* for its belated release and use of "non-Aryan" in place of the word "Jew." Their criticism, I would argue, can be traced back to *Mr. Smith*. They had only recently observed Hollywood's audacity in producing a controversial film that revealed the possibility of corruption in the Senate and targeted one of the leading isolationists in American politics. Hollywood, they implied, had shown great courage with *Mr. Smith*. With the release of *The Mortal Storm*, coinciding with the Nazis' triumphal march across Western Europe, the stakes were so much higher. Hollywood could do better, they insisted, as it had shown in Capra's depiction of American politics.

Mr. Smith and *The Mortal Storm* should be considered in tandem. Jimmy Stewart starred in both. He appeared at the time to carry Hollywood as far left and politically engaged as it dared to go. Will Hays, spokesman for the studios, had announced in March 1939 that Hollywood could now treat the issues of the day, addressing matters of "war and peace." It did so with *The Mortal Storm*. He added, it could also initiate "discussion of the values of our [...] democracy."[85] *Mr. Smith* had opened that conversation. Jimmy Stewart embodied Hollywood's new more political trend as 1939 turned to 1940. Playing Senator Jefferson Smith, he modeled civic courage with a stand on principle against overwhelming odds, confronting a kind of fifth column within the US Congress itself. *Mr. Smith*, taken as a whole, could be seen as a metaphor for the principled fight against a fascist takeover from within at the highest levels of government. Capra saw the film's relationship to the menace of fascism. He called it "a shot in the arm for all the Joes [...] that resent being [...] pushed around by all the Hitler's in the world."[86]

From Wheeler's perspective, *Mr. Smith* raised a number of other questions. Did Hollywood attempt to undermine the credibility of the Senate in popular consciousness or just the reputation of one senator in particular "from a Western state"? Wheeler, as noted, hoped to head the Democratic ticket in 1940. He had run for vice-president in 1924 and sought the same office in 1932. With his emergence as one of the most powerful figures in the Senate, Wheeler believed the time was ripe for him to claim the top prize. Three times in the film, Senator Paine is manipulated by a reference to "a national convention coming up." The first reference is the most pointed of all: "you're the logical man from the West for the national ticket," his co-conspirator tells him. In American politics in 1939, "the logical man from the West" could only mean the powerful senator from Montana. An accusation of corruption could sink Wheeler's chances for the presidency, starting with nomination to the "national ticket," as Edward Arnold, playing corrupt newspaper editor Jim Taylor, says temptingly in *Mr. Smith*.

Other issues were at stake. Both Wheeler and his close ally Republican Senator Gerald Nye of North Dakota had honed their national reputations on Senate investigating committees, that is, in revealing corruption and calling evildoers to account. Their personal reputations were critical to that role. Hollywood now seemed to say that Senate leaders were no better than those they had investigated. Having tarred the upper chamber's leadership with the stain of corruption, did Hollywood intend to compete with its members over whose voice would prevail in framing the urgent matters before the country just as war began in Europe?

Hollywood was not the isolationists' only competitor as war loomed. *Mr. Smith* raises another question. What role, if any, did the president play in a film potentially so damaging to one of his rivals for the nomination in 1940? Was Roosevelt conspicuous by his absence at the film's premier, attempting to hide his possible involvement? In any event the president came away unscathed from the controversies surrounding the film.

Capra believed the film threatened at least some members of the press as much as it threatened the politicians. The Washington pundits especially, he wrote, who "not only influenced government policy," but "made it" attacked *Mr. Smith* as representing "a new, perhaps superior power invading their empire—'film power.'" According to Capra the Washington press corps "envied and feared film as a rival opinion maker."[87]

The controversy over Capra's film dissipated. Hollywood came away unscathed and retained its monopoly over the most effective communications medium in the country. There was nonetheless one casualty from *Mr. Smith*. Even if, as Wheeler insisted, he and Roosevelt reconciled after the court fight, the premier of that film would have tested their cordiality given the president's emerging closeness to Hollywood. Their relations must surely have been strained, intensifying the conflict between the president and the isolationists.

If *Mr. Smith* was an opening salvo, more was to come. On June 20, 1940, another Jimmy Stewart film premiered. It offered a new twist sure to antagonize Wheeler. Adding insult to injury, from the senator's point of view Stewart's latest film, *The Mortal Storm*, committed two transgressions. It could be said to propagandize for war. Worse, it made heroes of embattled European Jews.

Two Appointments in One Day

To Senate isolationists it might have seemed on June 20 that the biggest show in town played not in a local movie theater but in their own chamber. That morning the president sent two critical, cabinet-level nominations to the Senate for its approval. He named Henry Stimson to be Secretary of War and Frank Knox to be Secretary of the Navy. His language was biblical in its efficiency. His message to the Senate read:

The White House. June 20, 1940
To the Senate of the United States:
I nominate Henry L. Stimson of New York to be Secretary of War. FDR
Same.
I nominate Frank Knox of Illinois to be Secretary of the Navy. FDR.[88]

Both towering figures in American public life, neither man needed identification beyond what the president provided in his letters of nomination that day. The new appointees were staunch Republicans; neither had supported FDR's domestic programs. Knox had run for Vice-president with Alf Landon in 1936 on an anti-New Deal platform. While Landon had wavered in his positions and avoided rigorous campaigning, Knox had taken a more aggressive approach. He, for example, had condemned the radical social engineering of the New Deal by accusing the president of "leading us toward Moscow."[89] After Roosevelt's landslide victory, Knox re-thought his hostility to the president and increasingly supported FDR's foreign policy.[90] In the week that France and Britain declared war on Germany, he publicly called on the president to form "a bipartisan cabinet."[91]

Stimson, also a staunch Republican, was a good choice for such a cabinet. He came thoroughly prepared to head the War Department. He had served as Secretary of War once before under Taft and as Secretary of State under Hoover just as Japanese aggression began against China in 1931. Roosevelt had taken Stimson's measure in early 1933 when the then Secretary of State had helped to negotiate the transition arrangements from Hoover's administration to FDR's.[92] Stimson impressed him then and continued to do so through the 1930s as an early and outspoken critic of the fascist regimes. In contrast, Secretary of War Harry Woodring, whom Stimson would replace, had repeatedly undercut military preparedness measures and opposed FDR's policy of shipping arms to France and Britain. Woodring argued that such generosity weakened American defenses. Stimson would have no such qualms. FDR could similarly trust Knox to assist in expanding the Pacific fleet to enable the navy to fight a two-ocean war.

The Stimson and Knox appointments turned the isolationists livid. Wheeler denounced Stimson for "secretly" colluding with twenty-nine others in drafting an advertisement "to propagandize the American people into taking steps that would lead this Nation to war [...]."[93] The advertisement had appeared in the *New York Times* two days earlier on June 18. Bennett Champ Clark, a staunch isolationist from Missouri who often worked in tandem with Senator Nye, gave his support to Wheeler, announcing that he too would never vote to confirm Stimson and Knox. "They are for war" and are certain to encourage "war propaganda and [the] war spirit," he fumed.[94] According to the *Times*, "Democratic isolationists [in the Senate] became so bitter in denouncing the President's appointments that it was necessary for the majority leader Alban Barkley to remind the body that Congress alone had the power to make war and that the Secretaries of the Navy and War had little to say in the matter."[95] Stimson nevertheless had already had quite a lot to say in the matter.

Henry Stimson

A Patrician ahead of His Time

Henry Stimson was every inch an America patrician. The son of a prominent surgeon, he graduated from Phillips Exeter and Yale. After completing Harvard Law School, he chose law as his profession and excelled at it. He also excelled in government service, appointed, as noted, Secretary of War before the First World War and Secretary of State afterward, on both occasions in the cabinets of Republican presidents. In between, he distinguished himself on the Western front, negotiated an end to the civil war in Nicaragua, and served as Governor-General of the Philippines. In the 1930s Stimson returned to Wall Street and the practice of law as he had done before he entered government service. For Stimson, as for Churchill, that period could be termed the "wilderness years." Both men were ahead of their time in warning of the rise of fascism. Susan Dunn emphasizes Stimson's early warning about Japanese aggression and outspoken internationalism in determining FDR's decision to make him Secretary of War in 1940.[96]

Another factor motivated Stimson's prescient contempt for the dictators. He disdained the revisionist consensus of the 1930s that had absolved Germany of guilt for her conduct in the First World War. But then so did FDR. David Kaiser maintains that the president's attitude toward Germany in 1939–40 merely reflected his position at the time of the First World War when "he had been an active, and indeed eager advocate of American involvement in the First World War."[97] Kaiser further notes that the future president "blamed that conflict on German aggression from the beginning."[98]

Stimson did the same. At least from early 1939 up to his appointment as Secretary of War, he condemned Hitler's policy and his intentions, at the same time challenging the revisionist consensus denying German guilt for the last war. Stimson saw a similarity between Germany's aggressive policy before the First World War and that of the Third Reich in the late 1930s. Almost single-handedly, the former Secretary of State reintroduced into the national discourse the rhetoric of 1919 regarding German war guilt. In doing so, Stimson spoke with unique authority. Doris Kearns Goodwin has called him "the patron saint of the Eastern establishment."[99] His stature transcended the traditional party divisions of American politics. The Democratic president took note of what he said. So did the German embassy.[100]

Stimson, for example, extolled the former Foreign Secretary of Great Britain, Sir Edward Grey, who had pursued a policy before the First World War "focused primarily on the 'German threat'."[101] Grey's memoirs, published in 1925, justifying his anti-German policy, had been decidedly out of step with the emerging consensus on Germany as just another victim of the war.[102] Stimson recounted that "for nine long years before the Great War [Grey] labored [...] against the constantly growing menace of Prussianized Germany." Now, the former Secretary of State warned, "the German mailed fist has far less velvet concealing it than in the years preceding 1914."[103] Stimson made it plain: German militarism had ignited the Great War, not colluding arms makers or conniving British politicians, as the isolationists argued. German militarism in a new and more menacing form might encourage war again.

Stimson frequently referred to the First World War in his statements, the very repetition suggesting the need to get it right after two decades of distortion. He also used the war as his reference point because as he said he knew it from personal experience: "I have witnessed the war as a participant and saw at close hand its sorrows and devastations," he lamented.[104] He joined the president in calling for the repeal of the embargo provisions of the Neutrality Law, which forbade the Chief Executive from providing arms to combatants. But Stimson did it his way, arguing from the perspective of the First World War. He reminded the public that Robert Lansing as Secretary of State in 1915 had justified such sales to belligerents on the basis of international law.[105] Again, the First World War provided the justification for his position, because he saw the crucial similarities between that conflict and the one that threatened in 1939. As in the Great War, Britain and France confronted German aggression while American sympathies for her fellow democracies vied with the impulse to remain neutral.

The Republican elder statesman had begun his newfound activism by applauding the president's State of the Union Address of January 1939. He wrote a substantial letter to the *New York Times* in response to the president's message dated March 6, 1939. Stimson must have mulled over his words carefully given the interval between his remarks and the president's. When he finally commented he spoke with assurance. He "gave sweeping endorsement to a foreign policy of 'affirmative action'" on the part of the president.[106] But Stimson did something more in his letter to the *Times*. He provided a moral framework for an "affirmative action" policy, echoing the idealism that had driven American participation in the Great War. The very principles of democracy were now under threat, Stimson warned. He said of the members of the Berlin-Rome-Tokyo axis, "it is hardly appreciated what a complete reversal of the whole trend of European civilization they represent [...] a radical attempt to reverse [...] the long evolution out of which our democracies [...] have grown."[107]

By "hardly appreciated" Stimson referred to the corrosive effect of the revisionist interpretation of the war. But he also referred to something else. The interventionist position in the United States in early 1939 remained on the defensive, Germany's intentions still a matter of debate. Stimson's lonely warnings recall those of Bottome and other anti-appeasers in Britain two years earlier at the time she tried to publish *The Mortal Storm* "when it was dangerous to do so."[108] Like the British novelist, Stimson espoused an outsider's answer to the German question, praising Sir Edward Grey, the bête noir of the revisionists[109] and reminding of "the German mailed fist." Bottome as novelist and Stimson as statesman both warned of the threat from Germany, as war loomed before Britain and the United States in early 1939. The message of one would soon reinforce that of the other.

Graduation 1940

Stimson's views reinforced those of the president. FDR, like the former Secretary of State, began to raise the larger moral issues posed by the rise of fascism in the course of 1939. In his address to Congress of September 21, 1939, on repealing the embargo provisions of the Neutrality Law, the president stated: "Destiny first made us, with our sister nations on this Hemisphere, joint heirs of European culture. Fate seems now to compel us [...] to maintain [...] a citadel wherein that civilization may be kept alive."[110] Both Roosevelt and Stimson used the same phrase: European culture/European civilization. The stakes could not be higher in the struggle with fascism. Both would agree that German militarism, "the mailed fist" with "far less velvet," had placed the democracies and the very civilization they embodied once more at risk.

That risk had only increased in the following year; by the spring of 1940, the "mailed fist" of German militarism had struck. Stimson came into his own during the graduation season of 1940. With courage and conviction, he went before the Yale graduates of that year to make the case for conscription, speaking to the very ones who would have to fight. As he had so frequently done in the past, he invoked the First World War. On June 17 he told a mixed assembly of Yale seniors and lower classmen who filled Sprague Hall, "It was only in the Great War that a system [of conscription] was put in which, being fair, universal and carefully selective, went through without any hitch [...] This was a vital, decisive factor in winning the war." Stimson insisted, "compulsory military training" was again necessary.[111]

The former statesman found an unconventional ally in popular culture. *The Mortal Storm*, opening just three days after Stimson's address at Yale on June 17, dramatized the evils of Nazism. The film appeared to support his call for conscription and to confirm the warnings he had given in the past year regarding Germany. Jimmy Stewart's role in the film provided the example of sacrifice that Stimson urged upon the class of 1940. Playing pacifist Martin Breitner, Stewart is compelled to choose between self-sacrifice and self-interest. His moment of truth occurs in the scene in the ski chalet, described earlier, that takes place one year after Hitler has come to power. Freya Roth (Margaret Sullavan) persuades Martin to join her along with her brothers and fiancé at the chalet, where they had so often met before politics divided them. The others, unlike Freya and Martin, now belong to the Nazi Party. When the crowd lustily sings, "Close Up the Ranks," with the words "No race on earth can keep our land from glory. We are by birth the rulers of the world," Martin and Freya sit stone faced and silent. A third individual among the patrons, the elderly schoolteacher Mr. Werner also sits silently. When a group of Nazis gathers around to intimidate him Martin steps in. "This man's a friend of mine," he says, adding just as firmly, "I don't think you want a brawl. It's eight against two." He accompanies the older man to the door. Martin justifies his intervention to Freya: "I can't stand by and see the old chap bullied," he tells her upon returning to the table. The words, "old chap," carefully chosen by Claudine West, to invoke Britain.

Freya's fiancé Fritz Maberg (Robert Young) then demands of Martin: "We want to know if you're going to join the party and work for Germany or herd with the pacifist vermin we're going to stamp out!" At that moment someone shouts, "They're beating the old school teacher!" Martin glares at Fritz: "You want to know if I intend to join your party, I can tell you now: the answer's no!" He rushes out to aid Mr. Werner. In the few minutes of the scene, *The Mortal Storm* enacted the choice before the class of 1940. Would the young and vigorous come to the aid of the old and vulnerable? Would the New World rescue the Old? *The Mortal Storm* dramatized the German question as Stimson had posed it since his letter to the *New York Times* in March 1939. Civilization was at risk before the onslaught of German aggression. Would the heirs of that culture, safe within the citadel of the Western hemisphere, respond?

William Allen White

The month before Stimson addressed Yale undergraduates in the commencement season of 1940, he joined the foreign policy pressure group that William Allen White, the esteemed editor of the Kansas *Emporia Gazette*, had begun to organize. White operated with Roosevelt's blessing as he had in undertaking a similar effort in the fall of 1939 when the president sought to repeal the Neutrality Laws.[112] White then joined Clark Eichelberger, a renowned expert on international cooperation and an advisor to the League of Nations, to form the Non-Partisan Committee for Peace through Revision of the Neutrality Law. The group quickly became known as the White Committee. Local affiliates formed. They and the national committee successfully pressured Congress to repeal the Nye legislation that forbade American aid to France and Britain. White had followed a political trajectory similar to Stimson's. Like Stimson, a staunch Republican, White joined the former Secretary of State in outspoken support of FDR's emerging stand against the dictators. And like Stimson, White harbored no illusions about Germany, fearing "the Germans" might soon "conquer Europe and turn their greedy eyes westward."[113]

Starting in May 1940, White and Eichelberger joined forces again and, using similar methods to those they had employed to help repeal the Neutrality Legislation, forged a new "White Committee." By June, with headquarters in New York, the second White Committee began to operate. Its stationery listed as members hundreds of prominent individuals whose names in small type ran the length of the left margin and covered the entire reverse side of the committee's letterhead. Within months the Committee had 700 affiliates around the country.[114] It could prove formidable in support of Roosevelt's foreign policy which increasingly bore the label "aid to Britain."

White, however, chose to withdraw from direct involvement in the committee's efforts.[115] He remained in Kansas writing the editorials that had earned him a national reputation as the sage of the prairie and one of the New Deal's staunchest supporters in the Republican Party. Adding to his reputation for bipartisan moderation, White also commented regularly on politics in such respected periodicals as *The Nation* and *Saturday Review*.[116] An outspoken Republican who had supported his fellow Kansan Alf Landon in 1936, White also contributed the appearance of bipartisanship to endeavors that belonged to the president's agenda and that most Republicans in Congress opposed.

Clark Eichelberger played a different role on the committee from that of White. He ran the daily operations in New York which included oversight of the numerous local affiliates. He had to make the far-flung membership feel a part of the larger organization. White, on the other hand, preferred to comment from afar, leaving to others on the committee that bore his name to act on his suggestions.

One of White's suggestions to Eichelberger concerned *The Mortal Storm*. It is not known when he saw the film. He sat at home the first weekend the film played nationally, catching up on his correspondence. By late summer, White had seen the film and become enthusiastic regarding the uses to which it could be put in support of the interventionist cause. He wrote Eichelberger that *The Mortal Storm* should be screened at meetings of all the local chapters to encourage enthusiasm for the tasks before them. He also raised the possibility of local chapters sponsoring screenings for their communities as a way of generating wider support for the cause of aiding Britain.[117] The film had already demonstrated its political usefulness when its release coincided with Stimson's call for conscription. White now suggested a broader application of the film's message.

White's enthusiasm for *The Mortal Storm* implied something more. He had discerned a role for Hollywood in the perilous summer of 1940. With 80 million Americans attending 17–18,000 theaters each week, the movies had acquired the potential to sway the public either for or against the engagement that White and his political allies advocated. Hollywood, by 1940, could do more than entertain, something White's rivals also perceived.

Charles Lindbergh

The Aviator and the Diplomat

Lindbergh rarely went to the movies. In 1939, he saw four films. In 1941, he spent New Year's Day watching newsreels and in September he saw *Sergeant York*. No information remains about his movie attendance in 1940. Whether he frequented the movies or not, Lindbergh possessed a well-informed source on current cinema. What he missed on screen his close friend, the diplomat William R. Castle, could recount. Castle was an avid moviegoer and commented often in his diary on the films he saw.[118] Through Castle, Lindbergh would likely have learned in detail about the so-called "war propaganda films" of 1940 and their content. Thanks to Castle, he did not have to see *The Mortal Storm* for himself to realize the danger from his perspective Hollywood now posed in providing propaganda for war.

The two men had first met in 1931 when Castle had assisted the Lindberghs with arrangements for their trip to the Far East which provided Anne Morrow Lindbergh with the material for her first bestseller *North to the Orient*, an account of their air travel across Canada and Russia to China and Japan.[119] The two men became political allies after the aviator returned from Europe in the spring of 1939, meeting on a regular basis to further the isolationist cause. Castle lived a short walk from the property the Lindberghs rented on Long Island. On August 23, 1939, Lindbergh noted in his diary "Walked to Bill Castle's home at 6:00 [...]."[120] He did so frequently. They also consulted regularly by phone. Castle encouraged Lindbergh to go public with his isolationist campaign. Lindbergh agreed. He again noted in his diary on September 10, 1939, "Phoned Bill Castle and Fulton Lewis. Decided to go on the radio next week."[121] Fulton Lewis was an isolationist radio commentator with close ties to the German embassy.[122] Five days later, on September 15, 1939, Lindbergh gave his first radio address on behalf of the isolationist cause.

In 1940, contacts between Castle and Lindbergh became more frequent. They both detested the president and staunchly opposed his interventionist foreign policy. They also shared strong antisemitic views which ran like a red thread through their respective diaries. Lindbergh, for example, often condemned what he perceived as Jewish influence in the media, noting that Castle and Fulton Lewis possessed the same view, "We are disturbed about the effect of the Jewish influence in our press, radio, and motion pictures."[123] While Castle joined Lindbergh in concern about Jewish influence in the media, in his diary he revealed a more personal dislike of Jews. Typical entries include: "He is a rather objectionable Jew [...] after he had talked a few minutes [...] I doubted whether I could stand much more of it."[124] A week later he attended a dinner party where "many unpleasant things were said about Jews [...]," implying that he shared those views or at least moved in circles where such views were commonplace.[125]

Lindbergh valued Castle's advice and respected his distinguished diplomatic career. A Harvard graduate, Castle had served as Ambassador to Japan. He had been Assistant, then Under Secretary of State. In the 1920s, he directed the Division of Western European Affairs in the State Department; in the 1930s he devoted himself to Asian affairs. He advised Secretary of State Stimson regarding Asia but broke with him over policy toward Japanese aggression. Stimson advocated sanctions against Japan, while Castle opposed them. He dismissed Stimson's appointment as Secretary of War on June 20: "the most unpleasant news [...] R[oosevelt] puts in the cabinet [...] the one American whom the Japanese consider, and rightly so, their greatest enemy."[126]

Given his antisemitism and favorable views toward the dictators, Castle surprisingly enjoyed *The Mortal Storm*. Instead of condemning the film's sympathetic depiction of Jewish characters and the call to arms against Nazism, he dubbed it "a beautiful picture." His wife informed him that it was "in many ways better than the book." Castle emphasized how well the film succeeded. He characterized it as

> a most deadly indictment of Nazi philosophy and acts arising there [...] It is admirably acted and has none of the usual Hollywood exaggeration. But it does make one loathe the Nazis and all they stand for with a very personal and energetic loathing.[127]

One can only speculate about the conversation that Castle may have had with Lindbergh as a result of such praise for the film. Lindbergh might remind him that with its sympathetic portrayal of German Jews subjected to Nazi persecution, *The Mortal Storm* confirmed the misgivings, shared by both men, about "Jewish influence in our press, radio, and motion pictures."[128] From Lindbergh's perspective, the film made a case for American intervention in the war in Europe, possibly to rescue Jews, but certainly to aid Britain also at the mercy of the Nazi juggernaut. The film could attract Lindbergh's attention for another reason: its sympathetic portrait of renowned Jewish physiologist Victor Roth. The scientist's research into the composition of human blood would recall Lindbergh's own work through the 1930s with Nobel Prize winner Dr. Alexis Carrel on human physiology and organ transplants.

Professor Roth vs. Professor Carrel

While Bottome on her own admission crafted the character of Professor Roth as a homage to Alfred Adler, she also appeared to juxtapose her protagonist to Lindbergh's mentor, the Nobel Prize-winning physiologist Alexis Carrel to the clear advantage of the hero of *The Mortal Storm*. For example, in *The Mortal Storm* Professor Roth confronts his students, now wearing Nazi uniforms, to affirm that "blood does not differ by race [...] Scientific truth is scientific truth," he insists. Roth's heroic stand can be understood as contesting eugenicist, racist views that the Nazis certainly advocated but that also prevailed in many quarters of the United States at the time. Alexis Carrel staunchly defended those views. According to Lindbergh's biographer Scott Berg, "Nobody in Charles Lindbergh's adulthood affected his thinking more deeply than Alexis Carrel [...] In Dr. Carrel, the hero found a hero [...] and Carrel found a son."[129] From 1931 to 1938, they worked together on laboratory experiments to sustain organs outside the human body. Driving Carrel's research with Lindbergh was a commitment to the eugenics movement and its goal of ultimately perfecting a "genetic elite" in part through the voluntary practice of sterilizing those "deemed inferior."[130] Carrel also hoped apparently to be able to create the perfect human specimen.

Carrel's ideas on eugenics were expressed in his treatise *Man, the Unknown* published in September 1935. There are conflicting views as to the emphasis of that work. Scott Berg describes it as "a subjective discourse on the human body and soul, full of scientific fact and metaphysical opinions."[131] The work included the dictum that "A great race must propagate its best elements."[132] Anne Morrow Lindbergh's biographer, Susan Hertog, emphasizes in contrast to Berg the harsh prescriptions in Carrel's work. She cites his statement on social deviants: "Prisons should be abolished. Criminals should be whipped, sterilized, or gassed."[133] Kenneth Davis, another biographer of Lindbergh, provides the harshest account of what Carrel advocated in *Man, the Unknown*.[134] According to Davis, Carrel stated the "unfit" should be euthanized with the "proper gasses."[135] While their emphases differ, all three biographers concur: Alexis Carrel's views excluded him from the ranks of nature's liberals. Davis and Hertog might argue as well that Carrel shared the basic tenets of Nazi racist ideology.

Whether Bottome confronted Carrel directly in *The Mortal Storm*, she certainly wrote it in part to condemn the ideas that Carrel had tried to popularize in his bestseller of 1935, *Man, the Unknown*. In revising the novel for an American audience, where eugenics had a stronger hold than in Britain, she made Professor Roth, like Carrel, a Nobel laureate.[136] Professor Toller in the British edition of the novel did not hold the prestigious award. Professor Roth, the protagonist in its American version, therefore possessed credentials equal to those of Lindbergh's mentor. In the United States with Lindbergh and Carrel in partnership, Bottome confronted two renowned and highly popular proponents of the racist eugenics she abhorred. Professor Roth's insistence in novel and film that blood does not differ by race, no group is inherently superior or inferior to another, dismantles Nazi racism as well as Carrel's version of inbred elitism.

It is very likely that Lindbergh learned of *The Mortal Storm* as a film through his friend Castle, whether he viewed it or not. According to his diary, Castle saw it in late July 1940, precisely when he was especially close to Lindbergh and consulting with him on isolationist strategy on a regular basis.[137] It is also quite possible that Lindbergh read one or more of the five pieces that *New York Times* film critic Bosley Crowther wrote on *The Mortal Storm* in 1940.[138] By December, Crowther had named the film to his list of ten best for the year, observing that "variety and quality are notable in the annual list of outstanding films."[139] Lindbergh read the newspaper regularly, judging it "among our best," even if, he observed, "one cannot by any means believe all it says."[140]

One can also speculate that Lindbergh knew of Bottome's novel. *The Mortal Storm* shared a place on *Publishers' Weekly* bestseller list in 1938 along with Anne Morrow Lindbergh's *Listen! The Wind* about the Lindberghs' flights over Africa in 1933. That coincidence would bring Bottome's work to their attention. Set in Germany, *The Mortal Storm* may have further piqued their curiosity just as they were considering settling permanently in Berlin in late 1938.

Lindbergh Stayed Home

Lindbergh spent most of the week in which *The Mortal Storm* was released home on Long Island. On Monday, June 17, he received a phone call "from someone connected with the Republican convention arrangements in Philadelphia, asking [him] if [he] would attend the convention. [He] replied that [he] would have more influence in [his] stand on the war if [he] did not go to Philadelphia."[141] The unpublished version of the diary contains no more information than what Lindbergh chose to reveal in print about the phone call.

What there is, however, is tantalizing. Did Lindbergh ever consider running for president, as Philip Roth suggests he might have in his novel *The Plot Against America*? The Republican convention was scheduled to open the following Monday, June 24, and remain in session through the rest of the week. Two issues might have bothered Lindbergh about the invitation to attend. Whoever called lacked sufficient status, from Lindbergh's point of view, to warrant mention in his diary. The invitation itself, coming at the last minute, hardly suggested a groundswell movement on behalf of the aviator. Lindbergh may have felt slighted, only an afterthought or too controversial rather than, as he saw himself, an appropriate star participant at such an event. Despite his status as a leading isolationist, he may have feared rejection in competition with other popular contenders such as Taft or Willkie.

Lindbergh's refusal to attend the 1940 Republican convention also suggests something else. While his outspoken defense of neutrality made him the de facto leader of the isolationists, he was also the target of accusations that he worked for Germany, an issue to be discussed at greater length in Chapter 8. Lindbergh's refusal to attend the Republican convention belies the charge that he covertly furthered German aims. Defeating Roosevelt and obtaining the presidency would surely have been part of Lindbergh's mission had he in fact worked for Germany.

On June 21, the first Friday that *The Mortal Storm* played nationwide, Lindbergh "spent the evening" reading his father's isolationist tract from the First World War "Why Is Your Country at War?"[142] He also read that evening, as he so frequently did, *History of Europe* by the esteemed Oxford historian and former head of New College, H.A.L. Fisher.[143] Lindbergh, however, misinterpreted the work. He saw the war that Hitler had launched as no different from Fisher's account of past European conflicts. The historian would never have affirmed that misunderstanding of his study. Fisher regarded the Nazi menace as a unique threat to European stability. Had Fisher not died in a London street accident two months earlier, he would have joined Churchill's cabinet at its formation in May 1940, thus playing an activist role. Like Henry Stimson, he saw the conflict with Hitler as not just another European war. Western culture and civilization were now under threat, a view shared by Bottome.[144]

Phyllis Bottome on June 20, 1940

On June 20, 1940, Bottome and her husband Ernan Forbes Dennis settled into their home in Cornwall, having just returned to England. They had been in the United States since September 1939 where they had gone on a lecture tour that was to last until August of the following year; but as the situation in France deteriorated and it appeared that England would be next, they agreed that they must return and fight for their homeland themselves if necessary. Bottome had in fact given a few lectures in 1940. She had instead resided in Hollywood, offering herself as an unpaid consultant to the production of *The Mortal Storm*. In early June she and Ernan hastened to New York to take ship for England.

They had seen a version of *The Mortal Storm* in MGM's New York offices, rushing from the screening to board the ship, by June 1940 the crossing a far from safe undertaking.¹⁴⁵ Having arrived safely, June 20 might otherwise have been a day of celebration. *The Mortal Storm* as film and novel had preoccupied Bottome for several years. Now both had come to fruition. Instead of celebrating, however, she wrote her closest friend in Hollywood, the producer Walter Wanger of the current reality in Britain that she and Ernan found upon their return. Having left at the onset of the phony war in September, they arrived to find Britain under threat of invasion. Bottome made only an oblique reference to the film in a letter that captures the high drama and sheer intensity of life in Britain in late June 1940. She, no less than the British government, begged for assistance, in her case calling on her deep friendship with Wanger.

> France has fallen, and with this clarification fresh needs have arisen. This country is now a fortress and we look across the ocean as beleaguered soldiers search the horizon for the sight or sound of a Friend. I think you are that Friend. I have been informed that I should ask you privately should you wish to undertake this great act of fellowship with Freedom to hunt out and collect all the Tommy-guns from California ranches that are procurable, and if this venture has your approval to make an offer of these guns direct to Lord Lothian [the British ambassador], who will tell you how they can best be forwarded to us.¹⁴⁶

She assured Wanger that his efforts would not be wasted. "England is now spiritually prepared as never in her Island history […]."¹⁴⁷

Bottome trusted and respected Wanger, one of Hollywood's most prominent producers, working at times for Paramount, at times independently. Much of Bottome's Hollywood career had been linked to him. He had brought her novel *Private Worlds* to the screen in 1935, earning Claudette Colbert an Academy Award nomination for her role in the film. He might have produced *The Mortal Storm,* but his controversial and unpopular film *Blockade* (1938), depicting the Spanish Civil War, had caused him financial difficulties. While living in Hollywood in the spring of 1940, Bottome and her husband dined frequently with Wanger and his wife the actress Joan Bennett. In April when Wanger was elected president of the Academy of Motion Picture Arts and Sciences, Bottome congratulated him: "It was one of the few rays of light I see in our dark day because I have learned to count upon both your enlightenment and your courage."¹⁴⁸ On the eve of war, a leftist, Dartmouth graduate of German-Jewish heritage had taken charge of the Academy.

Bottome invoked the just released *Mortal Storm* only at the end of her June 20 letter to Wanger. She recalled for him a speech that she gave to studio workers in 1938 at the time of the Munich crisis when she told them: "If the torch of Freedom falls out of our old and nerveless hand [meaning Europe]—catch it up-hold it high—fight for it—die for it—

keep it alight!"[149] It was the message of *The Mortal Storm*: those who were left had to continue the fight. The image also recalls the torchbearer statue given to Professor Roth by his students to honor him on his sixtieth birthday. Just as he had imparted enlightenment to them, it was incumbent on them to pass it on. The continuity of such Western values as scientific inquiry and freedom of expression dare not be broken, symbolized by the passing of a torch.

Bottome then called on Wanger to keep Hollywood in the fight. She asked him to remind studio workers of what she had told them less than two years earlier. But more significantly she wrote him, "I turn to you [...] and the Studios of Hollywood with which I have been proud and happy to cooperate. I ask for your courage in producing faithful, truthful, and dynamic films [...]."[150] By "faithful, truthful, and dynamic films," she meant the films that isolationists would soon attack for luring the United States into another European war. Interventionists as well as isolationists could remember that the First World War began as a propaganda war in the United States with lurid accounts of German atrocities, encouraging Americans to come to the aid of the Allies. Bottome urged Wanger as the newly elected president of the Academy of Motion Picture Arts and Sciences to ignite another war of propaganda. She sought Hollywood's total engagement in Britain's cause, not just the dramatization of one bestseller, even if it was her own.

Wanger's wife Joan Bennett had already joined the fight. In a few weeks Twentieth-Century Fox would release *The Man I Married*, set in Nazi Germany. Bennett played the duped wife who marries a man loyal to Hitler. Fox got cold feet over the original title, *I Married a Nazi*; but unlike MGM, which used the term "non-Aryan" in *The Mortal Storm*, Fox retained use of the word "Jew" in its first anti-Nazi film. When the pro-Nazi husband discovers that he is in fact a Jew, the script employs the term. Each studio had limits to its newfound political engagement in 1940. For Fox, it was the word "Nazi," for MGM, the word "Jew."

The front office of MGM, on the other hand, had not imagined that it would release *The Mortal Storm* in a week that saw such cataclysmic events as the fall of France and the initiation of large-scale German bombing of Britain. The timing of the film's premier ironically made the conservative and reluctant studio appear to be at the forefront of American efforts to aid Britain. But then the two British writers responsible for the film, Bottome as novelist and West as scriptwriter, had intended all along that the production aid Britain's cause.[151] They brought to the American public a story that cried out for American intervention in the struggle with Hitler. The Roth family of the film, like the British people, stood alone and vulnerable before the Nazis. In dramatizing the plight of a German-Jewish family succumbing to the Nazi juggernaut, Bottome and West created a cinematic metaphor representing the current state of Britain. As Bottome wrote Wanger pleading for weapons for the Home Guard, "we look across the ocean as beleaguered soldiers search the horizon for the sight or sound of a Friend." In late June 1940, Britain found more than one.

More "Fellowship with Freedom": Anglo-American Cooperation Begins

Serious Anglo-American cooperation began with the arrival in New York on June 21, 1940, of William Stephenson, Canadian by citizenship and an intimate of Churchill.[152] Stephenson had distinguished himself as an air ace in the First World War, and then made a career in British intelligence. "He had worked for Churchill, [...] monitoring German rearmament."[153] He arrived in New York in June 1940 just as *The Mortal Storm* began its first run. Britain, he could already see, had an ally in Hollywood on the question of intervention.

Stephenson's accomplishments once he arrived in the United States included establishing "the closest possible marriage between the FBI and British intelligence."[154] British intelligence operations on American soil in fact proliferated under his direction. He established American branches of British Naval intelligence as well as a branch for the Special Operations Executive (SOE). The latter conducted covert propaganda and had responsibility for "dirty tricks."[155] He also had charge of protecting American military supplies that were bound for Britain from German sabotage. That responsibility proved no small matter as the Germans strove relentlessly to interdict and destroy those supplies before they even crossed the Atlantic. Stephenson did far better than Bottome in acquiring weapons for Britain. In short order he "obtained some one million rifles and thirty million rounds of ammunition."[156]

Arguably, his most significant contributions came from the "close and enduring partnership" that he forged with Roosevelt's new intelligence aid, Colonel "Wild Bill" Donovan.[157] Together they provided the information that the president needed to justify providing Britain with fifty surplus American destroyers.

While Churchill had pushed Stephenson into his new role as his personal representative in the United States, "charging him to return to America as the head of British intelligence in New York," FDR's encouragement pulled him into that role as well.[158] The president blessed J. Edgar Hoover's "marriage" with British intelligence, while he masterfully navigated the destroyer deal through Congress in the midst of his own presidential campaign in the summer of 1940. Britain's "true friend on the horizon" first and foremost proved to be FDR.

FDR

The Question of the Third Term

Of grave concern to the British and certainly to Bottome in June 1940 was the impending presidential election. Dependent on Roosevelt's continuing support, the British dreaded the possibility of his refusal to run for a third time or even his defeat, that is, an American repudiation of the president's cautious but consistent partnership with Britain. Roosevelt's every decision therefore mattered to the fate of Britain. Unbeknownst to the British, or even the American electorate, by June 20, 1940, the president had in fact decided to defy an unwritten rule of American politics and to compete for a third term.

Roosevelt remained in Washington the entire day of Thursday, June 20. Supremely superstitious, he refused to initiate travel on a Friday if he could help it. The presidential train bound for Hyde Park did not therefore begin to move that Thursday, as was the usual practice, until exactly 11:59 p.m.[159] It pulled away at that precise moment with the president's closest political confidante, Harry Hopkins, on board.[160] Hopkins, however, was not to linger in upstate New York. He had a busy weekend ahead of him. FDR ordered him to Chicago to begin organizing his team for the Democratic national convention in that city set to open on July 15. While still insisting on absolute secrecy, the president was already planning his strategy to be nominated for an unprecedented third term. In announcing the Stimson-Knox appointments that day, the president had come as close as he ever would to declaring his candidacy before the Democratic convention convened. Willkie, the Dark Horse Front Runner of the Republicans, had after all declared his candidacy only a little over a week earlier on June 12. Roosevelt, even if most observers missed one purpose behind the tandem appointments, could do no less than answer his soon to be opponent.

The *New York Times* caught the president's intention. It noted a connection between the appointments of Stimson and Knox and a third term. The *Times* suggested the possibility that the president was already at work constructing his wartime cabinet. No other appointments after all could be more significant for such a body than the posts of Secretary of the Navy and Secretary of War. The *Times* observed: "Mr. Roosevelt's selection of the two Republican leaders brought the third-term [...] issue to the fore as at no time during recent months."[161] Bottome, like most people in Britain, watched from afar that summer helpless to contribute to another Roosevelt campaign, should there even be one.

Bottome and the American President

Bottome had one advantage over her compatriots. She enjoyed a measure of access to the president because of her husband's connection to the women in the Roosevelt family. Through Ernan, Bottome had long been acquainted with the entwined Delano and Roosevelt families. Ernan claimed FDR's favorite aunt, Dora Delano Forbes, as his godmother. He retained her friendship, having met her on his first trip to North America in 1912.

The two Delano sisters, Dora and FDR's mother Sara, counted among the many admirers of Bottome's activist paternal grandmother, the one-time abolitionist, Margaret MacDonald Bottome. Bottome herself had a special relationship with Ernan's godmother. When Ernan was wounded at the front in 1918, Bottome, then in Paris, had to make the difficult journey back to England where he lay in hospital. Dora, living in Paris, provided assistance and support on that harrowing wartime journey.

In the fall of 1931, Bottome came to the United States to negotiate with her American publisher Houghton Mifflin. She spent a week with Dora's sister Sara Delano Roosevelt, the mother of the then governor of New York.[162] Fresh from Munich, she brought up the subject of the Jews in Germany whose persecution she and Ernan had already begun to witness. Bottome recounted:

> Franklin's mother shared the social prejudices of her time against the Jews, but she had listened with sympathy when I told her of their persecution in Germany, and told me later on, "My dear, I know you'll be pleased to hear that when any of my friends speak against Jews to me now, I say, 'Please don't speak like this in my hearing or I shall never call you a Christian again! You're only a Gentile!'"[163]

The president was devoted to both his mother and her sister. Bottome believed that thanks to her friendship with both of them, she would have his ear.

She and her husband were invited to the White House in December 1939.[164] Already on a lecture tour for the British Ministry of Information to educate Americans on the war in Europe and Britain's need for aid, she seized the opportunity to educate the president as well. She would have had no more important listener than that audience of one. Bottome certainly urged more aid to Britain. She would have also spoken to him about the plight of the Jews under Hitler. *The Mortal Storm* was about to begin production in the following month, a conversational opener on both subjects. Yet to her profound disappointment, she did not see as much of the president as she had hoped. He managed to depart for a weekend at his country estate in upstate New York in stealth, without telling her of his plans, probably knowing that she would give him no rest either on the subject of aid to Britain or the plight of the Jews in Germany were she to accompany him.[165]

Did FDR See *The Mortal Storm*?

The question remains unanswered. According to Ms. Virginia Lewick, Franklin D. Roosevelt Library Archivist,

> We do not have a complete list of the films that may have been viewed in the White House [1940–1941], nor those films that we can verify FDR saw. We have a database called *FDR: Day by Day*. Often times, the word "Movies" is in the activity field, but no title given."[166]

According to Doris Kearns Goodwin, December 3–14, 1940, when the president sailed the Caribbean on the U.S.S. *Tuscaloosa*, "evenings were spent [...] watching movies."[167] Ms. Lewick kindly examined the ship's log for that trip and informed me that the president saw at least seven films on that "Inspection Cruise through the West Indies": *Northwest Mounted Police, I Love You, Tin Pan Alley, They Knew What They Wanted, Gateway to Panama, U.S. Navy 1940*, and *Arizona*. Joseph McBride, Frank Capra's biographer, adds *Mr. Smith Goes to Washington* to the list of films the president watched on board the *Tuscaloosa* in December 1940:

> On the last day of the cruise, December 16 [*sic*], the President watched *Mr. Smith Goes to Washington* for the first time; afterward he not only expressed his appreciation of the film to the aides and sailors who watched it with him, he also used it as a springboard for a pep talk on each citizen's responsibilities in a democracy.[168]

McBride's account makes no mention of the possibility discussed above that FDR already knew of Capra's film and encouraged its production as a way of embarrassing Senator Wheeler, who was parodied in the film. Although McBride errs on the dates of the president's post-election cruise to the Caribbean, what he writes suggests that even official records such as the log of the *Tuscaloosa* do not provide a complete account of the president's activity, particularly regarding leisure and entertainment.

One other person close to the president might have urged him to see it or at least exposed him to it. Secretary of the Interior Harold Ickes qualified as the movie buff in the president's inner circle.[169] In that sense, he was for FDR what William Castle was for Lindbergh. But Ickes possessed actual ties to the movie industry. He was well aware of *The Mortal Storm*, having approved filming on Mt. Rainier where the production team hoped to capture the downhill ski and other snow scenes in the summer of 1939. Ickes therefore became directly involved in the production of *The Mortal Storm* at an early stage of filming, even possessing knowledge of its well-guarded script.[170] But that was not all. He had his own library of recent films and could provide advance screenings in his home using film copies provided directly by the studios. Ickes, according to his unpublished correspondence, regularly screened such films for his friends. While he does not specifically mention *The Mortal Storm* in those letters, he and his wife frequently screened the "propaganda films" available in the summer of 1940 and could have shared the films or their content with the president.

A Very Busy Week in June

David Welky considered June 1940 "pivotal" in the momentous summer of 1940. While agreeing with that point, it is possible to refine it. June 20, 1940 and the days immediately surrounding it changed the terms of American foreign and domestic policy. The introduction of conscription bills in both houses of Congress, echoed in Stimson's speeches to Yale undergraduates that week, confirmed American engagement with the war in Europe. Conscription also meant that the technologically backward and inadequate American army would acquire new scrutiny and pressure to modernize.

More than the military had to modernize. On June 21, US and British intelligence joined forces with the arrival in New York of Churchill's emissary to the FBI William Stephenson. That same day, lulled by the soothing rhythm of the presidential train traveling north, Roosevelt and Hopkins discussed plans for the upcoming Democratic national convention where the president intended to launch his campaign for a third term. His two cabinet appointments made the day before foretold that he already understood that in his third term he would be a wartime president.

By the third week of June 1940, interventionist forces were far better organized than the proponents of isolationism. The White Committee had established its New York headquarters and begun to form local affiliates by the hundreds. Its prestigious membership list showed it to be the cause of the hour. The isolationists, led by a small cohort in the Senate, lacked a national organization to compete with the White committee. On June 20, members of the cohort revealed flaws that would haunt their cause even as they came to direct a national movement. They were quick to anger and lacked discretion when on the defensive. The majority leader of the Senate, Alban Barkley, had to restrain Senators Wheeler and Clark for their unruly anger over the Stimson-Knox appointments.[171] Gerald Nye vented his anger by calling on the president "to retire [...] and turn over his office [...] to the Vice-President John Nance Garner [...]."[172] None of them recognized the real import of the president's two cabinet appointments that day: he prepared both for war and a third term. Nor did they yet seem to recognize the implications of what they termed "the war spirit" and "propaganda for war" in recent Hollywood productions. The president enjoyed a growing partnership with Hollywood. The movies had become more than mere entertainment. Some of them appeared to promote official policy.

And then there was Lindbergh. The isolationists' ally Charles Lindbergh may have stayed home on the weekend of June 21, but he was a sleeping giant prepared to take to the road to keep the United States neutral. By the fall of 1940, with a national organization, America First, backing them, Lindbergh and his cohort were ready to confront the White Committee on its own terms. Like the isolationists in the Senate, several in the pay of the German embassy, Lindbergh had not yet set his sights on Hollywood as the main instigator of "propaganda for war." It would not take long, however.

Others already watched Hollywood warily, even those disposed to it. Bosley Crowther sat rewriting his review of *The Mortal Storm* on Friday or Saturday night, June 21 or 22, to submit a second version to the widely read entertainment section of the *New York Times* which would appear in the Sunday edition on June 23. Crowther sought to revise his initial review, to make it more in line with the complaints that his fellow movie critics had lodged against the film for having been released when its message was no longer timely. Unlike Crowther, his colleagues had witnessed the premier of *Mr. Smith Goes to Washington* back in October and seen the havoc a Hollywood production could raise in the US Senate itself. Why did MGM compromise with *The Mortal Storm*, delaying its production, the critics seemed to ask, when the smaller, more vulnerable Columbia Pictures had only recently pulled no punches with *Mr. Smith Goes to Washington?* Crowther could not let go of *The Mortal Storm*. He wrote about it again and again that year, a kind of talisman of what was both right and wrong with the all-powerful movie industry.[173]

The week *The Mortal Storm* opened changed the terms of war for Britain. Massive air raids over her largest cities began. Bottome not only scanned the horizon for a friend, as she wrote Walter Wanger, but also for incoming German bombers, even the advance force of a German invasion. *The Mortal Storm* punctuated all those events. Opening on June 20, the film began to run almost nonstop, continuing to be shown in most American cities late into the fall. Professor Roth could be seen denouncing the absurdist racism of "immature hoodlums" for at least the next six months.[174] Again and again, Martin Breitner came to the rescue of frail and vulnerable, "old chap," Mr. Werner, modeling intervention for young Americans. *The Mortal Storm* provided the backdrop of political engagement for the new world that opened in June 1940. Contrary to what the critics said, the film's release that month could not have been timelier.

Looking back from the vantage point of the early 1950s, Bottome called *The Mortal Storm* in 1940 "the book of the hour."[175] Given that date, she must have meant by extension the film as well. But the response to the film extended well beyond the immediate period of its release, whether it was the film of the hour or not. *The Mortal Storm* evoked a response across the political spectrum for the next eighteen months, from June 1940 to December 1941. The reaction to the film proved to be as complex as the effort involved in producing it.

Notes

1. *The New Republic*, "First Page Editorial," 102. No. 22 (May 27, 1940), 712.
2. Welky, *The Moguls and the Dictators*, 193.
3. The Third Reich did not break ties with MGM and Fox until August, but by then the official break with them was a mere formality.
4. Welky, *The Moguls and the Dictators*, 198–9.
5. Ibid. Welky describes the formation of the MPCC as the culmination of lengthy negotiations between the studios and the Roosevelt administration. Hollywood, on its part, did not want to be seen as compromising its artistic freedom (195–7).
6. For further discussion of this point, see Mary Gelsey Samuelson, "The Patriotic Play: Roosevelt, Antitrust, and the War Activities Committee of the Motion Picture Industry," Ph.D. diss. University of California, Los Angeles, 2014, where Samuelson argues that "the motion picture industry's close relationship with the Roosevelt administration played a key role in its ability to stave off the commencement of government action against the studios until the postwar period," Synopsis, 5.
7. *Congressional Record*. 76th Congress, 3rd session, vol. 86. Part 8 (June 13–July 8, 1940), 8676. Unless otherwise noted, all references refer to this volume for the day of June 20, 1940. Subsequent references to the *Cong. Rec.* will contain the abbreviation *CR* and the appropriate page number from the above volume.
8. *CR*, 8835.
9. "Reich Alone to Put Demands to France," *New York Times*, June 20, 1940. All citations to the *New York Times* can be found in the data base Pro Quest Historical Newspapers: New York Times (1851–2010). http://search.proquest.com.libpdb.d.umn.edu:2048/hnpnewyorktimes/advanced?accountid=811.
10. *The Goebbels Diaries, 1939–1941*. Fred Taylor, trans. and ed. (New York: G.P. Putnam's Sons, 1983), 122. Entry for June 16, 1940.
11. "The International Situation." *New York Times,* June 20, 1940, 1.
12. See discussion of the pre-war American naval build-up in David Kaiser, *No End Save Victory. How FDR Led the Nation into War* (New York: Basic Books, 2014), 114–15.
13. See Susan Dunn, *1940. FDR, Willkie, Lindbergh, Hitler—the Election amid the Storm* (New Haven: Yale University Press, 2013), 169–70. James Wadsworth (R-NY) introduced the bill in the House on the same day.
14. For discussion of the careers of Burke and Wadsworth, see Dunn, *1940*, 170–1.
15. See discussion in Doris Kearns Goodwin, *No Ordinary Time. Franklin and Eleanor Roosevelt: The Home Front in World War II* (New York: Simon and Schuster, 1994), 49–53 regarding those maneuvers.
16. Ibid., 49.

17 Ibid., 52.
18 "Sentiment to Aid Britain Is Growing," *New York Times,* September 22, 1940, cited in Dunn, *1940,* 67, 338. See also the discussion of pro-interventionist sentiment in the South in Joan E. Denman, "Senator Claude Pepper: Advocate of Aid to the Allies, 1939–1941," *The Florida Historical Quarterly*, vol. 83, no. 2 (Fall 2004), 127, 132.
19 Denman, "Senator Claude Pepper," 140.
20 CR, 8807. See also Denman, 133 for discussion of Pepper's concern about Florida in relation to Nazi influence in the Caribbean region.
21 CR, 8679.
22 Griffin's daughter in conversation with the author.
23 CR, 8680.
24 Ibid., 8815–16.
25 CR., 75th Congress, 2nd session, April 25, 1939, 4738.
26 Ibid., 4730–7.
27 Ibid., 4732.
28 Ibid., 4737.
29 Robert K. Murray, *Red Scare. A Study in National Hysteria, 1919–1920* (Minneapolis: University of Minnesota Press, 2009). See also US Senate Committee on the Judiciary. *German Propaganda:* Hearings before a Subcommittee of the Committee on the Judiciary. US Senate. 65th Congress. Second and Third Sessions, Pursuant to Senate Resolution 307. US Government Printing Office, 1919.
30 *Documents on German Foreign Policy, 1918–1945*, Series D, Vol. X, Thomsen to Foreign Ministry (FM) (July 18, 1940), 243.
31 Ibid.
32 Mary Hugh Gottsacker, "German-American Relations, 1938–1941 and the Influence of Hans Thomsen," Ph.D. diss., Georgetown University, 1968,103.
33 Ibid., 108.
34 Ibid., 2.
35 Ibid.
36 Mombauer, *The Origins of the First World War,* 52–3.
37 See especially Series D, v. X, 250–1, Thomsen to FM (July 19, 1940) & v. IX (June 20, 1940), 626.
38 Gottsacker, "German-American Relations," 1.
39 Series D, vol. IX, 625–6.
40 Ibid., 626.
41 Series D., vol. X, 250.
42 Ibid., 252.
43 Ibid., 260.

44 The group included, in addition to Nye, Bennet Champ Clark (D-MO), D. Worth Clark (D-ID), Charles W. Tobey (R-NH), and Burton K. Wheeler (D-MT). Their investigation of Hollywood as a propagandizer for war will be examined in Chapter 8.

45 *Vital Speeches of the Day*, Charles A. Lindbergh, "Appeal for Isolation. Let Us Look to Our Own Defense," (September 15, 1939), 751–2.

46 CR, 8701.

47 Hamilton Basso, "Burton the Bronc," *The New Republic* (April 22, 1940), 527.

48 Nye wrote, "Bone, Clark, and Vandenberg were hard-working members of the committee [to investigate the munitions industry.]" Homer T. Bone (D-WA), Bennett Champ Clark (D-MO), and Arthur Vandenberg (R-MI) were all leading isolationists by the end of the 1930s. Unpublished interview with Gerald P. Nye conducted by Wayne S. Cole on March 3, 1971, generously made available to the author by Donald Ritchie, Historian of the US Senate.

49 www.senate.gov/artandhistory/history/common/generic/Featured_Bio_BorahWilliam.htm

50 On Wheeler's selection as leader of the fight, see Jeff Shesol, *Supreme Power. Franklin Roosevelt vs. the Supreme Court* (New York: W.W. Norton & Co., 2010), 303.

51 Basso, "Burton the Bronc," *The New Republic*, (April 22, 1940), 527.

52 Ibid.

53 George Creel, *Rebel at Large. Recollections of Fifty Crowded Years* (New York: G. P. Putnam, 1947), 295.

54 Burton K. Wheeler with Paul F. Healy, *Yankee from the West* (Garden City: Doubleday & Co., Inc., 1961), 332.

55 Shesol, *Supreme Power,* 318.

56 Ibid., as cited in Shesol, 318.

57 A. Scott Berg, *Lindbergh* (New York: Putnam Publishing Group, 1998), 419. According to Berg, the FBI had Mrs. Wheeler under surveillance for her involvement with antisemitic organizations.

58 That year, for example, the President's birthday celebration at the end of January, a benefit for the March of Dimes, became a photo opportunity for the President and for celebrities to mingle with political power. See Christine Ann Colgan, "Warner Brothers' Crusade against the Third Reich: A Study of anti-Nazi Activism and Film Production, 1933–1941"; Ph.D. Diss., University of Southern California, 1985, 270–305.

59 Frank Capra, *The Name above the Title. An Autobiography* (New York: Da Capo Press, 1997), 272.

60 For discussion of Hollywood's new turn in 1939–40, see Bennett, *One World, Big Screen*, 1–88; Doherty, *Hollywood and Hitler, 1933–1939*, 311–50; Welky, *The Moguls and the Dictators*, 179–279.

61 Joseph McBride, *Frank Capra. The Catastrophe of Success* (New York: Simon and Schuster, 1992), 418 and Capra, *The Name above the Title*, 280.

62 Capra, *The Name above the Title*, 280.
63 Cf. Capra's account with that of his biographer who insists that Capra's version "was over dramatized." But the biographer offers no alternative eyewitness account. McBride, *Frank Capra,* 419.
64 Capra, *The Name above the Title,* 281.
65 Ibid.
66 "*Mr. Smith Goes to Washington,*" IMDb, "Trivia," accessed June 1, 2014. While the IMDb account is misleading in that Wheeler did not actually exit Constitution Hall in a huff, it does make clear that a crisis occurred in conjunction with the first public screening of the film.
67 Capra, *The Name above the Title,* 282.
68 Ibid., 286.
69 *Christian Science Monitor,* October 27, 1939, cited in Capra, 287.
70 Repeal of the embargo provisions of the Nye legislation passed on November 3, 1939. See the discussion in Davis, *FDR. Into the Storm,* 493–509.
71 See introductory credits to *Mr. Smith Goes to Washington.*
72 Marc Eliot, *Jimmy Stewart. A Biography* (New York: Crown Books, 2006), 123.
73 Ibid., 125.
74 All references in this paragraph are cited in Capra, 288. Capra also cites ten other reviews from newspapers in the United States and Britain.
75 Basso, "Burton the Bronc," 527.
76 *Mr. Smith Goes to Washington,* Screenplay: Sidney Buchman; Director: Frank Capra; Columbia Pictures, 1939.
77 Welky, *The Moguls and the Dictators,* 142.
78 See my "Communism and the Co-ops: Recruiting and Financing the Finnish-American Migration to Karelia," *Journal of Finnish Studies,* vol. 8, no. 1 (August 2004), 28–47. See also Auvo Kostiainen, *The Forging of Finnish-American Communism, 1917–1924. A Study in Ethnic Radicalism* (Turku, Finland: The Migration Institute, 1978). For Buchman's time in Duluth, 1902–19, when he forged an academic and athletic record in the public school system never equaled since, see "Hometown of Duluth Showers Its Honors on Producer Buchman," *Duluth News Tribune,* February 12, 1950, 39.
79 McBride, *Frank Capra,* 411–12.
80 For example, Duluth in the early twentieth-century possessed a large and prosperous Jewish community which provided the merchant and professional classes for a town otherwise divided between an immigrant working class, largely Finnish-American, and the newly rich who had successfully exploited the timber and mineral wealth of the state. Little Falls, on the other hand, had no Jewish community to speak of.
81 As cited in Capra, *The Name above the Title,* 288.
82 Ibid., 283.
83 Ibid., 283, 286.

84 McBride, *Frank Capra*, 422.
85 Bennett, *One World, Big Screen*, 50.
86 Capra, *The Name above the Title*, 289.
87 Ibid., 283.
88 CR, 8686.
89 *New York Times*, June 24, 1936, as cited in Shesol, 236.
90 Dunn, *1940*, 93.
91 *Chicago Daily News*, September 7, 1939, as cited in Dunn, *1940*, 93, 345.
92 Jonathan Alter, *The Defining Moment. FDR's Hundred Days and the Triumph of Hope* (New York: Simon & Schuster. 2006), 145–6.
93 CR, 8694.
94 CR, 8700.
95 "Capital Surprised," *New York Times*, June 21, 1940.
96 Dunn, *1940*, 95.
97 Kaiser, *No End Save Victory*, 30.
98 Ibid., 30.
99 Goodwin, *No Ordinary Time*, 71.
100 Hans Thomsen commented on Stimson's appointment in a telegram to Berlin on June 20, 1940. (Referred to in footnote 1, p. 255: Series D, vol. X.) He apparently did not mention Knox in that message; Stimson's appointment dominated his concerns. The telegram, while not indicated as missing, was not printed in vol. IX, the appropriate volume for a message dated June 20, 1940.
101 Christopher Clark, *The Sleepwalkers. How Europe Went to War in 1914* (New York: Harper Collins, 2012), 202.
102 Sir Edward Grey, *Twenty-Five Years, 1892–1916* (New York: Frederick A. Stokes Co., 1925).
103 Henry Stimson, "Letter to the Editor," *New York Times,* March 7, 1939, 1.
104 "Plea by Stimson," *New York Times*, September 16, 1939, 1.
105 Ibid.
106 "Stimson Supports U.S. Foreign Policy," *New York Times*, March 7, 1939, 1.
107 Stimson, "Letter to the Editor," *New York Times*, March 7, 1939, 1.
108 *The Goal*, 258.
109 It should be noted that Sir Edward Grey remains the bête noir of revisionists. Niall Ferguson, for example, in a recent interview blamed Grey for encouraging German aggression before the First World War.
110 Kaiser, *No End Save Victory*, 54.
111 "Yale, Brown Urge Military Training," *New York Times*, June 18, 1940, 1.
112 See account of Roosevelt's closeness to White and trust in him in John DeWitt McKee, *William Allen White. Maverick on Main Street* (Westport and London: Greenwood Press, 1975), 182–95.

113 William Allen White to Mrs. F. W. Bigler, June 22, 1940; William Allen White Collection (WAWC), Library of Congress Manuscript Reading Room, Series D. Box 15.

114 The papers of individual chapters along with correspondence between the New York headquarters and local offices can be found in the Archive of the Committee to Defend America by Aiding the Allies (MC #011) in the Seeley Mudd Manuscript Library of Princeton University.

115 Cf. McKee, *Maverick on Main Street*, 186: "White worked hard at his chairmanship … he was not the figurehead that the pro-German groups and the isolationists called him." The charge in fact sticks. White left running the committee to others as his correspondence for 1940 in the Library of Congress confirms.

116 See especially the following essays by White: "Pay Day in Politics," *The Saturday Review* (April 9, 1938), 10–11; "Shock Troops of Reform," *The Saturday Review* (April 8, 1939, 3–4); "Academic's America," *The Saturday Review* (May 28, 1938), 5; "How Free Is Our Press?" *The Nation* (June 18, 1938), 693–5.

117 White's correspondence with Eichelberger regarding *The Mortal Storm* was not found among his papers in the Library of Congress. Instead, see discussion of the film and his proposals to Eichelberger in Alex W. Burger to William Allen White, October 3, 1940, WAWC, Series D, Box 17, acknowledging an earlier letter to Eichelberger.

118 William R. Castle, Unpublished multi-volume diaries, covering the years 1918–60, can be found in Houghton Library, Harvard University; MS Am 2021. See especially vol. V (1940).

119 Susan Hertog, *Anne Morrow Lindbergh. Her Life* (New York: Anchor Books, 2000), 276.

120 Charles A. Lindbergh, *The Wartime Journals of Charles A. Lindbergh* (New York: Harcourt, Brace, Jovanovich, 1970), August 23, 1939, 245.

121 Ibid., September 10, 1939, 253.

122 See *German Diplomatic Documents*, Series D, v. IX, 258.

123 Ibid., August 23, 1939, 245.

124 Castle Diaries, vol. 5; January 22, 1940, 22.

125 Ibid., January 30, 1940, 56.

126 Ibid., June 29, 1940, 238.

127 Ibid., July 21, 1940, 261.

128 Lindbergh, *Wartime Journals,* August 23, 1939, 245.

129 Berg, *Lindbergh*, 223.

130 Hertog, 276.

131 Berg, *Lindbergh*, 337.

132 Ibid., 373.

133 Hertog, 276.

134 Kenneth S. Davis, *The Hero. Charles A. Lindbergh. The Man and the Legend* (London: Longmans, Green & Co., Ltd., 1960).

135 Davis, *FDR. Into the Storm, 1937–1940*, 348.

136 See Max Wallace. *The American Axis, Charles Lindbergh, and the Rise of the Third Reich* (New York: St. Martin's Press, 2003), 93–9 for discussion of the profound influence of the eugenics movement on American social policy, particularly in the 1920s and 1930s.

137 See especially Lindbergh, *Wartime Journals*, 245, 253, 271–2, 333, 335, 382, 390–1, 396, 409, and Castle's diary entry in vol. 5 for July 21, 1940.

138 Crowther's pieces for the *New York Times* that refer to the film or were devoted to it consist of the following: "'The Mortal Storm,' a Deeply Tragic anti-Nazi Film at The Capitol" (June 21, 1940), 23; "Lost Opportunity or Where Was Hollywood When the Lights in Germany Went Out?" (June 23, 1940), 22; "End of First Half: The Screen Has Run Up a Good Score at This Mid-Year Turning Point" (June 30, 1940), 29; "Problem in Defense. Robert Montgomery Challenges the Screen to Do Its Best by Propaganda Films" (November 3, 1940), 3; "Again the 'Ten Best'" (December 29, 1940), 25.

139 Crowther, "Again the 'Ten Best,'" *New York Times*, December 29, 1940, 25.

140 Lindbergh, *Wartime Journals,* April 24, 1939; 190. See also diary entry of September 16, 1939; 259 for his attention to the opinion of the paper. Lindbergh often began diary entries with *New York Times* headlines, such as the entry for August 29, 1941; 529.

141 Lindbergh, *The Wartime Journals,* June 17, 1940, 359.

142 Ibid., June 21, 1940, 360.

143 See, for example, Lindbergh, *Wartime Journals* December 16, 1938, 126; September 3, 1939, 250; September 11, 1939, 253; and November 20, 1939, 289.

144 The biographical details concerning H. A. L. Fisher come from his daughter, the late Mrs. Mary Bennett, formerly Principal, St. Hilda's College, Oxford, in conversation with the author.

145 See her account of that screening in the *New York Times*, "Speaking as One Who Should Know: A Novelist Talks about the Screen Version of Her Book," June 16, 1940, 3.

146 Phyllis Bottome to Walter Wanger. June 20, 1940. BL Add. Mss. 88921/3/3.

147 Ibid.

148 Phyllis Bottome to Walter Wanger. April 17, 1940. BL Add. Mss. 88921/3/3.

149 Phyllis Bottome to Walter Wanger. June 20, 1940. BL Add. Mss. 88921/3/3.

150 Ibid.

151 *The Mortal Storm* credits Claudine West along with two others with the script. West in fact bears nearly sole responsibility for the script as was explained in Chapters 4 and 5.

152 The account of Stephenson's work that follows is based on that of Nicholas Cull, *Selling War. The Propaganda Campaign against American "Neutrality" in World War II* (Oxford: Oxford University Press, 1995), 80–2.

153 Ibid., 81.

154 Ibid.

155 Ibid.

156 Ibid., 82.

157 Ibid.

158 Ibid., 81.

159 Alter, *Defining Moment*, calls FDR "the most superstitious President in American history," 244.

160 Doris Kearns Goodwin describes this arrangement and the departure on June 20 in *No Ordinary Time*, 72. She apparently did not know of the explicit timing due to the President's immense superstition.

161 *New York Times*, "Capital Surprised," June 21, 1940, 1.

162 Hirsch, *The Constant Liberal*, 176.

163 Bottome, *The Goal*, 185.

164 Eleanor Roosevelt in her column "My Day" for December 13, 1939 wrote, "Monday night [...] among our guests were Mr. and Mrs. Forbes Dennis, who are English friends of my mother-in-law." Cited in Hirsch, *Constant Liberal*, 397.

165 Bottome. BL Add. Ms. 78858.

166 E-mail communication from Ms. Virginia Lewick: virginia.lewick@nara.gov on Thursday, August 21, 2014.

167 Goodwin, *No Ordinary Time*, 192.

168 McBride, *Frank Capra, The Catastrophe of Success*, 412. McBride provides no confirming source on the showing of *Mr. Smith* aboard the *Tuscaloosa*.

169 The Papers of Harold Ickes, Manuscript Division, US Library of Congress. Ickes correspondences for 1940 alone are filled with references to the films that he saw or screened at his summer retreat in the Catoctin Mountains of Maryland.

170 The Papers of Sidney Franklin, Box 24, "The Mortal Storm."

171 CR, 8700.

172 Ibid., 8898.

173 In addition to his two reviews of *The Mortal Storm*, see his comments on the film in "Reflections of Passing Events in the Screen World" (*New York Times*, November 3, 1940) and in "The Screen World Marks the Passing of Another Year/Again the 'Ten Best'" (*New York Times*, December 29, 1940), 25. Crowther picked *The Mortal Storm* to be the fifth best film of 1940.

174 Ohio movie theaters, for example, advertised screenings of *The Mortal Storm* in the Cleveland *Plain Dealer* and the *Cincinnati Post* well into the fall of 1940.

175 Bottome, *The Challenge*, 397.

7

The Response to *The Mortal Storm*, 1940

The Civil War Analogy and *The Mortal Storm*: Substitute Discourse in Uncertain Times

The eighteen months from the release of *The Mortal Storm* in June 1940 until the attack on Pearl Harbor proved to be a unique period for Hollywood. The movie industry never appeared to have so much influence outside the domain of entertainment as it did in that critical period before the United States entered the war. It was certainly not a role that Mayer had intended MGM to play. Nor Publicity Director Howard Strickling. Strickling had delighted in the confusion the term "non-Aryan" caused nearly 300 first-time viewers in Pomona two weeks before *The Mortal Storm*'s release. But the studio could not control all the factors that affected how audiences might perceive the film nor what might give it influence beyond MGM's anodyne intentions. The mood of uncertainty in the country regarding Roosevelt's foreign policy provided one of those uncontrollable factors, as did the rapid advance of German armies in the spring of 1940.

The release of *The Mortal Storm* not only coincided with calamitous events, it appeared when the public, fearful about the future, embraced the past, precisely that part of the American past that had resonated with Bottome when she composed the novel in the mid-1930s. Lincoln and the Civil War had captured the country's attention by the second half of the decade. As noted earlier, fascination with the nineteenth-century conflict nearly eclipsed the once all-consuming passion for the revisionist approach to the First World War that had so intrigued Americans in the interwar period. In fact, interest in the Civil War "increased exponentially" through the 1930s, Merrill Schlier has written.[1] Sociologist Barry Schwartz similarly observed, "Lincoln's reputation [...] peak[ed] during the Great Depression and World War II."[2] Seminal events in the previous century had now acquired new political meaning.

In April 1940, the president had made good use of the civil war analogy, employing it publicly to question Lindbergh's patriotism. After Lindbergh made two speeches to large crowds, one in a Chicago arena and another in Madison Square Garden, touting German military superiority, Roosevelt called the former aviator a "copperhead," that is, a Northerner whose sympathies lay with the South. Lindbergh, FDR suggested, was already on the wrong side of history.

The emergence of the Civil War in the 1930s as a touchstone for Americans was not lost on Bottome. She astutely sensed the fascination with the nineteenth-century conflict that she encountered on her extended stays in the United States in that decade, perceiving how Americans used a kind of substitute language to frame political debate within the analogy the Civil War so readily provided.

The Civil War had in that decade indeed become part of the national discourse. It proved easier to allude to impending war through historical analogy than to name the threat directly. Bottome appeared to anticipate such rhetoric of indirection when she wrote her bestseller. As noted in Chapter 2, she constructed *The Mortal Storm* with *Uncle Tom's Cabin* in mind. Major as well as minor characters in her novel evoked equivalents from Stowe's work. Stowe's influence could be felt in Bottome's very crafting of a work of fiction to depict the victimization of a whole people. And in *The Mortal Storm* there is a civil war with brother fighting brother over whether to join the Nazi cause or not.

Bottome's work made another connection with the Civil War. The idea of her mentor, Viennese depth psychologist Victor Adler, that sibling rivalry on a geopolitical scale could become a source of war, civil war in particular, permeated *The Mortal Storm* as both film and novel where sibling conflict acquires political resonance. Some protagonists join the Nazi Party and others are determined to fight it. Familial conflict, as so often happened in the American Civil War, thus leads to violence in a larger arena. Recalling the Civil War even subliminally enhanced the political relevance of *The Mortal Storm* for an American movie audience when released in 1940.

But there was even more in *The Mortal Storm* to evoke the Civil War. Jimmy Stewart as Martin Breitner embodied the connection between the screen adaptation of Bottome's novel and Frank Capra's *Mr. Smith Goes to Washington*, a film filled with references to Lincoln. The year before as Senator Jefferson Smith in the Capra film, Stewart played a hero who finds the strength to fight his corrupt enemies in the Senate, heartened by nocturnal visits paid to the Lincoln Memorial. The film remained both popular and respected for its serious subject. Stewart entered the set of *The Mortal Storm* as the odds-on favorite to win the Academy Award as best actor for his role in *Mr. Smith*. Whether as Jefferson Smith or Martin Breitner, Stewart had become the voice on screen of those who saw fascism as a threat to our most cherished values. Cinema had suddenly become the greatest advocate of those values.

Ironically, Frank Morgan, fresh from the role of the wizard in *The Wizard of Oz,* is seen as the protagonist who linked *The Mortal Storm* to the broader realm of popular culture.[3] His wise and avuncular image from that role made his hounding by the Nazis appear all the more brutal. In 1940, however, few thought the popular film of the year before, set in the Land of Oz, would be of lasting impact. *Mr. Smith Goes to Washington* in 1939–40, on the other hand, was regarded as the film of the hour and sure to make an indelible impression on the culture. Jimmy Stewart, as the star of both, linked the import of *Mr. Smith* to *The Mortal Storm*. Both films conveyed how quickly and insidiously the corrosive effects of fascism could triumph.

The Civil War analogy held even after the United States went to war. It took on new meaning seen in the Pulitzer Prize winner for History in 1942, Margaret Leech's *Reveille in Washington*, the story of how the Civil War transformed a provincial backwater of a town into the capital of a nation consumed by conflict. The nineteenth century provided a model for the capital's transformation in a world war. And "reveille," from Leech's title, the military call to awake, confirmed that the sleep of the 1930s had given way to the rude awakening of war. In 1940, *The Mortal Storm*, a film that seemed "to lead this country into war," to cite Luci Neville in *The Galveston Daily News*, took on a political and historical life of its own, much as Mayer, Mannix, and Strickling had tried to contain it.

MGM Tries to Shape the Response to *The Mortal Storm*

Shortly before the film's release on June 10, MGM invited reporters from the movie industry's trade papers to preview it. Their reviews, appearing in some instances two weeks before those of the large metropolitan dailies of New York and Chicago, tried to set the tone of response and preempt criticism, by showing the industry's support for MGM's qualified forthrightness.

The trade papers referred directly or indirectly to the timeliness of the film, as though anticipating impending criticism in the timing of its production. The *Harrison Report*, for example, called *The Mortal Storm*, "the most powerful anti-Nazi film *yet* [italics mine] produced."[4] *Variety* similarly praised it as "the most effective film exposé *to date* [italics mine] of the totalitarian idea [...]."[5] The *Motion Picture Herald* also addressed the film's timeliness, observing "a few months or weeks ago [the] Hollywood press audience would have used the word 'propaganda' to describe the film and speculated on the policy prompting its manufacture. [Instead] the word was not heard at the screening."[6] In sum, most trade papers concurred on the film's timeliness, in contrast to the judgment of the major critics whose reviews would soon appear, condemning MGM for not having made such a film considerably earlier. And at least for now, the film had dodged the bullet of being labeled propaganda.

The *Hollywood Reporter,* in contrast, took an entirely different tack, but nonetheless extolled the film's virtues. It absolved the production of a greater vulnerability than the charge of being dated. The trade paper praised the film's courage, saying nothing, however, of its failure to employ the word "Jew," and thus distorting the whole point of Bottome's novel. The *Reporter* instead called *The Mortal Storm* "a fearless screen indictment of a system."[7] Many would hardly find the term "non-Aryan," "fearless." But MGM had carried the trade papers.

MGM Publicity: *The Lobby*[8]

The studio could expect no trouble from its own publicity department which provided a key component to a production. Advertising could make or break a film. It could also enhance or harm the image of the studio. The studio considered advertising so important that communication between MGM and theater managers about how best to present a production to the public went both ways.[9] Twice a year the movie company brought theater owners and managers to Culver City. They met the stars and observed the production end of the movie business.

The studio did something significant with those events. It listened, seeking information on the mood, tastes, and preferences of the moviegoing public. Unfortunately, such events were of little help with *The Mortal Storm*, which was like no other film MGM had previously produced. And then there was another problem. With events in Europe occurring so rapidly in the spring and summer of 1940, neither the studio nor the exhibitors could be certain that they would be able to judge the public mood accurately or predict how moviegoers might respond to the real-life drama in news reels on the screen.

As a result, there frequently occurred a distinct divide between the recommendations of MGM's publicity department about *The Mortal Storm* and the response of the regional press. That divide mirrored the initial conflict between Bottome and Franklin when the two had first discussed adapting *The Mortal Storm* to the screen in April 1939, Bottome insisting on remaining true to the politics of the novel and Franklin, more cautiously, arguing for emphasis on its romance. Just prior to the release of the film, W. R. Ferguson, head of the Department of Exploitation in MGM's publicity, unit sent out his advertising advice to theater owners and managers in *The*

Lobby, the studio's guide to publicity for a particular film or films. Ferguson devoted an entire issue to *The Mortal Storm*.

Contravening studio bosses as well as Franklin as producer, Ferguson explicitly told exhibitors to embrace the film's political message. He justified that approach as a show of solidarity with the patriotism now prominent under the current circumstances in Europe. "A new wave of patriotism is currently sweeping America [...] Perhaps you'd like the idea of exploiting *The Mortal Storm* as something all liberty-loving Americans should see and guard against happening here."[10] Ferguson's inflated style in *The Lobby* appeared at times overblown, bordering on bombast. The war in Europe framed his most hyperbolic observation: "The eyes of the world and the thoughts of the universe are focused on the catastrophic events in Europe."[11] Such language justified a potentially controversial film while suggesting the magnitude of the issues it evoked. Also important in the nervous atmosphere of the moment, the advertising language was intended to insulate the studio against "a charge of propaganda." After all, a week before the film's release, Mussolini declared war on France, already under blitzkrieg attack. In keeping with a martial tone, Ferguson employed such phrases as "preparedness is the keynote," "billions for defense," "support for the allies." A year earlier, such words and phrases would have been unthinkable. Now even one of MGM's publicity directors sloughed off the potential charge of propaganda.

Ferguson also urged the obvious tie-in of the movie with Bottome's bestseller. The movie business after all thrived off the success of the publishing industry. He advised, "Key a major part of your exploitation around the book."[12] Ferguson thought the point so important that, as noted above, he contracted with Garden City Publishing to produce a 79-cent edition of the novel to sell in theater lobbies where the film played. The MGM executive informed his clientele, "Half a million readers of *The Mortal Storm* would become 50 million theater patrons if you promote with all the force and power at your command."[13] He advised, invite "critics to compare the picture with the novel."[14] Any moviegoer with 79 cents could do the same. With a cheap version of the novel so readily available, movie patrons could see that a film about non-Aryans had begun as a story about Jews. It seemed, the publicity department had pre-empted the policy of the front office and even worked at cross purposes with the studio. The Roth family, for a mere 79 cents, moviegoers found, were Jews after all.

That point had larger implications. Ferguson had already begun sending advertising copy to theater owners before the "father-son" scene was finally cut. His initial recommendation regarding that scene—advertise it as "Little Rudi learns what it is to be a Jew," had become moot with the scene's removal.[15] But Ferguson had embraced the issue while it still appeared in the film.

Mayer's agony over the Jewish question nonetheless gave the film one advantage. It delayed *The Mortal Storm*'s going into distribution until

Hitler's invasions of Western Europe in April and May 1940. By then Americans began to recognize that German victories might put their own security at risk. Ironically, the word "Jew," so potent that it could derail the stability of a studio, certainly that of its head, by the summer of 1940, could probably have been employed with few of the repercussions that Mayer had so profoundly dreaded. Freya, Rudi, and their father could have been Jews against a real-life backdrop of Nazi conquest and atrocities. Such phrases as "political oppression" and "gripping story of Nazi-torn Germany" could be found in reviews of *The Mortal Storm* in the regional press.[16] They joined MGM's own advertising copy with its references to "preparedness" and "support for the Allies." The events of 1940 had changed the terms for the use of the word "Jew," even as MGM's studio head had struggled with himself over its use.

The war news was so potent in the summer of 1940 that the love angle of the film acquired political overtones. Ferguson recounted in *The Lobby* the closeness between Jimmy Stewart and Margaret Sullavan off the set. Stewart, an accomplished pilot, was teaching his co-star how to fly.[17] At the same time, Stewart had recently received a patent for a fuel injector pump sure to make airplane engines more effective in the maneuvers of combat. What previously might have been seen as hints at an illicit off-screen romance (Sullavan was married with two small children), an unthinkable revelation for MGM's prudish publicity department had instead become yet another example of a tie-in of the film to the reality of war and the need for Americans to prepare for it. The regional press therefore found itself in uncharted waters in assessing the film. No consistency prevailed in the smaller papers, although discussion of the romance in the film tended to dominate as a safe draw that would avoid controversy.

Regional and Local Papers Respond to *The Mortal Storm*

Many regional papers embraced the tie-in with Bottome's bestseller. They often simply incorporated MGM publicity supplied by theater managers, an approach they assumed would be cheap and noncontroversial. Echoes of *The Lobby* could be heard on the local level. Nor did the Jewish question, or lack thereof, seem to matter to the regional press. That attitude stood in stark contrast to *The New Yorker*, where, it will be remembered, John Moser, in his review of *The Mortal Storm*, mocked the use of "non-Aryan." John Soames, however, writing in the *Oakland Tribune*, stated simply that "... Frank Morgan is a Jewish scientist of great renown ...."[18] Soames, unlike most regional reviewers, condemned the film precisely for its politics. "It is not a pretty story that Miss Bottome tells in 'The Mortal Storm.' Sitting through its enactment is a rather grueling experience and, I feel, a rather unnecessary one; for I still feel that the theater is not a place for propaganda films or sociological lectures."[19] His position was unusual for the West coast. The region tended to sympathize with intervention because of Japanese aggression in the Pacific.

More circumspectly, the *Hutchinson Kansas-News-Herald* explained *The Mortal Storm* recounted the fate of a "family torn by racial conflict."[20] Perhaps in that way the reviewer sought to elide the language of the novel with that heard on screen. In the end, the Kansas paper was one of the few regional papers to even mention what for Bottome had been the whole point of the novel.

The *Iowa Recorder*, along with numerous other regional papers, while not resenting the film's politics, praised its romance. The paper mentioned the "political upheaval" of the film without condemnation but urged viewers to see it because it contained "as great a [love] story as 'Camille' and 'Romeo and Juliet.'"[21] Ferguson's clarion call to exhibitors and advertisers to engage with "the catastrophic events in Europe" tended to be ignored. Regional reviewers interpreted the film as just another MGM tale of romance.

Jimmy Stewart agreed with Ferguson about embracing the politics of the film even though in the summer of 1940, it seemed, he hardly had time for anything other than moviemaking. A week before the release of *The Mortal Storm*, the *Syracuse Herald* reported that Stewart was already preparing for his next film. He had been "signed to play opposite Katharine Hepburn in 'The Philadelphia Story.'" Stewart was indeed a busy actor in 1940. *The Philadelphia Story* was one of five pictures that he made that year after the release of *The Mortal Storm*, starring in three in October alone.

Yet he still found time for politics. It appeared that off-screen the actor sought to play the roles of Jefferson Smith and Martin Breitner, a sudden change of heart for Stewart. Despite living in Hollywood, a town, at least since 1936 galvanized by anti-Nazi sentiment, he had previously not been known for his political commitments. After the release of *The Mortal Storm* on top of *Mr. Smith Goes to Washington*, he became one of the most outspoken interventionists in the movie colony. In the summer of 1940, Stewart joined fellow stars at rallies urging aid for Britain whenever he had time between acting assignments.[22] But he also did something unique as an advocate for Roosevelt's interventionist foreign policy that no other star at the time was able to duplicate. The role of Martin Breitner made that possible. Jimmy Stewart took *The Mortal Storm* on the road, imparting explicit political meaning to the words of the one-time pacifist he played on screen, "That old chap's been decent to me. I can't stand by and see him bullied." In the summer of 1940, those words amounted to a clarion call to intervention on behalf of Britain, the "old chap." Stewart's off-screen role with the film also had to change the perception of *The Mortal Storm*. It could not be just another MGM romance after all.

Mr. Stewart Goes to Cleveland

Political rallies in support of Britain became a regular occurrence in the summer of 1940. Movie stars often provided the main attraction, encouraging American aid to the beleaguered island short of war. Such rallies featuring Hollywood stars probably took their inspiration from the war bond rallies of the First World War in which Charlie Chaplin, Douglas Fairbanks, and Mary Pickford were frequent participants. Pickford and Fairbanks's son, movie star Douglas Fairbanks, Jr., continued the tradition. On September 18, 1940, the younger Fairbanks told a rally in Chicago that "I am frankly pro-British. But only because I am pro-American."[23] Dorothy Thompson and the outspoken interventionist senator from Florida, Claude Pepper, joined him on the podium.

In participating in those "Hollywood rallies" that summer, Jimmy Stewart appeared to have taken an example from his recent movie roles. Bottome herself observed Stewart's heroic qualities, telling a friend, "I am extraordinarily lucky to have got James Stewart, who makes a magnificent hero [...]."[24] Off-screen, Stewart expressed something more. The *Hollywood Reporter* sensed his personal engagement with the parts he had played since the previous year and praised him for "giving complete sincerity of purpose to his belief in political freedom," in the role of Martin Breitner, for example.[25] The same could be said of his earlier role as Jefferson Smith. Stewart transferred the convictions expressed in those roles off-screen on behalf of aiding Britain. But first he made two seemingly nonpolitical films in short order: for Warner Brothers, a recent Broadway hit called *No Time for Comedy*. He spent all of July and part of August on another Broadway hit, *The Philadelphia Story*. While seemingly another lightweight stage comedy, the movie made with Hepburn carried its own interventionist message.

In mid-August, Stewart began to speak openly on behalf of Britain. At his first rally that summer, he joined Henry Fonda, Tyrone Power, and Olivia de Havilland on stage in Dallas to urge support for Britain. According to Stewart's biographer Marc Eliot, by late summer 1940, the actor participated frequently in pro-British, anti-Nazi rallies.[26] He was no exception. Hollywood stars on- and off-screen became one of the faces of intervention in the summer of 1940. The petitions and declarations of the Hollywood anti-Nazi League (HANL) and other Hollywood anti-Fascist organizations had given way to more public activism on the part of those with star power. That summer one could attend in short order an anti-Nazi film and a pro-interventionist rally. Jimmy Stewart combined both when he went to Cleveland in September 1940 to attend such an event, bringing *The Mortal Storm* with him.

The invitation to Stewart came from the local branch of the White Committee. Even earlier, members of the committee's national board in

New York had considered using *The Mortal Storm* in their rallies. White himself had been among the first to suggest it, writing to the committee's Executive Director Clark Eichelberger, who directed the committee's day-to-day operations, that *The Mortal Storm* would generate enthusiasm for their work and encourage enrollment.[27]

Sidney Franklin, on the other hand, gave an activist clergyman in Cleveland credit for the idea to use *The Mortal Storm* on behalf of intervention. The Reverend Dilworth Lupton led a Unitarian congregation. In the broader community he enjoyed respect as an outspoken liberal activist. His voice was also heard in the regular column he contributed to the *Cleveland Plain Dealer*. In one of those columns, he argued for the political significance of *The Mortal Storm*. "Have you seen *The Mortal Storm*," he asked his readers, many of whom were inclined toward isolationism like so many in the Midwest. "If I were a multi-millionaire," he told them, "I would make it possible for every man, woman, and child in America to see this great drama of the screen. It is the story of what Hitler and his fellow mad men can do to the human soul, and it is told without exaggeration."[28]

In Cleveland at least, Marjorie Fry responded to his wish, attempting to make the film available to the broadest audience possible in the city. She brought her considerable organizational skills to bear in joining *The Mortal Storm* to the cause of intervention. Fry, who chaired the local affiliate of the White Committee, had quickly turned the group into a model of grassroots activism on behalf of Britain. She not only threw herself into the work of the Cleveland chapter, she arranged events on behalf of the Toledo chapter as well.[29] But she did more than spearhead and oversee programs. With the emergence of the America First Committee in the fall of 1940, she urged gathering intelligence on its leadership to show their connections to right-wing and fascistic organizations.[30]

Fry proved indispensable to the Stewart visit. Recognizing that the original venue she had rented would not accommodate the expected crowd, she quickly booked the Public Auditorium to seat the numbers that her advertising blitz was sure to generate. In fact, nearly 10,000 people attended the screening and presentations, with Stewart as the main attraction.

Fry had help locally but also enjoyed assistance from the national organization of the White Committee. A member of the national organization, Alex Burger, explained to Chairman White how the event came about, a week after it took place.

> The Cleveland gathering, while perhaps suggested by Mr. Lupton's article, was really the idea of Professor Ted Smith of our field staff and Mrs. Marie [sic] Fry of Cleveland, both of whom worked heroically on the details. Smith in obtaining Stewart through MGM and Mrs. Fry in promoting attendance.[31]

It was unlikely that MGM assisted with Stewart's appearance given the determination of the studio's front office not to engage in any more political controversy over the film than absolutely necessary. Burger rightly noted, however, that effective local leadership had been crucial to the success of the event.

Ted Smith and Marjorie Fry made an effective team. He was a professor of international relations at MIT but had volunteered in the summer of 1940 to assist local chapters of the White Committee in organizing public events. He himself often spoke at those events as a foreign policy expert who could make the case for aiding Britain. He may have met Stewart at a pro-interventionist rally in August or September. He and Stewart were certainly then traveling in the same pro-interventionist circles.

While the engagement of movie stars in political causes went back at least to the First World War, the use of cinema in those causes was more recent. The idea came from the peace movement of the 1930s. Grassroots activists, especially in the mid-West, similar to Lupton and Fry, first suggested using Hollywood productions in the cause of peace. They sought to screen films outside of studio-owned theaters as part of open-air rallies to reach as many people as possible.[32] The screenings entailed no admissions charge. In the 1930s, anti-war activists held the moral high ground that by 1940 belonged to the pro-interventionists who supported aid to a by-then desperate Britain. In 1931, Mildred Scott Olmstead of the American branch of the Women's International League for Peace and Freedom (WILPF), for example, "created a list of peace films the organization would recommend to its members."[33] The list held a significant number, because from 1930 to 1934 Hollywood found that anti-war pictures, most notably *All Quiet on the Western Front*, did well with the public and at the box office. That film even played a role in the Nye Committee hearings of 1934 when it was re-released in the midst of them to support the Senator's conclusion that only the "merchants of death" had profited from the Great War. Over the next two years, so-called peace caravans traveled the country to show *All Quiet* and other anti-war films, providing their own projectors and screens.[34]

In that tradition, Fry and Smith determined to use *The Mortal Storm* in their cause. On the night of September 23, 1940, with Jimmy Stewart to introduce it, nearly 10,000 people in Cleveland viewed the MGM feature released three months earlier which quite a few must have already seen. Stewart spoke movingly of what was at stake. According to the *Cleveland Plain Dealer*, the star was "the highlight of the program, making a strong impression with his honest, unaffected delivery."[35] Stewart told the Cleveland audience:

> I don't pretend to be an authority on international politics [...] but I know there's a war going on and I hope it doesn't come over here [...] But it seems there are countries which didn't want war either, but which had

no choice in the matter-and the reason for that appears [...] they weren't prepared [...] It looks as if a lot depended on England, and I think, it's logical to suppose we ought to help England because she's doing more than anybody else to help.[36]

Having urged aid for Britain, Stewart closed on a disarming personal note. "I'm 32, not married, and I know how to fly a plane, so I guess nobody can accuse me of talking about an army somebody else is going to be in."[37] Stewart had announced that, like Martin Breitner, he was willing to come to the aid of those being bullied. And that he did so like Jefferson Smith, the character he played in *Mr. Smith Goes to Washington*, who went to fight for what he believed in, not as Senator Smith, but as Mr. Smith, everyman, because the fight belonged to all of us. Without saying so directly, the actor had referred to the army he was about to join. His draft number had been among the first 900 pulled a week earlier on September 16, 1940, the day the president signed the Selective Service Act. He had thirty days in which to report for his physical.[38] Stewart spoke in Cleveland knowing that he could soon be preparing for possible combat himself.

That fact probably stayed the disciplinary impulse of Howard Strickling, MGM's so-called "Fixer." Strickling acquired a copy of the Cleveland program, so carefully composed by Marjorie Fry. The MGM mogul had apparently been caught by surprise. In his memo to Franklin, to this day still clipped to the program in Franklin's files, he wrote circumspectly, "Thought you might be interested in the attached."[39] Try as it might, the studio had not been able to control its adaptation of Bottome's novel nor the film's co-star. Mayer finally recognized as much. With a gala send-off, he threw a surprise party for Stewart as he prepared to leave for the army.

Burger's account of the event to White, explaining that MIT professor Ted Smith of the White Committee's field staff had "obtained Stewart through MGM," proved inaccurate. If Strickling had not known of the event in advance neither did anyone else in the studio. Smith may have been the one to arrange for Stewart's appearance, bypassing MGM. Stewart's participation was not surprising. Since 1939, he had shown a deep commitment to the anti-fascist cause on screen. In the summer and fall of 1940, he displayed it off-screen as well.

Professor Smith himself played a prominent role in the program. He told the audience, *The Mortal Storm* "is a warning because it gives us a picture of what is meant by the destruction of democracy [...] in 'Mortal Storm' you have seen the permanent state of society when the Fascist and Nazi scheme prevails [...] this great picture [has] a shattering impact," warning that "until we are armed and prepared for a fearful war, let us recognize that the British Navy and the magnificent Royal Air Force are protecting us." The White Committee, Smith summed up, "urges all aid [to Britain] short of war."[40]

The event that night in Cleveland was draped in patriotism. It opened with an organ recital of "The Flag Speaks." Kate Smith had agreed to sing "God Bless America" but failed to appear. In her absence, the audience sang to a recording of Irving Berlin's anthem broadcast over the p.a. system.[41] The speeches of Smith and Stewart were the last events of the evening.

The message of the evening's program was twofold. Aid for Britain served the best interests of the United States and was therefore patriotic. Nor could *The Mortal Storm* be construed as propaganda designed to lure the country into another war on behalf of Britain. Britain instead sacrificed for us as well as for her own survival. As Stewart insisted to his mid-western audience, "a lot depend[s] on England [...] it's logical to suppose we ought to help [her]."[42]

In keeping with that message, the organizers informed the audience that its members had a responsibility to urge a policy of intervention on Congress. The back of the program contained instructions under the heading "Will You Help?" on how to contact members of Congress from Ohio. The organizers explained, "Effective action to aid our defense can be obtained by writing or wiring your elected representatives." The program then listed the names and addresses of the members of the Ohio congressional delegation. What better way for the White Committee to engage the public in its cause. At the same time, the committee could demonstrate to congressional isolationists that interventionist sentiment existed even in the heartland.

Leading isolationists included the junior senator from Ohio, Robert A. Taft, clearly a prime target of such mailings. Taft, in only two years in the Senate, had emerged as an outspoken isolationist. His views on foreign policy "except for his lack of anti-Semitism were almost identical to Lindbergh's."[43] In June, three months earlier at the Republican convention in Philadelphia, Taft had been a leading contender for the nomination. He opposed the president's determination to introduce peace-time conscription and labeled Stimson and Knox, both longtime Republicans, members of the Democrats' "war party."[44] A message to Taft in particular would serve notice regarding the strength of interventionist sentiment among his own constituents. It would also be sure to alert the Senate isolationists of the use to which Hollywood war pictures could be put.

Taft in all likelihood had already been exposed to the film. *The Mortal Storm* had opened in Philadelphia, just days before the Republican convention began in late June 1940.[45] The newsreels that accompanied it featured "bedraggled French troops in chaotic retreat."[46] In his study of the 1940 Republican national convention, Charles Peters argues that the film and the accompanying newsreels playing daily across the street from the convention venue would have given delegates, many of whom were isolationist and even taking money from Hans Thomsen in the German embassy, no respite from the interventionist side of the foreign policy argument.[47] A few months later the arrival of a barrage of notes and cards from his Cleveland constituents warned Taft that the film continued to resonate with the public.

The interventionist movement, however, lost the initiative that Stewart's visit to Cleveland provided. Marjorie Fry had intended to set an example for other White Committee affiliates. Alex Burger, in recounting to White the details of the Cleveland screening of *The Mortal Storm*, referred to similar events to be held in the near future. "One [...] is now being arranged for Detroit. It has also been suggested to several of our other chapters."[48] Records of local White affiliates to be found in Princeton University's Seeley Mudd Library, however, indicate no events similar to the one in Cleveland. The one planned for Detroit apparently did not take place. *The Mortal Storm* did not become the successor to *All Quiet on the Western Front* as the cinematic embodiment of the evolution in the American attitude toward Germany. Stewart himself was no longer available, rushing through the making of three films in the following month while preparing to be inducted into the army. White himself resigned as chair of the committee in January 1941, no longer so enthusiastic about aid to Britain, throwing the work of the national organization for a time into disarray.

The White Committee proved an unreliable sponsor in other regards. Large-scale events were expensive and local committees were often strapped for cash, because such a large percentage of affiliate dues were supposed to go to the national organization in New York.[49] Limited funds as well as weak local leadership did not encourage duplication of the Cleveland program. Few White Committee affiliates possessed a Marjorie Fry who could organize a major public event. Other stars, like Stewart, prepared to join the military or perform some type of war work. The interventionist cause itself was evolving. It found new strength with FDR's reelection. Shortly after that, interventionism acquired a new focus. Support for the Lend-Lease bill before Congress replaced other grassroots efforts of the White Committee affiliates.

The Cleveland event with nearly 10,000 attendees nonetheless raises the question of just how many did see *The Mortal Storm* in its first run in 1940. Figures for box-office gross are available and provide a comparative picture of the film's initial success.[50] It made $3.3 million in its first run, although according to Nicholas Schenck, head of Loew's Inc., MGM's parent company, "The picture took in $4 million."[51] Of the war pictures of 1940, *The Great Dictator* grossed the most at $10 million, but a Chaplin film could be said to be in a category of its own. After that came *Foreign Correspondent* at $4.1 million followed by *The Mortal Storm* at $3.3 or $4 million. *Shop Around the Corner* made a respectable $2.4. Well behind that was *Four Sons* at $2 million, *The Man I Married* (originally, *I Married a Nazi*) at $1.7 million, and *Night Train to Munich* at $1 million. The war pictures as a whole, with the exception of Chaplin's film, could not be labeled smash hits, certainly not when compared to *Gone with the Wind*'s $20 million.

John McDonald of the American Film Center wrote of *The Mortal Storm* in *Public Opinion Quarterly* that for the month that Stewart spoke in Cleveland: it "did not do badly, but fell short of normal expectations."[52] By comparison to other war pictures it may "not have done badly," but in comparison to the popular *Philadelphia Story*, for example, it did. *The Philadelphia Story* grossed $6.8 million, just below *The Grapes of Wrath* at $7.1 million. To be considered a financial success, *The Mortal Storm* would have needed to gross between $6 and $7 million.

But the success of *The Mortal Storm* in 1940 had to be measured in more than monetary gross or even number of theater attendees. It joined a trilogy of films that Jimmy Stewart made in 1939–40 that possessed timely political significance impossible to quantify. Pivotal scenes in *Mr. Smith Goes to Washington*, *The Mortal Storm*, and *The Philadelphia Story* addressed the dilemmas before Americans on the eve of a war they naturally found frightening. In *The Mortal Storm*, Stewart skis to the Austrian border, bearing the dying Freya Roth in his arms, shot by a Nazi patrol. In *The Philadelphia Story*, Stewart carries the drunken Tracy Lord (Katharine Hepburn), lord of all she surveys, from her family's spacious pool, while singing *Over the Rainbow* at the top of his lungs, a song that suggested fantasy and make believe. Taken together, the two films posed the choice before Americans in 1940. Were we secure in our isolation, rich, spoiled, with the luxury of nighttime swims and drunken parties, able to escape into sheer fantasy; or, did intervention in Europe's conflict compel us, because the Nazis would give no quarter, even to the most vulnerable among us? Stewart tied the two films together as the bearer of the heroine and the message in each. Similarly, Frank Morgan as Professor Roth tied *The Mortal Storm* to *The Wizard of Oz*, as did Stewart's rendition of *Over the Rainbow*. The two MGM films carried a similar message. A wicked witch threatened Dorothy. A far worse menace stalked Freya Roth and her family.

The political measure of *The Mortal Storm*, seen in Stewart's stirring use of the film in Cleveland, made Hollywood appear more dangerous than ever to the growing isolationist movement, soon to coalesce around the America First Committee. *The Mortal Storm* had shown in the heartland that box-office success could no longer provide the measure of a film's reach or its effect on public opinion. The isolationists took note. The week before the film's release, Lindbergh met over the course of two days with his cohort of isolationist senators. The group included Clark of Missouri and Burton K. Wheeler, the senior senator from Montana, who later played a prominent role in the investigation of Hollywood's "propaganda for war." The congressional isolationists were already discussing plans for counteracting what they termed war agitation and propaganda.[53]

Unbeknownst to Lindbergh and the isolationists, Hollywood was soon to withdraw from its dramatic political engagement of 1940 when it made explicitly anti-Nazi films, most released in the summer of that year. David Welky has observed that the "studios essentially abandoned the German cycle [of films set in Nazi Germany] after 1940."[54] The spate of anti-Nazi films released that year, about twenty out of more than 500 the studios made altogether, did not do well at the box office. Why should the studios tempt controversy for inadequate financial reward? Welky maintains. To isolationists, on the other hand, ignorant that "the German cycle" of films would soon be put on hold, *The Mortal Storm* in particular, had demonstrated how a Hollywood film could arouse interventionist sentiment in the public.

The *Cleveland Plain Dealer* called the film "emotional, theatrical" with "a vividly dramatic story."[55] The film had moved the activist liberal, the Rev. Dilworth Lupton as well as Lindbergh's close associate, the isolationist and former diplomat William Castle, who praised it lavishly in his diary. *The Mortal Storm* could breach the political divide in its popularity. But it could pose another danger. While Senator Taft, historian Charles Peters argues, advocated isolationism without supporting antisemitism, a whole cohort of isolationists in the Senate certainly did. They gathered around Lindbergh, sharing his antipathy to Jews. They saw the film's potential to do more than advocate for intervention. In utilizing the term "non-Aryan" this time, MGM merely threatened. Next time the studio would show the plight of "the Jews" and rouse public opinion without obfuscation. The antisemites took note.

Bottome Learns She Was Duped/Rabbi Eisendrath Weighs In

Bottome left the United States in the third week of June 1940, believing that MGM had retained the word "Jew" in the film and that her arguments sent to Franklin and Mayer had prevailed. The New York office of the studio had shown her the version of the film in which Margaret Sullavan, Irene Rich, Frank Morgan, and Gene Reynolds play the full "father-son" scene in Professor Roth's study with the use of the word "Jew" as well as the questionnaire on race that Rudi brings home from school plainly visible. She learned only in August that the film the studio distributed had depicted the hounding of non-Aryans and worst of all deleted the "father-son" scene. Bottome wrote Roger Scaife, her editor at Little, Brown & Co., of her anger and frustration. "Have you and Ethel seen 'The Mortal Storm'? To my intense regret they have suppressed the scene they showed me between father and son. It was the gist of the book and I am very sore about it."[56] Two weeks later her ire had not cooled. She told Israel Seiff, a good friend who served as managing director of Marks and Spencer, "I am bitterly grieved that after having shown it to me in New York, they suppressed the father and son talk that was the gist of the book."[57]

At the same time an overall sense that the film had succeeded in urging an end to American isolationism offered some consolation. Bottome wrote her boss at the MoI, Sir Frederick Whyte, Head of the American Division:

> It would amuse you to read the rage of the Pacifist and Communist papers against 'Mortal Storm.' Several of them say of the film [...] 'This is bringing America into the war'! Hardly a point on which its author feels disappointment. It really seems to have hit the Hour [...][58]

Ernan was just as enthusiastic, telling J. J. Lewellin, Parliamentary Secretary in the Ministry of Aircraft Production, that "'Mortal Storm' is doing better work for our cause than any other form of propaganda which has been devised."[59]

Other correspondents informed Bottome that the film played in North American movie theaters through the summer, "continuing to receive a good reception here."[60] Duff Cooper, the head of MoI, offered his praise, assuring her "the film [...] is a very great success."[61] "Our cause," as he termed it, was intervention; and *The Mortal Storm* was warming the North Americans to it.

Rabbi Eisendrath, who had showcased the novel before his congregation and urged his colleague Rabbi Magnin to pressure Mayer to purchase it, did not seem distressed by the studio's censorship. Another issue disturbed him when he saw it only in December, because, as he explained to Bottome:

> 'Mortal Storm' [...] seems to have shown in most of the Toronto houses throughout the summer months we were away. But just the other day it was shown again at one of the Neighborhood Houses and we rushed off with some of our friends to see it [...] all of us were moved anew [...].[62]

Eisendrath then compared the film to the novel, favoring the latter:

> No producer could do justice to your writing [it] cannot be translated by anyone, producer or actors to the silver screen [...] But within these limitations it was one of the most beautiful and worth-while pictures that we have ever seen.

Despite the absence of the word "Jew" and the "father-son" scene that Bottome dubbed "the gist of the novel," the film adaptation, Eisendrath maintained, still works.

His problem with the film lay with the issue of timing, the source of most criticism of the film in its first year.

My one lament is that it was not shown so very much earlier. I repeat my sense of chagrin that undoubtedly some of my coreligionists were responsible for the cowardly procrastination and deliberate delays in the making and release of this penetrating document which would have done so much to have awakened this continent [...] to the deeper implications [of] the moral menace of Naziism to which only now they are beginning to be roused.

Eisendrath ended with the thought that "what a pity that these millions who wept over the fate of Dr. Roth and his loved ones were not so moved years ago [...]."

The rabbi spoke with authority on the need to arouse the public about the Nazis years earlier. He had tried to do so through the 1930s, having visited Germany as early as the summer of 1933.[63] Bottome, as a "premature anti-Nazi," shared those sentiments while also decrying the loss of the "father-son" scene. At least by 1940, the film adaptation of *The Mortal Storm* had become a brief for American intervention. Eisendrath excoriated the long silence of his fellow Jews. Bottome, on the other hand, knew that Britain's fate hung by a thread. Only aid from North America could save her, and so the film was made to arouse that audience, despite Mayer's best efforts to keep it noncontroversial. Bottome could at last take comfort in the reaction of the film's trans-Atlantic audience, however belatedly it had occurred.

Belated or not, Rabbi Eisendrath still considered the film "exceptional." Bottome's rabbinical friend had nonetheless raised the issue of the timing of *The Mortal Storm*. Should the picture have been made much earlier to awaken somnambulant audiences to the threat before them, or was its appearance appropriate, just in time to make the case for intervention before the reluctant American public, with the Nazis preparing to invade Britain? The disagreement over timing occurred among those who valued the film. 1940 belonged to the friends of *The Mortal Storm*. In 1941, the production's enemies had their say, those who "the minute Hollywood admits that the swastika is not a device used exclusively in Navajo rugs, [...] begin hollering that Hollywood is leading this country into war [...]."[64]

Notes

1   Merrill Schleier, "Mr. Smith Goes to Washington: The Two Lincolns, Monuments, and the Preservation of Patriarchy," *Quarterly Review of Film and Video,* May 14, 2014. Online, p. 453. Accessed July 2, 2015.
2   Schwartz, *Abraham Lincoln and the Forge of National Memory*, xii.
3   "The Mortal Storm," *Wikipedia*, accessed May 9, 2018.
4   "*The Mortal Storm*," *Harrison Report*, June 22, 1940, 98.

5   "The Mortal Storm," *Variety*, June 7, 1940.
6   "The Mortal Storm," *Motion Picture Herald*, June 15, 1940, 42.
7   "The Mortal Storm," *Hollywood Reporter*, June 11, 1940.
8   *The Lobby* (MGM Publicity Dept.), summer 1940. The entire issue of the newsprint brochure is devoted to *The Mortal Storm*. *The Lobby* and other MGM publicity materials can be found in NARA (College Park), RG59. Decimal File 1940–4. 811.4054/125 to 811. 4054/406. Mortal Storm 12–13. Box no. 3809.
9   MGM produced a short subject film shown on Turner Classic Movies in 2017 devoted to the twice-yearly gatherings at the studio for theater owners and managers from which this information is taken.
10 *The Lobby*, summer 1940, p. 4.
11 Ibid., 1.
12 Ibid., 3.
13 Ibid.
14 Ibid., 2.
15 Ferguson's use of the adjective "little" suggests that he referred to the "father-son" scene as played by the 8–10-year-old Scotty Beckett before the lanky 16-year-old Gene Reynolds joined the cast, at the end of February.
16 See *Racine Journal Times*, June 25, 1940, 9, and *Ogden Standard Examiner*, August 14, 1940, 10.
17 *The Lobby*, 3.
18 "Story of Rise of Nazis at Fox Oakland," *Oakland Tribune*, June 28, 1940, 22.
19 *Oakland Tribune*, June 28, 1940, 22.
20 *Hutchinson Kansas-News-Herald*, July 28, 1940, 9.
21 *Iowa Recorder*, September 25, 1940, 2.
22 Eliot, *Jimmy Stewart*, 158. Stewart invited Henry Fonda, Tyrone Power, and Olivia de Havilland to the event at the Coliseum in Houston, Texas.
23 Fairbanks, *Salad Days*, 368.
24 PB to unknown correspondent. February 24, 1940. BL Add. Mss. 88921/2/1.
25 "Review of the Mortal Storm," *Hollywood Reporter*, June 11, 1940, 3.
26 Eliot, 158.
27 The Committee to Defend America by Aiding the Allies (White Committee) Papers. Series 1, Box 24, July 7, 1940. Seeley G. Mudd Manuscript Library, Princeton University.
28 Franklin, "We Laughed and We Cried," 288.
29 See clippings from the Toledo newspapers for the summer of 1940 to be found in the Committee to Defend America by Aiding the Allies (White Committee) Papers. Seeley G. Mudd Manuscript Library, Princeton University.
30 See memo of Marjorie Fry to the Cleveland White Committee to be found in White Committee Papers, Cleveland branch, Seeley Mudd Library, calling for

such intelligence gathering. Both the Princeton collection of White Committee papers and the Committee's archive in the Library of Congress, Manuscript Collection contain the same two-page single-spaced typed memo with short bios of the America First (AFC) leadership. The memo resulted from her recommendation along with her own intelligence gathering. Seeley G. Mudd Manuscript Library, Princeton University, White Committee Papers, Series 1, Box 24. William Allen White Papers, Manuscript Division, US Library of Congress, Box 14.

31 Burger to White; October 3, 1940; William Allen White Papers, Manuscript Division, US Library of Congress, Box 15.
32 See the discussion in John Whiteclay Chambers II, "The Movies and the Antiwar Debate in America, 1930–1941," *Film and History*, vol. 38, no. 1 (2006), 44–57.
33 Ibid., 45.
34 Ibid., 46.
35 Roelif Loveland, "Help Britain, Be Ready, Stewart Urges 9, 865," *Cleveland Plain Dealer*, September 24, 1940, 1.
36 Ibid.
37 Ibid.
38 Eliot, 159.
39 To be found in SAF, Box 9, folder #26.
40 Loveland, *Cleveland Plain Dealer*, "Help Britain," September 24, 1940, 5.
41 Ibid.
42 Ibid.
43 Charles Peters, *Five Days in Philadelphia, 1940. Wendell Willkie and the Political Convention that Freed FDR to Win World War II* (New York: Public Affairs, 2005), 4.
44 Ibid., 69.
45 Ibid., 68.
46 Ibid.
47 Ibid.
48 Alex W. Burger to William Allen White, October 3, 1940. US Library of Congress, Manuscript Division, William Allen White Papers, Box 15.
49 See financial records of White committee affiliates in Seeley Mudd which contain numerous complaints sent to the national headquarters about the requirement to make the affiliates pay local as well as national dues which were considerably higher.
50 The web site from which these figures were taken is no longer available. The numbers were given in 1940 dollars rather than equivalents with twenty-first-century values.
51 "Propaganda in Motion Pictures," Hearings before a Subcommittee of the Committee on Interstate Commerce. United States Senate. 77th Congress, 1st Session on S. Res. 152, September 1941 (hereafter Hearings), 328.

52 John McDonald, *Public Opinion Quarterly* (September 1940), 520.
53 Lindbergh, *Wartime Journals* (June 12 and 13, 1940), 356–7.
54 Welky, *The Moguls and the Dictators*, 227.
55 "Review of 'The Mortal Storm,'" *The Cleveland Plain Dealer* (September 20, 1940).
56 PB to Roger Scaife, August 12, 1940. BL Add. Mss. 88921/3/3.
57 Ibid., PB to Israel Sieff, August 28, 1940.
58 Ibid., PB to Sir Frederick Whyte, August 3, 1940.
59 Ibid., Ernan Forbes-Dennis to J. J. Lewellin, July 30, 1940.
60 Ibid., Helen Lambert to PB, September 9, 1940.
61 Ibid., 88921/2/8, Duff Cooper to PB, November 21, 1940. In this letter Cooper refers to visiting the set of *The Mortal Storm* while on a tour of the United States earlier in the year. Hollywood could then show off a film with an interventionist message to a visiting British dignitary.
62 Eisendrath's letter to Bottome, December 1, 1940, can be found in BL Add. Mss. 88921/3/3.
63 Rabbi Maurice N. Eisendrath, "Berlin Diaries," *Holy Blossom Pulpit*, vol. II, no. 3 (December 7, 1941), 5.
64 Lucie Neville, "'Fence Straddling is Out'-Says Hollywood as It Goes anti-Hitler," *Galveston Daily News*, July 29, 1940, 29. The piece showcased two films in particular: *The Mortal Storm* and *The Great Dictator* with two photos from the MGM production and one from Chaplin's film.

8

The Response to *The Mortal Storm*, 1941

1941

1941 held its own surprises. True, the American public could be caught off guard as it had been with Hitler's invasion of Western Europe in the spring of 1940, but it had by now grown used to the reality of warfare as long as it occurred elsewhere. The shock value of the previous year's events could not be replicated, even if the invasion of the Soviet Union in the third week of June 1941 came close. The West remained largely unaware of the murderous war against the Jews, subsequently known as the Holocaust, which began as soon as the German armies crossed the Soviet border. By July 30, they had pushed as far east as Kremenchug in Ukraine where, as elsewhere on Soviet territory, they slaughtered the Jewish population they encountered. Churchill called what was happening "a crime without a name." Few had begun to comprehend the magnitude of the crime or its particular target.

American politics had other concerns. With 1941, the drama of the presidential election was over. The isolationists, instead of accepting defeat with Roosevelt's re-election, returned to the fray more vocal than ever. At the same time, their most well-organized opponent had lost steam. Internal descension and White's resignation as chair from the committee named for him undermined the organization's work down to the local committees. Instead, the isolationist America First Committee, which formed in September–October 1940, on the model of the White Committee, unleashed a nationwide campaign. It held one rally after another where isolationist Senators, often joined by Charles Lindbergh, denounced the president's foreign policy as adventurist and dangerous.

But there was more to the isolationist campaign in 1941. And in that sense a new emphasis made its way into American politics that year, if not always publicly proclaimed. Lindbergh and the cohort of congressional isolationists who supported him acquired another target in their campaign to keep the country out of war. Hollywood became the focus of the isolationists' scrutiny.

The movie industry ironically drew back from the activism it had shown in 1940 in contrast to what the isolationists now said about it. In 1941, the isolationists a year out of step, turned to the studio heads, nearly all of whom were Jewish. They believed the moguls intended to corrupt the most popular form of entertainment in the country, making it into propaganda for war. A disturbing strain of antisemitism can be discerned among those who the year before had decried aid to Britain and urged American neutrality. The isolationists in 1941 determined to show that Hollywood, largely controlled by Jewish studio heads, manipulated the American public for their own ends.

One film "particularly" attracted their attention. It combined propaganda for war with the Jewish question. In 1941, *The Mortal Storm* acquired a new lease on life thanks to the attention congressional antisemitic isolationists, colluding with Charles Lindbergh, directed at it. By the fall of 1941, the picture whose box office had disappointed on its initial run was resurrected by its enemies to become the symbol of Hollywood's abuse of the motion picture medium. *The Mortal Storm* came into its own again slightly over a year after its release.

Mr. Lindbergh on the Ground

Almost two months to the day after Jimmy Stewart addressed a rally in Cleveland to encourage aid to Britain, Ambassador Joseph P. Kennedy spoke to a large audience of Hollywood luminaries at a luncheon hosted by the Warner brothers. Kennedy's listeners did not like what they heard. Most left in consternation, some in fear. The ambassador had raised a sensitive issue for the moguls. Douglas Fairbanks, Jr. reported to the president that Kennedy warned "the studio bosses that they should refrain from making pro-Allied, anti-Nazi films because people would say [they did so] because [they were] Jews."[1] The ambassador further claimed that the studios "antagonized the inevitable victor" by making such films.[2] Presumably Kennedy meant that the European market would be closed permanently to American films if the moguls openly opposed Hitler who would soon conquer Britain, he claimed, and therefore control the whole continent. Drew Pearson reported that the moguls left the luncheon "pop-eyed" at Kennedy's admonitions.[3]

Kennedy was not the only isolationist who viewed Hollywood warily as 1940 came to a close. On New Year's Day 1941, Charles Lindbergh did something he rarely did. The aviator went to the movies. He wanted to see newsreel coverage of his wife's Christmas eve radio address, encouraging food shipments to occupied France. Lindbergh was not pleased that the segment featuring his wife contained the caption "Shall We Feed Hitler's Europe?" In the published version of his diary, he briefly complained, "They never miss an opportunity to do something like that."[4] The "they" is not identified. Nor is there an ellipsis to indicate that a portion from the original entry is missing. In the unpublished diary, Lindbergh did identify the source of the caption. He wrote, "Probably Jewish influence in this case. They practically control the motion picture industry."[5]

But Lindbergh was not finished with the movies that day. Also missing from the published version of the diary was the fact that he "went to a second theater [one devoted to newsreels], where the theater was showing a résumé of 1940 war pictures ...."[6] As noted earlier, Lindbergh had no doubt received an enthusiastic report about *The Mortal Storm* from his friend and fellow isolationist William Castle. If he had not himself already seen the film, he learned still more about its focus on the Jewish question that New Year's Day. It would have stood out, among the other "German pictures" of 1940 where reference to Jews might get passing mention, if any at all. Lindbergh would have no trouble discerning who were the "non-Aryans," the principal subjects of the film.

He admitted in his diary that the isolationist cause had not done well in 1940. As 1941 began, he wrote, "we who are against American intervention have been slowly losing ground ...."[7] But the New Year presented a fresh start. The aviator returned to politics with renewed vigor. What drove his political activity is more apparent in his unpublished diary than in the expurgated version which did not appear until 1970. Scott Berg, Lindbergh's biographer, observes that "several omissions in the published texts [...] were substantive in nature [...] the bulk of these omissions centered on one subject: the Jews." He insists, however, that "most of the references express Lindbergh's affinity and admiration for them. But in so writing about a single tribe, he was segregating them in his mind from the rest of the nation; and to that extent he was, like many of his countrymen, antisemitic."[8] Lindbergh, in fact, harbored deeply held antisemitic views that, as it would turn out, were precisely what separated him from most of his fellow countrymen.

His antipathy for Jews, his diary revealed, intensified through the course of 1941. By May of that year, antisemitism drove much of his political activity which had begun with his return from Europe in April 1939 as an advocate for American isolationism. By mid-1941 he held the conviction that Jewish influence, particularly in the movie industry, would drive the United States to war. On May 1 he wrote, deleted from the published version of the diary, "Probably the Jews are the greatest single influence pushing us toward war [...] I think if it were not for the Jews in America, we would not be on the verge of war today." The crux of the problem, he observed, lay with their control of "most of our motion pictures."[9]

By mid-July Lindbergh's antisemitism had reached all-consuming importance. On July 11, in one of the longest entries, if not the longest, in his entire diary, he speculated on how to address the inordinate Jewish influence in American life. He decried Jewish control over our agencies of information "as well as Jewish influence in National affairs [...] far out of proportion to their numbers." He did, however, generously insist that in addressing the problem, "it is essential to avoid anything approaching a pogrom ...."[10] The comment recalls his correspondence with Ambassador Kennedy regarding *Kristallnacht*, the Night of Broken Glass. He and Kennedy had earlier deplored the violence of *Kristallnacht*, the so-called November pogrom of 1938. Kennedy wrote Lindbergh at the time, "So much is lost [in violence] when so much could be gained."[11] Lindbergh almost three years later had intensified his views, his stance on the Jewish question having hardened to dangerous proportions. He now determined "to combat the pressure the Jews are bringing on this country to enter the war."[12] He mused, a Senate investigation of "the groups agitating for war" would be one approach to unmask the extent of Jewish influence and its consequences.[13] From Lindbergh's point of view, such an investigation was vital, because as he told Henry Ford, "The country is still opposed to our entry [into war] but I am not sure how long people will be able to withstand the misinformation and propaganda that fills our press, our radio, and our motion pictures theaters each day."[14] Such an institutional approach, relying on congress, would presumably avoid the violence of a pogrom like *Kristallnacht* that he and Kennedy both deplored.

Scott Berg, on the other hand, insists that the aviator's antisemitism had only a limited influence on his political activity. Lindbergh, he notes, spoke only once in public about Jewish agitation for war. He addressed an America First rally in Des Moines on September 11, 1941, where he said the Jews' "greatest danger to this country lies in their large ownership and influence in our motion pictures, our press, our radio, and our Government."[15] It was no accident that Lindbergh mentioned Jewish influence in motion pictures first. He spoke at the rally in support of the Senate investigation of Hollywood that had begun two days earlier, an investigation that, as his diary revealed, he himself had encouraged and helped to initiate. Berg instead argues that "Lindbergh [in Des Moines] had bent over backward to be kind to the Jews."[16] If true, the aviator contradicted nearly a year's worth of increasingly hostile entries in his diary. Through 1941, Lindbergh had shown no such inclination toward kindness in the portions of his diary that addresses the Jewish question and have yet to be published.

Lindbergh's thinking had evolved in other matters as well. Since returning to the United States in early spring 1939, he had modified his views from opposition to Roosevelt's interventionist foreign policy to repeatedly warning that Jewish control of the media, specifically Hollywood, had generated unceasing propaganda for war. In other words, Hollywood, not the president, had become his bête noir. It is quite possible that Lindbergh intended the Senate hearings, like the Des Moines speech, to initiate a public campaign against American Jews and their alleged agitation for war. The language, certainly the sentiments that had been confined to his diary, would then enter the public sphere bolstered by his heroic image and reputation as an expert in military affairs, German prowess in particular.

Lindbergh's isolationist, antisemitic cohort in the Senate had undergone a similar evolution. Determined to uphold an isolationist foreign policy dating from the 1930s, by mid-1941 they prepared to charge that the Jews used their control of Hollywood to produce propaganda for war. In their private correspondence as well as in public statements, one picture in particular had caught their attention. Released "oh so late" in 1940, as Bosley Crowther had observed, *The Mortal Storm* had become timely at last and, by 1941, was still being shown, the target of antisemites both inside and outside of the Senate.

But it had become something more. It served as the primary cinematic example for those on either side of the foreign policy argument regarding Hollywood. For Hollywood, *The Mortal Storm* revealed how the movie industry could fulfill its patriotic obligation to the country during what Will Hays termed the current "ordeal of fire and destruction."[17] In his annual report for 1940 to the Motion Picture Producers and Distributors of America, compiled for public consumption, Hays listed the films that "reflected [...] the somber [...] aspects of the tragedy of Europe."[18] *The Mortal Storm* came first.

America First, similarly, gave the film pride of place. In the summer of 1941, the national organization called for a boycott of movie theaters that showed war pictures. It listed the offending titles. *The Mortal Storm*, "which showed Nazis terrorizing a Jewish scientist," came first on the isolationists' list of offending films.[19] Professor Roth had acquired his true identity, and the film continued to attract moviegoers. Even in its second year, the film still had a role to play. The box office disappointment of 1940 had within a year attracted the renewed attention of isolationists and interventionists alike who listed it first among the films to be boycotted or, on the other hand, as Will Hays would have it, viewed for best reflecting "the tragedy of Europe."

Preparation for the Hearings on Hollywood

Senator Wheeler

Few would expect to see the name of Burton K. Wheeler on a White House guest list even though Wheeler as chair of the Interstate Commerce

Committee (ICC) counted among the most powerful Democrats in the Senate.[20] For nearly a decade, the animosity between him and the president had steeped in the ambition both men shared in equal measure. By 1941, the *Time* magazine correspondent Frank McNaughton reported that Wheeler's attitude to the president bore all the characteristics of "a rancid venom."[21]

Roosevelt in turn had never liked Wheeler. He gave the vice-presidency to John Nance Garner in 1932 even though Wheeler, who had been among the first to endorse the New York governor for president, "desperately [...] wanted it."[22] With Wheeler up for re-election in 1934, FDR visited Montana but failed to campaign for him.[23] And then there was Wheeler's almost single-handed defeat of the president's court-packing scheme in 1937 followed two years later by the parody of Wheeler in *Mr. Smith Goes to Washington* courtesy of Roosevelt-friendly Hollywood. Small wonder Wheeler could write, "... the modern Benedict Arnold is the silver screen."[24]

On the one hand, the hearings on Hollywood in 1941, conducted by a subcommittee of Wheeler's ICC, could be labeled another chapter in the Senator's ongoing rivalry with FDR. On the other hand, the hearings were something more, having emerged from the conflict between interventionists and isolationists over the whole direction of American foreign policy since 1939. But not even those issues taken together encompassed the origin of the hearings.

Supported and encouraged by Lindbergh, Wheeler and his Senate cohort of isolationists came to regard Jewish influence in the media as a threat to the country. Their antisemitism by 1941 could not be ignored. According to the well-connected Washington correspondent of *The New Republic*, Michael Straight, Wheeler's negative attitude toward Jews had attracted so much attention that it "has often been the subject of public discussion [...]."[25] The FBI subsequently substantiated reports that Mrs. Wheeler shared her husband's "bitterly antisemitic" views.[26]

The same could be said of those closest to Wheeler in the investigation of Hollywood: Gerald Nye and Bennett Champ Clark. Their wives, like Mrs. Wheeler, joined the battle for isolationism armed with the same animosity toward Jewish influence in the media, Hollywood in particular, run by Jewish moguls. Both couples had been frequent dinner guests of the Wheelers since early 1939.[27] Mrs. Nye and Mrs. Clark came to be recognized as outspoken isolationists in their own right. They served on the national committee of America First. Together they ran the important Washington, D.C. chapter of the organization.

In the Senate their husbands sought authorization to investigate what they termed propaganda for war. Investigating Hollywood figured in a campaign they had waged since the so-called merchant of death hearings that Nye had chaired in the mid-1930s to blame weapons manufacturers for luring the country into the First World War. Nye's committee had ended its final report with the observation that if it had the authorization, it would have conducted "a study of propaganda techniques [in World War I] employed by belligerent powers to secure the sympathy of the United States."[28] But each time, starting in 1939, Bennett Champ Clark, who had served on Nye's munitions committee, proposed an investigation into one source of propaganda or another, Senate interventionists outmaneuvered him, voting in the Audit Committee, which they controlled, to withhold funds from his resolutions.

By the summer of 1941, much had changed for the Senate isolationists. Hollywood itself had provided a critical mass of films to investigate. And Wheeler was spoiling for yet another fight with the president who since 1939 had repeatedly beaten him. The senator had failed to save Nye's Neutrality legislation that year. He had hoped to run for president in 1940 but could not even come close to the nomination. FDR had gone on to provide weapons to Britain and to introduce conscription, all Wheeler had heartily opposed. The Montana Senator went so far as to say of the president's Lend-Lease bill: "It will plow under every fourth American boy." FDR had not minced words in his reply, calling Wheeler's statement "the rottenest thing that has been said in public life in my generation."[29]

Wheeler therefore had two targets. Hollywood was the first. He loathed the movie industry for the damaging portrait of him in *Mr. Smith Goes to Washington*. He hoped to damage Hollywood in turn, showing the country that the Hollywood studios in the guise of entertainment colluded in propagandizing for war. By implication, public opinion, agitated and misinformed, supported Roosevelt's aggressive and dangerous foreign policy. The president himself provided the second target. If Wheeler could weaken FDR's ally Hollywood, he believed he could undermine the president and slow the momentum of his leadership that had prevailed for the past two and a half years on behalf of intervention.

In January 1941, the senator suggested a new responsibility for the already powerful ICC that he had chaired since 1935. In the five years of his chairmanship, the committee had focused on monitoring the mineral wealth of the western states. Wheeler proclaimed a new subject of interest. He threatened to investigate the newsreels and their insidious propaganda for war, claiming that the interstate commerce of Hollywood fell within his committee's purview.[30]

Having spent much of the spring of 1941 appearing at rallies all over the country on behalf of America First, Wheeler and his Senate cohort, joined by Lindbergh, brought their message of a dangerous drift toward war to the doorstep of Hollywood itself. In June, they held a major rally at the Hollywood Bowl. That event was to be one of the last America First rallies until the fall. Starting in July, the isolationists prepared to hold hearings, bringing the authority of a Senate investigation to bear on the studios for propagandizing for war. Instead of the heads of companies that manufactured munitions such as Dupont and Morgan whom Nye had once grilled, the studio heads of Hollywood were to be called to account, not only for newsreels but for the feature films that accompanied them. Targeted were the moguls whom Ambassador Kennedy had warned nine months earlier to "refrain from making pro-allied, anti-Nazi films."[31]

John T. Flynn

Wheeler chose John T. Flynn to organize the hearings. Lindbergh, who knew Flynn well and had had lengthy discussions with him regarding the baleful influence of Hollywood, urged his appointment. Economist and journalist, Flynn had made major contributions to the munitions hearings as an expert consultant. He was both competent and trustworthy; he was also available. The year before, Flynn had been one of the highest paid journalists in the country. But in 1940 one publication after another dropped his column, including *Colliers, Harpers*, the Scripps-Howard newspaper chain. In November *The New Republic* let him go after seven years as a contributor because of his isolationist views. Flynn believed that the interventionists were blacklisting him to keep his views out of print, which they probably were.

In addition to his impeccable credentials as an isolationist, Flynn detested Roosevelt. He published a denunciation of the president just in time for the 1940 campaign in which he accused FDR of using his office to enrich his own family.[32] Other convictions recommended him for the job of overseeing an investigation of Hollywood. Flynn shared the concern of Lindbergh and his cohort regarding the motion picture industry. He was convinced that "the Roosevelt administration had a subterranean arrangement with the film industry to promote subtle, emotional, interventionist propaganda."[33]

Flynn's daughter tried to absolve her father of the charge of antisemitism that was leveled against so many isolationists as well as America First itself. Her father chaired the New York chapter of the organization where his record on antisemitism, however, was ambiguous. She insisted that he aggressively opposed the infiltration of the organization by "militantly antisemitic groups." Such groups were especially attracted to Flynn's well-heeled New York chapter.[34] Flynn, on the other hand, attempted to distance the organization from them, believing they gave the anti-war cause the appearance of a European fascist movement. At the same time, he believed that in 1941 a smear campaign directed against America First was well-funded by "an interlocking core of donors [...] in which foreign and Jewish names would predominate."[35]

Whether Flynn liked it or not, antisemitism, like mustard gas on the Western front, crept in and hung over the hearings, toxic and unmistakable. Even before the hearings convened, letters poured into Wheeler's office by the hundreds, praising the fact that congress had at last targeted the Jews of Hollywood.[36] Typical was the following: "Dear Senator: At last we are having some action against the Jews of Hollywood. Give them hell; they are vicious and deserve it."[37]

Flynn approached the hearings in a methodical and well-organized fashion, ably assisted by funding from "one of the largest contributors to America First," never named.[38] He hired a trusted staff of twelve from the New York chapter of the organization to assist him. He wrote the Senate resolution for the hearings which Clark and Nye introduced before the Senate referred it to the Interstate Commerce Committee. Wheeler obligingly supplied the funds for what was labeled a "preliminary investigation" by an ICC subcommittee which would then report to the committee as a whole. The full committee was to use the charges and information gathered by the subcommittee as the basis for a second round of hearings. Flynn left nothing to chance. He prepared the questions to be asked of witnesses. He wrote speeches on the forthcoming hearings for Nye, Clark, and Wheeler as well as the testimony that Nye and Clark were to give as friendly witnesses.[39]

John Wheeler

Along with Flynn's well-funded efforts, the subcommittee found inspiration from another, almost accidental source. Guidance came from someone more in tune with the unambiguous antisemitism of most subcommittee members. Wheeler's son John provided a memo that trumped the careful work of Flynn and his well-vetted staff. The younger Wheeler was a Harvard educated attorney who headed the America First chapter of southern California where his responsibilities included monitoring Hollywood. His surveillance amounted to preparation for the hearings on Hollywood. He summed up his work in a memo to his father dated August 10, 1941, a month before the hearings began.

While Flynn's efforts had treated each of the more than twenty war pictures of the past year equally, John Wheeler singled out *The Mortal Storm* as "among the worst" of Hollywood's films that propagandized for war. He warned, confirming the isolationists' great fear, that the studio that produced it threatened to continue its propaganda barrage. Wheeler provided the following details for his father:

> Nicholas Schenck [head of Loew's, Inc., parent company of MGM] [...] is the key figure in the motion picture business [...] Louis Mayer, while head of MGM, takes orders from Schenck [...] I am told that [...] Mayer [...] has always been against the propaganda pictures but Schenck is the one who gave the orders [to make them]. MGM has [therefore] made more of the propaganda pictures than any of the other [studios]. Among the worst of the pictures is "The Mortal Storm," which was produced by

Victor Saville who came here from England after the war started. He is I am told [...] born in Russia.[40]

Wheeler continued by recounting how theater owners were bribed as a way of "getting movie theaters to show pictures like 'The Mortal Storm,' 'Escape,' etc."[41]

Up to a point Wheeler's informant or informants had supplied accurate information. According to Mayer's biographer Scott Eyman, "Nick and Joe Schenck between them [...] maintained more power than anybody else in Hollywood."[42] Joseph Schenck ran United Artists as well as Twentieth-Century Fox. While Mayer, even as head of MGM, had to defer to Nicholas Schenck. Schenck, happily for Mayer, regarded him as "a brilliant studio chief."[43] Pleasing Schenck may have been one reason that Mayer decided to make *The Mortal Storm*, despite John Wheeler's observation that the head of MGM opposed the propaganda pictures. The MGM producer Pandro Berman confirmed the difference between them, observing "L. B. [Mayer] was rabidly anti-Communist [...] He was the 'Mister Republican' of MGM and Nick Schenck in New York/was 'Mister Democrat.'"[44] Expurgating *The Mortal Storm* satisfied Mayer's instincts, making it pleased Schenck.

Schenck, on the other hand, emphasized Mayer's control over MGM in his testimony before the Hollywood hearings. He told the ICC subcommittee that Mayer had "a great brain [...] as a producer" and had been "in charge of production" at MGM since the death of Irving Thalberg in 1936. Schenck added, "he is the best man in our line of business by far."[45] In other words, Schenck relied on Mayer's production judgment. But, as Schenck's daughter remembered it, when her father, based in New York, said, "Come East," Mayer went.[46] In that sense the younger Wheeler was correct. Nicholas Schenck had ultimate authority over MGM.

Wheeler erred, however, on the role of Victor Saville in the production of *The Mortal Storm*. Saville only took over as producer of the film in March 1940, well after West and Franklin had shaped it. He continued in that capacity for the next two and a half months until shooting was complete in mid-May. Saville himself claimed to have simultaneously directed the film at that time. No evidence exists to confirm that claim (see Chapter 5). Wheeler's naming Saville as producer, however, had a distinct purpose. He emphasized that one of the British exiles in Hollywood, notorious for interventionist sentiments, had played a major role on the film. Saville's own heritage enhanced his negative influence. Having been "born in Russia," according to Wheeler, he was no doubt Jewish, compounding his sin of being a British expatriate. As a Jew and an Englishman, the producer of *The Mortal Storm* was a propagandist for war twice over.

Of all the subcommittee members, D. Worth Clark, Democrat from Idaho and the chair, made the most of Wheeler's memo. Largely ignoring Flynn's carefully crafted questions and guidelines, Clark based the interrogation of the moguls in the third and final week of the hearings on the information that the younger Wheeler supplied. The questioning that week proved to be the most controversial. It quickly provided the source of the subcommittee's demise.

D. Worth Clark (D-ID)

Senator Wheeler appointed D. Worth Clark to chair the "Hearings on Propaganda in Motion Pictures." A relative newcomer to the Senate, Clark was elected to that body only in 1938, having served two terms in the House. In that brief legislative career, he had shown himself to be a committed isolationist. In the spring and summer of 1941, he traveled the country with Wheeler and other Senate members of the isolationist cohort to speak at America First rallies. They were often joined by Lindbergh and his wife along with novelist Kathleen Norris and film star Lillian Gish, the only Hollywood entertainer on the board of America First.

In June, John Wheeler's southern California branch of America First arranged for their final rally at the Hollywood Bowl. Clark appeared to play the lead role in the event. He was introduced as a "pretty good substitute for Bill Borah," to audience laughter and applause.[47] According to the *Los Angeles Times,* Clark then spoke in a manner reminiscent of his mentor, the recently deceased senior senator from Idaho, William Borah, who had died in January of the year before. Clark criticized the administration's foreign policy "in blunt, incisive words." He condemned "the repeal of the arms provisions of the Neutrality Act [...]," and insisted that the United States had "insulted Germany, Japan, and Italy" without provocation. Speaking on Hollywood's doorstep, Clark also denounced the effect of the studios' "'propaganda' machine."[48]

Clark's Hollywood Bowl speech proved revealing. It indeed showed the influence of the late Senator Borah. Clark, like Borah, belonged to a distinctive group in the Senate, bonded by foreign policy. He adhered to Lindbergh's isolationist allies in that body. In the commencement season of 1940, when renowned speakers urged the cause of intervention before Ivy League graduates, Clark traveled to the Midwest and spoke on behalf of neutrality to the graduates of Notre Dame, his alma mater. By the end of the year, he had denounced Roosevelt's newly proclaimed program of Lend-Lease. Borah had similarly led a cohort known as the Irreconcilables who uncompromisingly opposed the Treaty of Versailles.[49] They saw its provisions as certain to impose constraints on the conduct of American foreign policy. Borah also condemned the treaty for its vindictiveness which he believed would undermine the new Weimar Republic. By the same token, he denounced the war guilt clause in the treaty and belonged to the school that held the Allies as responsible for the Great War as Germany.

Those opinions discouraged Borah from taking a critical attitude toward Nazi Germany in the 1930s.

Clark, a Democrat and devout Catholic, might have been expected to seek a mentor in someone other than Borah on both counts; but the two senators from Idaho bonded. Borah had urged the Wilson administration to pressure the British on Irish independence while negotiating in Paris. In 1936, he had not supported the Republican nominee for President Alf Landon. Many thought that he would jump parties and vote for Roosevelt.

Clark diverged from Borah with his reference to the Hollywood "propaganda machine." Borah had been no outspoken defender of persecuted European Jews, but neither was he an antisemite. Clark's pointed reference to Hollywood propaganda was readily seen in the context of Wheeler's threats against the studios made since the start of the year. Clark, who had been appearing with Wheeler at anti-interventionist rallies since the spring, suggested at the Hollywood Bowl, that the studios were now to be the focus of those opposed to war.

Other Subcommittee Members

In addition to Clark of Idaho, Wheeler appointed Charles W. Toby (R-NH), C. Wayland Brooks (R-IL), and Homer T. Bone (D-WA) to the subcommittee. All were known isolationists and part of Wheeler's cohort on the full ICC. Bone had served on the original Nye Committee as had Bennett Champ Clark of Missouri. Seriously ill, Bone remained in the hospital during the hearings and did not participate. Brooks had very little to say and as early as the first day had begun to distance himself from the proceedings, stating, "I was not put on this committee at my request-merely as a Member of the Senate to try to get some facts."[50] Nye and Clark of Missouri, on the other hand, gave such lengthy testimony—a day each—that they could be said to be serving on the subcommittee ex officio. Although as non-members of the ICC, they could not be appointed to one of its subcommittees.

Tobey, already well known for his antisemitism, spoke frequently. Michael Straight, the Washington correspondent for *The New Republic,* labeled the New Hampshire Senator "a virulent antisemite," whose Judeophobic comments he had witnessed the year before.[51]

Wheeler somewhat surprisingly appointed the junior Senator from Arizona, Ernest W. McFarland, a Democrat, only eight months in the Senate and a relative unknown, to the subcommittee. In his recent Senate campaign, McFarland had defeated Henry Fountain Ashurst, whom he condemned for Ashurst's "ties to East coast bankers like the renowned Jewish financier Bernard Baruch."[52] Such a reference to Baruch's Jewish identity would explain why Wheeler regarded McFarland as a potential political ally. According to McFarland, the Montana Senator rewarded him with appointments to ICC subcommittees that addressed issues of mass communication.⁵³ From Wheeler's perspective among those issues must have been Jewish control of the media.

Wheeler, however, erred in his assumptions regarding McFarland's views. Despite the Arizona senator's campaign reference to east coast Jewish bankers, he proved to be a one-man wrecking ball on the Hollywood subcommittee, taking as his target the blatant antisemitism of so many participants. Wheeler also failed to perceive another quality that should have disqualified McFarland for membership on the subcommittee. The Arizona senator possessed a sense of humor. As a subcommittee member, McFarland regularly mocked other members or witnesses whose comments readily conveyed not only the antisemitism they harbored but also their ignorance of how the movie business actually operated. Wheeler must have expected that the Arizona senator, who had spent the last six years as a Superior Court judge in his home state, "would keep his mouth shut" on the high-profile Hollywood investigation subcommittee. McFarland instead chided his Senate colleagues for failing to see the very films they derided. Subcommittee members, along with Nye and Bennett Clark, had relied on Flynn's lengthy synopses, making them vulnerable to the point that McFarland raised regarding their basic ignorance of what the film industry had in fact produced.⁵⁴ His often hostile and outspoken remarks, calling his colleagues on the subcommittee to account, delighted the press and other observers who attended the hearings.⁵⁵ In the end, Chairman Clark, along with Senators Tobey and McFarland, for different reasons, dominated the questioning with the junior senator from Arizona regularly showing himself to be at odds with his isolationist Senate colleagues who did not bother to hide the antisemitism so many of them shared.

Certain they would convince the public of Hollywood's insidious intent and the threat that it posed to the country, the antisemitic lawmakers naively launched the hearings they had so long sought. The very formation of the subcommittee energized them, and they rallied around Wheeler. He and his cohort would at last have a platform to convince the public of the nefarious intentions of the studio heads. Chairman Clark's enthusiasm could be seen in an incautious statement that he made shortly before the hearings opened. In a singular lack of restraint, he recommended that the United States "should as a way of protecting the hemisphere from incursion take over control of all Latin America and Canada by establishing puppet governments" there.⁵⁶ The suggestion did not go over well in the press or elsewhere, already revealing that the hardcore isolationists were out of step with public opinion.

Clark nonetheless as scheduled firmly gaveled the hearings into session at 10:15 a.m. on Tuesday, September 9, 1941, in the Caucus Room of the Senate Office Building with over 500 people in attendance. It was seven years and five days since the Nye Committee had convened to investigate the merchants of death. The Clark subcommittee now took up its mantle to reveal the identity of those who would again lure the country into war for their own profit.

The Hearings on Propaganda in Motion Pictures, September 1941

Momentous Events in the Atlantic

Armed conflict at sea accompanied the opening of the hearings on September 9. On September 4, U-boats had attacked the destroyer USS *Greer*, which responded with depth charges. Adding to the tension, on the day the hearings convened, the Germans sank an American owned freighter with the loss of twenty-four lives. The president did not address those events until September 11. The death of his mother on September 7 had forced the delay in his response. Speaking to the nation in a Fireside Chat, he termed the "Nazi submarines [...] the rattlesnakes of the Atlantic" and announced that "U.S. warships [...] would [now] fire on Axis warships west of his declared defense line without warning."[57] The line extended well into the Atlantic, east of Greenland as well as Iceland. We were claiming much of the Atlantic Ocean as our own. The historian David Kaiser has argued, Roosevelt's statements that evening "amounted to a declaration of war at sea."[58]

Lindbergh Weighs In

On the same evening that FDR addressed the deteriorating situation in the Atlantic, Lindbergh spoke to an America First rally in Des Moines. He gave what has come to be known as his "Des Moines speech." Broadcast nationwide just minutes after the president spoke, the speech laid out Lindbergh's case against the culprits who he claimed were driving the country to war against its own self-interest and better instincts. The aviator said nothing about the critical issues the president had just addressed. Instead, he spoke in support of the hearings on Hollywood that he had proposed to his Senate allies two months earlier as a way to reveal and condemn those who propagandized for war. Ignoring the momentous words of the president, he insisted the threat to peace lay here at home which more than once in the speech he attributed to the Jews.

He proceeded to denounce in public what had figured so prominently in his diary for the past nine months, namely the claim of insidious Jewish influence in the media. He stated that "the majority" of Jews do not "stand opposed to intervention."[59] Because of that "their greatest danger to our country lies in their large ownership and influence in our motion pictures, our press, our radio, and our Government." With the exception of the reference to Jewish influence in government, Lindbergh had been making the same point since his first speech on foreign policy in September 1939 when he asked his audience to consider who owns the communications media in the country. As for the reference to Jews in government, it had become an antisemitic trope of the 1930s that Jews had inordinate influence with Roosevelt, whom they allegedly advised on the "Jew Deal."

Lindbergh further charged that "the leaders of both the British and Jewish races [...], for reasons which are not American, wish to involve us in the war." But he insisted that he was "not attacking either the Jewish or British people," only their leaders. Except that he had stated, contradicting himself, that "the majority [of] Jewish people" do not "stand opposed to intervention." In effect, the Jewish leadership in control of the media along with the majority of Jews who concurred with them united, "for reasons which are not American," in supporting intervention.

The speech could not help but attract attention. Lindbergh gave it on behalf of America First to a national audience that had already tuned in to hear the president. He brought into the open the antisemitism that critics of America First had accused the organization of harboring. The Des Moines speech did damage to Lindbergh, to be discussed below, as well as to his allies. It appeared to confirm the charges of Judeophobia that so readily clung to Wheeler and his Senate cohort and by extension to the hearings themselves. Some might ask, had the ideology of the Third Reich begun to intrude on American political life?

The president had given his own answer to the identity of the enemy and the source of the threat before the American people. He had all but declared war on the rattlesnakes at sea. Those who made war on Hollywood still had to prove their point.

Nye and Clark of Missouri Testify

Nye then Clark of Missouri dominated the first two days of the hearings, September 9–10. The privilege of speaking first recognized their many attempts since 1939 to investigate propaganda for war. Appropriately, Senate Resolution 152 that called for the current investigation (written by Flynn) bore their names.

The two quickly established the main themes of the hearings. Nye based himself in large measure on John Wheeler's memo. He denounced at length a single picture: *The Mortal Storm*. Speakers sometimes paired the film with *Manhunt* or *Escape,* both released in 1940, as similarly blatant examples of propaganda; but no film over the course of the eight-day hearings received as much attention as *The Mortal Storm*. Clark, on the other hand, basing himself on Flynn's approach, focused on the moguls' monopoly of the industry which enabled the studio heads to turn the country's "17,000 theaters into 17,000 daily and nightly mass meetings for war."[60] Clark like Flynn assumed a monolithic character to the movie industry. It was the message of the Justice Department's lawsuit that had hung over the moguls for two years, July 1938 to June 1940, and attempted to divest the studios of ownership of the numerous movie theaters around the country.[61] Clark vowed to "do everything in [his] power to bring about once and forever, the utter destruction of the monopolistic grasp of this handful of men on the screen," most of whom, he might have added, were Jewish.[62]

Both men nonetheless objected to the charge of antisemitism that was repeatedly leveled at them. The Missouri Senator denounced the accusation of Wendall Willkie, the moguls' legal consul, that he and Nye were "actuated by 'racial prejudice,' or, to be more exact by what has come to be known as antisemitism."[63] Willkie, even though hired to defend the movie industry before the subcommittee, had been ordered to remain silent during the hearings. In defense against Willkie's charge, Clark insisted that he still bore the scars of his conflicts, "not so many years ago" with the Ku Klux Klan of Missouri.[64]

Nye found it more difficult to absolve himself of the charge. He had only a month earlier given a speech to an America First rally in St. Louis in which he indicated "the men who dominate the major film companies [while] a storm of boos and derisive cries arose after the mention of each studio head."[65] In its account of the event, the *St. Louis Globe-Democrat* neglected to mention that in pronouncing the names of the Hollywood moguls, Nye had, according to an eyewitness, "drolly exaggerated their most Hebraic sounding syllables, with pauses to encourage his inflamed hearers to shout and hiss."[66]

As if to confirm the charge of antisemitism, Nye devoted a portion of his testimony to denouncing *The Mortal Storm*, using it as an example to show how the baleful combination of Jewish influence and British propaganda had motivated production of the recent spate of war pictures, Lindbergh's point two days later in his Des Moines speech. The British-Jewish collusion came together in the person of Victor Saville who, John Wheeler had insisted in his memo, was a "Russian born [i.e., Jewish] British agent" responsible for the film. Nye informed the subcommittee that

> Frank Borsage [sic] an American director was directing a war propaganda film titled, "The Mortal Storm." Borsage was not satisfactory or sufficiently brutal in directing the production […] Saville [therefore] took over the task[67]

Nye, like Wheeler, portrayed Saville not only as "brutal," but as an agent of the British government. To confirm his point, he reported that there is a "persistent rumor […] that Saville is a British agent operating on motion picture lots."[68] The British Ministry of Information arranged for his visa so that he might represent the interests of that ministry in Hollywood, according to Nye. Borzage quickly challenged Nye's charge that he had been removed as director of *The Mortal Storm*. He wired Willkie that he "started and finished direction of 'The Mortal Storm' and was at no time removed from directorial duties."[69]

Despite having waited several years for an appropriate stage from which to denounce propaganda for war, Nye and Clark made ineffective use of the platform once they had acquired it. They spent a significant portion of their testimony on the defensive, trying to fend off charges of antisemitism. Nye at times almost ludicrously appeared to confirm them. He did raise the curtain on the one film the hearings were increasingly to target, even if he did not know who had directed *The Mortal Storm*.

Flynn, Fidler, and Fisher Testify

Flynn testified on Thursday, September 11. That evening Lindbergh spoke in Des Moines. Jimmie Fidler and George Fisher, self-proclaimed gossip columnists, rounded out the docket on the next day of the hearings, Monday, September 15. Flynn's carefully laid plans for organizing the investigation had so far gone awry. Nye and Clark had bogged down, facing well-deserved charges of antisemitism and, in Nye's case, proclaiming a glaring factual error regarding the director of *The Mortal Storm*. Fidler and Fisher had their own drawbacks. They could offer little on the inner workings of Hollywood other than to complain that the moguls harassed them when they criticized one or another propaganda picture, although both admitted to having seen no more than three of them.

Fidler denounced *The Great Dictator,* "obviously made for [...] slinging insults at two foreign rulers [and] should never have been made." "And 'The Mortal Storm' by MGM," Chairman Clark prompted him about the film's motivation. "That is very definitely propaganda," answered Fidler.[70] Fisher similarly told the subcommittee, "I am complaining largely about pictures like 'Escape' and 'The Mortal Storm,'" although he too found *The Great Dictator* objectionable as propaganda.[71]

Flynn gave a distinctive picture of the movie industry, emphasizing its monopolistic cohesion which facilitated an organized conspiracy among the moguls. Like Clark of Missouri, most of whose testimony Flynn had written, he promised to do all he could to destroy "the monopolistic grasp" by which the moguls controlled the movie industry. Flynn insisted on behalf of the subcommittee as a whole that it would "restore freedom of speech which has been destroyed by these men."[72] He, along with the two gossip columnists, acted as a bridge between Nye and Clark, on the one hand, and the main act to come. The "handful of men" who held the movie industry in their "grasp" were about to be called before the subcommittee to speak for themselves.

The second round of hearings, starting on September 23 after a week-long recess, like the first round, lasted four days.[73] The subcommittee finally got down to the business it had promised to conduct in the first place. Chairman Clark took over to grill the moguls themselves. The hearings for the first time began to resemble those held by the Nye committee when the North Dakota Senator had interrogated captains of industry for enhancing their fortunes with the manufacture of weapons of war. With the moguls called to testify, the hearings on Hollywood now caught the public's attention in a way they had not in their first four days. Relying on John Wheeler's memo with its emphasis on *The Mortal Storm* as "one of the worst of the propaganda pictures," Chairman Clark gave the hearings the focus they had previously lacked. His emphasis on *The Mortal Storm* again raised the specter of antisemitism, already so ineptly denied by Nye and Senator Clark from Missouri.

Compelling too were the witnesses. Some of the most powerful men in the country, possessing, it would seem untold wealth—the creators of the Hollywood dream factory—gathered in one room to defend themselves before the US Senate against the charge of turning entertainment into propaganda. Hollywood might have written the script.

Mr. Schenck and Mr. Warner Go to Washington

Nicholas Schenck, since 1927 president of Loew's Inc., the parent company of MGM, testified first after the subcommittee resumed hearings on September 23. In Schenck, the antisemites on the subcommittee, Chairman Clark and Senator Tobey, in particular, believed that they had a prize witness. The younger Wheeler, in his memo to his father, had described Schenck as "the key figure in the motion picture business [...] the one who gave the orders [to make] the propaganda pictures."[74] Clark was determined to showcase Schenck's role, and just as damning, to reveal that he had colluded with Harry Warner, the president of Warner Brothers, to make *The Mortal Storm*. The chairman would thus nail the issue of collusion among the moguls and reveal the true origins of the one Hollywood production (so far) to devote itself to persecution of the Jews.

Clark operated with inadequate information. Neither Flynn nor John Wheeler had supplied the subcommittee with an accurate picture of how Hollywood actually functioned with rival studios and competing business models instead of overarching collusion and solidarity. In the case of MGM, New York City was the home of its parent company. The studio made its films on the west coast. Those at MGM responsible for producing *The Mortal Storm* were based in Culver City. Mayer, Eddie Mannix, Howard Strickling, certainly Sidney Franklin, who, along with Claudine West, had crafted the film's adaptation, were not called to testify. They held the answers to questions regarding the film's production. Clark's frustration, therefore, was to mount in the third and final week of the hearings.

It could not have been lost on the moguls why, in the first week of testimony, *The Mortal Storm* had emerged as a film of particular interest to the subcommittee. One witness emphasized the evils of *That Hamilton Woman*, another decried *The Great Dictator*, but all of them, sometimes prodded, affirmed their disgust with *The Mortal Storm*, "the most powerful anti-Nazi picture yet produced."[75] And, it might be added, the only one to focus on the Jewish, that is, non-Aryan, question in Nazi Germany. Senator Clark of Missouri had merely advertised the subcommittee's motivation in denying his and Nye's "racial prejudice [...] or to be more exact, [...] what has come to be known as antisemitism."[76] Clark insisted, "This suggestion [of antisemitism on our part] was completely exploded [...] by Senator Nye."[77] The moguls knew better.

Testifying in his distinctive Russian accent, Nicholas Schenck faced harsher and more extended questioning than any other mogul.[78] Yet he never seemed able to satisfy Chairman Clark's curiosity regarding the origins of *The Mortal Storm*. Clark did not appear to comprehend that although Schenck had run MGM for the past fourteen years, the managerial and business side of affairs comprised his domain. He had overseen the formation of MGM in 1924 and remained the dealmaker of the company. Despite such responsibilities a crucial gap remained: Schenck made no decisions on production. He left those to Mayer, and Mayer remained in California.

Howard Dietz, the other MGM mogul who testified, like Schenck, did not make production decisions. He too was based in New York City and worked so closely with Schenck that he was considered "a Schenck man" within MGM.[79] The two were sure to present a united front before the subcommittee, both with plausible deniability regarding the production decisions for *The Mortal Storm*. By the final week, the hearings had turned into a duel between Chairman Clark, the Harvard educated attorney from Idaho Falls, and Loew's president Nicholas Schenck, who had spent his first twelve years, along with his family, managing to survive outside the Pale of Settlement, in the river towns along the Volga, a fractious and rebellious region of the Tsarist empire.

On the first day of questioning Schenck, Chairman Clark quickly began to focus on *The Mortal Storm*, lifting the curtain on his concern about that film in particular. No matter what his subject of inquiry, the chairman came back to that film. The Idaho Senator began with how films were booked and distributed. The chairman insisted that *The Mortal Storm* was made under government pressure then forced on theater owners and managers.[80] Schenck adamantly denied the point. But Clark needled, "The exhibitor [...] of course would not turn down a picture like 'Mortal Storm'?" John Wheeler in his memo had revealed that theater owners were bribed to show the propaganda pictures.

On the second day of Schenck's testimony, September 24, Clark continued to focus on *The Mortal Storm*, but took a different tack, namely raising the question not of government pressure in making the film but of collusion among the moguls to make it. At the same time, Chairman Clark revealed the origin of his questions and the motivation behind the hearings themselves. At a critical moment, Clark disclosed that of all the so-called propaganda films, *The Mortal Storm* in particular had caught the attention of Senate isolationists whose barely disguised antisemitism lay just beneath the surface. "There is one picture particularly which [...] several witnesses have alleged [...] was a war propaganda picture,"[81] Clark stated, naming *The Mortal Storm*. The senator from Idaho had finally played his hand.

Clark proceeded to address the motives behind making it. He questioned Schenck relentlessly for one full afternoon. The questioning of the day before had carried a less aggressive tone. On the second day of Schenck's testimony, matters were different. Clark grilled Schenck repeatedly about *The Mortal Storm*. No other film mentioned by the subcommittee received such intense scrutiny nor the same amount of uninterrupted testimony.[82] Having learned the day before, the government, as Schenck insisted, had nothing to do with decisions surrounding *The Mortal Storm*, Clark now sought to establish Schenck's responsibility for the film and, if he could, Schenck's collusion with Harry Warner in the production. Schenck denied both points. Clark asked, "Did you approve *The Mortal Storm* as a picture?" Schenck simply sidestepped the question and praised the film as well. "I only loved it after I saw [...] it," he answered Clark.[83]

To Clark there was nothing to love about *The Mortal Storm*. He told Harry Warner during his testimony that "I do not think [...] that a picture like *Manhunt* and a picture like *The Mortal Storm* have any place in the moving-picture industry."[84] When Schenck argued that the latter film depicted the truth of what was actually occurring in Germany Clark countered, "But do you think that the fact that [...] a movie [...] that portrays the truth is a justification [...] for" it?[85] Clark argued that a true representation or not, *The Mortal Storm* "incited hatred [...] for [...] the German people."[86]

In justification for his point, the senator quoted almost verbatim from the memo of complaint that Hans Thomsen, German Chargé d'Affaires, had submitted to the State Department in protest against *The Mortal Storm* and *Four Sons* shortly after their release. Clark did not reveal that he quoted a German diplomat. Thomsen had written Secretary of State Cordell Hull on July 16, 1940:

> I am obliged to direct your Excellency's attention to the [recently released] films 'Mortal Storm,' produced by Metro-Goldwyn-Mayer Co. and 'Four Sons,' produced by Twentieth-Century Fox. Both pictures are in all their details deliberate attempts to arouse public sentiment and hate in this country against the German people and their government.[87]

Clark, like Thomsen earlier, implied that both studios had violated their own production code which forbade less than "respectful treatment" of "the rights, history and feelings of any nation."[88]

The Idaho Senator then raised a related issue, but one with ominous implications. He asked Schenck, "Do you think a picture like *The Mortal Storm* tends to create unity and harmony among [...] racial groups in the U.S.?"[89] Clark did not specify which racial groups he had in mind, but he appeared to share Lindbergh's idea expressed in the Des Moines speech that such distinctive groups existed and some, like the Jews and the British, were conducting themselves with insidious intent. Even more disturbing, Clark's questioning reinforced a sense of Jewish otherness, racially based, according to Nazi precepts, that hung over the hearings.

The chairman used the conception of a distinctive Jewish identity to charge collusion among the moguls in the making of propaganda films via their monopoly of the movie industry. He asked Schenck whether he had discussed "the production of these pictures as a policy" with Mr. Warner or other producers at "your producer association meetings."[90] The head of Loew's denied that such discussions ever took place. Schenck's denial notwithstanding, Senator Clark of Missouri provided details on how the alleged collusion among the moguls operated. "[...] five or six men can sit around the table together or contact each other on the telephone and tell this nation what 80 million can see and hear in 18,000 theaters each week."[91] His Idaho colleague added his complaint, "a group of financial men [...] own and control an industry" and conspired together. Few would have trouble discerning that by the "five or six" "financial men," both senators meant Jews.

The next day, Thursday, September 25, it was the turn of another mogul, Harry Warner, president of Warner Brothers. Despite Schenck's denial of collusion with that studio, Warner too was grilled about his possible role in the production of *The Mortal Storm*. The notion was absurd. Warner Brothers could only view *The Mortal Storm* as a competing product from a rival studio. Harry Warner might agree with Chairman Clark that the film should never have been made but only because it competed for an audience with his studio's productions. As for colluding with Schenck in particular, Harry Warner observed, to no avail, that he "had seen more of Mr. Schenck in this room than" he had "in [the past] three years" in Hollywood.[92]

The Senate isolationists who conducted the Hollywood hearings appeared to embrace the notion of a Jewish conspiracy described in The Protocols of the Elders of Zion, circulated by Henry Ford in the 1920s and 1930s. By 1940, Jewish moguls had been cast in the role of the Jewish elders. They used their monopoly of the production, distribution, and exhibition of motion pictures to seduce the American public into war. The truth lay elsewhere. Competitive business rivals who barely spoke to each other, Harry Warner insisted, were not about to collude even in a war on screen against the Nazis.

Warner further attempted to explain that the studios were more than competing rivals. They operated by different business models. Schenck's "policy in operating his business is so different from ours that there is no comparison," he tried to tell Chairman Clark.⁹³ Schenck himself denied that the pictures under attack had anything to do with propaganda: "in no way can I agree with you that [...] *The Mortal Storm, Escape,* and *Flight Command* are any propaganda pictures."⁹⁴ On that point Warner agreed with Schenck. "We have not produced any pictures [...] to incite anybody to war," he insisted.⁹⁵ Their words fell on deaf ears.

Senator Sheridan Downey, the junior Democratic Senator from California, also spoke in the third week to defend one of the most important industries in his state. Downey had earlier had his own run-in with Hollywood when serving as Upton Sinclair's running mate in Sinclair's 1934 campaign for governor. The moguls had banded together, Mayer and Thalberg being particularly active, to defeat what they charged was in fact a socialist ticket even though Sinclair and Downey ran as Democrats. Those events behind him, Downey now testified before the subcommittee in defense of a key industry in his state. He insisted that the films alleged to purvey "insidious propaganda" did not. Rather, "the antipathy of the audience to nazi-ism evoked [them], and not vice versa."⁹⁶ Similarly, Harry Warner argued two days after Senator Downey spoke, on what was to be the last day of testimony, that "the only sin of which Warner Brothers is guilty is that of accurately recording on the screen the world as it is or as it has been."⁹⁷

Overnight the press turned the moguls into heroes. The cautious businessmen of Hollywood had stood up to their accusers. Columnist Sidney Skolsky, writing in the *Hollywood Citizen News,* stated, "Hollywood is proud of the way Warner and Nicholas Schenck conducted themselves. They [...] were a credit to the industry and to themselves." ⁹⁸

In 1939, Bottome had called the moguls cowardly, even self-destructive for their reluctance to depict the truth of Nazism. To the extent that the studios made anti-Nazi pictures, they only did so belatedly and reluctantly in the belief that the public expected it of them and would go to see such films, justifying the cost of production and controversy the films were sure to generate. Ironically, the moguls had become heroes despite having recently dropped production of the so-called propaganda pictures because when released in 1940 they had not proven popular with the public after all, as Senator McFarland tried to point out to his fellow subcommittee members.⁹⁹ The Nye Committee of the mid-1930s met for three years and generated three significant pieces of legislation on neutrality. The subcommittee on Hollywood, faced with public ridicule and the opposition of witnesses, collapsed after only eight sessions in three weeks.

The real story about Jews as a group lay elsewhere. It ended in tragedy, not in farce. The horrible truth echoed in the "noticeable Russian accent" of Nicholas Schenck. It could have been heard in Claudine West's first version of the script for *The Mortal Storm* where she had predicted the fate of Europe's Jews. Amélie Roth asks in alarm, "Doesn't Hitler mean to kill all the Jews?" In the third week of September 1941, that prediction was about to come true for the Jews of Kiev and those not very far away, in the town of Dymer where Louis B. Mayer had been born.[100] The command of SS Einsatzgruppen C, whose units were responsible for the murder of Soviet Jews in Ukraine, gathered in Kiev, occupied by the Germans since September 19. The occupiers met to determine the fate of the city's Jews. On Friday, September 26, the day that D. Worth Clark adjourned the hearings "subject to the call of the Chair,"[101] the SS made the decision to annihilate Kiev's Jewish population, beginning on Monday, September 29. The massacre, just outside the city limits at the ravine of Babi Yar, took two days. It was the Nazis who conspired; and their aim was murder, massive and genocidal. Even the expurgated version of *The Mortal Storm* had become timely at last.

Timely at Last

Speaker of the House, Sam Rayburn, gleefully told the Washington Bureau Chief for *Time* magazine, Frank McNaughton, "This [the collapse of the Senate hearings on Hollywood] will affect the outcome in damned near every congressional district that is now represented by an isolationist."[102] *The Mortal Storm* came into its own in the fall of 1941, no longer belated or even passé, as some critics had charged the year before. It joined the other anti-Nazi films named in the hearings, acquiring renewed popularity along with distinctive political significance in the heated atmosphere fueled by naval confrontation in the Atlantic and increasing truculence on the part of the Japanese in the Pacific.

Public opinion too had shifted in a year's time. The change in attitude registered in Lindbergh's damaged reputation. After the Des Moines speech, Lindbergh the isolationist had become Lindbergh the Fascist sympathizer. The question of censoring Hollywood also failed to capture public support. That possibility had been one of the motivators in the formation of the ICC subcommittee. The *Freeport, IL Journal Standard,* for example, condemned the hearings as just that—a prelude to censorship. It editorialized, "The whole question is much bigger than the right of Hollywood to put out 'The Mortal Storm' or 'Escape' or 'The Great Dictator,' or similar pictures. The question is really the old, old question of censorship."[103] *The Journal* of Lewiston, Maine best captured the public contempt for the hearings. It simply asked, "Doesn't the public [...] deserve a rest from such as Nye and Clark?"[104]

Two weeks after Chairman Clark adjourned the subcommittee seemingly indefinitely, *Time's* Frank McNaughton interviewed the chairman. "Off the record," the dejected Senator from Idaho and would-be successor to William Borah admitted to the reporter, "things have not gone well."[105] Nor did it seem that the subcommittee would soon resume the hearings. McNaughton also reported to his editor that Scott Lucas (D-IL), chairman of the Senate Audit and Control Committee, "refused to cover the committee's expenses." He intends to withhold payment "until the committee winds up its tragicomic act."[106] Nor did it seem that Senator Wheeler had any intention of keeping the subcommittee solvent. The subcommittee hearings were finished as was the possibility of an investigation of Hollywood by the full ICC.[107] Wheeler's original intention had been to use the revelations of the subcommittee to force the hand of the interventionists on the full committee to join the attack on Hollywood.

Clark formally announced on October 8 that "the Committee will meet again in the near future subject to the call of the chair."[108] The press took that announcement to mean that the "film probe hearings" had been "put off indefinitely."[109] Committee members had lost interest in subjecting themselves to withering attacks in the press for being antisemitic or advocating government censorship of the movies. Even worse, accusations of both. Frank McNaughton in his off-the-record conversation with Chairman Clark learned that the senator could no longer even "get a quorum. [...] Brooks of Illinois is out speaking; bald, shrewish Charles N. Tobey [...] is taking the rest cure [...] and Clark doesn't want to start holding hearings with only himself and that expert-needler Ernest W. McFarland [...] holding the fort."[110] The subcommittee had simply come apart in failure and embarrassment.

Almost as disturbing as the relentless press attacks, Charlie Chaplin figured among those to be called on October 6. The members may well have recognized that if Nicholas Schenck and Harry Warner could embarrass them, they would be no match for the creator of *The Great Dictator*. *U.S. Week, A National Journal of News and Opinion* observed, "Charlie will not need to double as Der Fuhrer. Members of the subcommittee [...] can be counted on to vie for that part."[111]

Clark did not formally dissolve the subcommittee until December 18, shortly after Pearl Harbor. He informed Chairman Wheeler that with the United States now at war, "matters covered in 'Senate Resolution 152'" were either "moot" or "controversial." In the case of the latter "it is believed by your subcommittee that in the interests of national unity it would not be desirable to report in detail upon them at this time."[112] What Clark really meant was that he intended to save the erstwhile isolationists further embarrassment. His restraint did not help. In the election of 1944, Nye, along with Clark of Idaho and Clark of Missouri, went down to defeat. Wheeler lost his seemingly impregnable Senate seat in 1946. Brooks lost his in 1948. Only Tobey was returned to the Senate by New Hampshire voters into the early 1950s, but isolationism had cost the others their political careers.

Clark never submitted a report to Wheeler on the work of the subcommittee. The Government Printing Office issued a transcript of the hearings in 1942, and that remains the only official record of what for the isolationists had become a debacle. They came away labeled antisemites or censors. In some cases, both. Hollywood at least temporarily had come out the winner in its first major confrontation with Congress.

Editorial commentators across the country united in condemnation of the hearings, but more particularly they found the Senate isolationists at fault. The *Christian Science Monitor*, for example, argued that the "main value" of the hearings "is to disclose what a world of fantasy isolationism lives in."[113] Even worse, the strongest criticism came from newspapers in states whose electorates had sent members of the subcommittee to the Senate. The *Kansas City* (MO) *Journal* assailed the co-author of Senate Resolution 152, Bennett Champ Clark, for his role in the hearings: "Missouri is ashamed that its senior senator is not above such despicable business. It concludes reluctantly that Bennett Clark, who had a chance to be a distinguished Senator, prefers to be a hawker in the vestibules of democracy."[114]

Nor was Chairman Clark spared. The newspaper of his hometown, the *Idaho Falls Post Register*, took the head of the subcommittee to task. "The isolationist-sponsored Senate investigation of the moving picture industry chairmaned by Idaho's D. Worth Clark bids fair to menace as many democratic processes as it defends."[115]

In the fall of 1941, *The Mortal Storm* enjoyed a new lease on life. As a novel it had not become *The Uncle Tom's Cabin* of the twentieth-century, as Bottome had hoped. As a film it had not become the *All Quiet on the Western Front* of interventionism, as the White Committee had hoped. But the 1940 pro-interventionist, "non-Aryan" version of the film succeeded at one thing. It became the defiant, patriotic vehicle of 1941.

Sidney Skolsky reported on September 19, with the Clark subcommittee still in session, that

> Because of the "investigation," there has been a demand by the public and exhibitors to see some of these "horrible propaganda pictures." "The Mortal Storm," for example, is the top feature on a "request program" at the Weltern Theater [in the capital].[116]

The film that had been labeled "a box office disappointment" the year before had come into its own.[117] The newfound popularity of other war pictures confirmed the point. *Film Daily* reported, "Warners' 'Underground' mentioned by the Senate subcommittee [...] is now averaging a gross of 167%, with indications it will be among Warners' 10 top grossers of the year. Interest has resulted in another spurt, with many exhibitors re-booking."[118]

The hearings, contrary to the intention of those who convened them, had resurrected the whole genre of war pictures. In the first week of October,

Warners negotiated with William L. Shirer to purchase his *Berlin Diary*. MGM bought Helen McInnes's *Above Suspicion* the week before. A genre that, as recently as August, had been perceived as box office poison had once again attracted the attention of the studios.[119] The war pictures had come into their own, as it turned out, not in 1940, but in 1941 thanks to Wheeler and his isolationist cohort in the Senate.

Nor had the phrase, "gigantic engines of propaganda," used repeatedly by subcommittee members during the hearings, managed to capture the public imagination. The phrase, coined by Flynn, never resonated as he had hoped. It lacked the uncompromising lethality of the earlier one: "merchants of death," employed so successfully to label weapons manufactures. That phrase took four syllables to do the job in 1934. In 1941, in Flynn's phrase, ten labored the point. Flynn claimed the moguls weaponized the movies. In effect, their propaganda drove men to fight whereupon they encountered what the munitions manufacturers produced. The moviemakers had joined the weapons makers as merchants of death.

The phrase was more trouble than it was worth. It was cumbersome; and, it seemed, none of the isolationists could quite get it right nor even agree on what it meant. More than one version was heard throughout the hearings. Chairman Clark, for example, charged that "75% of the better-known newspaper columnists in this country have attacked and smeared this subcommittee."[120] He referred to such attacks as a "conspiracy" on the part of the "gigantic engines of propaganda."[121] Yet Clark and other subcommittee members also used the phrase to apply specifically to Hollywood. The subcommittee chairman accused Harry Warner, the president of Warner Brothers, of attempting to use "this vast engine of the moving pictures to destroy nazi-ism."[122] He further charged Hollywood with organizing "this vast and powerful engine of propaganda," that is, "the moving picture industry to incite the people to war and hatred."[123] In Clark's version, the gigantic engine of propaganda constituted both the movies and any part of the media that attacked the isolationists. How could the public be certain exactly what the isolationists meant by the phrase or what they attacked in using it.

Even if the studios traded in propaganda, they produced entertainment and supplied information that had sustained their audiences through one of the worst decades, so far, in American history. The subcommittee failed to convince the public to hobble the defining medium in popular culture with censorship. And certainly not for the reason Wheeler's cohort insisted on: to rein in Jewish moguls who colluded to take the country to war. Homing in on *The Mortal Storm*, "the worst of the propaganda pictures," had tainted members of the Senate rather than the moguls. In reluctantly purchasing the rights to *The Mortal Storm* then producing a version of it designed to confuse, Mayer had in spite of himself benefitted his own studio and his Hollywood rivals in the opinion of the public.

Lindbergh suffered the worst defeat of all. The aviator had inspired the investigation of Hollywood and publicly supported it in his Des Moines speech given to coincide with the opening of the hearings. Both America First, which he had helped to organize, and his allies in the Senate, who since 1939 had enjoyed his support, now turned on him. Lindbergh reported in his diary, "My Des Moines address has caused so much controversy that Gen. Wood [national chairman] has decided to hold a meeting of the America First National Committee in Chicago. I must of course attend."[124]

Wood was not alone in demanding an explanation. Lindbergh's strongest supporters condemned the speech. Flynn lamented to the America First leadership that "It seems incredible to me that Col. L., without consulting anyone, literally committed the America First movement to an open attack upon the Jews [...]."[125] Even the worshipful Nye admitted, "at first I wished the colonel had not been so direct."[126] "Wheeler pleaded for tolerance and understanding" of Lindbergh, who, he claimed, was engulfed in "a smear campaign."[127] But the Montana Senator, like Nye, publicly failed to support the aviator's contention of the Des Moines speech that the Jews, the British government, and the Roosevelt administration were leading us to war. The Lone Eagle, in the fall of 1941, was more alone than ever. Or was he?

German Involvement?

For numerous members of the press there seemed to be an obvious connection between those in Congress opposed to intervention and an insidious partner abroad. They were not alone. Their readers either assumed or at least found plausible that Nazi influence had figured in the Hollywood hearings. Editorial commentators frequently noted the possibility. The *Louisville Courier-Journal*, for example, queried, "Supposing some films have been anti-Hitler, why this solicitude [for Hitler] in the United States Senate?"[128]

More directly, three of the most prominent columnists in American journalism charged Berlin with complicity in the hearings. Dorothy Thompson labeled them "the greatest Nazi propaganda stunt ever pulled off in the United States."[129] Michael Straight of *The New Republic* called the hearings part of "an organized campaign of intimidation and terror [...] undertaken in America against the Jews [and] *closely directed from Berlin* [italics mine]."[130] Drew Pearson claimed outright the organizers of the hearings had ties to Germany.[131]

But did they and if so, what did those ties amount to? The Nye investigations of the previous decade certainly provided one source for the hearings, and while sympathetic to the idea of German innocence, had no direct ties to the German government. Their intent to expose the merchants of death and thereby explain the origins of the First World War belonged to the larger context of revisionist understanding of the war. That interpretation blamed the allies and absolved Germany for the conflict. One could nonetheless charge indirect German involvement as a result of the government's attempt to mold public opinion since 1919. Berlin, as noted, aggressively encouraged revisionism, establishing a whole division within the Foreign Ministry to underwrite those who furthered the cause of German innocence and condemned the harsh terms of the Treaty of Versailles. But the cautious diplomats in the German embassy, like Hans Thomsen, would think twice before insinuating themselves into a congressional hearing.

The original Nye hearings of the 1930s and the Hollywood investigation were indeed connected. Nye himself and Clark of Missouri as well as Tobey of New Hampshire had all served on the Nye Committee as had John Flynn, an advisor to both Nye's hearings and the investigation of Hollywood five years later. The isolationists held that instead of British propaganda luring the United States into war, as had happened in 1917, in 1941 an alleged Jewish conspiracy, undertaken by Hollywood moguls, connived to entice the country once more into an unnecessary war. *The Mortal Storm* with its positive depiction of Jews provided the best confirmation of the charge. And Hans Thomsen had funneled money to the three Senators named above, among others. But by 1941 that practice had stopped. At the time of the Hollywood hearings, the German embassy had only a skeleton staff and was under intense FBI scrutiny.[132]

Lindbergh, on the other hand, possibly possessed the strongest ties to the German Embassy. His close friend Truman Smith would have supplied the link. As the American military attaché in Berlin, Smith hosted the aviator on the six visits he made to Germany in the late 1930s. Their closeness is well documented in Lindbergh's *Wartime Journals* and unpublished diary and was well known. Lindbergh noted in both versions of his diary that Smith was "one of the many people who are rumored to have written my [radio] addresses."[133] They agreed on German military prowess and shared an affinity for Nazi ideology. As a member of the board of *Reader's Digest*, Smith had facilitated publication of Lindbergh's article "Aviation, Geography, and Race" in that periodical where Lindbergh wrote of a coming race war to defend white supremacy.[134]

Smith returned to the United States in 1939 at the same time as Lindbergh. He took up the position of "special consultant to the army on Germany."[135] In that capacity he met regularly with Friedrich von Beotticher, Military Attaché of the German Embassy in Washington. Von Boetticher and Hans Thomsen worked closely together. Lindbergh, whom they regarded as "a true friend of Germany," figured frequently in their dispatches to Berlin. Von Boetticher at one point urged Thomsen to warn Berlin to forbid favorable references to Lindbergh in the German press, lest he appear to be a Nazi agent, leaving open the question whether he was or not.[136] Through Von

Boetticher, Smith could act as a go-between connecting Lindbergh to the German Embassy.[137]

Lindbergh, on the other hand, never refers in his diary to any contact with the German embassy, either directly or indirectly. He returned from Europe in April 1939, a man seeking a mission. His partner in scientific research, Alexis Carrel, was soon to leave for France. He had largely exhausted his role as an aviation pioneer. Very quickly he began to move in political and military circles, advocating American neutrality in an impending conflict that he regarded as detrimental to the white race, as he explained in his *Readers Digest* article.

Lindbergh's role in the next two years had less to do with German interests than with his own festering antisemitism and white racism which the aviator carefully charted in print, on the radio, and in the unpublished portions of his diary. The published version of his diary refers to numerous meetings with John Flynn where they discussed Jewish control of the media. Entries in his unpublished diary make especially clear that in the summer of 1941 he urged Senator Wheeler to hold the Hollywood hearings.[138] The Des Moines speech alone, which coincided with their opening and was made to justify them, revealed his involvement.[139]

The scholarly literature, on the other hand, absolves Lindbergh of involvement with the hearings.[140] While much can be made of D. Worth Clark's accusations to Nicholas Schenck that *The Mortal Storm* defamed Germany, quoting Hans Thomsen, the hearings as a whole echo Lindbergh that the Jews of Hollywood were luring the country into war.

That Lindbergh might have been a German agent is furthermore belied by the fact that he refused to attend the Republican convention in 1940, even when invited to do so (see Chapter 6). Surely any self-respecting agent would have seized the opportunity to defeat Roosevelt and assume the presidency. Lindbergh similarly condemned the moguls not because they were rivals of Goebbels and the German film industry that he headed. He condemned them as purveyors of war, justifying his toxic attitude toward Jews by a high-minded desire to prevent the country's involvement in conflict. There is no direct evidence that Goebbels or the German embassy played a role in the sad and destructive evolution of the aviator's thought on the Jews as war approached. More likely, Lindbergh did it all on his own.

One other possible source of German influence deserves mention. Since the spring of 1933, Georg Gyssling, the German Consul in Los Angeles, had closely monitored Hollywood. Starting in 1936 his dispatches had gone directly to Goebbels, who took over German cinema in that year. But there is no evidence of a connection between Gyssling and John Wheeler, who directed America First in Los Angeles. Wheeler denounced *The Mortal Storm* to his father because it propagandized for war with a subtext of philosemitism, abhorrent to the isolationist and antisemitic contingent that the Wheelers belonged to. Gyssling and that contingent might not have been natural allies. He "was a Nazi, but not an antisemite," according to Steven Ross.[141] Chaplin, for one, was not reassured. He wrote, "The Nazi consul, whom I met [...], did his best to be engaging. But I gave him a wide berth."[142] Whatever the truth about Gyssling, once so powerful and threatening to the studios, he was already back in Germany by the time of the hearings.

The New Realism

Drew Pearson was correct in one regard: some of the organizers of the hearings had taken money from Hans Thomsen. But to what end? For propaganda that had failed?[143] The isolationists badly miscalculated American sentiment and the mood of the country by 1941. The pro-German revisionism of the 1920s and 1930s, or what was left of it, died in the Hollywood hearings. Even an antisemite like William Castle admitted that he would choose the Roth family over the Nazis. To what degree Berlin encouraged the members of the subcommittee on propaganda in Hollywood behind the scenes remains an open question. But Berlin's influence in 1941 was nothing like what it had been on the eve of the nominating conventions in the summer of 1940.

Without doubt, one particular MGM film enraged the subcommittee members. *The Mortal Storm* provided the hearings with focus, directing their animus at the only feature film so far devoted to the plight of Europe's Jews. By 1941, its rhetoric, visual as well as spoken, gave expression to an emerging consensus as to Germany's real intentions. The German government put to sea the "rattlesnakes of the Atlantic," and Harry Warner insisted his studio merely "recorded on screen the world as it is or as it has been." Public opinion would hardly support censorship of that.

The Hollywood hearings did encourage a new realism in American political discourse. The Civil War analogies so recently in use as a kind of substitute language, a quasi-denial, quasi-acknowledgment of the war that loomed ahead, gave way before the new reality of US participation in an undeclared war in the Atlantic. Ironically, Wheeler's subcommittee which sought so desperately to condemn intervention encouraged the new realism, posing the question before the country in stark terms, "Whose side are we on?" By September 1941, sober reality had begun to prevail and one of the sources of the new attitude had been growing contempt for an antisemitic cohort in the Senate purveying conspiracy theories about Hollywood.

A symbol of that new realism arose on the fifth day of the hearings, September 15, in the midst of gossip columnist Jimmy Fidler's testimony.[144] The Clark subcommittee had to switch rooms for the afternoon session to make way for the Special Committee to Investigate the National Defense Program, chaired by the junior Senator from Missouri Harry Truman, a staunch interventionist.[145] The so-called Truman Committee had been meeting since April. Tireless in his efforts, Truman had flown the committee all over the country to inspect as many military facilities as time would allow. As David McCullough has noted, every time they took off and landed, they could see the Pentagon under construction just outside the city. The military was growing at every turn.[146] Truman's committee had started with seven Senators. Success bred success. By the end of the summer three more had joined. Also telling, Truman's committee had enlarged its staff and increased the number of investigators who reported to it. The public was riveted by the accounts of graft, incompetence, and cost overruns that the committee revealed.[147]

In the clash for space in the Senate Office building that hot and steamy September afternoon, isolationists confronted interventionists. Truman's sober sense of the new reality contrasted with the inflammatory charges against Hollywood moguls made by Clark's committee. Symbolism and practicality converged. The subcommittee on propaganda had to relinquish the large and airy third floor Senate Caucus Room that afternoon to the committee on national defense and find a smaller room in which to grill its witnesses.

The progressive *New Republic* captured the American public's change in attitude. "The United States should," it insisted, "immediately declare war on the Axis."[148] By the fall of 1941, the statement did not arouse controversy. Mired in antisemitism and atavistic battles over the origins of the First World War, the isolationists had yet to catch up with the new reality as the year drew to a close. The hearings discredited the isolationists themselves rather than the moguls whom they had targeted for humiliation. Conspiracy theories regarding the source of propaganda for war, or, in contrast the possible collusion of isolationists with Berlin, all issues raised or implied by the hearings, did not survive the Japanese attack on Pearl Harbor.

The repercussions of the hearings nonetheless proved significant. The so-called "German" pictures of 1940, that is, those set in Nazi Germany, temporarily received a new lease on life in the fall of 1941. *The Mortal Storm* especially so. The film had its third incarnation that year. The script of 1939 with the word "Jew" intact had never reached the screen. The pro-interventionist, "non-Aryan" film of 1940 had become a defiant, patriotic vehicle by the fall of 1941, capturing the mood of determination that pervaded the country as war approached.

There were other repercussions. A genre that had been perceived as box office poison only two months earlier had once again engaged the studios. But the fad did not last. By 1943, Hollywood prepared to cease making war pictures. The public, the studios deemed, had had enough of them and needed a rest from the war at least at the movies. As for *The Mortal Storm*, it had already been condemned for being behind the times, "late, oh so late," said Bosley Crowther when it was released. The film never became what Bottome had hoped for the story. It was not the *Uncle Tom's Cabin* of antisemitism, nor did it replace *All Quiet on the Western Front* as the embodiment in film of a moral position on war. Thanks in part to the Cleveland branch of the White Committee and Jimmy Stewart, it did figure in the debate over intervention in 1940. The following year the film enjoyed renewed prominence because of the fixation on it of Chairman Clark encouraged by Senator Wheeler's son John. Clark's insistence on collusion among the moguls in making it advertised his outdated isolationism when the American public already prepared for war. The film had contributed to the political demise of the hardcore isolationists by the end of the 1940s. Lindbergh's political career had already crashed and burned with the Des Moines speech made in support of the Hollywood hearings.

Timely at last in 1941, within a year *The Mortal Storm* would again be labeled passé. What contemporaries could not then realize, the film when made was not already dated but genuinely ahead of its time. It would be decades before Hollywood discovered the Holocaust and with that, once more gave the Jews a prominent place on the silver screen. The film nonetheless remains the first significant attempt in American popular culture to bring word of the impending Holocaust to the attention of the public and to warn of what the Nazis portended should they succeed in conquest of the New World as well as of the Old. It also remains a window as well into the complexities of awakening the country on the eve of entry into the Second World War.

Notes

1. Fairbanks, *Salad Days*, 366.
2. Dunn, *1940*, 269.
3. Cited in ibid.
4. Lindbergh, *The Wartime Diaries of Charles Lindbergh* (January 1, 1941), 436.
5. Yale University Library, Manuscripts and Archives, Charles A. Lindbergh Papers, MS 325, Series V, Box 216, Folder 587.
6. Ibid.
7. Lindbergh, *Wartime Diaries*, 437.
8. Berg, *Lindbergh*, 385.
9. Yale, Lindbergh Papers, MS 325, Series V, Box 216, Folder 595.
10. Ibid., July 11, 1941.
11. See Amanda Smith, *Hostage to Fortune. The Letters of Joseph P. Kennedy*, J. P. Kennedy to Charles Lindbergh, November 12, 1938, 301.

12 Yale, Lindbergh Papers, MS 325, Series V, Box 216, Folder 595, July 11, 1941.
13 Ibid.
14 FBI File 65-11449-94 as cited in Douglas M. Charles, *J. Edgar Hoover and the Anti-Interventionists. FBI Surveillance and the Rise of the Domestic Security State, 1939–1945* (Columbus: The Ohio State University Press, 2007), 73–4.
15 Cited in Berg, *Lindbergh*, 427.
16 Berg, *Lindbergh*, 427.
17 Will H. Hays, *Annual Report*, "Motion Pictures and Total Defense," to Motion Picture Producers and Distributors of America, March 31, 1941, 38.
18 Ibid., 5.
19 See, Justus D. Doenecke (ed.), *In Danger Undaunted. The Anti-Interventionist Movement of 1940–1941 as Revealed in the Papers of the America First Committee* (Stanford: Hoover Institution Press, 1990), 35 and 69. See also *America First Bulletin*, nos. 452 and 453 (July 30, 1941) and no. 501 (August 19, 1941) on the boycott and the listing of *The Mortal Storm* first.
20 Appointed to the committee in 1935, in six years Wheeler had turned it into his power base in the Senate.
21 Harry S. Truman Library, Papers of Frank McNaughton, Box 2, Frank McNaughton to David Hulbard, November 3, 1941. I want to thank historian David Welky for generously supplying me with copies of the McNaughton Papers.
22 Shesol, *Supreme Power*, 319.
23 Ibid.
24 Burton K. Wheeler, *America First Committee Bulletin*, no. 627 (October 14, 1941).
25 Michael Straight, "The Antisemitic Conspiracy." *The New Republic* (September 22, 1941), 362.
26 Berg, *Lindbergh*, 419, cites the confirming FBI reports on Mrs. Wheeler.
27 Elizabeth Wheeler Colman, *Mrs. Wheeler Goes to Washington* (Helena, MT: Falcon Press Pub. Co., Inc., 1989), 173–4. According to her daughter, Lulu Wheeler in early 1939 helped to forge the isolationist cohort in the Senate by a series of well-timed dinner invitations to the Clarks, Nyes, and a handful of others who could fit around their ten-seat dining table.
28 John Edward Wiltz, "The Nye Committee Revisited," *The Historian*, vol. 23, no. 2 (February 1961), 227. See also US Senate, Munitions Industry, Senate Report 944, 74th Cong., Sess. 1 and 74th Cong., Sess. 2, Part 6, p. 1.
29 Kenneth S. Davis, *FDR. The War President, 1940–1943* (New York: Random House, 2000), 98–9.
30 Wheeler had clearly embraced the attitude toward propaganda for war that Nye and Clark had long warned about. According to Wheeler's daughter, Clark's wife Miriam, a regular at her mother's dinner parties, believed that "the British propagandists [...] will try again to instill in the public fear and

hate of the Germans—a repeat performance of the [nineteen] teens." Colman, *Mrs. Wheeler Goes to Washington*, 175–6.

31 Fairbanks, *Salad Days*, 366.
32 John T. Flynn, *Country Squire in the White House* (New York: Doran & Co., Inc., 1940), 108–12.
33 Michelle Flynn Stenehjem, *An American First. John T. Flynn and the America First Committee* (New Rochelle: Arlington House Publishers, 1976), 147.
34 Ibid., 57.
35 Ibid., 147.
36 The full collection of letters can be found in the files for Senate Resolution 152, Box 86 in NARA (DC).
37 Ibid., Edward Sieger to Senator Wheeler, August 1, 1941.
38 Cole, *Gerald P. Nye*, 187. Flynn's financial arrangements in the preparation for the hearings can be found in Box 21 of his papers in the University of Oregon Knight Library. None of those documents reveal the name of the anonymous donor.
39 Stenehjem, *An American First*, 149.
40 John Wheeler to Burton K. Wheeler, August 10, 1941, Files of Senate Resolution 152, Box 86, NARA (DC).
41 Ibid.
42 Eyman, *Lion of Hollywood*, 127.
43 Nicola Schenck, daughter of Nicholas Schenck to Scott Eyman, *Lion of Hollywood*, 129.
44 Basinger and Wasson, *Hollywood. The Oral History*, 153–4.
45 Hearings, 245.
46 Eyman, *Lion of Hollywood*, 129.
47 *Los Angeles Times*, "Throng Hears Lindbergh in Fight on War," June 21, 1941, 7.
48 Ibid.
49 "William Borah," Wikipedia, www.wikipedia.org. accessed September 2, 2023.
50 Hearings, 64.
51 Michael Straight, "The Antisemitic Conspiracy," *The New Republic*, September 22, 1941, 362.
52 Carr, *Hollywood and Anti-Semitism*, 268.
53 Ibid., See also *Ernest W. McFarland, Mac: The Autobiography of Ernest W. McFarland* (published by author, 1979), 62.
54 James E. McMillan, "McFarland and the Movies: The 1941 Senate Motion Picture Hearings," *Journal of Arizona History*, vol. 29, no. 3 (autumn 1988), 279. See also Carr's account of McFarland's role on the committee in his *Hollywood and Anti-Semitism*; and Karen K. Kroman, "Ernest

W. McFarland," in John Myers (ed.), *The Arizona Governors, 1912–1990* (Phoenix: Heritage Publishers, 1990), 99–108. The transcript of the hearings is full of McFarland's put-downs and needling of his fellow subcommittee members. See, for example, McFarland's taking Nye to task for his St. Louis speech, a month before the hearings opened. Hearings, 60.

55 McMillan, "McFarland and the Movies," 277–302.
56 *New York Times*, July 30, 1941, 8.
57 Kaiser, *No End Save Victory*, 276.
58 Ibid.
59 All citations from the Des Moines speech are from Berg, *Lindbergh*, 426–7.
60 Hearings, 71.
61 For an account of the lawsuit, see Welky, *The Moguls and the Dictators*, 63–9, 163–4, 198.
62 Hearings, 77.
63 Ibid., 68.
64 Ibid.
65 Ibid., 1.
66 Ibid., 9–11. Nye quoted Dr. John Sherman, President of Weber College in Florida. He condemned the accuracy of Sherman's account. The Weber College President had called Nye's speech "an un-American appeal to antisemitic prejudice" (p. 11) which Nye denied before the subcommittee.
67 Hearings, 54.
68 Ibid.
69 *Variety* printed an excerpt of Borzage's letter to Willkie on September 15, 1941, no page.
70 Hearings, 170–1.
71 Ibid., 201.
72 Hearings, 96.
73 The gap in the hearings that occurred between Monday, September 15, and Tuesday, September 23, remains unexplained. Neither the transcript nor the documents available in the archive of the subcommittee, that is the files of Senate Resolution 152, reveal the cause of a full week's recess in the midst of the hearings. Nor has correspondence between the committee and the studio heads come to light, although negotiations between the two sides may have accounted for the delay. For a day-by-day account of the sessions, see Chris Yogerst, *Hollywood Hates Hitler! Jew-Baiting, Anti-Nazism, and the Senate Investigation into Warmongering in Motion Pictures* (Jackson: University of Mississippi Press, 2020), which relies heavily on contemporary newspaper accounts. Yogerst does not address the seven-day gap in the hearings.
74 John Wheeler to Burton K. Wheeler, August 10, 1941, Files of Senate Resolution 152, Box 86, NARA (DC).

75 "The Mortal Storm," *Harrison Reports* (no date), read into the record of the Hearings, 176.
76 Hearings, 68.
77 Ibid.
78 According to Scott Eyman, "Nick and Joe Schenck had a strong fraternal resemblance [and] noticeable Russian accents." (Eyman, *Lion of Hollywood*, 127). According to Neal Gabler, "And though the brothers had arrived in this country at the same time and Joe was the elder, Nick spoke with a thick accent while Joe had no accent whatsoever." (Gabler, *An Empire of Their Own*, 113). Nick indeed must have had a Russian accent as two sources concur.
79 Eyman, *Lion of Hollywood*, 192.
80 See especially the exchange in Hearings, 275.
81 Hearings, 323.
82 Ibid., 323–4.
83 Ibid, 324.
84 Ibid., 328.
85 Ibid., 330.
86 Ibid., 323.
87 NARA (College Park) RG 59. 811.4061. Mortal Storm/Box 1. Thomsen to Hull. July 16, 1940. Thomsen had channels of communication with isolationist Senators, Wheeler's cohort in particular.
88 Cited in Welky, *The Moguls and the Dictators*, 4.
89 Hearings, 323.
90 Ibid., 334.
91 Ibid., 77.
92 Ibid., 381.
93 Ibid.
94 Ibid., 271.
95 Ibid., 376.
96 Ibid., 339.
97 Hearings, 449.
98 *Hollywood Citizen News*, "The Week in Review," September 27, 1941, Page F, 8th Day in Academy of Motion Picture Arts and Sciences, Press Clipping File on the Senate Sub-Committee on War Film Hearings, vol. I, August 1 through October 15, 1941, ed. Donald Gledhill (Academy Executive Secretary), henceforth Academy Clipping File. Page numbers for newspaper clippings are rarely visible. Internal page numbers for the collection are given as letters of the alphabet in sequence for each day of the hearings and then doubled if needed.
99 Hearings, 62.
100 Eyman, *Lion of Hollywood*, 18.

101 Hearings, 449.
102 Truman Library, McNaughton Papers, Box 1, Frank McNaughton to David Hulburd, October 23, 1941.
103 Cited in *The Film Daily* for September 25, 1941. Academy Clipping File.
104 Academy Clipping File, p. E, Lewiston (ME) *Journal* (no date), as cited in *The Film Daily*, "U.S. Dailies Editorially Rake Senate Witch Hunt," September 25, 1941.
105 Truman Library, McNaughton Papers, Box 1, McNaughton to Hulburd, October 10, 1941.
106 Ibid.
107 *The Evening Star,* October 9, 1941, Academy Clipping File, p. QQ.
108 See *The Film Daily*, October 9, 1941 and *The Evening Star*, October 10, 1941, Academy Clipping File, p. QQ for recognition that Clark was in fact shutting down the hearings.
109 Ibid.
110 Truman Library, McNaughton Papers, Box 1, McNaughton to Hulburd, October 10, 1941.
111 "Nye Sets a Stage, But Chaplin Stars," *US Week*, September 27, 1941, Academy Clipping File, p. H.
112 NARA, US Senate ICC. Senate Resolution 152, Box 86. D. Worth Clark to Burton K. Wheeler, December 18, 1941.
113 *Christian Science Monitor,* no date, as cited in *The Film Daily*, "Nation's Editors Press Fire on Propaganda Probe," October 1, 1941, Academy Clipping File, p. S.
114 Ibid., *Kansas City (MO) Journal*.
115 Ibid., *Idaho Falls* (IDA) *Post Register.*
116 Sidney Skolsky, *Times Herald*, September 19, 1941 (excerpt), Academy Clipping File (Second Recess), p. B.
117 Frederick C. Othman, "Pure Propaganda Is Box Office Poison," Los Angeles *Daily News*, September 18, 1941, Academy Clipping File, p. DD.
118 September, 23, 1941, Page E, 8th Day, Academy Clipping File.
119 See *Variety*, October 3, 1941, for the turnaround in Hollywood's attitude toward war pictures. Academy Clipping File, p. HH.
120 Hearings, 137.
121 Ibid. See also John E. Moser's interpretation of the phrase in "'Gigantic Engines of Propaganda': The 1941 Senate Investigation of Hollywood," *Historian*, vol. 63, no. 4 (summer 2001), 731–51.
122 Hearings, 372.
123 Ibid., 379.
124 Yale, Lindbergh Papers, MS 325, Series V, Box 216, Folder 597, September 15, 1941.

125 *In Danger Undaunted*, Flynn to Robert E. Wood and R. Douglas Stuart, Jr., September 12, 1941, 395–6.
126 Reported in New York *Journal-American,* September 17, 1941, Academy Clipping File, p. EE.
127 Wheeler was quoted in *Variety*, October 3, 1941, Academy Clipping File, p. P.
128 *Louisville Courier-Journal*, no date, as cited in "Nation's Editors Press Fire on Propaganda Probe," *The Film Daily*, October 1, 1941. Academy Clipping File, p. S.
129 Dorothy Thompson, "On the Record-Collusion," *Cleveland Plain Dealer,* September 12, 1941, Academy Clipping File, p. G.
130 Michael Straight, "The antisemitic Conspiracy," *The New Republic*, September 22, 1941, Academy Clipping File, p. I.
131 Drew Pearson and Robert S. Allen, "Washington Merry-Go-Round," Los Angeles *Daily News,* September 24, 1941, Academy Clipping file, Fifth Day, p. E.
132 See Alfred M. Beck, *Hitler's Ambivalent Attaché* on Thomsen's congressional network, 172.
133 Lindbergh noted in his (published) diary that Smith was "one of the many people rumored to have written my radio addresses." Entry for May 29, 1940, 352.
134 Charles A. Lindbergh, "Aviation, Geography, and Race," *Reader's Digest*, vol. 35 (November 1939), 64–7. See also Beck, 148 on Smith's involvement with *Reader's Digest.*
135 Robert Hessen (ed.), *Berlin Alert. The Memoirs and Reports of Truman Smith* (Stanford: Hoover Institution Press, 1984), xviii.
136 See Beck, Hitler's *Ambivalent Attaché*, 163. See also references to Lindbergh in *Documents on German Foreign Policy, 1918–1945* (Series D), vols. IX and X. The War Years, 1940 (Washington, DC: US Government Printing Office, 1956 and 1957). For example, Hans Thomsen and Friedrich von Boetticher to Foreign Ministry, October 16, 1940, Top Secret, *Documents on German Foreign Policy*, Series D (1918–1945), vol. X (Washington, DC: US Government Printing Office, 1957), 308. Thomsen and Boetticher reminded the Foreign Ministry that "Lindbergh, his speeches and his connections with leading German personages [should] not be mentioned in the press, in speeches and discussions, etc."
137 See denials of such a link in Alfred M. Beck, *Hitler's Ambivalent Attaché. Lt. Gen. Friedrich von Boetticher* (Washington, DC: Potomac Books, Inc., 2006), 161, including an account of the author's correspondence with Lindbergh on the issue.
138 Yale, Lindbergh Papers, MS 325, Series V, Box 216, See especially entries for July 1941.
139 Ibid., Folder 597, September 15, 1941.
140 See David Welky, *The Moguls and the Dictators*: "Lindbergh had nothing to do with [the 1941 Senate] hearings," 307. John Moser insists that "Lindbergh

in no way associated with the motion picture investigation," 740 in "The Celluloid War," *The International History Review*, vol. 24, no. 1 (2002). Todd Bennett similarly maintains that the aviator "was not affiliated with the investigation into the film industry,"100 in "Gigantic Engines of Propaganda." See also my review of David Welky, *The Moguls and the Dictators* in *The Space Between: Literature and Culture, 1914–1945*, vol. 7, no. 1 (2011), 141–4.

141 Steven J. Ross, *Hitler in Los Angeles* (New York and London: Bloomsbury Press, 2017), 125.

142 Charles Chaplin, *My Autobiography* (New York: Pocket Books, Inc., 1966), 421.

143 By 1940, Goebbels and Hollywood had vastly different, one could say, competing images of the Jew onscreen. Whose image would prevail? If Goebbels had a hand in the hearings, by discrediting the moguls he also discredited their version of the Jewish question. See my Phyllis Bottome's "The Mortal Storm: Film and Controversy" in *The Space Between, Literature and Culture, 1914–1945*, 39–58.

144 *Hearings*, 449.

145 David McCullough, *Truman* (New York: Simon & Schuster, 1992). See pp. 254–89 for discussion of Truman's investigation into procurement contracts, 1941–1943.

146 Ibid., 264.

147 Ibid., 264–5.

148 Anonymous, *The New Republic*, vol. 105, no. 19 (November 10, 1941), 603.

Epilogue

Hollywood Almost Missed the Bus, Again

At the time of its release in 1940, Bosley Crowther had criticized *The Mortal Storm* for not having been produced in 1935 or at least in 1937. As a result, "Hollywood has missed the bus," he wrote. The Pulitzer Prize-winning playwright and Roosevelt speech writer Robert E. Sherwood used the same phrase in a communication to producer Samuel Goldwyn about a picture the mogul hoped to make shortly after the war ended. Sherwood expressed his doubts about the proposed picture: "I […] urge that you consider very seriously whether you want to go ahead with this picture. It isn't merely a question of my reneging on a job that I agreed to—it is the major problem of your investing a lot of money in a picture which […] will be doomed to miss the bus."[1] Time proved neither Crowther nor Sherwood correct in his assessment. *The Mortal Storm* turned out to be timely in 1940 and for different reasons again in 1941. *The Best Years of Our Lives,* the picture Sherwood nearly reneged on, remains one of the best Hollywood ever produced.

Yet by the middle of the war, Hollywood had decided that war pictures and presumably those about the war's aftermath were no longer what the public wanted to see. With such films as *Confessions of a Nazi Spy* and *The Mortal Storm*, Hollywood had reluctantly declared war on Nazi Germany before the US government did. Similarly, Hollywood decreed the war over before the fighting stopped. The decision to abandon the whole genre of war-themed pictures appropriately enough coincided with the death of Claudine West. She died on April 12, 1943, having refused all visitors for several weeks. Among those who tried to call was Greer Garson, whose film career up to then West had largely written.² The day after West succumbed, probably to lung cancer, *The Hollywood Reporter* ran the banner headline, "The Studios Plan for Post-War Era."³ The article that followed revealed that the major studios were already anticipating a shift "in public taste away from war pictures."⁴

The decision would have been a blow to West. Since 1939, she had almost exclusively produced scripts for war pictures. Partnered with Sidney Franklin, she had seen her career take off with *Good-bye, Mr. Chips,* released in that year. By 1943 she belonged to the well-paid elite among Hollywood scriptwriters.⁵ The work not only gave her financial security, she loved it. She contributed almost to the end, leaving the set of *The White Cliffs of Dover* on February 27 for the last time. As a British expatriate, devoted to England her friends teased her, she had been the obvious choice to write the script for that particular war picture which extolled the Anglo-American bond in two world wars. But the war picture bonanza of the past four years was soon to disappear. Had West been able to return to MGM, her career would never have been what it was when she left.

The movie companies intended to follow "the Government's 'win the war first' policy" for the next eight months to a year. After that, by 1944, both Warner Brothers and Paramount intended "to submerge the war angle in favor of straight entertainment."⁶ The article on the studios' new plans cited William Dozier, once Bottome's agent in the sale of *The Mortal Storm* to MGM, now head of the Story Department at Paramount. Dozier pointed to Paramount's patriotic releases and then confirmed, "The bulk of our future films will underscore entertainment and the stories will ignore the current conflict."⁷ Hollywood, according to Dozier, was taking its cue from the bestseller lists which reveal "the public is tiring of war yarns," and prefers instead "sheer romantic or escapist entertainment."⁸

But did such lists accurately reflect the public mood with the war still raging? The moguls seemed to be looking ahead with undue haste, even before the Allied invasion of Europe, in their determination to "ignore the current conflict." On the other hand, studio heads had succeeded not only by reflecting public taste; they were also adept at anticipating it. They intended to do the same now.

By 1944, so the plan went, the producers would have already remade themselves in preparation for the post-war era. The effort might be more difficult for some than for others. West and Franklin, for example, since 1938 had produced nearly all war-themed pictures, pioneering in the case of *The Mortal Storm*, hugely successful in the case of *Mrs. Miniver*. Such pictures, Jack Warner and Bill Dozier now argued, were already passé. *Casablanca* and *Yankee Doodle Dandy* had narrowly made it through production at Warners. In 1943, the studio intended to phase out war-themed pictures entirely.⁹

Dozier and Warner were right that Hollywood would have to adapt once again to changing public taste. They were wrong regarding what the public might want in a year's time. In the midst of war, they failed to anticipate the frightened, noir mood of veterans and the public alike, both suffering from the many versions of combat fatigue. The studios might have meant one thing by combat fatigue in 1943, that is, a surfeit of war pictures. Two years later, the term meant the neuroses of exposure to combat coupled with survivor's guilt. At the same time, one did not need to go into actual combat to experience the stress and anguish associated with the trauma of war. The studios did not anticipate that combatants and civilians both faced burdens of re-adjustment in 1945. The altered taste in movies reflected it. "Audiences craved [...] social realism [...] after World War II." They wanted "dramas about alcoholism and mental illness and antisemitism and racism [...]," wrote film historian Mark Harris.[10]

Not all the moguls misread the attitude of the American public after the war. In 1945, as noted above, Samuel Goldwyn invited Robert E. Sherwood to produce a script about one of the most painful issues confronting the American public in the post-war era, namely the readjustment of traumatized war veterans. Goldwyn wanted Sherwood to base the script on MacKinley Kantor's recent blank verse novel on the subject, *Glory for Me*.

Sherwood politely but firmly turned him down on the grounds of timeliness. "... in all fairness, I should recommend to you that we drop it, [because] by next Spring or next Fall, this subject will be terribly out of date." Sherwood further argued that the picture would arouse considerable resentment by suggesting that maladjustment was typical of all returning servicemen. In sum, Sherwood advised Goldwyn not "to invest a lot of money in a picture which [...] will be doomed to miss the bus."[11]

Goldwyn prevailed. Sherwood relented; and together with director William Wyler they produced *The Best Years of Our Lives*, which captured the public mood in the years after the Second World War. Readjustment proved to be the work of the whole country. *The Mortal Storm*, on the other hand, had captured the mood of the American public on the eve of war. It conveyed the sense of mission and moral energy that underlay the politics of 1940. Bottome had captured that spirit when she wrote a friend at the time, "The Nazi regime is not a mere change of politics; it is a systematic attack on the moral law of the universe."[12] The film would be heavy baggage to carry into the post-war era, as some who had contributed to it were to find.

The Harsh Realities of Victory

Bottome, as noted earlier, was a novelist of war, largely the First World War, "my war," she called it. But her formative years had occurred even earlier: in the preceding century when her values and sensibility emerged in a Victorian childhood. War's end, when it came in 1945, could be described as the dawn of a whole new century, so great were the changes wrought by the Second World War. Bottome would have to adapt to what amounted to her third century.

She painfully discovered that her fame in 1940 had not survived the war. Hints that her status as the author of *The Mortal Storm* might not be long-lived nor as significant as she had hoped occurred with the film just beginning its first run. In the summer of 1940, she attempted to acquire permission from the MoI to publish a psychological analysis, Adlerian naturally, of Lindbergh. She sought a respected American publication such as *The Atlantic* for a piece to be titled "The American Fuhrer."[13] As an employee of the MoI, she required the ministry's permission to send the essay abroad for publication.

The ministry would have none of it. Her immediate supervisor in the American Division, Sir Edward Whyte, refused her request to send the piece with the comment "America ought to look after her own black sheep." Better not to publish such an essay "over the name of a British writer."[14] She promptly went over his head to Duff Cooper, the minister himself. Cooper had his secretary rebuff her. Bottome then submitted the piece to Harold Nicholson, then one of numerous bureaucrats in the ministry. Nicholson promptly lost it.[15] "Would it be possible for your secretary to hunt once more for my article upon [sic] Lindbergh?" she asked plaintively.[16] Alan Hodge, probably in the midst of reading proofs for his history of the interwar period, written with Robert Graves, and titled *The Long Weekend*, could only sympathize. "I am extremely sorry to have to tell you that in spite of further searches we cannot find your article on Lindbergh."[17] Bottome claimed that she had no other copy. The Ministry had effectively managed to shut her down.

The post-war period afforded few opportunities for the life of purpose she had known before the conflict. The new circumstances were reflected in the content, even appearance of her correspondence. On the eve of war, she had filled thin sheets of paper with petitions that Churchill enter the government and demands that Chamberlain be removed. She wrote fiery letters to newspapers in the North. She hectored MPs on a regular basis, driven by a sense of righteousness in her mission. All of that changed after the war. The thin nibs carrying watery ink in the late 1930s gave way to wide points that bled strong ink into commercial cards on heavy paper. Such communications recorded Bottome's social engagements. Gone were the desperate pleas on behalf of Austrian refugees and the denunciations of a sell out at Munich.

Worst of all, her American publisher no longer treated her as one of its most valued contributors. She told Roger Scaife, her friend and editor at Little, Brown & Co. that she had grown dissatisfied with the company's "handling of [her] books."[18] By that she meant the company's unwillingness to promote them to her satisfaction. She surmised that they did not "care for [her] Adlerian ideas" and "prefer to back books with a less moral and leftist tendency."[19] Bottome had rarely written works with a "leftist tendency," except perhaps the British edition of *The Mortal Storm* with Hans's perorations extolling Stalin. Her difficulty lay precisely with the moral fervor that had stood her in good stead as a "premature anti-Nazi" and salesman of a controversial novel to reluctant studio heads. The fervor of the 1930s played badly in the post-war world which sought recovery rather than causes.

Bottome instead entered the post-war period with her pre-war sensibilities and drive intact. Adding to her woes, Scaife's position at Little, Brown & Co. had grown insecure. He was not only her editor whose judgment she trusted regarding the American readership, but she relied on his support within the company. "I have had the feeling," she wrote him that "you and I stood and fell together at Little, Brown."[20] She candidly lamented, it did "not seem to be the case" that Scaife could continue to provide "the backing" he had "always" been able to offer.[21]

The last straw for Bottome proved to be Little, Brown & Co.'s rejection of the first volume of her autobiography titled *Search for a Soul*. Her agent Ann Watkins explained that a memoir devoted to a childhood and adolescence lived before the two world wars would not attract an American post-war readership. Bottome had fired Watkins in the past only to quickly reemploy her. Within two years they parted permanently.[22]

She did no better in an attempt to reconnect with Hollywood after the war. She wrote Sidney Franklin proposing three of her novels that she thought could successfully be adapted to the screen. She suggested her 1941 novel *Heart of a Child*, a parable of dictatorship as a means to "bring simple morality home to the great public."[23] She also offered *Old Wine* on "the revival of Vienna after the First World War" and the "much lighter" morality tale on "French life called 'Advances of Harriet'."[24]

If Franklin replied, his response has not been retained in Bottome's archive. Of the three novels that Bottome suggested, only *Heart of a Child* was subsequently adapted for the screen. The British company of J. Arthur Rank produced it a decade later in 1957.[25] To Bottome a consolation prize that would never reach a broad and lucrative American market. Six years later, she published the third volume of her autobiography, *The Goal*, which ends in 1937, just before *The Mortal Storm* was published in the United States and adapted for the screen two years after that. Bottome herself never recounted the story of *The Mortal Storm* in its American incarnation, a gap this book has tried to fill.

She and Ernan lived in Jamaica for several months in 1947 and again from 1949 to 1950 when Ernan ran a boys' school like the one they established in Austria in the late 1920s. The island in fact proved to be a kind of post-Second World War Vienna for Bottome. She found one more cause that she could turn into fiction. She attacked the racial prejudice all too prevalent among British colonials in the Caribbean. Titled *Under the Skin*, it was filled with characters recovering from the wounds of war. It sold well enough but failed to reach the screen despite Bottome's composition of a script.[26]

Sidney Franklin: Grieving for Claudine West

Franklin too had difficulty adapting to the post-war world. A week before Claudine West died, he wrote Kenneth MacKenna what her loss would mean. MacKenna had been part of Franklin's production team and present when Bottome offered advice on the adaptation of her novel shortly after MGM's purchase of *The Mortal Storm*. Franklin confided:

> I already miss her terrifically ... the loss will be very keen for some time, and it also puts me in the position of being completely without someone to write my scripts for me—that is, someone who thinks much the same way as I do.[27]

Franklin referred to the unique role West had played on his production team. She had in effect been the creative spirit behind the group that he led at MGM, often working directly with him. Her last day on the set, the one for *The White Cliffs of Dover*, as noted, was February 27, 1943. The studio waited a year to release the film, doing so without enthusiasm. It was the kind of war picture MGM no longer intended to promote.[28]

A year and a half later, Franklin again confided to MacKenna, now serving in the Army Signal Corps:

> I miss you ... more so than ever now since Claudine isn't with me anymore; it has been an awful struggle to find a writer—a permanent one on my staff to take her place in any sense of the word. In fact, I haven't anyone.[29]

Franklin grieved for more than West. He never did replace her to continue, as he thought, business as usual. By 1945, that would have meant finding a scriptwriter who could have adapted to post-war uncertainties in entertainment, including the impending competition with television. And then there was the brutal scrutiny of congressional investigations to which Hollywood was now subjected, including Hollywood's own version of censorship in the form of the blacklist. The changed financial picture for Hollywood and a new and insidious censorship both within and without made another stable partnership such as he had enjoyed with West highly unlikely. By 1953 Franklin had ceased production work altogether.

Bottome and Franklin faced a problem common to many artists after 1945 whose careers had thrived in the interwar period and during the war that followed. They needed to remake themselves in the post-war period; few could.[30] In the case of *The Mortal Storm*, only one major contributor managed the feat. Jimmy Stewart became a different kind of actor, largely by embracing the new mood and anxieties of the public as well as recognizing that he too had been changed in a similar fashion by the war. The role of pacifist Martin Breitner that Stewart had taken in the film paradoxically played a significant part in his post-war transformation.

Jimmy Stewart and the Trauma of War

In 1940, Jimmy Stewart had been one kind of actor, both on- and off-screen. Extending his role as the heroic Martin Breitner, he had gone to Cleveland to tell an audience of nearly 10,000, "I think we ought to help England ... because she's doing more than anybody else."[31]

Two film scholars, Tim Palmer and Colleen Glenn, have recently addressed Stewart's post-war transformation as an actor. Palmer has observed that Stewart did what he needed to do to maintain a career in Hollywood after 1945.[32] The actor, according to Palmer, underwent a "post-war transformation ... completely revising the terms of his stardom ...."[33] As a result, he repeatedly assumed the role of "characters in the throes of crisis both physical and psychological."[34] He was able to do so, the film scholar further argues, because "during the 1940s and 1950s, Stewart quite literally became a different man."[35] Palmer's descriptive account of the remade Stewart, certainly accurate, offers no explanation for why the actor should so dramatically transform himself.

Colleen Glenn provides the explanation for Stewart's post-war transformation.[36] She addresses the dynamic that made Stewart after 1945 into "a different man." Glenn argues that the key to Stewart's psychological and artistic metamorphosis lies precisely in his wartime service when, after nineteen missions as a bomber pilot over Germany, he suffered a mental breakdown and ceased to engage in further combat operations. His military career was far from over, however. He quickly adapted to service on the ground and was rewarded with promotion to colonel. "Lingering combat fatigue," nonetheless, plagued Stewart well into the 1950s, seen in his post-war films where his roles rarely deviated from an established pattern.[37] Those films, Glenn argues, can be interpreted as a form of "the compulsive repetitions that typifies trauma."[38] In his collaborations with director Anthony Mann, Stewart made Westerns in which he repeatedly played "an ex-soldier suffering from post-traumatic stress disorder."[39] Similarly, in the films he made with Hitchcock, Stewart "plays a World War II veteran grappling with his past who unintentionally becomes involved in a murder."[40] In effect, Stewart sought roles that met his personal needs as a shell-shocked veteran and were consonant with them.

But such roles met more than Stewart's own needs, and here lay the source of the actor's post-war success. The parts he played also met the needs and addressed the experiences of numerous Americans after 1945. Glenn cites Willard Weller, who warned in 1944 that "Every veteran is at least mildly shell-shocked."[41] The same could be said of the entire population of the country which found individuals adapting slowly and, in some cases, reluctantly to post-war life. Stewart therefore paid a high price for his post-war success, basing it on the convergence of his on-screen persona with his own painful wartime experiences and lingering psychological trauma.

One of Stewart's films, made in 1956 and released in 1957, appears to belie the contention that the actor repeatedly portrayed a veteran afflicted with his own PTSD in his post-war movie career. In *The Spirit of St. Louis*, Stewart played the youthful Charles Lindbergh in 1927 at the time of his historic flight from New York to Paris. Playing Lindbergh, who had not even served in the First World War, could not possibly be construed as one of Stewart's roles as a maladjusted veteran.

Or could it? In fact, one can argue that the war intruded even on Stewart's role as Lindbergh. The actor had found yet another part perfectly consonant with his post-war anxieties. But he had to fight for it. In 1956, the politics of 1940 returned to haunt him in a controversy over who would be cast to play Lindbergh. Stewart himself was an unlikely choice. Lindbergh agreed with the producer Leland Hayward, the former husband of Margaret Sullavan, Stewart's co-star in *The Mortal Storm* and a longtime close friend, that the actor at forty-seven was too old to play the aviator at twenty-seven. Lindbergh at first insisted on the young and handsome John Kerr "far closer [to him] in age and temperament than Stewart."[42] But Kerr refused the honor, objecting to "Lindbergh's isolationist soft-on-Hitler activities prior to World War II."[43]

After Anthony Perkins and Martin Milner refused the part, Lindbergh agreed to meet with Stewart; but as Kerr's refusal had shown, pre-war politics had not been forgotten. Stewart and his wife dined with Lindbergh. The casting question remained unresolved. They dined a second time, Stewart significantly accompanied by Margaret Sullavan. If Lindbergh harbored doubts about Stewart's politics, Sullavan, who had been taught to fly by Stewart, could confirm the actor's reverence for Lindbergh's achievements in aviation, if not the conservative evolution in her friend's politics.[44]

Lindbergh, Stewart, and possibly Sullavan had indeed evolved since the pre-war years. In 1941, Lindbergh had become an outcast after the Des Moines speech that he gave in support of the Senate investigation of alleged pro-war propaganda in Hollywood, encouraged by American Jews and the British government. Public opinion and the press quickly condemned both the aviator and the Senate isolationists. Lindbergh's political demise followed on the heels of Stewart's emergence as a proponent of intervention. Earlier overshadowed by such outspoken interventionists in Hollywood as Melvyn Douglas and Douglas Fairbanks, Jr., Stewart in 1940 quickly made up for lost time. His role in *Mr. Smith Goes to Washington* and *The Mortal Storm* galvanized him into political engagement.

The Mortal Storm proved the more useful. When he took the film on the road at the invitation of the Cleveland branch of the White committee with his lanky, boyish appearance and his celebrity, Stewart could remind his audience of Lindbergh who too spoke to large rallies with a political message. Stewart's call to aid Britain and encourage American rearmament, in contrast to Lindbergh's message of America First, won the public's favor.

Stewart's role in *The Mortal Storm* had another consequence. His gung-ho spirit in support of intervention, on full display in Cleveland, arguably contributed to his wartime breakdown. The actor flew into combat with a mindset that could not prepare him for the brutal reality of the air war in Europe, nor could his role in Hollywood. From the mid-1930s, he had embraced the make-believe of moviemaking and immersed himself in the acting profession in the Golden Age of Hollywood. In contrast to his best friend Henry Fonda, who disdained it, Stewart thrived in the studio system. He subsequently reminisced about that innocent, pre-war period of his career:

> I was just wrapped up by the whole idea of [Hollywood] where make-believe took place [...] every once in a while you'd look and there was Garbo and there was Gable and I had a tiny little part with Jean Harlow and the whole thing was a wonderful experience for me [...] I never [...] said [...] they're taking advantage [of me] [...] It was all a learning process for me and I enjoyed every minute of it.[45]

Naïve and determined, he went to war, contributing to the mass death of German civilians whom he could picture from his role in *The Mortal Storm*. He also had to take "responsibility for the deaths of men in his command" (Colleen Glenn, 33). Combat transformed Stewart, who had played the one-time pacifist Martin Breitner, into a very different character, traumatized and conflicted about intervention which he had advocated so enthusiastically before he actually fought.

Stewart emerged from his breakdown a changed man, advocating a different brand of politics. He nonetheless remained in the military and became an exemplary performer in the chain of command, soon promoted to colonel and ending his career as a general and spokesman for the Strategic Air Command. The former liberal interventionist had come to embrace the Cold War and Vietnam-era politics of anti-Communism for which he became known. Like other victims of trauma, he espoused conservative, even at times authoritarian, politics, seeking security in obedience after defiance and protest before the war.

Lindbergh's reputation, if not his conservative politics, had changed too, although as Kerr's refusal of the role of the aviator had shown, not everyone had forgotten Lindbergh's pre-war association with Nazism. During the war, however, he had served admirably in the Pacific where his skills in long-distance flying had been welcome. He had (illegally as a civilian) flown fifty combat missions and was credited with providing recommendations and advice to navy pilots regarding fuel consumption which gave them significant advantage over the Japanese in the long-distance air war in the Pacific. Lindbergh could once again claim the status of a hero.

And then there were the changes in Hollywood itself. When Stewart and Sullavan sat down to dine with Lindbergh in 1956, the HUAC investigations into Hollywood, some would argue, had confirmed the charges that the aviator and his allies had made against the moguls in 1941. The script had been modified but not the Hollywood Jews as the target of accusations. A large number of Jews, particularly those in the Screenwriters Guild, had encouraged Communists and their propaganda to infiltrate entertainment in America, so some in congress now charged. The whole country took note; and, unlike 1941, fear permeated Hollywood over the accusations. The perpetrators of the Hollywood blacklist and the new generation of congressional investigators had succeeded beyond the wildest dreams of the pre-war Senate isolationists in their denunciations of Hollywood as a purveyor of propaganda.[46] Lindbergh had simply been ahead of his time.

That had been true in 1927. Military observers were quick to see "the frightening implications of progressive aviation" which Lindbergh's flight portended (Eksteins, *Rites of Spring*, 263). In *The Spirit of St. Louis*, Stewart not only dramatized Lindbergh's survival but he also recalled his own wartime experience, reprising it in the role of the first man to fly solo across the Atlantic. In 1927, the aviator had triumphed by careful calibration measured down to the last gallon of fuel, struggling against the elements but more particularly at war with the distance between one continent and another. Lindbergh's flight, while it may have recalled the aerial combat of a decade earlier, as Modris Eksteins suggests, sooner resembled the combat of the Second World War, predicted when Lindbergh traversed the distance from one continent to another in reaching Paris. The quest to cross the Atlantic and the air battles of the Great War diverged over a fundamental issue. The aerial combat of the First World War occurred over short distances and encounters were of relatively brief duration, limited by the fuel capacity of the early planes. Lindbergh's trans-Atlantic flight served as a harbinger of the distances that pilots would face in Europe and the Pacific in little more than a decade. The aces of the Great War could not have imagined the scale of the air war in the Second World War. Stewart had survived over Europe, traversing the distance between British airfields and the industrial centers of Germany. His bombing raids where distance and fuel consumption posed the same threats that Lindbergh had faced could therefore be said to resemble Lindbergh's successful trans-Atlantic flight repeated with every mission.

Stewart had still more in common with Lindbergh, who had survived his own air-born combat. A new front in the 1920s had opened in the sky, and the casualty rate was high. Two French aces from the war had disappeared going west across the Atlantic only weeks before Lindbergh succeeded from the opposite direction.[47] Decades later, at dinner with the two stars of *The Mortal Storm* when the aviator relented and let Stewart reenact his flight, the actor simply took on the role of another combat veteran. As Lindbergh, Stewart came as close to portraying himself in combat as he ever did after the war. Colleen Glenn, on the other hand, argues that Stewart carefully refused any combat roles, instead reprising his wartime experience only as a veteran. It would seem, however, that the one role Stewart fought so keenly to play was in its own way that of a participant in combat who survived the distance between one continent and another.

Stewart, as the consistently conservative Lindbergh, also played another role. He vanquished the messages of his pre-war films of engagement: intervention in *The Mortal Storm*, indifference as frivolity in its companion *The Philadelphia Story*. In playing Lindbergh, he also appeared to break with the renowned predecessor of those two films, *Mr. Smith Goes to Washington*, where the potential for fascism to masquerade as political corruption is depicted.[48] By the 1950s, the actor had embraced the conservative politics he would have disdained in 1940. In 1957, with the starring role in *The Spirit of St. Louis*, Jimmy Stewart confirmed that he had indeed remade himself artistically as well as politically, the only major contributor to *The Mortal Storm* to do so after 1945.

Timely Once More

As a novel, *The Mortal Storm* was considered "premature." The critics complained that once adapted to the screen, it lagged behind events. Antisemites saw the film with its use of "non-Aryan" as a threat. "Jew" next time, they feared. Still others regarded the use of "non-Aryan" as a fatal flaw, a destructive compromise. More recently, Mayer's tremulous decision of 1940 has become a source of mockery.[49]

One cannot help but ask how much more provocative would a version made from Claudine West's original script have been? And how much more might that version have contributed to the isolationist vs. interventionist debate in 1940? What might that version have meant for discussion regarding the plight of Europe's Jews that year when both the Lodz (April) and the Warsaw (November) ghettos were sealed? Similarly, what might a remake of the film made from West's original script mean today? Few, if any, in the audience would twist in their seats at the sound of the word "Jew." The film nonetheless retains its relevance. In successfully "dramatizing the brutality of the Third Reich," as Susan Dunn observed, *The Mortal Storm* raises issues for our own time.⁵⁰

In 1940, Bottome insisted to Sidney Franklin that "What is being a Jew [...] is the crux of the book and the crux of the world today [...]. I would make the Jew question utterly clear." She earlier told Franklin's production team, "it's [the novel] about an attack on all that's good and decent." She called the Nazis "wolves." Their descendants howl today in the form of the radical right and the mainstream politicians who take inspiration from its violence prone adherents.⁵¹ Bottome's use of *Uncle Tom's Cabin* seems similarly prescient. As David S. Reynolds has explained, a great deal of Southern literature has been written in objection to the novel and the negative picture of the American South that it painted. Bottome took the opposite view. She jumped into defense of the abolitionists whose work remained far from over when she wrote, shortly after her trip to Virginia in 1932.

"Premature anti-Nazi" that she was, she also wrote to raise the issue of antisemitism which had turned deadly before her very eyes. She insisted that there is no alternative to taking sides when baying predators threaten the moral order. *The Mortal Storm* on screen in black and white suggested just how stark the choices were in 1940, a message Bottome had hoped to convey when she sold the novel to MGM a year earlier.

Similarities between that time and ours encroach on whatever complacency we still possess. I wrote this book not far from where Sidney Buchman attended high school in Duluth, MN. There his English teacher, Mira Southworth, was the first to recognize his talent as a writer and urged him to develop it. We are all the beneficiaries. The heroes of 1940 remain our models to this day because so much has not changed since the eve of the Second World War.

Notes

1. Rocky Lang and Barbara Hall (eds.), *Letters from Hollywood. Inside the Private World of Classic American Moviemaking* (New York: Abrams, 2019), 135.
2. Greer Garson to Gavin Lambert, January 8, 1950, SAF, Box 24.
3. Anonymous, *The Hollywood Reporter*, vol. LXXII, no. 45 (April 13, 1943), 1.
4. Ibid., 3.
5. West's salary had climbed steadily since the mid-1930s. When she contributed to the script for *Ninotchka* in 1939 she earned $850/week. By *The White*

Cliffs of Dover, her last film, her salary had risen to $1500/week, placing her among the elite of Hollywood scriptwriters. Her total salary for that film was $34,583.33. She had earned $22,508.33 for *The Mortal Storm* only three years earlier. For *Mrs. Miniver*, she was indeed the highest paid writer at $18,000, nearly twice that of any other writer on the production except for James Hilton, who received a flat $25,000 to attach his name to the film. See SAF. Box 23/24, 5.

6   *The Hollywood Reporter*, April 13, 1943, 3.
7   Ibid.
8   Ibid.
9   Ibid.
10 Mark Harris, *Five Came Back. A Story of Hollywood and the Second World War* (New York: The Penguin Press, 2014), 440.
11 Robert E. Sherwood to Samuel Goldwyn, August 27, 1945 in Lang and Hall (eds.), *Letters from Hollywood*, 134–5.
12 PB to a friend Tobey S. November 23, 1938. BL Add. Mss. 88921/3/1.
13 PB to Israel Sieff. August 28, 1940. BL. Add. Mss. 88921/3/3. The title alone would have put her at odds with her friend Dorothy Thompson, who had labeled Lindbergh "the American Fuhrer" following his first radio address in September 1939.
14 Sir Edward Whyte to PB. June 12, 1940. BL Add. Mss. 889214/7.
15 PB to Victor Waybright. July 15, 1940. BL Add. Mss. 88921/4/7.
16 PB to Harold Nicholson. August 12, 1940. BL. Add. Mss. 88921/4/7.
17 Alan Hodge to PB. August 13, 1940. BL Add. Mss. 88921/4/7.
18 PB to Roger Scaife. September 16, 1946. BL Add. Mss. 88921/4/1.
19 Ibid.
20 Ibid.
21 Ibid., September 26, 1946.
22 See Hirsch, *The Constant Liberal*, 343–6 on the end of their professional connection.
23 PB to Sidney Franklin. SAF: Box 24, Sack 13. Undated/internal evidence suggests spring 1947.
24 PB to Sidney Franklin, July 15, 1947. SAF: Box 24, Sack 13.
25 See Hirsch, *The Constant Liberal*, 338.
26 Hirsch, *The Constant Liberal*, 308–16.
27 Sidney Franklin to Kenneth MacKenna. April 7, 1943. Box 19, Sack 5.
28 In addition to MGM's objection to another war picture, *The White Cliffs of Dover* faced government opposition to its release. Sidney Franklin told Kenneth MacKenna, "... the OWI [Office of War Information] took a couple of cracks at us. Whereas I thought I would get a medal from both England and America, they seem to think I might cause an international crisis. So I am

now endeavoring to correct a few things that they think might be bad ..." Box 19, Sack 5, April 7, 1943. The film, not released until 1944, depicted a romance between a British soldier and a young American with much clever banter supplied by West on the frequent clashes between the two cultures.

29 Sidney Franklin to Kenneth MacKenna. December 17, 1944. Box 19, Sack 5.
30 The exceptions were the great directors John Ford, George Stevens, John Huston, and William Wyler. See Mark Harris's collective biography, *Five Who Came Back*, of those four and Frank Capra, whose creative work, with the exception of *It's a Wonderful Life*, was over after 1945.
31 Roelif Loveland, "Help Britain, Be Ready, Stewart Urges 9,865"; *Cleveland Plain Dealer* (September 24, 1940), 1.
32 Tim Palmer, "Star Interrupted: The Reinvention of James Stewart," in Kylo-Patrick R. Hart (ed.), *Film and Television Stardom*, (Newcastle: Cambridge Scholars Publishing, 2008), 43–57.
33 Ibid., 43.
34 Ibid.
35 Ibid., 51.
36 Colleen Glenn, "The Traumatized Veteran: A New Look at Jimmy Stewart's Post World War II Vertigo," *Quarterly Review of Film and Video*, vol. 31 no. 1, (2014), 27–41.
37 Ibid., 28.
38 Ibid.
39 Ibid., 33.
40 Ibid., 35.
41 Willard Weller, *The Veteran Comes Back* (New York: Dryden Press, 1944), 84–90, 115.
42 Eliot, *Jimmy Stewart*, 286.
43 Eliot, *Jimmy Stewart*, 286.
44 On Stewart's teaching Sullavan to fly, see *The Mortal Storm* issue of *The Lobby* (1940) distributed by the MGM Publicity Department, "Mortal Storm" file, NARA, College Park, MD.
45 "Interview with Jimmy Stewart," Papers of Howard Teichmann, Box 59, folder 1. 1980–1981. Library of Congress. Manuscript Division.
46 For full discussion of these events, see Thomas Doherty, *Show Trial. Hollywood, HUAC, and the Birth of the Blacklist* (New York: Columbia University Press, 2018).
47 See Eksteins on the aviation risks of the 1920s, 263–4.
48 See my "Phyllis Bottome's *The Mortal Storm* in Film and Controversy," *The Space Between*, vol. 6 no. 1 (2010), 45 for the relationship between *The Mortal Storm* and *The Philadelphia Story*.
49 Movie schedules in the *New York Times* of a decade ago cautioned television viewers about the references to "non-Aryans" under attack by the Nazis

in the film. In the scholarly literature, see for example the discussion in Bernard F. Dick, *The Star-Spangled Screen. The American World War II Film* (Lexington: University of Kentucky Press, 1985), 70–2 on the use of "Jew" vs. "non-Aryan." Dick was unaware about the conflict over which term to use in the film.

50   Susan Dunn, *A Blueprint for War. FDR and the Hundred Days That Mobilized America* (New Haven: Yale University Press, 2018), 142.

51   See Laurance Tribe, "Constrain the Court-Without Crippling It," *The New York Review of Books* (July 27, 2023), 53. Tribe discusses Jeffrey Toobin's research into this matter. See also Toobin's *Homegrown: Timothy McVeigh and the Rise of Right-Wing Extremism* (New York: Simon and Schuster, 2023.

ESSAY ON SOURCES

Inspired by David Welky's "Essay on Sources" in *The Moguls and the Dictators* (pp. 395–403), I am offering a discussion of the most relevant sources I have utilized in a discursive format rather than an alphabetical listing of undifferentiated items. While my focus has remained on one film of 1940, *The Mortal Storm* and the novel that preceded it, at the same time the novel and its film drew on issues that go as far back as the mid-nineteenth century. Bottome also wrote in response to the controversies of the interwar period which in turn cannot be understood outside of the First World War itself. Below are some of the sources, on those and related subjects, that contributed the most to this book.

European Archives

Berlin. I sought information on Georg Gyssling, the German Consul in Los Angeles, 1933–41 in two archives: the **Foreign Ministry Archive** and the **Bundesarchiv**. According to Gyssling's personnel record in the Foreign Ministry Archive, upon termination of his diplomatic career in Los Angeles, he returned to Germany where he contributed to the counterfeit operation to duplicate American currency, a commodity he must have known well. See also Steven Ross, *Hitler in Los Angeles. How Jews Foiled Nazi Plots against Hollywood and America* (New York: Bloomsbury Press, 2017), pp. 336–8 on Gyssling's post-American career. According to an anonymous archivist in the *Bundesarchiv*, direct incendiary hits on the Ministry of Propaganda in April 1945 destroyed Gyssling's reports from Los Angeles which starting in 1936 went directly to Goebbels rather than to the Foreign Ministry. That particular bombing raid thus did irreparable damage to both the History of Hollywood and the History of German cinema.

London. Bottome's personal papers can be found in the **Manuscripts Reading Room of the British Library**. She was a meticulous correspondent, that is, a kind of self-promoter through letter writing. She kept copies, even alternative drafts, of the letters she sent. Much of it is typed, but her handwriting is readily decipherable. I am convinced from the amount of detail in the second volume of her autobiography that she must have kept a diary, but none exists in the material I consulted. Her correspondence with Duff Cooper, Rabbi Eisendrath, and some of her closest friends is available here. There is also much on her relationship to the Viennese depth psychologist Alfred Adler. Her hectic, intense, at times angry negotiations with MGM to purchase the rights to *The Mortal Storm* can be found here as well.

National Archives. Most of what I know about British codebreakers in the First World War, I found in unpublished memoirs here. An archivist warned me that all but 10 percent of the material on Hollywood and Britain had been culled. Much, I discovered, on their trade relations and British movie censorship remains.

Colindale. RAF Archives. According to Claudine West's obituary in *The Times*, she had five brothers who served in the RAF. Their surname would have been Godber; but, alas, I found no service record of any of her siblings in the RAF archive.

US Archives

Harvard University. Houghton Library. I consulted the diary of William R. Castle, diplomat, close friend, and confidant of Lindbergh. He was also well-connected with the Republican Party and a member of its National Committee. If he was involved in the telephone call to Lindbergh on June 17, 1940, inviting him to the upcoming national convention, Castle makes no mention of it in his otherwise-candid diary.

Yale University. Sterling Memorial Library. Manuscripts and Archives. Lindbergh's diaries as well as those of his wife Anne Morrow can be found here. The permission of their daughter, Reeve Lindbergh, is required to consult them. Both Lindbergh and his wife saw their diaries ultimately as public documents and worked carefully on their presentation. Nonetheless, the extent of Lindbergh's antisemitism, well-documented in his diaries, has never appeared in print. His *The Wartime Journals of Charles A. Lindbergh* (New York: Harcourt, Brace, Jovanovich, Inc., 1970) contains little of the evolution in his intensifying antisemitism through the course of 1941.

Beineke Rare Book and Manuscript Library. Contains Bottome's correspondence with an often-incoherent Ezra Pound, with whom she remained close.

Princeton University. Seeley G. Mudd Manuscript Library. Contains the archive of the White Committee (1940–1), the pro-interventionist (in the form of aid to Britain) organization named for William Allen White, editor of the *Emporia Gazette*. The records for each branch, altogether hundreds throughout the country, are extensive. Most useful for my purposes were those of the Cleveland Branch which document plans for Jimmy Stewart's visit and the involvement with it of Chairman Marjorie Fry.

Washington, D.C. U.S. Library of Congress. Manuscript Reading Room. Papers and correspondence of William Allen White. Some duplication of the White Committee material in the Seeley Mudd Library at Princeton, but White's own correspondence as a promoter of *The Mortal Storm* proved invaluable. The unpublished version of Harold Ickes diary contains reference to his extensive movie viewing in 1940 not found in the three-volume published version (see below). Teichmann Papers. Teichmann conducted interviews with Henry Fonda and those close to him, including Jimmy Stewart, in 1979–80.

National Archives and Records Administration (NARA). Washington, D.C. Contains the records of the Senate Interstate Commerce Committee (ICC) under Burton K. Wheeler's chairmanship. That collection includes the papers generated by Senate Resolution 152, creating the Subcommittee to Investigate Propaganda in Hollywood. The public's reaction to the investigation can be gauged by the hundreds of letters Wheeler's office received. **College Park.** Contains extensive State Department documents relevant to Hollywood. There were three boxes alone devoted to *The Mortal Storm,* including the disintegrating copies of *The Lobby* that I was able to consult.

Los Angeles. Margaret Herrick Library of the Academy of Motion Picture Arts and Sciences. Contains the papers of the Production Code Administration (PCA) which complement censorship materials found in the National Archives (London). The library contains an extensive script collection. I consulted twenty versions of the script for *The Mortal Storm*, alone. It possesses hundreds of stills of the film taken of the sets and the actors, on and off camera. The photos remain in pristine condition, save the bent and torn one of Professor Roth's study, I would argue passed repeatedly around Mayer's inner circle and the focus of the debate over use of the word "Jew" in the film. These photos are unavailable for reproduction.

Eugene, Oregon. University of Oregon. Special Collections and University Archives. The Papers of John T. Flynn, head of the New York Chapter of America First and organizer of the ICC Subcommittee Hearings on Propaganda in Hollywood (September 1941). Flynn's extensive correspondence along with details of the planning for the hearings and their organization. Flynn regarded the hearings as a chance to unveil the propaganda machine of Hollywood as opposed to the insistence of John

Wheeler, who regarded *The Mortal Storm* as the most dangerous of the propaganda films and therefore, he insisted, what should be the primary target of the ICC subcommittee.

Duluth, MN. Duluth Public Library. Newspaper Clipping Collection on Sidney Buchman. Contains over 100 clippings from the local press on Buchman and his family dating from the late nineteenth century, meticulously maintained by Librarian David Ouse.

Papers of Sidney Franklin (SAF) held in private hands. Fifty-six bankers' boxes of memos and correspondence relevant to Franklin's career at MGM. His work with Claudine West is detailed as is the salary information for every film he produced. One can follow the trajectory of West's career (1936–43) by her increasing salary in those years. By the end of her life, she was among the highest paid writers in Hollywood. Franklin's family is currently in negotiation with the Margaret Herrick Library for purchase of this most valuable collection. It was a privilege to consult it.

Sources by Topic

Overview and Background. On the First World War and interwar revisionism, that is, the movement to absolve Germany after the Treaty of Versailles, I would recommend Annika Mombauer, *The Origins of the First World War. Controversies and Consensus* (London: Pearson Education Limited, 2002). It is excellent on the German "innocence campaign," which seduced a whole generation of American historians.

Must reading on German motivations in the First World War, the war's aftermath, and the whole *zeitgeist* of the interwar period is Modris Eksteins, *Rites of Spring. The Great War and the Birth of the Modern Age* (Boston: Houghton Mifflin Co., 1989). An astute cultural history with much insight into the Lindbergh phenomenon as well.

On the significance of Lincoln and the Civil War for American popular culture and politics in the interwar period, see Barry Schwartz, *Abraham Lincoln and the Forge of National Memory* (Chicago: University of Chicago Press, 2000) and Merrill Schlier, "Mr. Lincoln Goes to Washington: The Two Lincolns, Monuments, and the Preservation of Patriarchy," *Quarterly Review of Film and Video*, vol. 31 (2014), 452–68.

The best book, I believe, on the origins of modern antisemitism is George L. Mosse, *The Crisis of German Ideology: The Intellectual Origins of the Third Reich* (New York: Schocken Books, 1981). On the Dreyfus Case, I turned to fiction: Robert Harris, *An Officer and a Spy* (New York: Vintage Books, 2014). For an overview of antisemitism in the United States, the best book remains, Leonard Dinnerstein, *Anti-Semitism in America* (Oxford: Oxford University Press, 1994).

The subject of Hollywood is gargantuan. I consulted all the secondary sources Welky lists in his "Essay on Sources," most published in the 1990s. But much of that has been superseded by Welky's own *The Moguls and the Dictators* (2008) and by Thomas Dougherty, *Hollywood and Hitler, 1933–1939* (New York: Columbia University Press, 2013). Even more recently two excellent source collections have been published: Rocky Lang and Barbara Hall, *Letters from Hollywood. Inside the Private World of Classic American Moviemaking* (New York: Abrams, 2019) and Jeanine Basinger and Sam Wasson, *Hollywood. The Oral History* (New York: HarperCollins, 2022). The latter, while fascinating, cries out for an index.

Rescuing Claudine West. After Phyllis Bottome, Claudine West is the central figure in the story of *The Mortal Storm* as a film; yet there is nothing reliable about her in print. Mistakes large and small abound regarding her role as the primary writer of the adaptation of Bottome's novel as well as her writing of *Mrs. Miniver* and her contributions to other films of the time such as *Ninotchka* and *Random Harvest*. She very nearly wrote Greer Garson's career. Disappointing, for example, is Mark H. Glancy's *When Hollywood Loved Britain. The Hollywood "British" Film, 1939–45* (Manchester: Manchester University Press, 1999), which addresses West's contributions but is filled with errors, such as she merely "assembled" the scenes provided by other writers.

I have tried to restore West to her rightful place in the history of Hollywood but can offer no further reading beyond my own: this book and the articles mentioned below. West's house, high in Beverly Hills, recently changed hands for $4 million. Surrounded by foliage and a carefully maintained garden, the house, with the upstairs bedroom overlooking the street where she often wrote, looks very much as it did when cared for by the Mexican couple she hired as cook and gardener. Past photos confirm: it looks the same as when she bequeathed it to Dr. Blanche Slagerman in April 1943.

Phyllis Bottome. Of the material in print by or about Bottome, one should begin with her three-volume autobiography: *Search for a Soul* (New York: Reynal & Hitchcock, 1948), *The Challenge* (New York: Harcourt, Brace and Co., 1953), and *The Goal* (London: Faber and Faber, 1962). *The Goal* is by far the most important of the three, providing insights into the origin of her major fiction, her relations with her husband, Alfred Adler and his school of psychologists, and other close friends. As a kind of fourth volume to her autobiography, there is *From the Life*. See especially the essay on her grandmother, Margaret Bottome.

Bottome's fiction is extensive. Recommended, in addition to *The Mortal Storm* (Evanston: Northwestern University Press, 1998 [1937/1938]), are the novels *Old Wine* (Evanston: Northwestern University Press, 1998 [1925]), *Private Worlds* (London: Penguin Books, Limited, 1934/1937), and *Under the Skin* (New York: Harcourt, Brace and Co., 1950). *Under the Skin* permits one to compare the continuities and discontinuities in Bottome's thinking on a number of questions before and after the Second World War. Phyllis Lassner and Marilyn Hoder-Salmon have provided excellent introductions to the Northwestern University Press reprints of *Old Wine* and *The Mortal Storm*. In addition to their astute treatment of those two works, their essays can serve as an introduction to all Bottome's fiction.

The secondary literature on Phyllis Bottome is limited. Pam Hirsch's *The Constant Liberal* (London: Quartet, 2010) provides an overview of her life and work. It is especially good on her British heritage. I also recommend my first essay on *The Mortal Storm*, "Phyllis Bottome's *The Mortal Storm*: Film and Controversy," *The Space Between: Literature and Culture, 1914–1945*, vol. 6, no. 1 (2010), pp. 39–58 for an overview along with one I wrote with Phyllis Lassner titled "An anti-Nazi Special Relationship: British Writing, Hollywood Filmmaking and *The Mortal Storm* (1940)," pp. 49–68 in Nathan Abrams, *Hidden in Plain Sight. Jews and Jewishness in British Film, Television, and Popular Culture* (Evanston: Northwestern University Press, 2016). Most recently I published an essay on Bottome's symbiotic relationship with Alfred Adler titled "Phyllis Bottome—An Intermodernist under Treatment in the Age of Modernism: Tuberculosis and the Embrace of Alfred Adler's Depth Psychology," *The Space Between: Literature and Culture, 1914–1945*, vol. 17 (2021), no pagination. See also Phyllis Lassner's very fine *British Women Writers of World War II. Battlegrounds of Their Own* (New York: St. Martin's Press, Inc., 1998) and Judy Suh's *Fascism and Anti-Fascism in Twentieth-Century British Fiction* (New York: Palgrave Macmillan, 2009).

Bottome drew on *Uncle Tom's Cabin* in writing *The Mortal Storm*. I found most helpful for background on Stowe's novel and its impact, David S. Reynolds, *Mightier Than the Sword. Uncle Tom's Cabin and the Battle for America* (New York: W.W. Norton & Co., Inc., 2011) and Eric Foner, *Gateway to Freedom. The Hidden History of the Underground Railroad* (New York: W.W. Norton & Co., Inc., 2015).

Franklin Roosevelt and American Politics on the Eve of War. My go-to biography on FDR was Vols. 4 and 5 of Kenneth S. Davis's magisterial account of the life: *FDR. Into the Storm, 1937–1940* and *FDR. The War President, 1940–1943* (New York: Random House, 1993 and 2000). I would also single out Samuel I. Rosenman, *Working with Roosevelt* (New York: Harper and Brothers, 1952). Rosenman was FDR's main speechwriter for seventeen years. Robert E. Sherwood, *Roosevelt and Hopkins. An Intimate History* (New York: Enigma Books, 2008). Sherwood also wrote speeches for FDR, and Hopkins was the president's closest confidant on the eve of war. Harold Ickes's perspective was always enlightening. See his three-volume *Secret Diary*, especially vol. 3, *The Lowering Clouds, 1939–1941* (New York: Simon and Schuster, 1954). On the 1940 election and numerous related topics, I recommend Charles Peters, *Five Days in Philadelphia* (New York: Public Affairs, 2005), Susan Dunn, *1940. FDR, Willkie, Lindbergh, Hitler—the Election Amid the Storm* (New Haven: Yale University Press, 2013), and Doris Kearns Goodwin, *No Ordinary Time* (New York: Simon and Schuster, Inc., 1994).

On the isolationist movement in general, I would recommend Justus D. Doenecke (ed.), *In Danger Undaunted. The Anti-Interventionist Movement of 1940–41 as Revealed in the Papers of the America First Committee* (Stanford: Hoover Institution Press, 1990) along with two works by the historian of American isolationism on the eve of the Second World War, Wayne S. Cole, *Senator Gerald P. Nye and American Foreign Relations* (Minneapolis: University of Minnesota Press, 1962) and *Roosevelt and the Isolationists, 1932–45* (Lincoln: University of Nebraska Press, 1983). Also important on the isolationists vs. interventionists debates, see the *Congressional Record*, vol. 84–7, 1939–January 1942 (76th–77th Congresses).

Charles Lindbergh and **Burton K. Wheeler** figured among the president's most prominent opponents. Neither could be said to have approved of *The Mortal Storm*. For anyone interested in Lindbergh, two books are essential: A. Scott Berg, *Lindbergh* (New York: G.P. Putnam's Sons, 1998) and *The Wartime Journals of Charles A. Lindbergh* (New York: Harcourt, Brace, Jovanovich, Inc., 1970). Both diverge on the extent of Lindbergh's antisemitism to be found in his unpublished diaries located at Yale. I would also recommend Robert Hessen (ed.), *Berlin Alert. The Memoirs and Reports of Truman Smith* (Stanford: Hoover Institution Press, 1984). As a complement to the latter, Alfred M. Beck, *Hitler's Ambivalent Attaché. Lt. Gen. Friedrich von Boetticher in America, 1933–1941* (Washington: Potomac Books, Inc., 2006). Lindbergh's close friend Truman Smith worked directly with von Boetticher. There is much on Lindbergh in volumes IX, X XI, and XII of *The Documents of German Foreign Policy*, Series D (Washington: U.S. Government Printing Office, 1956–8). See also, Edith Gottsacker, "German-American Relations, 1938–1941 and the Influence of Hans Thomsen," Ph.D. Dissertation: Georgetown University, 1968.

Wheeler was a determined opponent of both Hollywood and the president. On Wheeler's battle with Roosevelt over the Supreme Court, best is Jeff Shesol, *Supreme Power* (New York: W.W. Norton & Co., 2010). On his battle with Roosevelt over intervention, see Marc C. Johnson, "Franklin D. Roosevelt, Burton K. Wheeler, and the Great Debate," *Montana the Magazine of Western History* (Winter 2012), pp. 3–22. There is also Wheeler's autobiography with Paul F. Healy, *Yankee from the West. The Candid Story of the Freewheeling U.S. Senator from Montana* (Garden

City: Doubleday & Co., Inc., 1962). His daughter, Elizabeth Wheeler Colman, wrote a biography of her mother with the provocative title *Mrs. Wheeler Goes to Washington* (Helena, MT: Falcon Press Publishing, Inc., 1989), showing a measure of defiance in response to the Capra film starring Jimmy Stewart. Most significant of all for *The Mortal Storm*, Wheeler gave the hearings on propaganda in Hollywood a home with his Interstate Commerce Committee. The transcript of the hearings is available as "Propaganda in Motion Pictures," Hearings Before a Subcommittee of the Committee on Interstate Commerce, U.S. Senate, Seventy-Seventh Congress on S. Res. 152 (September 9–26, 1941) (Washington: U.S. Government Printing Office, 1942). The Academy of Motion Picture Arts and Sciences published a collection of newspaper clippings chronicling the press coverage and response to the hearings: Academy of Motion Picture Arts and Sciences, Press Clipping File on the Senate Sub-Committee on War Film Hearings, multiple volumes, August 1 through October 15, 1941, ed. Donald Gledhill (Academy Executive Secretary). Of the growing secondary literature on the hearings, I would recommend the still highly relevant, Steven Carr, *Hollywood and Anti-Semitism. A Cultural History up to World War II* (Cambridge: Cambridge University Press, 2001) along with James E. McMillan, "McFarland and the Movies: The 1941 Senate Motion Picture Hearings," *The Journal of Arizona History*, vol. 29, no. 3 (Autumn 1988), pp. 277–302 and John E. Moser, "'Gigantic Engines of Propaganda': The 1941 Senate Investigation of Hollywood," *Historian*, vol. 63, no. 4 (Summer 2001), pp. 731–51. Finally, must reading on the hearings are the papers of *Time* magazine correspondent Frank McNaughton in the Harry S. Truman Presidential Library, generously supplied to me by David Welky.

Margaret Sullavan and Jimmy Stewart. The most important book on Sullavan remains the memoir of her daughter Brook Hayward titled *Haywire* (New York: Alfred A. Knopf, 1977). I also found informative the biography by Jan Herman of her former husband, William Wyler, *The Life of William Wyler. A Talent for Trouble* (New York: De Capo Press, 1997). There are two recent books on Stewart's wartime service: Starr Smith, *Jimmy Stewart, Bomber Pilot* (St. Paul: Zenith Press, 2005) and Robert Matzen, *Mission. Jimmy Stewart and the Fight for Europe* (Pittsburgh: GoodKnight Books, 2016). See also Marc Eliot, *Jimmy Stewart. A Biography* (New York: Harmony Books, 2006) and Scott Eyman, *Hank and Jim. The Fifty-Year Friendship of Henry Fonda and James Stewart* (New York: Simon and Schuster, 2017). But most important on Stewart are the articles by Tim Palmer, "Star Interrupted: The Reinvention of James Stewart" in *Film and Television Stardom*, edited by Patrick R. Hart (Newcastle: Cambridge Scholars Publishing, 2008), pp. 43–57 and Colleen Glenn, "The Traumatized Veteran: A New Look at Jimmy Stewart's Post World War II Vertigo," *Quarterly Review of Film and Video*, vol. 31 (2014), pp. 27–41.

INDEX

1936 Olympics 14, 49
1936 presidential election 14, 82, 83

Abe Lincoln in Illinois 3
Ablow, Rachel 55
abolitionism 4, 45–8, 50–1, 59, 68
Academy Awards 24 n. 67, 213, 230
Academy of Motion Picture Arts and Sciences 194, 213, 214
Adler, Alfred 3, 28, 30, 35–9, 49–50, 89–91, 142, 210, 230
    antisemitism and 49–50
    biography of 83
    as character in *Old Wine* 35–6
    concept of sibling rivalry 28, 39–45
    conversion to Christianity 49, 72 n. 80
    Individual Psychology of 36–9. *See also* Adlerian psychology
    as model for Roth 138
    personal and political in 70 n. 48
    sibling rivalry and 70 n. 48
    visit to Cardiff Mental Hospital 39
Adler, Raisa 49–50, 72 n. 80
Adlerian analysis 47, 48
Adlerian psychology 36–45, 64, 89–91, 292
African Americans 3, 46–7, 55
All Quiet on the Western Front 165, 238, 241, 273, 280
Allies 12
Ambler, Eric, *Background to Danger* 94
America First Committee (AFC) 2, 220, 237, 242, 249, 252–7, 259, 262–3, 275, 277, 297
American Film Center 242
American Revolution 55

Americanism 80
Anderson, Ellis 141, 154
Anglo-American cooperation, beginning of 215
Anschluss 54, 67–8, 77, 78, 83
Anthony, Susan B. 59
anti-German sentiment 190, 193
anti-Nazi films 103–4, 116–17, 136, 138–9, 151, 166–7, 231, 241–3
anti-Nazism 9–10, 87, 142, 235. *See also* anti-Nazi films
antisemitism 2, 5, 67–8, 76–80, 141, 154, 177, 243, 250, 267, 277–8
    Bottome and 29–36, 41
    depiction of 179
    Dreyfus case 65–8
    fears of arousing 96
    Flynn and 256
    increases with onset of Great Depression 96
    isolationism and 250, 253–61, 279
    Lindbergh and 191, 208–9, 240, 251–3, 262–3, 274–5, 277
    notion of Jewish conspiracy 208–9, 269–70
    Sullavan and 168
    US Congress and 193, 194, 253–61, 263–5, 271–5
appeasement 4, 91, 92, 98, 187–8
aristocrats 57–8
Arizona 218
Arliss, George 127
Arnold, Edward 197, 200
Ashurst, Henry Fountain 260
The Atlantic 292
Austria 54, 56, 67, 102

Babi Yar, massacre of 271
backlash, fear of 152
Bankhead, John Hollis II, 186
Barkley, Alban 195–6, 202, 219
Barnes, Harry Elmer 12, 15–16
Barnes, Howard 9, 199
Baruch, Bernard 260
The Battle Hymn of the Republic 4
Bäumer, Paul 11
Bavarian Soviet Socialist Republic or "Red Republic" 85
Beckett, Scott 157, 158, 246 n. 15
Beecher, Henry Ward 47
Bennett, Joan 213, 214
Bennett, Todd 286–7 n. 140
Beotticher, Friedrich von 276–7
Berg, Scott 210, 251, 252
Berg-Allenberg agency 105
Berlin, Irving 239
Berman, Pandro 117–18
The Best Years of Our Lives 289, 291
Bethlehem Steel 13
Billington, Louis 73–4 n. 103
Billington, Rosamund 73–4 n. 103
The Birth of a Nation 2, 19, 52
Bishop of Chichester 76
blacks, in Canada 55
blitzkrieg 173–4, 177, 187, 233
Block, Al 152, 159, 162
Blockade 16, 24 n. 67, 213
Boehnel, Bill 9, 15–16, 199
Bone, Homer T. 260
Borah, William E. 16, 192, 259–60, 272
borders 52–5
Borzage, Frank 147 n. 56, 157, 171, 172–7, 179, 264
Bottome, Francis 47
Bottome, Margaret MacDonald 4, 46–7, 217
Bottome, Phyllis 17, 34, 156, 212, 216, 235. *See also* Bottome, Phyllis, works of
  Adler and 3, 28, 30, 35, 36–9, 142, 210
  Adlerian analysis with Seif 36–9, 47, 48
  Adlerian psychology and 36–9, 47, 48, 292

  agenda of 166
  Americans and 68
  antisemitism and 29–36, 76–80
  aristocrats in 57–8
  battle over substitution of "non-Aryan" for Jew 144
  biography of Adler 83
  Carrel and 210–1
  closing deal with MGM 104–6
  consulting on film 122–32, 137–8
  creative vision of 19
  depth psychology and 138
  as Dreyfusard 65–8
  education of 65–6, 67
  Eisendrath and 95–101, 243–5
  escapes Vienna before *Anschluss* 78, 83
  fascination with Civil War 229–30
  FDR and 216–17
  feminism and 58–61
  formative years of 291–2
  Franklin and 232, 243, 293, 295, 300
  Hollywood and 80, 213, 214
  invited to White House 217–18
  involvement in film production 105–6, 116, 122–32, 123, 212
  Jewish community and 95–101
  Jewish question and 65–8
  on June 20, 1940 212–15
  learns she was duped 243–5
  leaves Munich for Vienna 48
  on lecture tour 95, 217
  lectures given by 212
  Little, Brown & Co. and 7, 8, 19, 83, 86, 87, 102, 171, 243, 292–3
  Magnin and 100–1
  Mayer and 170–1, 243
  Mitchell and 9–10
  mixed-race characters in 55–7
  as novelist of war 27–74
  Nuremberg Laws and 29, 31
  perception of Civil War 4
  protests changes to adaptation 168–72, 270, 300
  public lectures by 92–3, 94, 98, 99–100

redemption in 62–5
revisions to sell film to Hollywood 75–6
Sandburg and 4
selling film to Hollywood 75–113
sense of mission and 126
servants in 61–2
short-lived fame of 292
sibling conflict and 28, 37–8
Stowe and 51–2
success of 27
in Swiss Alps 40–1
Swiss Alps and 132
Thompson and 76, 77–8, 107 n. 23
tour in United States 68
tuberculosis and 71 n. 55
US South and 45–8
views *The Mortal Storm* release 212–15
visit to Cardiff Mental Hospital 39
visit to United States 45–8, 68
visits to United States 76
Wanger and 220
Watkins, Ann 293
working for British Ministry of Information 9–10, 22 n. 17, 125–6, 146 n. 34, 217, 244, 264, 292
World War I and 27, 38, 125–6
Bottome, Phyllis, works of
The Depths of Prosperity 77
Devil's Due 37, 41, 132
The Goal 17, 171–2, 293
Heart of a Child 293
"I Accuse" 78
From the Life 107 n. 23
"Love and Marriage" lecture 99–100
Masks and Faces 171
The Mortal Storm (novel). See *The Mortal Storm* (novel) (Bottome)
Old Wine 27, 29–36, 41, 46, 67, 77, 293
Private Worlds 3, 27, 28–9, 37, 39–45, 75, 76, 88, 90, 213
Search for a Soul 38, 293
Under the Skin 294
"What Is Propaganda?" 92–3

Bottome, William 47
Boyer, Charles 127
Breen, Joseph I. 153–4, 156, 159, 162, 169, 175
Brent, Earl 162, 175
Britain 1, 4, 17–18, 54–5, 65, 186, 275, 296–7
  aid to 207
  American attitudes toward 178
  Anglo-American cooperation and 215
  Anschluss and 67–8
  appeasement in 91, 92
  British Board of Censors 153
  deteriorating situation in 187
  FDR and 215, 216
  Fugitive Slave Act and 50
  German threat to 17–18, 187, 196, 202, 204, 213–15, 220, 233, 250
  political rallies in support of 236–43
  propaganda and 276
  public attitudes in 27
  rally for 236–43, 250
  Stewart speaks on behalf of 236–43
  Stowe and 50, 68
  supported by US South 188
  war effort and 125–6
Britain-Jewish collusion, accusations of 264
British intelligence 215
British-Jewish collusion, accusations of 269, 276
British Navy 215, 239
Brontë, Charlotte, *Jane Eyre* 28–9, 39–40, 44, 45, 84
Brooke-Wilkinson, J. 153, 154
Brooks, C. Wayland 260, 272
Brown Shirts 119, 135–6, 177
Brownlow, Kevin 145 n. 30
Buchan, John 22 n. 17, 125–6, 146 n. 34
Buchan, Susan 126
Buchman, Sidney 198, 199, 300
Buffalo Courier-Express 79
Burdekin, Katharine 19, 25 n. 81
Burger, Alex 241

INDEX 315

Burke, Edward 187
Byrnes, James F. 191

Caldwell, Idaho 188
Canada 54–5, 95, 97
   blacks in 55
   Fugitive Slave Act and 50, 52–3, 55
   war spirit in 93
capitalism 86, 87
Capra, Frank 118, 194, 195, 196, 197, 198, 199, 200, 201, 218, 230
Cardozo, Benjamin 96
Carrel, Alexis 209, 210–1, 277
Casablanca 290
Castle, William R. 208–9, 211, 218, 243, 251, 278
censorship 104, 125, 137, 138–9, 151, 153–4, 198, 243–5, 274, 278, 294
Chamberlain, Neville 80, 292
Chaplin, Charlie 18, 104, 109 n. 54, 152, 166, 236, 241, 265, 267, 272, 278
Chic, Chas 136
Chicago, Illinois, banning of *Professor Mamlock* in 151
Chicago Tribune 9, 16
China 202
Christian Science Monitor 195, 273
Churchill, Winston 20, 97, 126, 146 n. 37, 215, 219, 292
Civil War 2–4, 229–31
   analogy with World War I 52, 278
   fascination with 229–30
   FDR and 230
   The Mortal Storm (film) and 230–1
Civil War analogy 278
   FDR and 230
   The Mortal Storm (film) and 230–1
Clark, Bennett Champ 202, 254, 260, 261, 263–5, 266, 267, 268–9, 272, 273, 276, 281 n. 27, 281–2 n. 30
Clark, D. Worth xiii, 1, 219, 242, 255, 257–60, 263–9, 271–4, 277, 278, 279, 280
Clark, Miriam 281–2 n. 30
Clark, Mrs. 254

Cleveland, Ohio 236–43, 280, 297
Cleveland Plain Dealer 237, 238, 243
codebreaking 124–5, 126, 146 n. 37
Cohn brothers 195
Colbert, Claudette 75, 213
Colston Leigh lecture bureau 76
Columbia Pictures 195, 220
Communism 80–3, 84, 85–7, 95, 119, 139, 151, 198, 298
Communist Party 198
concentration camps 77, 79, 116, 119, 141, 159, 160, 179. *See also specific camps*
Confessions of a Nazi Spy 103, 115, 134, 169, 173, 289
Congress of American Mothers [Against War] 188
Congressional Record 189
conscription 185, 187, 188, 205, 207, 219, 239, 255
Cooper, Duff 75, 92, 95, 244, 292
Corbaley, Helen 102, 112 n. 134, 152, 156, 158
Court of St. James 18
Creel, George 193
Cromwell, John 3
Cronin, A. J. 95
Crookes, Beth 147 n. 56
Crowther, Bosley 8, 9, 10, 13, 14, 15, 16, 22 n. 8, 199, 211, 220, 253, 289
Culver City, California 232, 266
Cummings, Jack 118
Czechoslovakia 54, 98, 103, 115, 178

Dachau 119, 165
Dale, Esther 164
Darius, Mellie 66, 67
Davis, Kenneth 107 n. 26, 210
Delano family 217
Democratic National Convention 185, 191, 216, 219
Democratic Party 20, 82, 134, 191, 192, 200, 202
Denmark 19
depth psychology 28, 36–9, 44, 138, 230
Der Angriff 49

Der Stürmer 48–9
Des Moines, Iowa, AFC rally in 252, 253, 262–3, 269, 275, 277, 280
Detroit, Michigan 241
Dick, Bernard 102
Die Grosse Politik der Europaischen Kabinette (*The High Politics of the European Cabinets*) 12
Dieckhoff, Hans 189–90
Dies, Martin 80, 82
Dietz, Howard 267
Dinter, Arthur 48
Disraeli, Benjamin 156
Dodd, William E. 96
Doherty, Thomas 139
Donat, Robert 127
Donovan, "Wild Bill" 215
Douglas, Melvyn 297
Downey, Sheridan 270
Dozier, William 105, 290, 291
Drax, Admiral Reginald 80
Dreyfus case 65–8, 127, 152
Dumont, Hervé 147 n. 56, 175, 176
Dunn, Susan 203, 300
Dupont 13, 255
Dymer, Ukraine 271

Eichelberger, Clark 206–7, 237
Einstein, Albert 140, 157
Eisendrath, Maurice N. 95–104, 106, 122, 243–5
Eksteins, Modris 10–1, 18, 19, 22–3 n. 27, 298
Eliot, Marc 196, 236
émigrés 140–1, 160–1, 165. *See also* Jewish refugees
Emile Zola 67
empathy, transition to 55
Emporia Gazette 206
Englebrecht, Helmuth C. 13–14
Entente 20
Erens, Patricia 96
Escape 1, 270
eugenics 210–1
Evian Conference 15–16, 78, 107 n. 26
Eyman, Scott 152, 179, 258, 284 n. 78

Faber, Geoffrey 7, 8
Faber & Faber 68
Fairbanks, Douglas, Jr. 166, 236, 250, 297
Fallada, Hans 173
Farley, James 195
fascism 9, 15, 17, 44, 77, 200, 202, 205, 231, 239, 256. *See also* Nazism
Fay, Sidney Bradshaw 12
FBI 193, 215, 254
Federal Theater Project 85, 109 n. 54
feminism 58–61, 73–4 n. 103, 87, 142, 143–4
Ferguson, W. K. 167
Ferguson, W. R. 232–3, 234, 235, 246 n. 15
Fidler, Jimmie 265–6, 278
film. *See also* film industry; war films; *specific films*
  anti-Nazi 103–4, 116–17, 136, 138–9, 151, 166–7, 231, 241–3
  German Expressionist 141
  power of 125–6
  propaganda and 125–6
  Soviet 138
  Weimar 141
Film Daily 273
film industry 220, 274. *See also* Hollywood
  advertising and 232
  censorship and 104, 125, 137, 138–9, 151, 153–4, 198, 243–5, 274, 278, 294. *See also* Production Code
  Production Code and 104, 129, 137, 138–9, 151, 153, 154. *See also* PCA (Production Code Administration)
  race laws and 50
  spies in 193–4
  studio system and 198. *See also* moguls; *specific studios*
  trade papers of 231–2
  US politics and 1
Finnish American communities 198
Fisher, George 265–6

Fisher, H. A. L. 212
Fitzgerald, Penelope 125
Flight Command 270
Florida 188
Flynn, John T. 256–9, 263–6, 274, 275, 276, 277
folk culture 63
Fonda, Henry 236, 297
Forbes, Dora Delano 217
Forbes Dennis, Ernan 28, 31, 46, 48, 80, 83, 92–3, 95, 102, 212, 216–17, 293–4
    acquaintance with Delano and Roosevelt families 217
    Adler and 35, 38–41
    invited to White House 217–18
    Thompson and 77–8
Ford, Ann 86
Ford, Henry 252
Ford, John 3
Foreign Affairs 78
Foreign Correspondent 241
Fortune magazine 13
Foster, Lewis R., *The Gentleman from Montana* 196
Four Sons 268
France 12, 65, 233
    antisemitism in 65–8
    German aggression toward 1, 186–7, 196, 202, 204, 214
    Jewish question in 66
    Treaty of Versailles and 12
Franco, Francisco 16
Franco-Prussian War of 1870–1 66
Frankau, Pamela 94
Frankel, Glenn 5
    The Searchers 5
Frankfurter, Felix 96
Franklin, Sidney xii, 19, 233, 237, 239, 301–2 n. 28
    adaptations by 258, 266
    Bottome and 122–32, 123, 131, 168, 169–70, 171–2, 232, 243, 293, 295, 300
    circumspection of 127–8, 130
    location shooting in Switzerland and 135–7

    MGM and 106, 116, 118–20, 141–2, 144, 145 n. 18, 145 n. 30, 147 n. 58, 151, 153, 157, 159, 165
    rejoins production 178–80
    replacement of 172–6, 177
    response to criticism of *The Mortal Storm* 16–17
    seeks permission to film on Mt. Rainier 133–5, 133
    West and 120–1, 120, 121, 124, 174–6, 182 n. 43, 290, 294–5
Fraser, Duncan 186
Freed, Arthur 118
Freeport (IL) *Journal Standard* 271
Freud, Sigmund 44
Friedman, Dave 159
Froeschel, George 136, 141, 154, 156
Fry, Marjorie 237, 238, 241
Fugitive Slave Act 48–51, 52

Gabler, Neal 97, 284 n. 78
Galveston Daily News 231
Garden City Publishing 233
Garner, John Nance 192–3, 219, 254
Garson, Greer 119, 289–90
Gateway to Panama 218
Gau 49
German Communist Party 139
German embassy 188, 189, 190, 203, 240, 276
German Foreign Office 190
German identity 163
German innocence campaign 11–2, 190, 203–4, 275
German question 206
Germany 1–2, 4–5, 9, 10, 14, 15, 17, 96–7, 196. *See also* Nazi Germany
    absolution of 19
    German militarism 205
    image rehabilitation and 12, 14–15
    public attitudes in 27
    public opinion and 193–4
    Reichstag fire in 139
    Treaty of Versailles and 11–2
    war guilt and 259
    World War I and 11–2, 27, 48

Gestapo 49, 51, 163
Gish, Lillian 259
Glenn, Colleen 295–6, 299
Godber, Ivy 145 n. 23. *See also* West, Claudine
Goebbels, Joseph 48–51, 71 n. 65, 85, 91, 165, 166, 186–7, 277
   The Mortal Storm (film) and 48, 72 n. 83
   Rassenschande and 48–9
   Sullavan and 166–7
Goldsmid-Abrahams, Ernest 119
Goldwyn, Samuel 113 n. 142, 289, 291
Gone with the Wind (film) 76, 241
Good-bye, Mr. Chips xii, 118, 119, 122, 123, 290
The Good Earth 122
Goodwin, Doris Kearns 187, 203, 218
Gordon, Donald 7
Goulder, John 141
The Grapes of Wrath 242
Gratten, C. Hartley 12
Graves, Robert 29, 292
Great Depression 2, 96, 229–30
The Great Dictator 18, 109 n. 54, 152, 241, 265, 267, 271, 272
Grey, Edward 203–4, 205
Griffin, William 188
Griffith, D. W. 2, 52, 166
Gulf of Mexico 188
Gyssling, Georg 71 n. 65, 277–8

Hall, J. H. 95
Hanighen, Frank C. 13–14
Harris, Mark 291
Harrison Report 231
Havilland, Olivia de 236
Hays, Will 104, 116, 137, 143, 173, 200, 253
Hayward, Leland 164, 165, 296
hearings on "Propaganda [for war] in Motion Pictures" xii–xiii, 1–2, 253–87, 281 n. 27, 281–2 n. 30, 282–3 n. 54, 283 n. 66, 284 n. 78, 284 n. 87, 286–7 n. 140
   antisemitism and 263–5, 271–5
   German involvement in 275–8
   preparation for 253–6
   repercussions of 279–80
Hebrew Union College 97
Hecht, Ben 96
Heine, Heinrich 140, 156, 157
Hepburn, Katharine 179, 235, 236, 242
Hertog, Susan 210
Herwig, Holger 11
Hilton, James 122
Hindenberg, Paul von 139
Hirsch, Pam 35, 46
Hitchcock, Alfred 295
Hitler, Adolf 8–10, 47, 123, 130, 136, 154, 158, 162, 177, 180, 237, 250, 275
   Anschluss and 54, 67–8, 77, 78, 83
   appointed chancellor 139, 151
   attack on Soviet Union 4–5
   Bottome and 36–7, 217
   failed presidential bid in 1932 13
   interventionism and 214
   invasion of Europe 19, 104, 173–4, 186–7, 188, 234, 249
   isolationism and 189–90
   Jewish emancipation and 140
   Stimson's condemnation of 203, 212
Hoder-Salmon, Marilyn 87, 88
Hodge, Alan 29, 292
Hollywood 5, 80, 151. *See also* film industry
   accused of "missing the bus" 8–9
   advertising and 232
   almost missed the bus 289
   anti-Nazi films and 151, 152, 235, 260
   Bottome and 213, 214
   censorship and 198
   conspiracy theories about 278
   decrees the war over 289–90
   draws back from activism 250
   FDR and 194–201
   Goebbels and 166–7
   historical moment and 186
   influence of 229
   interventionism and 207–8, 215, 219, 220, 236–43

isolationism and 200, 250–3
Jews and 95–6, 250–3, 254
legislation against 199
Lindbergh and 277
McCarthyism and 294, 298
neutrality and 116–17
partnership with Washington 186
patriotism and 253
political realism and 104
politics of 75–6
post-war transformation of 298
preparation for hearings on 253–61
Production Code in 104
propaganda and 91–3, 99, 101–2
red scare and 82–3
selling *The Mortal Storm* to 75–113
spies in 193–4
studio system and 82–3, 198. *See also* moguls; *specific studios*
trade papers and 231–2
US Congress and 194–201, 220. *See also* hearings on "Propaganda [for war] in Motion Pictures"
US Justice Department's antitrust lawsuit and 186, 197
war effort and 1, 236–43
Wheeler and 193–201
Hollywood Anti-Nazi League (HANL) 85, 152, 154, 236
Hollywood Bowl, AFC rally at 255, 259, 260
Hollywood Citizen News 270
Hollywood Reporter 105, 232, 290
Holocaust 96–7, 249, 270–1, 280
Holt, Rush D. 191
Holy Blossom Temple x, 95, 97, 98, 99, 100–1
homosexuality, persecution of 119, 120
Hooker, Isabella Beecher 59
Hoover, Herbert 202
Hoover, J. Edgar 215
Hopkins, Harry 82, 216, 219
Horst Wessel song 161–2, 163, 174, 175, 177
Houghton Mifflin 217
House Un-American Activities Committee (HUAC) 82, 294, 298

Hughes, Charles Evans 193
Hull, Cordell 268
Hutchinson Kansas-News-Hearld 235

Ickes, Harold 82, 133–5, 147 n. 50, 147 n. 51, 147 n. 54, 218–19
Idaho 188
Idaho Falls Post Register 273
I Love You 218
Independent German Social Democratic Party 85
intermarriage 48–50, 142, 166
International Alliance of Theatrical Stage Employees (IATSE) 91–2
internationalism 199
"interracial intercourse" 72 n. 66
Interstate Commerce Committee (ICC) 253–4, 255, 257, 258, 260–1, 263–6, 271
interventionism 15, 185, 193, 209, 214, 220, 273, 278
FDR and 186, 275
Hollywood and 207–8, 215, 219, 220, 236–43
vs. isolationism 2, 177–8, 188–201, 204–5, 219, 236–44, 251–3, 255–6, 258, 279, 296–7, 299
politics of 177–8
Iowa Recorder 235
Irreconcilables 259
Iseiva, Irene 129
isolationism 13–14, 87, 91, 177, 199, 249–50, 276, 277
antisemitism and 250, 253–61, 279
bipartisan support for 190–1
demise of 280
Democratic Party and 191, 202
Hollywood and 200, 250–3
vs. interventionism 2, 177–8, 188–201, 204–5, 219, 236–44, 251–3, 255–6, 258, 279, 296–7, 299
Lindbergh and 197–9, 208–9, 212, 219–20
Republican Party and 190–1
US Congress and 16, 185, 191–2, 203–4, 219, 271–8, 281 n. 27

isolationists, US Congress and 202
Italy 15

J. Arthur Rank 293
Jamaica 293–4
Jameson, Storm 25 n. 81
Janssen, Werner 24 n. 67
Japan 15, 96, 202
The Jazz Singer 96
Jewish-American press 95
Jewish community 95–101
Jewish identity 84–5, 130, 139, 151–9, 269
Jewish question 66, 117, 125, 129–30, 151–72, 176, 177, 180, 250, 251
    Bottome and 33–4, 65–8
    Lindbergh and 252
    PCA and 154
    politics of 151
    as refugee crisis 15–16
    US indifference to 14–17
    woman question and 73–4 n. 103
Jewish refugees 15–16, 77, 78, 116, 140–1, 160–1
Jewish self-effacement 96
Jewishness 130, 139. See also Jewish identity
Jews 251, 267, 296–7. *See also* antisemitism; Jewish identity
    American 95, 152
    erasure of 158–63
    erasure vs. representation of 2, 5, 117, 141, 144, 151–63, 167–74, 177–8, 180, 199, 209, 214, 229, 232–4, 243–5, 267, 276, 279, 299–300
    expunged from film 151–2
    Hollywood and 250–3, 254
    influence in the media and 250–61, 277
    McCarthyism and 298
    mentioned in film 279
    in Minnesota 224 n. 80
    perceived influence of 208–9
    persecution of 2, 217. *See also* antisemitism; Holocaust
    representation of 5

Kaiser, David 203, 262
Kane, Edward 162, 175
Kansas City (MO) *Journal* 273
Kantor, MacKinley 291
Katz, Sam 118, 136
Kennedy, John 18
Kennedy, Joseph P. 250, 252, 256
Kerr, John 296, 298
Kiev, Ukraine 271
King, William H. 189
Kirschway, Frida 80, 102
Kitzbühel, Austria 38
Knopf, Edwin 118
Knox, Dilthy 125
Knox, Frank 4–5, 185, 187, 201–2, 216, 219, 225 n. 100, 240
Konitz, Germany 5
Kremenchug, Ukraine 249
Kristallnacht 2, 14–15, 16, 77, 78, 79, 138, 165, 190, 252
"Kurfurstendamm riots" 49

La Follette, Robert 192
Labour Party 9
Ladies Home Journal 46
Laemmle, Carl 165
Laemmle, Walter 165
Lambert, Mervyn 119
Landon, Alf 202, 207, 260
Lane, Allen 7
Lassner, Phyllis 40, 87, 88
Latin America 188
L'Aurore 66
Lawson, John Howard 24 n. 67
League of Nations 206
lebensraum, conquest of 161
Lee, Gypsy Rose 16
Leech, Margaret, *Reveille in Washington* 5, 231
legality gone awry 48–51, 65–8
Lend-Lease bill 241, 255, 259
Lenfilms 140
Lerner, Max 21
Lewellin, J. J. 244
Lewick, Virginia 218
Lewis, Fulton 208
Lewis, Michael 77

Lewis, Sinclair (Hal) 77, 78, 80, 104, 107 n. 23
Lewiston, Maine *Journal* 271
Liberal Party 9
Liberty League 14, 82
The Life of Emile Zola 127, 152
Lincoln, Abraham 2–3, 4–5, 230
Lincoln Brigade 2
Lincoln Memorial 3, 230
Lindbergh, Anne Morrow 208, 210, 211, 250–1, 259
Lindbergh, Charles 2, 77, 164, 191, 193, 199, 208–12, 218, 242, 249–53, 255–6, 277
  addresses Des Moines rally 252
  at AFC rallies 259
  antisemitism and 208–9, 240, 251–3, 262–3, 274–5, 277
  as aviator and diplomat 208–9
  Bottome's analysis of 292, 301 n. 13
  Carrel and 209, 210–1
  "Des Moines speech" of 262–3, 265, 269, 271, 275, 277
  FDR question's patriotism of 230
  Flynn and 256
  Germany and 198, 276
  hearings on "Propaganda [for war] in Motion Pictures" and 286–7 n. 140
  Hollywood and 277
  isolationism and 197–9, 208–9, 212, 219–20
  Kristallnacht and 252
  The Mortal Storm (film) and 208, 209
  at the movies 250–1
  neutrality and 212, 219–20
  played by Stewart in *The Spirit of St. Louis* 296
  political demise of 271, 275, 296–7, 298
  radio addresses by 208
  refused to attend Republic convention 277
  Republican Party and 211–2
  return to politics 251–3
  stays home for RNC 211–2
  trans-Atlantic flight of 298–9
  Wheeler and 254

Lindley, Ernest K. 15
Litchfield, John 147 n. 56
Little, Brown & Co. 7, 8, 19, 83, 86, 87, 102, 171, 243, 292–3
Little Man What Now 173
Lloyd George, David 146 n. 34
The Lobby 232–4
Locke, Eric 135, 136
Locker Lampson, Oliver 76
Lodz ghetto, sealing of 15, 299
Loew's, Inc. xiii, 134, 136–7, 241, 257, 266, 267, 269
Loew's Theater, Washington, D.C. 186
Logan, Josh 164
Longerich, Peter 49
Los Angeles Jewish Community Committee (LAJCC) 152
Los Angeles Motion Picture Committee 152
Los Angeles Times 259
Louisiana 187, 188
Louisville Courier-Journal 275
Loyalists 16
Lucas, Julian 77
Lucas, Paul 127
Lucas, Scott 272
Luce, Clare Booth 122, 182 n. 43
Lumet, Sidney 151–2
Lupton, Dilworth 237, 238, 243

MacInnes, Helen 94
MacKenna, Kenneth 126–9, 294, 301–2 n. 28
Magnin, Edgar 97, 98, 99, 100–4, 106, 122, 244
The Man I Married (originally *I Married a Nazi*) 2, 214, 241
Manhunt 268
Mann, Anthony 295
Mannix, Eddie 118, 134, 136, 143, 165, 174, 179, 231, 266
Margaret Herrick Library 141, 175, 198
Marie Antoinette 122
Marxism 95
Mayer, Louis B. 85, 97, 102, 229, 231, 266
  benefits MGM in spite of himself 274

birthplace of 271
Bottome's protests to 170–1, 243
compromises of 166, 167
Congressional hearings and 270
efforts to avoid controversy 244–5, 257, 258, 299–300
heavy-handedness of 164
Horst Wessel song and 162
inner circle of 179
Jewish identity and 154–5, 177, 233–4
PCA and 153–4
production of *The Mortal Storm* and 116–19, 127, 130, 134, 143, 151–4, 156, 158–9, 165
re-instatement of father-son scene 163
replaces Franklin 172–6
West and 176
McBride, Joseph 218
McCarthyism 294, 298
McCord, Maida 45–8, 105, 171
McCullough, David 279
McDonald, John 242
McFarland, Ernest W. 260, 261, 270, 272, 282–3 n. 54
McInnes, Helen 274
McKenna, Kenneth 122
McNaughton, Frank 254, 271–2
Mendelson, Felix 156
MGM (Metro-Goldwyn-Mayer) xii–xiii, 2, 5, 8, 14–15, 20, 50, 68, 85, 97, 294
ambivalence of 141
approves release of *The Mortal Storm* 180
attempts to shape response to film 231–2
audience survey by 178, 180
Bottome and 34, 168–72, 243–5
censorship and 243–5
closing deal with 104–6
compromises of 220
division of labor at 118
father-son scene and 154–8
feature films as vehicles for female stars 88
hearings on "Propaganda [for war] in Motion Pictures" and 266–71
hesitation of 151–2
hires Ross Federal Research Co. 178, 180
Jimmy Roosevelt and 194
The Lobby publication 232–4
Music Department 177
Nazi Germany and 221 n. 3
"producer system" at 118
production of *The Mortal Storm* 115–49, 151–84
publicity and 232–4
publicity department of 232–4
purchase of film rights 19, 101, 102–4
refusal to refer to "Jews" 243–5
release of *The Mortal Storm* (film) 93, 212–15
replacement of Franklin 172–6
response to *The Mortal Storm* and 229, 239, 241–2, 257–8, 265, 266, 274, 278
selling film to 76, 101–4
Stewart's appearance in Cleveland and 237–8
Story Department 102
suppression of the word "Jew" 214
war propaganda films and 301–2 n. 28
West and 176–8, 290
Mielziner, Leo 122
Millis, Walter 13
Milner, Martin 296
Minnesota 198–9, 224 n. 80
Mischling status 52, 57, 69 n. 16
Mitchell, Chalmers 9–10, 125
Mitchell, Margaret, *Gone with the Wind* 3–4, 52
mixed-race characters 55–7
moguls 85, 96, 97, 102–4, 113 n. 142, 116–17, 139, 152, 171, 194, 250–1, 254, 256, 289, 291. *See also specific moguls*

accusations of collusion against 266–71, 274, 276, 277, 279, 280
Congressional hearings and 254, 256, 259, 266–71
control of film industry and 134
hearings on "Propaganda [for war] in Motion Pictures" and 266–71
McCarthyism and 298
turned to heroes by the press 270
universal themes and 99
Morgan, Frank 2, 20, 158, 171, 231, 242, 243, 255
The Mortal Storm (film) xii–xiii, 50, 165, 167, 177, 200, 217, 251, 274, 278, 297
   1939 version 115–49
   accused of defaming Germany 277
   as anti-Nazi film 151
   attempts to shape response to film 231–2
   audience survey about 178, 180
   belatedness of 8–10, 13–16, 199
   Bottome's reaction to 93, 212–15
   Castle and 209
   censorship of 153–4
   Civil War analogy and 229–31
   consultation with Bottome on production 122–32
   critics of 7, 16–17, 27, 220, 232, 289, 299–300
   delayed distribution of 233–4
   delayed production of 220
   draws attention of isolationists 250, 253, 263–5, 266–71
   erasure vs. representation of Jews in 117–21, 141, 144, 151–63, 167–74, 177–8, 180, 199, 209, 214, 229, 232–4, 243–5, 267, 276, 279, 299–300
   father-son scene in 152–3, 154–8, 159, 162–3, 166, 172, 177, 179, 233, 243–5, 246 n. 15
   FDR and 218–19
   feminism in 143–4
   fictional origins of 27–74
   filming mountain scenery 132–5
   Goebbels and 48, 72 n. 83
   hearings on "Propaganda [for war] in Motion Pictures" and 263–5, 266–71
   historical moment and 185–228
   interventionism and 185, 209
   Jewish identity in 154–8
   Kristallnacht and 79
   labeled passé 280
   Lindbergh and 208, 209
   MGM approves release of 180
   new lease on life 273, 279
   onset of *blitzkrieg* during 173–4, 177
   possible protest on set of 163–8
   production of 9
      in 1939 115–49
      in 1940 151–84
      Franklin rejoins 178–80
      replacement of Franklin 172–6
   Professor Mamlock as model for 137–42
   as propaganda 180, 277–8
   publicity and 167, 232–5
   in rallies for Britain 236–43
   reception of 7–9, 14–17, 19, 27, 220, 229–48, 232–5, 249
   regional and local papers respond to 232–5
   release of 1, 19–20, 185–228, 229–30, 289
   reversals of 1939 and 115–17
   reviews of 220, 231–2
   safe choices and 117–21
   selling to Hollywood 75–113
   selling to MGM 101–4
   singled out by Wheeler 257–8
   success of 241–2, 244
   Swiss terrain and 135–7
   tie-in with novel 233, 234–5
   timeliness of 8, 14–15, 16, 19–20, 220, 232, 271–5, 299–300
   timing of 7–26, 27, 180, 232, 244–5, 253, 289
   uniqueness of 2
   as vehicle for patriotism 273

versions of 151–3
White and 207–8
The Mortal Storm (novel) (Bottome)
  5, 9, 30, 31, 40–2, 48–52, 68,
  75–113, 204–5, 210–1, 239
 Adler in 210
 Adlerian themes in 35, 36–9, 43,
  89–91, 142
 anti-Nazism and 87, 142
 antisemitism portrayed in 41
 aristocrats in 57–8
 as bestseller 19
 Carrel in 210–1
 editons of 7, 52, 54, 68, 73 n. 89,
  75–6, 80–91, 94–5, 108 n. 49,
  109 n. 58, 210–1
 expansion of Freya portrait in US
  edition 87–9
 father-son scene in 168, 169–70
 feminism and 58–61, 87, 142
 fictional origins of 27–9
 film adaptation of. See *The Mortal
  Storm* (film)
 Jewish identity in 84–5
 Mischling status in 69 n. 16
 mixed-race characters in 55–7
 mountain scenery in 132
 Nazism in 58
 nineteenth-century inspiration for
  44–5
 Norse mythology and 64–5
 as novel of protest 51–65
 Nuremberg Laws in 58
 as propaganda 91–3, 94, 95, 99,
  101–2
 reception of 7–8, 52, 73 n. 89, 76,
  94–5, 167
 redemption in 62–5
 reissuing of 167
 revision of for US edition 75–6,
  83–91, 94–5
 selling to Hollywood 101, 290
 servants in 61–2
 sibling rivalry in 89–91
 success of 27, 76, 167
 tie-in with film 233, 234–5
 timeliness of 299–300
 universal message of 99–100
 US sales of 95
 as a work ahead of its time 7–10
Moser, John 234, 286–7 n. 140
Mosher, John 9
Mosse, George 48, 72 n. 66
Motion Picture Herald 231–2
Motion Picture Producers and D
  Motion Picture Committee
  Cooperating for the National
  Defense (MPCC) 186
Motion Picture Producers and
  Distributors Association
  (MPPDA) 104, 116, 139, 253
mountain scenery, filming of 132–5,
  133
MPCC 221 n. 5
Mrs. Miniver xii, 124, 129, 290
Mr. Smith Goes to Washington 2, 3,
  194–201, 218, 220, 230–1,
  239, 242, 254–5, 297, 299
Mt. Rainier 133–5, 133, 218
Mulhausen, Alsace 165
Muni, Paul 67, 127
Munich, Germany 47–8, 49–50, 67,
  85, 165, 217
Munich Agreement of 1938 104, 115
Munich crisis 213–14
munitions manufacturers 13–14, 192,
  254–6, 274
Mussolini, Benito 9, 233

The Nation 16, 21, 78, 79, 92, 102,
  193, 194, 207
National Park Service 133–5, 133, 147
  n. 51
National Press Club 195
Nazi Germany xii, 1, 3, 5, 67, 104, 113
  n. 142, 151, 188, 280
 1936 Olympics and 14–15, 49
 anthem of 161–2, 163, 174, 175,
  177
 appeasement of 4, 91, 92, 98, 187–8
 attacks on Britain 187
 attacks on France 186–7
 banning of cast members from 164
 Foreign Ministry of 12, 189
 German Foreign Office 11–2
 Hollywood and 221 n. 3

invasion of Europe 234
invasion of Soviet Union 96–7
involvement in hearings 275–8
Kristallnacht and 102
launching of *blitzkrieg* 173–4
Lindbergh 198
Nazi propaganda 189–91
portrayal of 127–30, 214
takeover of Czechoslovakia 98, 103, 115
US Congress and 275–8
Nazi Party 49
Nazism 7–8, 17, 19–20, 76, 85, 95, 98, 102, 209–12, 217, 291.
See also antisemitism; Nazi Germany
American racism and 47–8
Bottome and 27, 36–7, 45–6, 58, 63
Britain and 17–18
homosexuals and 119, 120
Kristallnacht 14–15, 16, 77, 78, 79
as legalized pogrom 152
in *The Mortal Storm* 61–2, 65
in *The Mortal Storm* (film) 123, 126, 154, 161–2, 164, 173–4, 180, 239, 276, 278
racial theories of 140
Netherlands 19
neutrality 116–17, 186–8, 250, 259, 270
end of 96–7
Lindbergh and 212, 219–20
neutrality campaign of 1930s 13–14
official policy of 15
regional divide on 188
US Congress and 13, 14, 189, 190, 192, 195. See also Neutrality Acts
Neutrality Acts 14, 204, 206, 207, 255, 259, 270
Neville, Luci 231
New Deal 14, 82, 202
new realism 278–80
The New Republic 16, 20, 21, 68, 78, 79, 185, 192, 254, 256, 275, 279
New York Daily Mirror 197
New York Dramatists Guild 83

New York Herald Tribune 15, 77, 80, 95, 199
New York Times 8, 11, 94, 96, 104, 138, 186–8, 190–1, 199, 202, 204, 211, 216, 220
New York World-Telegram 9
New Yorker 9, 234
newsreels 1, 193, 208, 240, 251, 255, 255–6
Next Time We Love 164, 165
Neyfak, Nicky (Nicholas Nayfack) 136–7
Nicholson, Harold 292
Night Train to Munich 241
No Time for Comedy 236
Non-Partisan Committee for Peace through Revision of the Neutrality Law 206
Nordoff, Charles 95
Norfolk, Virginia 45–8
Norris, Kathleen 259
Norse mythology 64–5
North Dakota 189
Northcote, Muriel 39–40
Northwest Mounted Police 218
Norway 19
Nugent, Frank 8, 104, 138, 158, 199
Nuremberg Laws 2, 14, 48–52, 57–8, 69 n. 16, 85, 119, 142, 154–6, 166
Nuremberg Race Laws 29, 31
Nye, Gerald P. 13–14, 189–90, 192, 195, 200, 202, 219, 238
hearings on "Propaganda [for war] in Motion Pictures" and 261, 267, 272, 281 n. 27, 281–2 n. 30, 282–3 n. 54, 283 n. 66
Neutrality Acts and 14, 204, 206, 207, 255, 259, 270
Nye Committee hearings and 260, 266, 270, 275, 276
testimony of 263–5
Wheeler and 254–7
Nye, Mrs. 254

Oakland Tribune 234–5
Offenbach, Jacques, *Tales of Hoffman* 159

INDEX

Olmstead, Mildred Scott 238
optimism 106
　end to 80
　false 76–80
　unwarranted 91
Orr, William A. 133, 134, 136
Orwell, George 17–18
Ouspenskaia, Maria 129
Over the Rainbow 242
Overman Committee 189

Pabst, G. W. 140
Palmer, Tim 295–6
Paramount 1, 173, 290
Parsons, Louella 105–6, 115, 122
Pasternak, Joe 118
patriotism 233, 239, 253, 273
PCA (Production Code Administration) 153, 154, 156, 159, 175
Pearl Harbor
　alert issued for 187
　attack on 1, 2, 96, 229, 272, 279
Pearson, Drew 250, 275, 278
Penguin Books 7
Pepper, Claude 188, 189, 236
Perkins, Anthony 296
Perkins, Frances 82
Peters, Charles 240, 243
Philadelphia, Pennsylvania 240–1
The Philadelphia Story 235, 242, 299
philosemitism 277
"phony war" 154
Pickford, Mary 166, 236
Poland, German aggression toward 178
political discourse, new realism in 278–9
Potter, Stephen 80, 103, 122
Pound, Ezra 17
Power, Tyrone 236
press 199, 270, 271–2. *See also specific outlets*
Preston, Jim 195
Princeton University 241
Private Worlds (film) 75, 76, 213
Private Worlds (novel) (Bottome) 88, 90
　Adlerian psychology in 39–45
　sold to Hollywood 75, 76

Production Code 104, 129, 137, 138–9, 151, 153, 154. *See also* censorship; PCA (Production Code Administration)
Professor Mamlock 137–42, 151
Progressive Party 192
propaganda xii, xiii, 91–3, 94, 95, 139, 180
　accusations of 189, 191–2, 233, 235
　film and 125–6
　Hollywood and 99, 101–2
　The Mortal Storm (novel) as 91–3
　"propaganda film" 219
　war effort and 125–6
　as weapon of war 9–10
protest literature 5
Protocols of the Elders of Zion 269–70
public opinion 94, 193–4, 196, 255, 271, 274, 276, 278, 279
Public Opinion Quarterly 242
Publishers' Weekly 8, 10–1, 12, 18, 19, 75, 211
Pulitzer Prize 3, 4, 5

race laws 14, 50. *See also* Nuremburg Laws
racism 14, 50, 210–1. *See also* antisemitism
　American 47–8
　exposure to 45–8
　Nazism and 47–8. *See also* Nuremburg Laws
Rains, Claude 197
Rameau, Hans 136, 141, 154, 156, *See also* Anderson, Ellis
Random Harvest xii
Rapaport, Herbert 140–1
Rassenschande 48–9
Rayburn, Sam 271
reading public, American 12
red baiting 81–2
red scare 80–3, 95
redemption 62–5
refugees 15–16, 77, 78, 116, 126, 140–1, 160–1
regional press 232–3, 234
Remarque, Erich Maria 18, 19, 173

All Quiet on the Western Front
    10–1, 19. *See also All Quiet on the Western Front* (film)
Republican National Convention 190, 240, 277
Republican Party 14, 20, 82, 201–2, 207
    isolationism and 190–1
    Lindbergh and 211–2
revisionism 11–2, 13, 203–4, 229, 275–6, 278
Reynolds, David S. 52
Reynolds, Gene 157, 158, 172, 175, 243, 246 n. 15, 300
Rhys, Jean 70 n. 50
Rich, Irene 157, 171, 243
RKO 3, 80
Rogerson, Sidney 189
Rohm purge 119
Romantic Movement 63
Rooney, Mickey 170–1, 172
Roosevelt, Franklin D. 1, 15, 133, 262, 263
    1936 presidential election and 82, 83
    appointments by 96, 185, 187, 201–2, 219
    birthday celebration of 223 n. 58
    Bottome and 216–17
    Britain and 215, 216
    Civil War analogy and 230
    court packing attempt by 192–3, 194, 201, 254
    Democratic National Convention and 216, 219
    election to third term 249
    Evian Conference and 107 n. 26
    films seen by 218
    foreign policy of 187–8, 192–3, 196, 202, 205, 229, 252, 255, 259
    Germany and 203
    Hollywood and 194–201
    interventionism and 186, 192–3, 275
    isolationists and 256
    Kristallnacht and 102, 190
    Lend-Lease bill and 255, 259
    Lincoln's relevance to 4–5
    The Mortal Storm (film) and 218–19
    Mr. Smith Goes to Washington and 194–201
    New Deal and 14, 202
    "quarantine speech" 15
    red scare and 81–2
    signs Selective Service Act 239, 255
    State of the Union address 135, 204
    third term and 134, 147 n. 50, 185, 216, 219
    Thompson and 78
    US Congress and 187, 191, 254
    US Supreme Court and 192–3, 194, 201, 254
    on U.S.S. *Tuscaloosa* 218
    Wheeler and 192, 194, 197–8, 201, 253–4
    White and 206–7
Roosevelt, Jimmy 194
Roosevelt, Sara Delano 217
Roosevelt family 217
Roper, George 45–8
Rosenman, Samuel 80–3
Ross, Steven 278
Ross Federal Research Co. 178, 180
Roth, Philip 211
Roth, Victor 209, 210–1, 214
Royal Air Force 239

Saint-Amour, Paul K. 22–3 n. 27
Sandburg, Carl 4
Saturday Review 7, 94, 207
Saville, Victor 106, 172–7, 258, 264
Scaife, Roger 19–20, 83, 102, 171, 172, 243, 292–3
Schacht, Hjalmar 49, 50
Schaefer, George 80
Schenck, Joseph 136–7, 258, 284 n. 78
Schenck, Nicholas xiii, 241, 257, 258, 266–71, 272, 277, 284 n. 78
Schlier, Merrill 229
Schwartz, Barry 2, 229–30
Screen Writers' Guild 119, 298
Script Writers' Guild (SWG) 83
Seif, Leonard 36–9, 47, 49
Seiff, Israel 243–4

Selective Service Act 239, 255
Sergeant York 208
servants 61–2
Sherman, John 283 n. 66
Sherriff, R. C. 82–3, 145 n. 18
Sherwood, Robert E. 3, 289, 291
Shesol, Jeff 193
The Shining Hour 164
Shirer, William L. 274
Shop Around the Corner 164, 241
The Shopworn Angel 164
sibling rivalry 3, 28, 37–8, 39–45, 70 n. 48, 230
Sinclair, Upton 68, 78
Skolsky, Sidney 270, 273
Slagerman, Blanche 120
Smith, Amanda 47
Smith, Helmuth Walser 5
Smith, Kate 239
Smith, Ted 238, 239
Smith, Truman 276–7
So Ends Our Night 166, 167
Soames, John 234–5
Social Security Act 187
Southern, Jane Spence 94
Southwest Airlines 164
Southworth, Mira 300
Soviet Union 4–5, 81, 96–7, 138, 249
Spain 2–3, 9, 16
Spanish Civil War 2–3, 9, 16, 213
Special Operations Executive (SOE) 215
The Spirit of St. Louis 296, 298
Spokane Spokesman Review 197
St. Louis Globe-Democrat 264
St. Paul Dispatch 79
Stack, Robert 164, 175
Stalin, Josef xii
Stanton, Elizabeth Cady 59
Steinbeck, John 4
stenograficheskie otchëty xii
Stephenson, William 215, 219
Stevens, George 80
Stewart, Jimmy 230–1, 234, 280
   address Cleveland rally 236–43, 250
   aviation and 164
   dinner with Lindbergh 298, 299

The Mortal Storm (film) and 2, 3, 19, 129, 147 n. 56, 163–5, 168, 171, 175, 177, 197, 200, 201, 205–6
   in *Mr. Smith Goes to Washington* 194, 196–7, 200, 201
   politics and 178, 235, 236–43, 297–8, 299
   post-war transformation of 295–9
   wartime breakdown of 297–8
Stimson, Henry 185, 187, 203–6, 207, 212, 216, 219, 225 n. 100, 240
   appointment of 201–2
   graduation address in 1940 205–6
   as patrician ahead of his time 203–5
Stowe, Harriet Beecher 44, 66, 84
   abolitionism and 68
   aristocrats in 57–8
   Bottome and 51–2
   in Britain 68
   Canada and 55
   feminism and 58–61, 74 n. 104
   Fugitive Slave Act and 50–1, 52, 55
   mixed-race characters in 55–7
   redemption in 62–5
   servants in 61–2
   Uncle Tom's Cabin 3, 5, 28, 39, 45–65, 68, 71 n. 55, 230, 273, 280, 300
Straight, Michael 254, 275
Streicher, Julius 48–9
Stresemann, Gustav 12
Strickling, Howard 179–80, 229, 231, 239, 266
Struss, Karl 117
Struthers, Jan 124
studio system. *See also specific studios*
   censorship and 198
   spies in 193–4
Sturm abteilung or S.A. 119, 136, 161, 162, 177. *See also* Brown Shirts
Sullavan, Margaret 143, 147 n. 56, 155, 171, 175, 205, 234, 243, 296
   as anti-Nazi crusader 166–7
   antisemitism and 163–5, 168

Borzage and 173
dinner with Lindbergh 296, 298, 299
Goebbels and 166–7
Jewish question and 163–5, 168
personal exposure to Jewish question 163–4, 165
political activism of 166–7
power of 165–6
Universal Studios and 165–6
Sulzberger, Arthur Hays 96
Swiss Alps 40–1, 132, 147 n. 56
perilous terrain of 135–7
shooting on location in 135–7, 147 n. 56, 176, 179
Syracuse Herald 235
Syracuse Post-Standard 79

Taft, Robert A. 240, 241, 243
Taft, William Howard 202, 212
Texas 187
Thalberg, Irving 68, 118, 152, 173, 270
That Hamilton Woman 267
theater managers 232–3, 234
theater owners 232–3, 258
They Knew What They Wanted 218
Thompson, Dorothy 76, 80, 83, 107 n. 23, 236, 275, 278, 301 n. 13
The Depths of Prosperity 77
"On the Record" column 77
"Refugees: A World Problem" 78
Thomsen, Hans 189–91, 225 n. 100, 240, 268–9, 276–7, 284 n. 87
Three Comrades 164, 173
Time magazine 254, 271–2
Tin Pan Alley 218
Tobey, Charles W. 191, 260, 261, 266, 272, 276
Toller, Ernst 84, 109 n. 54, 210
Tracy, Spencer 127
Treaty of Versailles 11, 12, 259, 276
Trubey, Elizabeth Fekete 59, 61, 74 n. 104
Truman, Harry 278–9
Turgenev, Ivan 44, 66
Twentieth-Century Fox 2, 3, 214, 221 n. 3, 258, 268

U-boat attacks 187, 262
Underground 273
United Artists 24 n. 67, 166, 258
United Front Spain 2–3
United States 68, 173
Anglo-American cooperation and 215
Bottome's visits to 45–8, 68, 76
optimism in 76–80, 91
public attitudes in 27
regional divide on neutrality in 188
revisions to references to in novel 86–7
war spirit in 93
Universal Studios 165–6
University Players 164
University of Virginia 14
Uruguay 188
US Commerce Department 199
US Congress 200, 259–63
antisemitism 253–61
antisemitism and 256
conscription bill and 185, 187, 219
corruption in 194–200
FDR and 187, 191, 254
Germany and 275–8
hearings on "Propaganda [for war] in Motion Pictures" xii–xiii, 1–2, 262–87
Hollywood and xii–xiii, 1–2, 199, 200, 262–87
House Un-American Activities Committee (HUAC) 82, 294, 298
isolationism vs. interventionism in 16, 185, 188–201, 202, 203–4, 238, 240–1, 242, 255, 272–8
Kristallnacht and 16
Lend-Lease bill 241
McCarthyism and 298
neutrality and 13, 14, 189, 190, 192, 195
preparation for hearings and 253–61
regional divide in 188
Truman Committee 278–9

US Department of Interior 133–5, 136, 218–19
US Department of the Navy 201–2
US House of Representatives
    conscription bill and 187
    House Un-American Activities Committee (HUAC) 82, 294, 298
US Justice Department 134, 186, 197, 199, 263–4
US military 187, 219
U.S. Navy 1940 218
US Senate 186, 187
    anti-Roosevelt faction in 192–3
    antisemitism and 253–61
    Audit and Control Committee 272
    conscription bill and 187
    FDR's appointments and 201–2
    Foreign Relations Committee 16
    hearings on "Propaganda [for war] in Motion Pictures" xii–xiii, 1–2, 259–87
    Hollywood and 194–201, 220
    Interstate Commerce Committee (ICC) 199, 253–4, 255, 257, 258, 260–1, 263–6, 271
    investigation into Hollywood 252–61
    investigation of pro-war propaganda 296–7
    isolationism vs. interventionism in 2, 16, 191–2, 202, 219, 242, 255, 271–5, 281 n. 27, 296–7
    Judiciary Committee 193, 194
    neutrality campaign of 1930s and 13–14
    Nye Committee hearings 238
    passes Neutrality Acts 14
    preparation for hearings and 253–61
    Resolution 152, 263, 272, 273
    rivalry with FDR 254
    Truman Committee 278–9
US South 45, 61–2, 300
    Bottom and 45–8
    social system in 56
    support for Britain 188
US State Department 268

US Supreme Court 192–4, 254
    FDR and 192–3, 194
    Roosevelt, Franklin D. and 201
    vacancy on 96
US War Department 201–2
U.S. Week, A National Journal of News and Opinion 272
USS *Greer* 262

Valman, Nadia 73–4 n. 103
Vansittart, Robert 4
Variety 231
victory, harsh realities of 291–4
Vienna, Austria 48, 54, 56, 67, 77, 78, 83
Viertel, Salka 120
Villard, Oswald Harrison 78

Wadsworth, James 187
Wanger, Walter 24 n. 67, 105, 213, 214, 215, 220
war, trauma of 295–9
war effort
    Britain and 125–6
    Hollywood and 1, 236–43
    propaganda and 125–6
war films 208, 219, 231–3, 235, 238, 241–2, 250, 289–90, 301–2 n. 28 *See also specific films*
    censorship of 104, 125, 137, 138–9, 151, 153–4, 198, 243–5, 274, 278, 294 *See also* censorship
    congressional hearings and 253–8, 266–70, 273–4, 279
    Hollywood and 260
    suspension of 173
war guilt 259
Warner, Harry 266, 268, 269–74, 278
Warner, Jack 134, 152, 250, 270, 290, 291
Warner Brothers 67, 97, 103–4, 115, 127, 134, 173, 236, 250, 266–74, 278, 290
Warsaw ghetto, sealing of 15, 299
Washington Post 188
Watkins, Ann 105
Weingarten, Larry 118
Welky, David 186, 219, 221 n. 5, 243

Weller, Willard 296
Welles, Sumner 107 n. 26
Wessel, Horst 161
West, Claudine 106, 116, 119–20, 135, 145 n. 18, 145 n. 30, 151–4, 163, 165, 168–9, 171, 214
  adaptations by 170, 206, 258, 266, 270–1, 299–300
  agenda of 166
  censorship and 125
  as codebreaker in World War I 124–5
  consulting with Bottome 122–32, 123, 131, 137–8
  continued influence of 176–8
  continuity provided by 176–8
  death of 143, 147 n. 58, 174, 289–90, 294–5
  Franklin and 120–1, 120, 121, 124, 174–6, 182 n. 43, 290, 294–5
  grieving for 294–5
  illness of 142–4
  location shooting in Switzerland and 135–7
  Mayer and 176
  MGM and 176–8, 290
  modifications by 155–7, 158, 159, 167, 170, 174–5, 180
  obituary of 145 n. 17
  pacing of script and 182 n. 43
  personal exposure to Jewish question 163
  politics of intervention and 177–8
  salary of 300–1 n. 5
  sense of mission and 126
  Swiss Alps and 132–3
  World War I and 124, 125–6
Wheeler, Burton K. 202, 218, 219, 242, 272–4, 277, 278, 280, 281–2 n. 30, 284 n. 87
  antisemitism and 253–61
  FDR and 192, 194, 197–8, 201, 253–4
  Hollywood and 194–201
  Lindbergh and 198, 254
  Mr. Smith Goes to Washington and 194–201
  preparation for hearings and 253–6
  Supreme Court and 192–4

Wheeler, John 193, 257–9, 263, 266, 267, 277, 280
Wheeler, Lulu 193, 254, 281 n. 27
White, William Allen 206–8, 219, 220, 249
The White Cliffs of Dover xii, 142–3, 290, 294, 301–2 n. 28
White Committee 219, 220, 236–43, 249, 273, 280, 297
Whyte, Edward 292
Whyte, Frederick 93, 106, 244
Willkie, Wendall 212, 216, 264–5
Wilson, Carey 118
The Wizard of Oz 2, 76, 231, 242
Wolf, Frederich 140–2
woman question, Jewish question and 73–4 n. 103
Women's International League for Peace and Freedom (WILPF) 238
women's suffrage 59
Wood, General Robert E. 275
Woodring, Harry 202
World Telegram 199
World War I 9, 10, 14, 18, 20, 38, 48, 124, 125, 187, 198, 254–6, 279
  aerial combat during 298–9
  approach of 52
  Bottome and 27, 125–6
  changing attitudes toward 10–1
  Freud's search for origins of 44
  munitions manufacturers and 13–14, 192, 254–6, 274
  origins of 275–6
  revisionism and 4, 11–2, 203–4, 229, 275–6, 278
  sibling rivalry and 70 n. 48
  war bond rallies during 236
  war guilt and 259
  West and 124, 125–6
World War II
  aerial combat during 298–9
  approach of xii, 1, 4, 5, 51–65, 229, 262
  onset of 116–17
  victory in 291–4
Wyler, William 165, 291

Yankee Doodle Dandee 290
You Can't Take It with You 194
Young, Robert 140, 164, 167, 171, 206
Young Mr. Lincoln 3

Zanuck, Darryl 134
Zimbalist, Sam 118
Zola, Émile 44, 67
    Dreyfus case and 66
    "J'accuse" 66, 68

www.ingramcontent.com/pod-product-compliance
Lightning Source LLC
Chambersburg PA
CBHW070012010526
44117CB00011B/1536